Language and Body in Place and Space

ALSO AVAILABLE FROM BLOOMSBURY

Corpus Approaches to the Language of Sports, edited by
Marcus Callies and Magnus Levin
Sports Discourse, Tony Schirato
Multilingual Baseball, Brendan H. O'Connor
*How Language Shapes Relationships in Professional
Sports Teams*, Kieran File

Language and Body in Place and Space

Discourse of Japanese Rock Climbing

Kuniyoshi Kataoka

BLOOMSBURY ACADEMIC
LONDON • NEW YORK • OXFORD • NEW DELHI • SYDNEY

BLOOMSBURY ACADEMIC
Bloomsbury Publishing Plc, 50 Bedford Square, London, WC1B 3DP, UK
Bloomsbury Publishing Inc, 1385 Broadway, New York, NY 10018, USA
Bloomsbury Publishing Ireland, 29 Earlsfort Terrace, Dublin 2, D02 AY28, Ireland

BLOOMSBURY, BLOOMSBURY ACADEMIC and the Diana logo
are trademarks of Bloomsbury Publishing Plc

First published in Great Britain 2023
This paperback edition published 2025

Copyright © Kuniyoshi Kataoka, 2023

Kuniyoshi Kataoka has asserted his right under the Copyright, Designs
and Patents Act, 1988, to be identified as Author of this work.

For legal purposes the Acknowledgements on p. vii constitute
an extension of this copyright page.

Cover design: Elena Durey
Cover image © Katerina Sergeevna/Getty Images

This work is published open access subject to a Creative Commons Attribution-NonCommercial-NoDerivatives 4.0 International licence (CC BY-NC-ND 4.0, https://creativecommons.org/licenses/by-nc-nd/4.0/). You may re-use, distribute, and reproduce this work in any medium for non-commercial purposes, provided you give attribution to the copyright holder and the publisher and provide a link to the Creative Commons licence.

All rights reserved. No part of this publication may be: i) reproduced or transmitted in any form, electronic or mechanical, including photocopying, recording or by means of any information storage or retrieval system without prior permission in writing from the publishers; or ii) used or reproduced in any way for the training, development or operation of artificial intelligence (AI) technologies, including generative AI technologies. The rights holders expressly reserve this publication from the text and data mining exception as per Article 4(3) of the Digital Single Market Directive (EU) 2019/790.

Bloomsbury Publishing Plc does not have any control over, or responsibility for, any third-party websites referred to or in this book. All internet addresses given in this book were correct at the time of going to press. The author and publisher regret any inconvenience caused if addresses have changed or sites have ceased to exist, but can accept no responsibility for any such changes.

A catalogue record for this book is available from the British Library.

A catalog record for this book is available from the Library of Congress.

ISBN: HB: 978-1-3503-1947-9
PB: 978-1-3503-1951-6
ePDF: 978-1-3503-1948-6
eBook: 978-1-3503-1949-3

Typeset by Jones Ltd, London

For product safety related questions contact productsafety@bloomsbury.com.

To find out more about our authors and books visit www.bloomsbury.com
and sign up for our newsletters.

CONTENTS

List of Figures vi
List of Tables vii
Preface viii
Acknowledgments x
Notes on Romanization and Transcription Conventions xii
List of Abbreviations xiii
Glossary of Climbing Terminology xv

1 Language and Body in Place and Space 1

2 Theories and Approaches 15

3 Rock Climbing as a Site of Embodied Institution 43

4 Affordances in Rock Climbing 61

5 *Ue* and *Shita* in Horizontal and Vertical Space 79

6 The Body and Deictic Verbs of Motion in Imaginary Space 107

7 Poetic Construction of Vertical Space and Chronotopic Analysis of "Fall" Experiences 137

8 Views from Mountaineer Ethics and Deviations 171

9 Conclusion 193

Notes 199
References 209
Index 231

FIGURES

1.1	Canonical and climbing settings	5
1.2	Risk and recognition of climbing styles	6
1.3	Locations of data collection	10
2.1	"The cat is _____ the truck"	22
2.2	Four major types of perspective-taking	27
2.3	Possibilities of verbal/gestural perspectivization	28
2.4	Classification of gestures	29
2.5	Components of a gesture unit	29
2.6	"Distance" between C-VPT and O-VPT	30
2.7	Ethnopoetic formation of a narrative text	36
3.1	Climbing gear (quickdraw and belay device)	48
3.2	Skeletal formation of route climbing	51
3.3	Climber–belayer coordination	52
3.4	Belaying postures	54
3.5	Belayer's reactions against a fall	56
3.6	Climbing as institutionalized interaction	58
4.1	Recognition and prestige of climbing styles	64
4.2	Lunge move on "polygon"	68
4.3	Undercling move	71
4.4	Flow of extensions	76
5.1	Axial shifts and projections	90
5.2	Pointing, manner, and path gestures in the negotiation of meaning	91
5.3	"Move upward"	91
5.4	Situation of instruction-giving	93
5.5	Orientations of carabiner	94
5.6	Correct and wrong ways of clipping a rope	94
5.7	Side view of quickdraw in projected vertical space	99
5.8	Bodily axis rotation in the environment	100
6.1	Default use for COME and GO: Japanese and English	110
6.2	M Route and H-S Route on Central Face of Peak 4	111
6.3	Schematic map of the approach trails in Section 3	127
6.4	Synthetic view of denotational and interactional texts	134
7.1	Spatial configuration and gestural perspectives	153
7.2	Correspondence between rhetorical components and places	155
8.1	Cline of "interference" in reporting	175
8.2	A cultural model shared by participants	187
8.3	Repertoires of K and M's reported speech	191

TABLES

2.1	Three perspectives and related notions	23
2.2	Viewer-oriented spatial frames of reference reconsidered	25
2.3	Denotational and interactional texts	39
4.1	Factors of prestige in climbing styles	64
4.2	Spatial concepts of UE/MAE	65
5.1	If X is Y, then Z	98
5.2	Accommodation to intersubjectified corporeality	102
6.1	Sequence of *iku/kuru* across Participants in Section (a)	129
6.2	Sequence of *iku/kuru* across Participants in Section (b)	131
6.3	Sequence of *iku/kuru* across Participants in Segment (c)	132
6.4	Different experiential status as to spatial segments	133
7.1	Profile of crevasse-falling narrative	146
7.2	Profile of "massive fall" narrative	160
8.1	Types of quotation in English and Japanese	176

PREFACE

The work presented in this book is an accumulation of many years of research on discourse, space, and gesture conducted partially for my dissertation and mainly as my ongoing research topic. This book investigates what everyday and extraordinary spatial experiences are made accountable interactively, how perception and cognition of space emerge discursively from the vertical plane, and when and how the identity of the rock climber is constructed through language and action. Although the target audience is Japanese, the book is also intended for students and communities of discourse analysis, who are interested in language, space, and the body. I hope it will be of interest also to those who study the Japanese language and Japanese society, regardless of whether they are keen on rock climbing. In all cases, this book is aimed at undergraduate and graduate students in educational and research institutions.

Although the research on which this book was originally based was the author's doctoral dissertation submitted to the University of Arizona, the current book has been revised and updated substantially, and includes new chapters that draw on recent research. My long-term, though intermittent, focus has been specifically on climbers' interactions, spatial descriptions/depictions, and stories of near-death experiences in mountaineering and rock climbing. These themes are related very closely to my mountaineering experience and frustration in my youth, as well as to the climbing environment in Arizona, where I chose to pursue my Ph.D. In addition, my choice of climbing as the field for my research was heavily concerned with the worldwide interest in spatial cognition in linguistics, anthropology, and related fields in the 1990s. At that time, linguistic analysis was based largely on the spatial lexicon of the horizontal plane, with the result that the language use of climbers whose activities take place in the vertical space was an unexplored niche. In addition, linguistic and anthropological studies on space have been conducted in a variety of languages and regions, but a discourse analysis of vertical space is still a rare commodity by and large.

Furthermore, in narrative research during the 1990s, the challenge still lay largely in working out how to overcome the "Observer's Paradox" and collect spontaneous, natural narratives. As is well known, sociolinguist William Labov tried to address this constraint by asking people to share their near-death stories, of which there is no shortage among rock climbers. Although the discussion of the validity of data is now largely obviated, space discourse is still a recurrent topic in the field of narrative studies. In that sense, climbers' talks seem to be an ideal site for connecting theoretical interests and actual language use in space. Jane Hill, my late mentor, helped me to realize that continuing to take an interest in local ways of doing things should be one's very first motivation. This is the reason why I remain engaged with this topic.

However, it is sometimes frustrating to collect data—I cannot climb with the research participants while carrying cumbersome data-collection equipment! It is only recently that lightweight action cameras and durable batteries have been made available. Also, in my early years of research in climbing, I was not fully ready to analyze the video-recorded data due to my lack of expertise in multimodal analysis. I retrieved my old data for this book, and (re)analyzed them. This process delayed the launch and completion of this book much longer than I wished. Fortunately, I managed to take a year's sabbatical at the same time as the Tokyo Olympic Games 2020 (2021), in which rock/sport climbing was adopted as an official entry for the first time. This coincidence prompted me to finish, at least partially, this book. .

Rock climbing is now more popular than ever around the world. With that in mind, this book attempts to reveal some previously unexplored facets of the activity, elaborating on interactionally institutionalized and intersubjectively promoted aspects of rock climbing, as well as demonstrating how climbers' identity and ideology are vividly constructed and performed through climbing talks. Above all, I hope the book helps readers to realize how climbers mediate horizontal and vertical environments and make sense of them through climbing instruction, narrative, and gossip, as well as their heated discussions of unexpected incidents. While acknowledging that this book involves methodological skews and flaws, I sincerely hope it will appeal not only to climbers, but also to those interested in outdoor activities.

Kuniyoshi Kataoka
April 30, 2022

ACKNOWLEDGMENTS

This book would not exist without the generous help and support of my friends, climbing partners, family, and colleagues. Above all, I am greatly indebted to my fellow climbers for allowing me to participate in climbing with them. Data collection for this book was made possible through the networks of those local climbers. Among those I greatly appreciate are, first, the members of the Tokai Alpine Club, who were the major source of the present data and human resources. Particularly helpful were Masatoshi Ito, Seiyuu Soumiya, Osamu Tanabe (deceased), Masafumi and Takako Soga, Naoto Kanada, Hidehiro Nimura (deceased), Shin'ichi Izuchi, Hiromi Shimohara, Osamu Kawaguchi, and Hiromasa Ogawa. I would also like to express my gratitude to Masanori Hoshina and regular members of *Hatenko*, a now-closed climbing gym in Nagoya, as well as to Masami and Toshiko Sasaki, the owners of Tonai Lodge in the Suzuka Mountains, and many regular guests at the lodge for their generous support in data collection. In particular, I am indebted to the members of the Nisshin Bears Climbing Club for providing me with invaluable opportunities for gathering data and information. In particular, Seiji Maki (deceased), Naoko Matsuoka, Tomotaka Nakayama, Takashi Sakurai, Kazuhiro Manda, Mitsunori Iwata, and Ririko Katsu have been important sources of the data, not to mention the other club members.

There is no end to the list of my "mentors" in the academic aspect of this book. First, I would like to express my sincere appreciation to my late mentor, Jane Hill, for her understanding and encouragement of this seemingly absurd project. She will be my eternal role model and source of inspiration. My gratitude extends to the faculty members and students of the interdisciplinary program in Second Language Acquisition and Teaching (SLAT) at the University of Arizona, especially Adrianne Lehrer, Tsuyoshi Ono, Susan Philips, Shoji Takano, Miki Shibata, Noriko Iwasaki, and Akiko Kato, with whom I have shared a great deal of happiness in my professional career. I also have gained a great deal of intellectual inspiration and influence through direct and indirect interactions with Dell Hymes, William Bright, Stephen Levinson, Michael Silverstein, Alessandro Duranti, Charles Goodwin, Niko Besnier, and Nick Enfield. Without these path-breaking pioneers in the fields, this book would have been something completely different.

After returning to Japan in 1998, I was able to construct academic networks through the help of Harumi and Sachiko Tanaka and Hiroshi Yoshikawa. At the same time, another spiritual mentor in Japan, Sachiko Ide, kindly established an academic connection for me with Yasuhiro Katagiri, Yoko Fujii, Kaoru Horie, Myung-Hee Kim, Kishiko Ueno, Sotaro Kita, William Hanks, William Beeman, Jacob Mey, Jef Vershueren, Gunter Senft, Li Wei, Scott Saft, and many others, for whom I cannot thank enough. I have also worked individually with Kazuko

Shinohara, Keiko Ikeda, and Kaori Hata, with whom I collaborated on separate volumes of papers that we co-edited with a Grant-in-Aid for Scientific Research (KAKENHI) in Japan. Above all, I would like to express my gratitude to my research colleagues who have advanced discursive and linguistic anthropological approaches in Japan; specifically, Keiko Matsuki, Risako Ide, Wataru Koyama, Masataka Yamaguchi, Makiko Takekuro, Takeshi Enomoto, Yuichi Asai, Toshiaki Furukawa, and Gaku Kajimaru for offering me unfathomable intellectual stimuli. I would also like to thank Kazuyo Murata and Ayako Namba for their collaboration, and Nobuhiro Furuyama for providing me with valuable information and precise advice in writing up Chapters 3 and 4 of this book. I am especially indebted to the insightful and constructive comments by Risako Ide, Masataka Yamaguchi, Makiko Takekuro, and Takeshi Enomoto on several chapters in the book. I also appreciate the valuable comments and suggestions from my research colleagues in Japanese Association of Sociolinguistic Sciences (JASS) and the Nagoya-de-Socio (NDS) Research Group, and Carol Sonenklar and Lisa Carden for carefully reading and editing my manuscript. All errors and misconceptions are of course my own.

Several chapters of the book were supported by a JSPS KAKENHI Grant-in-Aid for Scientific Research (B) (#23320090) and (C) (#25370499, #22520413), as well as by a research fund of The Institute for Research in Humanities and Social Sciences, Aichi University (IRHSA). Chapters 5 and 6, which began as selected portions of previously published articles, have been revised significantly. I am grateful to the publishers of these articles for giving me permission to reproduce them here: "On Intersubjective Co-construction of Virtual Space Through Multimodal Means: A Case of Japanese Route-finding Discourse," in *Approaches to Language, Culture, and Cognition: The Intersection of Cognitive Linguistics and Linguistic Anthropology* (Masataka Yamaguchi, Dennis Tay, and Ben Blount, eds.), Palgrave Macmillan, 2014: 181–216 (Chapter 5); "Co-construction of a Mental Map in Spatial Discourse: A Case Study of Japanese Rock Climbers' Use of Deictic Verbs of Motion," *Pragmatics* 14(4), 2004: 409–38 (Chapter 5); "Gravity or Levity: Vertical Space in Japanese Rock Climbing Instructions," *Journal of Linguistic Anthropology* 8(2), 1998: 222–48 (Chapter 6); and *Zatsudan to goshippu no hazama de: Kihan to itsudatu kara kangaeru*, "In the Middle of Small Talk and Gossip: A View from Norms and Deviations,' in *The Kaleidoscope of Small Talk: A Linguistic Approach* (Kazuyo Murata and Risako Ide, eds.), Hituzi Shobo, 2016: 281–307 (Chapter 8). I am also grateful to anonymous reviewers of the manuscript for their constructive comments, as well as Morwenna Scott and Laura Gallon of Bloomsbury Academic for their timely support, and Balsa Indexers for their help with indexing.

Last but not least, I would like to warmly thank those who have supported me over the years, especially my family, Kayoko, Ryo, and Aoi, as well as my late parents and parents-in-law.

NOTES ON ROMANIZATION AND TRANSCRIPTION CONVENTIONS

In transcribing Japanese text, I have followed the Hepburn style of Romanization. Long vowels are represented by duplicating a single vowel. (In the case of extra lengthening beyond the normal length, the lengthening notion (:) is added.) However, this practice is not strictly followed for commonly used words: e.g., Tokyo rather than Tookyoo.

Keys to textual transcription (modified from Du Bois et al. 1993: Jefferson 2004):

.	final contour	,	continuing/listing contour
..	pause about 0.2 s or less	...	pause bet. 0.3 to 0.6 s
... (1.0)	pause about 0.7 s or longer	?	appeal
!	booster	↑	raised tone
-	restart	--	abandoned utterance (no restart)
> <	sped-up delivery of word within	< >	slowed-down delivery of word within
=	latching	°	reduced volume of word within
[ ]	speech overlap	:	lengthening
@	laughter	(( ))	researcher's comment
word	underline for emphasis	x	indecipherable mora
<x x>	uncertain hearing	<Q Q>	quotation quality
<@ @>	laugh quality		

Keys to gestural transcription (modified from Kendon 2004):

~~	preparation	***** (dotted underline)	pre-stroke hold
*****	stroke	***** (solid underline)	post-stroke hold
-.-.-.-.	recovery	bh	conducted by both hands
rh	conducted by right hand	lh	conducted by left hand
hd	conducted by head	| |	gesture phrase boundary
/	internal boundary for stoke	1, 2, 3, ..	number of repeated gestures
ê	glance/gaze	ʊ	nod

ABBREVIATIONS

ACC	accusative
ARA	affordance-reading ability
C-VPT	character viewpoint
COM	complementizer
COMP	complementizer
CON	conjunctive
COND	conditional
CONT	continuous
DAT	dative
DM	discourse marker
DVM	deictic verb of motion
FP	final particle
FOR	frame of reference
GEN	genitive
HON	honorific
IMP	imperative
INJ	interjection
INS	instrumental
IRE	initiation-response-evaluation
IU	intonation unit
LOC	locative
NEG	negative
NOM	nominalizer
O-VPT	observer viewpoint
PASS	passive

PRF	perfective
QM	quotation marker
QP	question particle
SB	subject
TOP	topic

GLOSSARY OF CLIMBING TERMINOLOGY

aid a use of means other than the action of hands, feet, and body.
anchor a means by which climbers are secured to a cliff; it can be natural (rock spike, flake, or a tree) or placed (a bolt, a peg, a nut/cam, or something similar).
arête an outside corner of rock, usually a narrow ridge of rock, ice or snow.
belay the procedure of securing a climber by use of a rope.
biners *see* carabiners.
bolt an artificial anchor placed in a hole drilled for that purpose.
bucket a handhold large enough to fully latch onto, like the handle of a bucket.
carabiners aluminum alloy rings equipped with a spring-loaded snap gate.
crack climbing to ascend on a rock by wedging body parts into a natural fissure in the rock wall.
crux the most difficult section of a climb or a pitch.
drop knee a technique that allocates the weight on the outside of one foot with the opposing foot supporting against another hold.
dyno a lunge move.
flash to lead a climb on the first attempt after having received prior information (or beta).
free solo to climb using hands and feet only; no rope.
free/free climb to climb using hands and feet only; the rope is used only to safeguard against injury.
gaston to maintain friction against a hold by pressing outward toward the elbow (often regarded as a reverse side pull).
gear the general name used for climbing equipment.
grade the "difficulty rating" given to a climb.
hangdog to rest on the rope or a piece of protection for a rest as you climb.
jam to wedge hands, feet or other body parts into a crack.
layback a method of ascending a crack or edge where the hands grip and pull while the feet are used to provide counterforce.
lead to be first on a climb; to lead a route, placing protection.
mantel a technique for which downward pressure is applied with the hands to a ledge, lifting the body high enough to raise the feet on that same ledge.
onsight to lead a climb on the first attempt without prior practice or information (or beta) of the route or moves.
pitch the section of rock between belays.
pro(tection) any equipment or anchors used for arresting falls.
quickdraw a short runner used to attach a rope to a bolted anchor with carabiners.
redpoint to lead a climb without falling or putting weight on the rope, regardless of number of attempts.
runout the distance between two points of protection, often referring to a long stretch of climbing without protection.
sidepull a hold that needs to be pulled sideways or that pulling action.
slab a large, featureless, off-vertical inclined sheet of rock.
smear to stand on the front of the foot and gain friction against the rock.
stance a standing rest spot, often the site of the belay.
top-rope to belay from a fixed anchor point above the climb.
traverse to move sideways, without altitude gain.

(Based on Long 2010: see also https://en.wikipedia.org/wiki/Glossary_of_climbing_terms)(Last accessed 29 November 2022)

1

Language and Body in Place and Space

1.1 Introduction

Spatial movement on horizontal and vertical planes is an action as old as human history. It is enacted to gain access to food and prey, to find a safe living space, and to seek a more habitable environment. This book revisits some major topics that have been discussed keenly in sociolinguistics and linguistic anthropology over the past thirty years, and attempts to offer new insights by focusing on a novel research area and activity—rock climbing. Rock climbing is a proactive activity based on free will and physical creativity. A climbing party typically consists of a climber (who leads the route) and a belayer (who applies tension to the rope to catch the climber in case of a fall). At the same time, certain protocols set by expert knowledge must be relied upon rigorously to ensure the safety of participants during the activity.

This book thus intends to demonstrate how language and the body in rock climbing are involved and mobilized for holistic activities that: (1) are maintained within institutional constraints; (2) are accomplished through intersubjective and intercorporeal exchanges; and (3) are carried out in accordance with culturally preferred "texts" including language, the body, and the environment in general. What I mean by these statements are that, first, rock climbing is achieved verbally and (inter)actionally according to institutionally particularized conventions to secure the activity's efficiency and safety. In that sense, it is akin to discourses that take place in courtrooms, classrooms, and medical encounters. Second, given the nature of rock climbing, the discourse therein heavily concerns the mutual engagement with and commitment to the key actions of climbing and belaying, for which intersubjective and intercorporeal understanding is essential for the informed interpretation of their actions. Thus, the range of investigation not only holds the climbing participants in scope but inevitably also incorporates the researcher, who is a participant observer as well as an interpreter of the event. Finally, climbing discourse reveals culturally significant aspects of what it means to be a climber through a particular formation of experience, or broadly defined "text." In the present data, Japanese rock/alpine climbers talk about climbing routes, partners, expeditions, and accidents as if they constitute what they are/were themselves, representing part of their identity and their community ethics.

Space and place have been an important theme in linguistics, sociolinguistics, linguistic anthropology, and discourse analysis since the 1990s, and have attracted extensive research interest. However, as the focus has been mainly on activities and movements in horizontal space, very few empirical studies have addressed the concept of extraordinary experiences in vertical space. This book discusses how everyday spatial experiences are realized (at least for rock climbers) verbally and nonverbally; the kind of perceptions that emerge from being in an extraordinary terrain; and how identity as a "climber" is expressed in climbing discourse. These themes will be addressed through accumulated observations of and participation in climbing activities. Although the intersection of language, the body, the equipment, and the environment is also a long-standing theme in the social sciences, it remains untrodden terrain that promises new insights by investigating rock climbing as a sport and an adventure. The insights will provide language researchers with an opportunity to reconsider the plasticity of language use and the diversity of experience by showing how both language and the body reflect and adapt to a gravity-laden activity.

Before I tackle those issues, it would be helpful to briefly review the history and the key concepts of rock climbing, as the activity is practiced less than other major sports. In what follows, different types of rock climbing—such as alpine climbing, free climbing, aid climbing, free solo, and bouldering, among others—will generally be called "climbing" unless there is a special need for differentiation.

1.2 A Very Brief History of Mountaineering and Rock Climbing

Humans have been present in the mountainous regions since prehistoric times. As late as 1991, a 5,300-year-old mummy named Ötzi was discovered in a glacier in the Ötztal Alps. It is clear, however, that in centuries past, people did not climb mountains purely for the "rush" of ascending peaks or routes, as is often thought to be the driver behind modern alpinism. As the literature has shown, many ancient peoples associated mountains with supernatural or religious concepts and thought they were inhabited by gods or demons. People were generally fearful about approaching mountains in those days and if they climbed them at all, it would have been for religious motivations, as a result of conflict, or to hunt and gather plants and animals, or to excavate mineral resources.

As the years passed, however, in Europe people threw off their superstitious shackles and began to pave the way for modern mountaineering, in which enthusiasts find infinite joy in the very act of climbing mountains. The forerunner of modern alpinism is said to be the Italian poet Petrarch. In April 1336, he climbed Mont Ventoux (1910 m) in Vaucluse, Southern France, with his brother and wrote a collection of letters, *epistolae familiars*, about the experience (Macfarlane 2003). His description of his amazement on seeing the vista from the summit is considered the first record of an individual climbing a mountain for personal fulfillment and one of the reasons why he is called the "father of alpinism."

In a broad sense, alpinism refers to mountaineering as a whole, but in particular to modern mountaineering and its ideology. Modern mountaineering, which began in the late eighteenth century, emphasizes the joy of climbing mountains and the benefits of the activity to the body and mind, which were believed to make life more fulfilling (Hansen 2013). Alpinism is also an ideology that aims to cultivate the technical skills of mountaineering and the knowledge of how to approach mountains in a holistic manner. Backed up by these beliefs, rock climbing has developed as a means of reaching the summit of a mountain in the European Alps. Along the way, it has also gained its own *raison d'être* as self-realizing leisure pursuit and a means by which participants can achieve their full potential.[1]

Although modern mountaineering declined temporarily during and after the Second World War, the 1950s saw a worldwide rush towards first ascents of 8,000-meter peaks in the Himalayas (there are fourteen), including Mt. Annapurna (8,091 m) by a French team in 1950, Mt. Everest (8,849 m) by a British-led team in 1953, and Mt. Manaslu (8,163 m) by a Japanese team in 1956. Not long after those historical ascents, Reinhold Messner, an Italian mountaineer, ascended all fourteen 8,000-meter peaks in 1986. He broke from traditional expedition-style mountaineering by advocating and practicing the "alpine-style" climb, characterized by self-sufficiency, such as carrying one's own food and equipment rather than using fixed ropes, porters, or supplemental oxygen. This trend also marked the start of a gradual decline in expedition-style mountaineering and opened the door to the commercial expeditions that would begin in the 1990s.

On the other hand, in Japan, mountain climbing developed alongside mountain worship and religion. There are many legends that link the ascent of mountains with religious beliefs, such as Mt. Hakusan (2,702 m), first scaled by the monk Taicho in 717, Mt. Tateyama (3,015 m), whose summit was allegedly reached by Saeki Ariyori in 701, and Japan's highest mountain, Mt. Fuji (3,776 m), which is said to have been climbed in the late tenth century (Kikuchi 2003; Suzuki 2015). Through the Kamakura period (1185–1333) and the Muromachi period (1336–1573), asceticism practiced by priests in mountain temples continued to flourish throughout Japan (except on the northernmost island, Hokkaido), following the ridge paths of each mountain range.

An epoch-making event occurred in 1874, when William Gowland, Robert William Atkinson, and Ernest Mason Satow became the first foreign party to climb Mt. Rokkō (931 m) in Kobe using ice axes and spiked boots. Gowland climbed Mt. Yarigatake (3,180 m) and Mt. Hotakadake (3,090 m) in 1881 and named them the "Japanese Alps" (Kikuchi 2003). In 1889, Walter Weston, a British clergyman, introduced tents, ropes, and other equipment to Japan, and on his recommendation, the first mountain club in Japan (later known as the "Japan Alpine Club") was established in 1905 by Kojima Usui and others. It is widely assumed that this year marked the beginning of modern alpinism in Japan.[2] Spurred on by the trend, the number of people climbing the Japanese Alps began to increase and mountaineering in general became particularly popular in the Taisho era (1912–26) (Haneda 2010).

In the post-war era, the first ascent of Mt. Manaslu (8,163 m) in 1956 by a Japanese expedition team was considered an historical event and triggered another nationwide mountaineering boom. From then until the 1980s, alpine climbing, with the ultimate goal of climbing the Himalayas, became the mainstream option in Japan, mainly among university alpine clubs and domestic mountaineering federations. In the 1980s, however, American-style free (and big wall) climbing and

European-style free climbing on short, hard routes were introduced and began to take hold in Japan. In addition, the gradual acceptance of "alpine-style" mountaineering in the 1980s changed the focus of Japanese mountaineering and spurred the decline of expedition-style alpine climbing—although it is still practiced avidly by some alpine clubs and federations.

Historically speaking, alpinism has encompassed a variety of outdoor activities aimed at climbing high mountains, but has since branched into distinct genres such as ice climbing, sport climbing, bouldering, buildering, and indoor climbing, among others. In addition, modern mountaineering displays sport-like but has as its sole focus the act of climbing, and in this respect, it differs fundamentally from religious mountaineering or mountaineering for war, hunting, surveying, and/or research. In particular, rock climbing has gained huge popularity around the world as an "alternative sport" (also termed "extreme sport," "lifestyle sport," and "adventure sport"). Sports climbing has also come to be associated with specific attention to its acrobatic practices and representations, especially when it made a new entry into the Olympic games in 2020.

In academia, outdoor activities have come to be seen through novel angles such that they shed new light on how humans and nature can interact in harmonious ways, bridging the permanent dichotomous split between "human–nature" and "mind–body" and affording overlooked possibilities for re-capturing them in a reciprocal manner (cf. Rossiter 2007; Latour 2004). Specifically, because of the possibilities inherent in climbing—in which perceptual, cognitive, physiological, technological, and environmental milieus meet and merge—the activity provides opportunities to work holistically and across disciplines, thereby offering a novel way of considering the intertwined network of humans and nonhumans.

1.3 Climbing Situations and Styles of Climbing

As background for the following discussion, let us review how a climbing situation differs from what is called a "canonical setting for speech" (Levelt 1989: Figure 1.1 (a)). A canonical setting is one in which "the interlocutors are relatively close to each

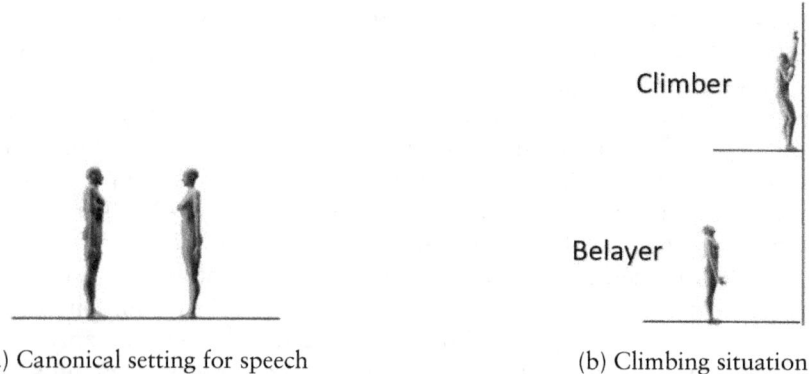

(a) Canonical setting for speech   (b) Climbing situation

FIGURE 1.1 *Canonical and climbing settings.*

other and mutually visible. They share both gravity and important aspects of the visual frame" (Levelt 1989: 49). In our case, however, this normative assumption needs to be modified for a rock climbing setting, which can be alternatively described as "aligned F-formation" (Kendon 1990) on staggered levels (see Figure 1.1 (b)).

These differences provide substantial research resources for the study of bodily movements, topological/coordinative expressions, and the interface between humans, bodies, and tools in the vertical plane (see Chapter 5). More specifically, these perceptual differences could be spelled out to a climber and belayer (who secures safety of a climber with rope) in the following ways:

1

(a) Orientation: The climbing situation is fundamentally based on a face-to-back or "aligned" (Hill 1982) orientation, while the canonical setting is based on a "face-to-face" or "facing" (ibid.) orientation.

(b) Gravity-sensitivity: The climber has to function in a precarious environment where gravity exerts a load on many body parts, whereas the belayer perceives gravity practically while on his/her feet, as in the canonical setting.

(c) Body axis: The climber's body axis is approximately parallel to the vertical plane of the rock surface. The belayer's body axis is perpendicular to the horizontal plane (as in the canonical encounter). Their axes are parallel, but on staggered levels.

(d) Field of view: The climber's field of view is limited on the vertical plane, but s/he can have a bird's-eye view of where the belayer is located on the horizontal. The belayer's perspective is approximately the opposite, providing a (rotated) bird's-eye view of the vertical plane.

Climbing a vertical plane is different in several crucial aspects from residing on the horizontal plane: In the vertical space, gravity can cause a fall, which could be fatal depending on the distance traveled. This is not normally the case on the horizontal plane, however. Also, although feet and legs primarily drive the movement forward on the horizontal plane, various body parts are used to move upward in the vertical space, appropriating protrusions, holes, cracks, and other physical features as "holds" (see Chapter 4). Moreover, since the angle of the viewing direction can be shifted variably, such tilting of the visual trajectory may induce a merger of the horizontal and vertical dimensions to different degrees (Chapter 5).

The previously mentioned conditions can vary depending on the style of climbing. Among various styles of rock climbing, sport climbing is the cutting-edge style in that the participant pursues purely technical refinement and physical strength in a safety-assured environment. As an official entry at the Tokyo Olympic Games 2020 (2021)), sport climbing was divided into three different styles: "bouldering," "lead climbing," and "speed climbing," the last of which is a special style practiced only for competitions[3] Despite their commonalities in climbing movements, lead climbing and bouldering should be technically separated because the former is usually performed in a "party" style (often two members) on a relatively high rock/wall formation and utilizes ropes, harnesses, and other protective devices to protect against a fatal fall, while the latter is usually conducted solo without any equipment (except for climbing shoes, chalk bags, and/or bouldering mats) on smaller rock formations or artificial rock walls.

With regard to the relationship between climbing style and social evaluation, the risk and recognition increase in correlation along the cline of "top-rope," "bolted protection," "traditional protection," and "free solo," which is based on the degree of safety and stability of "protection" (Langseth and Salvesen 2018: Figure 2).[4] As the name implies, free solo involves climbing a route without a rope or any protective devices and is undoubtedly the most adventurous and dangerous style (see *Free Solo*, the Academy-Award-winning documentary film (2018) about Alex Honnold's feat on El Capitan). On the other hand, top-rope is the safest and the most reliable method of climbing, with the rope running through a securely set anchor system at the top of a climb so that the belayer is ready to catch the climber at any time. Although only the climber's skills tend to be emphasized, both the climber's and belayer's expertise are crucial and need to be developed steadily to ensure both safe climbing and the healthy dissemination of climbing knowledge to newcomers.

Figure 1.2 (from Langseth and Salvesen 2018, with modification) generally applies to American-style free (and big wall) climbing in which natural, removable protections (nuts, cams, copperheads, etc.) are still widely used. European-style free climbing is largely limited to the "bolted protection" category. As far as all bolt-protected and some naturally protected routes are concerned, other styles are more precisely distinguished. The most acknowledged style among them is to "onsight" a route—i.e., to climb a route from bottom to top on the first attempt and without prior knowledge, such as watching others climb the route or doing any research of the moves.[5] The next highly acknowledged style is called "flash," which is to climb a route from bottom to top on the first try, but *with* prior knowledge of the route. "Redpoint" is the next common style and involves leading a route from bottom to top without falling or using protections. Still, it does allow for a rehearsal of "top-roping" and/or "hangdogging" before the attempt. These three styles are generally regarded as "leading a route," but climbing a route by top-roping is not. Accordingly, in the case of lead climbing, each style requires specific expertise on the part of the climber and the belayer respectively (see Chapters 3 and 4).

In bouldering, "problems"—specific routes—are also graded, and often require boulderers with specialized skills to use maximum effort. Thus, it normally takes

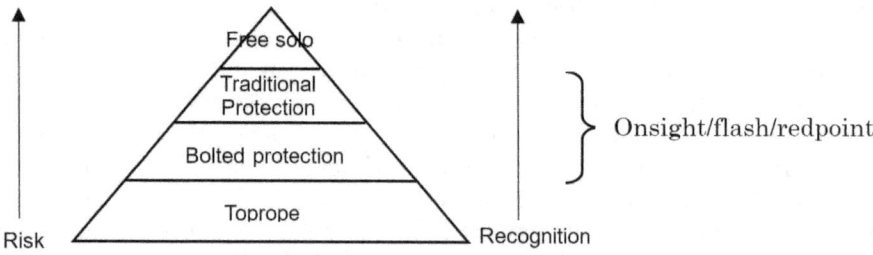

FIGURE 1.2 *Risk and recognition of climbing styles (Langseth and Salvesen 2018, CC-BY 4.0).*

boulderers several attempts to clear a "problem" unless its grade is much lower than their present level (see Chapter 4). As is often the case with lead climbing, climbers can use any features on/in the rock as "holds" as far as they find them useful. Thus, the number of attempts matters—i.e., the fewer the attempts, the more respect one receives. These conditions are somewhat different from those for indoor gym climbing and climbing competitions, where the number of holds used is restricted and specified. This means that the ability to "read out" holds from the environment may be reduced for some climbers, which renders solving a bounder problem at a climbing gym largely equivalent to producing a result in a physical performance test.

In outdoor climbing, however, climbers sometimes climb multiple pitches on a long route to reach the top or the end point. In such a case, party-style climbing is usually adopted. When the first climber—the leader—reaches an anchor point on the route, s/he now belays the follower from above in a top-rope manner. An anchor often consists of bolts nailed in the rock face or can be created on the spot by using protection devices such as "nuts" and "cams" and/or sewn slings hitched around trees or rocks. When the follower reaches the leader, the leader will hand the follower a set of necessary protection devices (known as a "rack" of gear). The follower then becomes the leader and climbs the next pitch. (However, if the climbers are not equally proficient, the previous leader continues on the next pitch.) This process continues until they reach the top or the end of the route (see Chapter 3).

There also exist competing ideologies between long-established traditional climbing processes and fast-developing sport climbing styles. In the turmoil of such shifts lies the question of to what extent the style used in the first ascent should be adhered to, especially in regards to the use of bolts as a protection device—a debate often called "bolt wars" (Bogardus 2012).[6] In the late 1960s and early 1970s, most US rock climbers were socialized into an ethic called "clean climbing." Those "clean" climbers basically espoused two ethical precepts: (1) to refrain from harming the rock; and (2) to "leav[e] a route unchanged so others may enjoy the creation of those who made the first ascent" (Robbins 1971: 61, cited in Bogardus (2012: 6)). Currently, the style for climbing varies according to the manner in which a climber ascends a route, ranging from a traditional, clean style (in the US) to the sports approach that originated in France and is widely practiced in Japan. In other countries, such as the UK, more audacious climbs on poorly protected routes have long been undertaken. In a sense, the style that a climber employs is a manifestation of their self-identity and/or cultural background (see Chapter 8).[7]

1.4 The Relevance of Climbing to Language and Discourse Studies

While theory is important, some of its utility will be lost if it is not better integrated into empirical research that explores people's everyday experience and lives. This book is no exception. Theoretically, spatial experience can be "iconic" and "indexical" (cf. Peirce 1955). Movement in space is often discussed in terms of a "cognitive/mental map"—a term that suggests that a concept of space is cartographic and therefore iconic. However, real places where people live are saturated with indexical values, and certain "qualia" (Harkness 2015) is attached to entities and experiences in the environment. These conceptual differences correspond in parallel to those between "navigation" and "wayfinding," as distinguished by Ingold (2000). In the case of mountaineering and climbing, the vertical space is conceived canonically in terms of "(spatial) frames of reference" (Levinson 1996a, 1996b, 2003) with which the movement therein is captured through geometric relations characteristic of navigation based on the Euclidean relationship. However, the act of climbing, or "wayfinding" on a route, consists of various moves and actions that center around particular "places" on the route such as holds, the crux, and protections, among others. These topological features are inevitably accompanied by indexical values constructed in the actor's lived space. For example, micro holds and cruxes would provide climbers and belayers with a sense of danger and caution, while bucket holds and protections provide a sense of security and relief from danger. In this respect, "places" are closely associated with affective and social significance.

At another intersection lies the gap between proximal and distal communication, both literally and metaphorically. The literature on mountaineering and climbing is abundant and encompasses (non)fictional works, periodicals and reports, travelogues, essays, editorials, and interviews, all of which are readily available today. Despite the apparent plethora of talks about climbing and mountaineering, real conversation rarely takes place during climbing activities except in urgent situations. Moreover, most climbers behave individualistically in physically separated environments. At the same time, however, a vast amount of *tacit* communication is taking place behind this facade, based on shared knowledge and expertise through aural, visual, and physical representations. Related to that distinction, this book exclusively addresses primary resources, such as verbal and physical interactions in/about climbing activities and people's near-death narrative experiences, while resources such as written texts and literature published after climbing activity are treated as secondary.

The phenomena examined in this book have similarities to Goodrich's (2004) investigation into rock climbing activities, although that study included only sparse discussion of specific utterances. Strongly influenced by Ingold's (2000) phenomenological approach to physical activity in space, Goodrich sees climbing as an activity that expands and inscribes itself in ways that adapt to the environment. Thus, spatial understanding developed through climbing emerges as a physical simulation rather than a mental representation. Among discourse-oriented studies, Kataoka (1998b) would be one of the forerunners, as he discussed the semantic expansion of the spatial lexicon negotiated between climbers and belayers from an enactive and phenomenological perspective. In another line of research, Human, Kriek, and Potgieter (2007) primarily used the method of conversation analysis to examine climbers' interaction from the perspective of discursive psychology. They investigated how rock climbers use laughter as a discursive tool to manage the difficulty of the climbing experience—although the scope of their analysis is narrow, and the data they address are limited.

Given the paucity of discourse-oriented research in climbing, the ethnography of mountaineering is an empirical juncture between primary and secondary resources. Since it requires a great deal of time, effort, and dedication, such works are not numerous, and those that focus on language and the body during climbing activities are even fewer. Ortner's (1999) pioneering ethnography of the sherpa was a representative example. In the past, climbing in the Himalayas was often a form of manifestation of nationalism and/or ethnic pride, and the sherpas (a term that was once used for a specific mountain tribe, but has been extended to include porters and operators engaged in Himalayan mountaineering) are now considered to be unique beings at the mercy of the ethnic, social, economic, political, and recreational forces of modernity. As such, they have attracted the interest of many anthropologists and ethnographers (e.g., Oh 2016; Miller 2017). Even in Japan, several ethnographies have been written about them (e.g., Kano 2001; Furukawa 2020). Also, the relationship between gender and mountaineering, particularly in high-altitude and/ or extreme climbing activities, has been institutionalized as a form of manifestation of masculinity as well as a system that excludes females. Gender studies focusing on this issue have increased in recent years (Robinson 2008; Dilley and Scraton 2010; Wigglesworth 2021).

Given the social impact of climbing, these issues are undoubtedly important for contemporary mountaineering and climbing.[8] This book, however, attempts to connect the inside and the outside, or the cognitive and the social, with more discourse-oriented approaches, highlighting the interaction of language, the body, and the environment. Building on this principle, I aim to fill the aforementioned gaps between theory and practice, primary and secondary data, and proximal and distal communication. As theoretical bases, I draw specifically on recent findings and models in linguistics, anthropology, and psychology, such as the typological classification of "spatial frames of reference" (Levinson 2003) and features of spontaneous gestures (McNeill 1992, 2005), as well as an ecological psychology concept called "affordance" (Gibson [1979] 2015; Reed 1996; Chemero 2003), and recent phenomenological and discursive investigation of "intersubjectivity" and "intercorporeality" (Ingold 2000; Meyer et al. 2017; Merleau-Ponty 1962). These ideas are approached eclectically and geared toward interactional and multimodal analyses of climbing communication (cf. McNeill 1992, 2005; Goodwin 2000, 2017; Mondada 2016).

To begin, the spatial lexicon in climbing is a case in point. The use of spatial terms is expected to not only encode perceptions in the immediate context, but to also represent linguistic relativity phenomenon called "collateral effects" (Sidnell and Enfield 2012; Enfield 2015). Equally, the use of tools (or climbing equipment) is another important issue in climbing because the expertise required to use them inherently involves knowledge and experience maximally relevant to the context (Carr 2010). In these respects, language, tool use, and the body in the lived space can never be examined sufficiently without recourse to intersubjectivity and intercorporeality. Reasoning and cognitive processes seen in climbing need to be verified empirically by attending to actual use of language and the body.

Narrative analysis is another important issue in this book. By investigating climbers' near-death and fall incidents, I argue that responsibility and authority in experience seeps covertly through the "denotational" (propositional) and "interactional" (indexical) text formation (Silverstein 1993, 2004; Agha 2007a). Also, since places in climbing are experience-filled and value-laden, the shift of narrated (and narrating) spatial events leads to representing distinct "chronotopes" (Bakhtin 1981; Perrino 2007, 2011; Blommaert 2015; De Fina and Perrino 2020). Thus, as the audience moves through the narrated space—whether it is real or imaginary—each place emerges with different perceptions and stances.

In addition, narrations of climbing experiences tend to be constructed in terms of highly (ethno) poetic formations (Hymes 1981, 1996, 2003; Kroskrity and Webster 2015), both verbally and nonverbally. In order to verify the assumption, co-speech gestures are simultaneously analyzed using multimodal analysis methods (Streeck et al. 2011; Goodwin 2017). Finally, I analyze highly contestable gossip about a climber who is believed to have caused the death of his climbing partner (cf. Besnier 2009) and follow the process in which the target of the gossip comes to be ostracized socially in terms of a cognitive model (D'Andrade 1998) that is shared based on community ethics and norms. All of these themes, combined with the concepts briefly introduced, cut into the interaction of climbing, the body, and the environment.

1.5 Data Collection Method and Participants

The data used in this book have been collected intermittently in Japan from the mid-1990s until 2021 and are based on fieldwork and linguistic ethnography. The data were collected in three different locations (Figure 1.3): a traditional rock-climbing area in Japan (around Mt. Hotakadake in the Northern Japanese Alps in Nagano Prefecture; a developing free-climbing area, Horai in Aichi Prefecture; and a free-traditional mixed area, Mt. Gozaisho in the Suzuka Mountains range in Mie Prefecture), all of which are popular and widely known among Japanese rock climbers. Additional data were collected at two indoor climbing gyms in Aichi Prefecture.

FIGURE 1.3 *Locations of data collection.*

Data collection for this book was made possible through the networks of an alpine club and a climbing community to which the author belongs. Approximately thirty interviewees were audio- or video-taped. The data also include interviews with world-class alpine climbers and free climbers who were active in the 1990s and 2000s. However, I concluded that some of the original data were inappropriate due to the sensitive nature of the content, and thus I excluded them from analysis. Part of the data has now been re-examined and included in the present analysis.

This study focuses on rock climbers' linguistic descriptions and bodily depictions, which I believe are highly sensitive to orientational and spatial configurations of the vertical dimension. Specifically, three types of data are investigated: (1) audio-/video-tape of immediate interactions in climbing; (2) audio-/video-tape of "near-death" narrative experiences; and (3) written data, such as mental map drawings and published and unpublished documents concerning the geographic areas.

In the first type of data, the participant observation method was used to obtain ethnographically valid data. Basically, the researcher accompanied the participants and conducted audio-/video-recording of their verbal and nonverbal behaviors, while also taking precise fieldnotes of the activity under investigation. For the second type of data, semi-structured interviews were conducted. The informants were audio-/video-taped when they narrated their near-death and wayfinding experiences in climbing and mountaineering or at any critical moments in the activities. The relationship between the interviewer and the interviewee was invariably casual, or at least informal, because the interviewees were basically acquaintances and friends of the interviewer. When the interviewees were complete strangers, they were acquainted prior to the session by an intermediary (a friend of a friend), who stayed and joined the session as an active participant, rendering the situation less formal and information more accessible. The first and second types of audiovisual data were later transcribed, though not completely, according to a modified transcription system based on Du Bois et al. (1993), Jefferson (2004) (for verbal data), and Kendon (2004) (for nonverbal data), totaling more than 100 single-spaced pages of Japanese transcripts. The third type of data includes map drawings of the critical scenes by some of the participants, as well as published route maps and articles in magazines, periodicals, and guidebooks aimed at rock climbers—however, these data were mainly for consultatory use.

1.6 Structure of the Book

This book consists of a preface and nine chapters. Chapter 1 (this chapter) concisely introduces the background of mountaineering and climbing and touches on the possible connections to discourse studies. The merit and significance of focusing on language use in/about climbing is outlined and connected broadly to sociolinguistic and linguistic anthropological theories and methods.

In Chapter 2, major theories and concepts to be applied to the following analysis are reviewed in the order of "inter-X" (X being action, subjectivity, and corporeality), "spatial frames of reference" (FoRs), "gesture and narration," "poetics in/of interaction," and "place and chronotope," emphasizing the contemporary significance of these notions in discourse analysis and linguistic anthropology. These approaches will be employed eclectically for a multimodal analysis of language, the body, and tools/materials in context.

Chapter 3 begins the substantive analysis and provides an overview of the process by which rock climbing is carried out, pointing out the similarity of the climbing system to the mechanism of certain institutional discourse. It also examines the participants' skills involved in carrying out "climbing and belaying" from the belayer's perspectives. Specifically, belayers' expertise in "how to catch" a falling climber is analyzed closely, showing that it is essential to make context-dependent reactions for avoiding unwanted consequences.

In Chapter 4, the concept of "affordances" in ecological psychology is applied to the data of climbing instruction with an assumption that vertical space provides a special "niche" for climbers, and that various holds on the wall serve as "affordances" from the environment. By analyzing a situation in which expert climbers teach novices how to solve a problem/move, I confirm that the construction of "fields of promoted actions" is important for a learning environment. Based on these results, I also show that climbing is an activity in which the actor's perception, knowledge, dexterity, and skill are inextricably connected.

Chapter 5 provides an analysis of how technical instruction from expert climbers to novice climbers is achieved verbally and nonverbally. The focus here is the use of the vertical lexicon *ue/shita* ("up/down") in the first-aid training session for climbers and an expert climber's *in situ* instruction to avoid "back-clipping" (an incorrect way of clipping a rope into a carabiner). As will be shown in these case studies, experts' instruction to a novice is accomplished through a series of spatial and bodily managements in ways to divert from the ordinary spatial axes, which suggests that even the robust perception of verticality may be overridden by contextual requirements.

Chapter 6 examines identifying the location of a fall accident that a participant suffered during the data collection. Here, spatial frames of reference, perspective-taking, physical representations, and experiential statuses are shown to be intertwined intricately. Specifically, multiple participants are shown to collaboratively construct a holistic spatial image through deictics and the transitions of the *origo*. In particular, I confirm that multimodal resources are abundantly invested in the wayfinding activity, in which a poetic configuration emerges through an "interactional" text.

Next, Chapter 7 conducts an (ethno)poetic multimodal analysis of participants' narratives of fall experiences. In particular, it becomes evident that the "near-death" narratives that feature critical and long-distance falls are told through ethnopoetic structuring and rely on culturally preferred formations common in Japanese. I also emphasize that narratives of such contested experiences are saturated with chronotopic values differentiated by distinct physical viewpoints, while at the same time they are aligned with certain narrative components.

Chapter 8, the final analysis-based chapter, concerns the functions of specific gossip that occurred inadvertently and evolved into debate on how one should hold accountable someone involved in a "suspected" accident. I follow the process that led to the denunciation of a deceased climber's partner, whose lack of responsibility might have been the cause of an unfortunate death on a wintry mountain. The key issue is how such gossip escalated to accusation through the manipulation of specific metaphors and quotations, augmented implicitly and incrementally by an ideology (or climbing ethics) shared among "wholesome" climbers.

Finally, in Chapter 9, I confirm the general importance of investigating the intertwined nature of language, space, and the body through rock climbing. As a human activity based on a fixed protocol, rock climbing should consist of overt strategies and covert expertise for achieving the specified interaction. Based on the findings and claims in preceding chapters, I conclude that, in an environment where specific spatial expressions and bodily depictions are foregrounded, it becomes clear which features are enhanced and which are retained as essential semiotic signs, revealing the core characteristics of everyday actions.

All things considered, I argue that in activities such as climbing rocks and mountains, facets of interaction exist that have been both naturalized and particularized. Based on the analysis of a non-Western language such as Japanese, I draw attention to the significance as well as the possible limitations of recent discursive theories and concepts, and aim to contribute to their refinement from an eclectic perspective. In Chapter 2, I review such major theories and concepts that are applied and (re-)considered in the succeeding chapters.

2

Theories and Approaches

2.1 Introduction

This chapter provides an overview of the theoretical foundations and methods of application that form the basis of the analysis in this book. The theme that runs throughout its chapters is a multimodal and multi-layered analysis of language and the body in rock climbing. The significance of the theme comes from the fact that rock climbing takes place mainly outdoors or in large indoor spaces and involves spatial descriptions and physical movements on the vertical as well as horizontal plane. In addition, rock climbing is an involving—sometimes deadly—spatial experience that is deeply concerned with perception and affect and thus directly related to some of the recent research themes on language and discourse; namely, "spatial frames of reference," "gesture and narration," "poetics in/of performance," and "chronotopes in climbing." Under these themes lie specific features that are contingent on climbing discourse: the three types of "inter-X"; i.e., inter-action, inter-subjectivity, and inter-corporeality. These concepts are closely related and loom large in tacit communicative achievement on which rock climbing rests. These issues will be touched on first.

2.2 Inter-action, Inter-subjectivity, and Inter-corporeality

The act of "climbing" is undoubtedly central to the activity of rock climbing, but it is inevitably paired with "belaying"—the activity of securing the climber against unavoidable incidents, such as falling and subsequent dangers. Although climbing and belaying are often performed at a distance, their activity is mutually dependent, and in this sense they are highly interactional. In addition, those participating in the climb are expected to follow a shared protocol, not only in terms of what they say, but also in terms of what they accomplish, exercising their accumulated skills and conforming to the implicit institution of rock climbing. For that purpose, an act of "putting oneself in others' shoes" is essential on occasions such as giving precise instructions to one's partner, offering advice on how to avoid danger, investigating the cause of a fall accident, or sharing a near-death experience. That is, "intersubjective" and "intercorporeal" immersion are prerequisites. Since these activities are accomplished largely through linguistic, aural, visual, and kinetic channels, a multimodal analysis is indispensable to precisely examine and represent the expertise involved in rock climbing in general. In the following, some theoretical backgrounds and approaches for such analysis are first reviewed.

In representations of expert knowledge and actions, the primary medium is often vision. Obviously, it plays a crucial role in discursive achievement of ordinary talk (Goodwin 1981; Rossano 2013) as well as in scientific representations (Latour and Woolgar 1987; Coopmans et al. 2014) and professional work/duties (Goodwin 1994, 2017; Heath and Luff 2000; Mondada 2003; Matoesian and Gilbert 2018), to name just a few. As has been argued meticulously in these studies, the use and application of "professional vision" (Goodwin 1994) is coupled with ongoing utterances to elaborate on how and what to see and focus on. For example, Goodwin (2000, 2017), summarizing an interactional process between expert and novice geographers, asserted that the process starts with giving a structure to a complex perceptual field by finger-pointing and other "focusing" techniques. The geographers then make a particular target object ("figure") stand out from its surroundings ("ground"), linking the structure to a concept shared within the community, and classifying it as an object of investigation. In so doing, the structure is made continuously salient and available as a medium for the practice of recording and classification. In a similar vein, rock climbing is also a primordial site wherein the "expert" vision and (re-)action come to the fore to sensitize the precaution for imminent danger. Further, multiple perceptions are found to be situated in the sequence of actions, and it is evaluated, revised, and applied to preceding actions as well as preparations for upcoming consequences (Iwasaki et al. 2019; Cekaite and Mondada 2020).

Such "expert (re)action" is often coupled with what is called "ascription" (Levinson 2013; Seuren 2018), the notion of which renders ordinary and unnoticed conduct in rock climbing accountable. In this regard, Levinson (2013) recommended the term "action ascription" instead of "action recognition" because the latter creates an assumption that an action can be correctly identified when it is executed as a turn. In the climbing practice, the relationship between a climber and a belayer is akin to that of a speaker and a listener, although the mode of interaction is overwhelmingly nonverbal. Thus, a particular action is assumed to fulfill the requirement of a turn if it constitutes necessary features in the sequence of the overall procedure, to which a belayer would adequately react. Usually, a judgment is made continuously in a chain of actions, and if they are not modified in subsequent turns, it is understood that an appropriate action has been conducted. To secure safety in climbing, the action ascription is implicitly customized, and it operates on shared knowledge and institutional constraints, both of which cannot be adequately explained without investigating a chain of conduct in the process.

–Unlike an ordinary conversation, the participants' roles (climber and belayer) are fixed rigidly and, as will be shown in Chapter 3, they follow the action sequence of the "beginning–middle–end," as defined in a traditional Aristotelian narrative model. During climbing, a leader makes relevant actions according to which a belayer reacts in appropriate manners such as taking in/out slack rope or "catching" a climber with a belay device in case of a fall. In addition, the distance between a climber and a belayer gradually increases as the climber ascends, even beyond the bounds of vision. Attention to this type of physically distal (but perceptibly proximal) participation would pose fundamental questions about the difference in and similarity to the online/telecommunication (e.g., Mondada 2012; Mirus and Keating 2003; Keating and Sunakawa 2010), and reveals yet a broader potential to bridge between/among sports/gaming activities as a form of institutionalized practice.

Rock climbers also engage in covert "multitasking," rather than "multiactivity," for the ultimate purpose of completing a climb (cf. Haddington et al. 2014).[1] Rock climbing is a goal-oriented activity in which each task consists of purposefully structured actions, and it has a recognizable starting point and a definite end point. In order to accomplish a climb, a climber and a belayer use different equipment to adapt to changing conditions and environments, mostly relying on visual, and sometimes tactile, sensoriality with minimal verbal exchanges (cf. Mondada 2016, Iwasaki et al. 2019). In so doing, the participants engage in more than one activity at a time. They make preceding and following activities relevant by orienting to the timing, order, and arrangement of those activities developing and emerging *in situ*, with concurrent actions contributing to a single purpose.

The point of departure for examining the institutional nature of rock climbing interaction would be Drew and Heritage's (1992b) scope and features of institutional talk (see also Heritage 2005). There they proposed, referring to Levinson's (1992) notion of "activity types," that institutional interaction is "informed by goal-orientations of a relatively restricted conventional form," and exhibits "special and particular constraints on what one or both of the participants will treat as allowable contributions to the business at hand"—the features largely shared in other settings such as education (Mehan 1979), legal procedures (Matoesian 2001; Coulthard and Johnson 2010), news interviews (Heritage and Greatbatch 1989), service encounters (Zimmerman 1984; Kidwell 2000), and so forth. Likewise, in climbing, tasks can be set, structured, and distributed among participants, and such tasks require specific skills that are appropriated to the expected roles, actions, and responsibilities. Thus, it is "associated with inferential frameworks and procedures" specific to the context (Drew and Heritage 1992: 22). Such institutional constraints in climbing are closely examined in Chapter 3.

These institutional constraints do not work in a void, but in an intersubjective realm of interaction. Many researchers are now deeply aware that the emergence and development of human sociality is not simply a matter of maturation, but rather is fundamentally motivated by, and geared toward, full-fledged human interaction (e.g., Enfield and Levinson 2006). Undeniably, one major precondition of the process is a concept of intersubjectivity (Merleau-Ponty 1962; see also Zlatev et al. 2008, Meyer et al. 2017, Lindstrom et al. 2021). In social and cognitive sciences, this phenomenological notion has been heavily incorporated into ethnomethodology, anthropology, and interactional studies. In fact, many sociologists and anthropologists in the 1960s and 1970s built much of their work on the phenomenological foundations in order to investigate the emerging nature of everyday interaction (e.g., Garfinkel 1967; Goffman 1959; Cicourel 1973), and such a tradition persistently continues in current endeavors (Ingold 2000; Csordas, 2008; Gillespie and Cornish 2009; Duranti 2009, 2010).[2]

Duranti (2010), for instance, defined it in plain terms and argues for its renewed importance in language and communication studies as follows:

For Husserl, intersubjectivity means the condition whereby I maintain the assumption that the world as it presents itself to me is the same world as it presents itself to you, not because you can "read my mind" but because I assume that if you were in my place you would see it the way I see it. This is captured by the notion of *Platzwechsel*, that is, "trading places" or "place exchange," which is made possible by empathy.

DURANTI, 2010: 6

Duranti also emphasized that although intersubjectivity has often been regarded as something that must be "achieved," it is "not a product or an effect of communication but a condition for its possibility" (Duranti 2010: 9). Although this book looks into achieved aspects of interaction specifically, it will be confirmed that the phenomena at issue are made possible only by the participants' being then and there, in a certain formation, for a common goal, with intersubjectivity as a precondition to communication. In that respect, intersubjectivity does concern more of "the possibility of being in the place where the Other is" (Duranti 2010: 1), and hinges upon a condition of what may be called environmental affordances. Ingold (2000: 264)) further made a crucial point of inseparability of the self and the other (including the environment), stating that "(w)e live in visual space from the inside, we inhabit it, yet that space is already outside, open to the horizon. Thus the boundary between inside and outside, or between self and world, is dissolved." I focus on such perceptually and experientially integrated phenomena emerging in rock climbing discourse.

The notion of intersubjectivity has also been extensively applied to various branches of the cognitive sciences and anthropological studies based on a premise that it serves as a cognitive foundation for developing sociality (Rogoff 2003; Tomasello 2008), revealing that even neonates could manifest the burgeoning features of intersubjective intentions (Nagy 2008; Frank and Trevarthen 2012). Further, because of the crucial property of taking others' perspectives, intersubjectivity is thought to be a defining feature of the human species (and possibly enculturated apes) (Tomasello 1999; Tomasello and Carpenter 2007). In addition, because of its encompassing nature, intersubjectivity has been extensively recapitulated as "distributed cognition" (Hutchins 1995), "joint attention" (Moore and Dunham 1995; Tomasello 2008), "shared intentionality" (Tomasello and Carpenter 2007), and various versions of "the X mind," where X could be readily replaced by, say, "embodied," "discursive," "social," or "shared" (Zlatev et al. 2008).

All of these tenets are highly pertinent to, and typically concerned with, the phenomena I consider in this book. In fact, the phenomena to be analyzed in Chapters 4, 5, and 6 are largely analogous to what Zlatev illustrated as the (full) "third-order mentality," which is heuristically paraphrased as "I see that you see that I see X" (Zlatev 2008: 227). Fuchs (2013) further mentioned that the second-person perspective (2PP) mediates between the first-person and third-person perspectives (1PP and 3PP respectively), and it is acquired developmentally. The key to development, Fuchs said, is the second-person interaction, which serves as an intermediary for acquiring 1PP-dependent "self-consciousness" and 3PP-dependent "other-consciousness" through joint attention and taking the perspective of others in cooperative and collaborative situations. Such a perspective is always held implicitly, and develops into a higher-level point of view that becomes explicitly conscious through the metaperspective.

A critical awareness here is that the "inner (or psychological)" and the "outer (or physical)" may not be so clearly separated. Rather, one cannot escape the influence of the other in that they mutually ride into each other through (inter)subjective and somatic correspondences (Merleau-Ponty 1962; Meyer et al. 2017). What mediates the "inner" and the "outer" is the body in space, which lays the groundwork for the social, cognitive, and neurobiological underpinnings (Johnson 1990; Van Wolputte 2004; Iacoboni 2009). According to Meyer et al. (2017), intercorporeality is postulated to serve as the most basic form in human social interaction, and various types of cooperative actions such as gazing, hugging, kissing, and speaking are typically achieved through joint attention and taking others' perspective in cooperative and collaborative situations. Now, more interdisciplinary attempts need to be made to incorporate these notions into an integrated approach to language, the body, and the environment, in which rock climbers typically and intensively participate. Thus, the theorem of intercorporeality is the other side of the same coin and should not be considered as a revised version of the mind-body split.

The idea of intersubjectivity is highly compatible with the idea of "affordance," which was originally defined as "what it *offers* the animal, what it *provides* or *furnishes*, either for good or ill" (Gibson [1979] 2015: 119), but more plainly as "an action possibility formed by the relationship between an agent and its environment" (*Encyclopedia of the Sciences of Learning* 2012). For example, Chemero (2003, 2008) maintained, based on Heft's (2001) view that Gibson's ecological psychology is a direct inheritance of William James's radical empiricism, that affordances are properties of an environment having perceived functional significance for an animal. Affordances are percepts rather than concepts and are always the core content of what is perceived. Gibson was also concerned with a problem inherent in the idea of "pure experience," especially about the possibility of what James called "the problem of two minds" perceiving the same object—a critical issue of intersubjectivity. If you and I perceive an affordance in the environment, our experiences (and perceiving minds) overlap. That being the case, our minds are not private nor separate—a tenet that also leads to socially distributed cognition. Through this line of argument, Chemero (2003) maintained that what we perceive is not in the environment alone but that affordances are "relations between particular aspects of animals and particular aspects of situations." (Chemero 2003: 184).

Japanese philosopher Ichikawa (2010 [1996]) made a similar argument with his notion of *mi-wake* ("corporal division"): "In other words, the body dividing the world with the body is at the same time the body being divided through the world. It is a co-incidental event, and a phase of a situation. . . . . While the body is segmented by the historically and socially segmented semantic world, it re-segments the world by itself, and is simultaneously re-divided by the re-segmented world" (Ichikawa 2010 [1996]: 26, my translation). Thus, the body, as the origin of perception, is divided into the orientations of "up" and "down," "front" and "back," and "right" and "left," which have a qualitatively specific valence. However, this specificity is "gradually neutralized by behavioral shifting of the center and representational de-centering" (ibid: 26). In other words, by repeatedly trans-locating the origin and axes of the coordinate system, the internal structure of the system is neutralized, and a homogeneous quantitative coordinate space is established. Such a space would be equivalent to an intersubjectified/intercorporeal space.

Also, the Japanese notion *ba(sho)* ("place/space/context") in/of discourse is represented as the source of all these perceptions. Instead of seeing the individual as an independent cognizer, actor, or practitioner, the Theory of Ba (Hanks et al. 2019) emphasizes that an un(/pre)conscious sense of co-presence exists among participants; it is culturally and historically constructed, handed down, and reinforced and renewed (including bodily knowledge) in the process of transmission. The sharing of such perception is in line with the concept of the "historical body" (Nishida [1941] 1989; Scollon and Scollon 2004), which has been long sought in Zen/Buddhist thought, and defines the place where Husserlian "intersubjectivity" unfolds (see also Lusthaus (2003), who pointed out fundamental affinities between Husserl and Merleau-Ponty's phenomenology and Yogachara School of Buddhism).[3] This type of communication is characterized by an ontology of "mutual dependence, impermanence and ultimately non-separation" (Hanks et al. 2019: 64). Such a state of being represents the pre-cognized sharing of the "primary Ba"—"place"—which holds intersubjectified participants. On the other hand, what I will analyze here focuses on a different level of "place," or the "secondary Ba," in which a process of categorial information unfolds and serves as the locus for "articulation, categorization and distinction" (Hanks et al. 2019: 65), the understanding of which cannot be fully established without the sharing of the "primary Ba." In other words, the ways in which Ba is shared among participants through collaborative wayfinding, are modes of emergence of the primary Ba. There, sharing of subjectivity and corporeality is not enough—sharing of situational awareness of Ba is also essential.

These approaches to people's perception and experience give us thought-provoking and challenging clues to analyzing the discursive practice in rock climbing and will be tackled in Chapters 4, 5, and 6.

2.3 How Space is Perceived, Conceived, and Represented

2.3.1 Spatial Perspectives and Spatial Frames of Reference (FORs)

Since rock climbing is conducted in space, discourse therein inevitably necessitates specific means to describe and depict it. One of the essential means is the use of a "spatial frame of reference" (FOR), an important concept connecting perspective-taking and bodily representations, and closely related to gestural and narrative performances. Referring to the integrated phenomenon, I occasionally use the term "perspectivization," which is meant to represent the act of perspective-taking realized through various semiotic means, whether conscious or unconscious. It is a practice through which people grasp and interpret things in space and their relations, states, and events. Although the term "perspective-taking" is often used, it smacks of a conscious and active manipulation and often fails to encompass unconscious and culture-specific styles of grasping and utilizing spatial relations. I thus use the term "perspectivization" to alleviate such discomfort.

Multiplicity of perspectivization is also a central issue in the study of deixis and "shifters" (Jakobson 1960). Deixis indexes the locus of the cognitive base (= *origo*), which can never be separated from the context of utterance (e.g., Fillmore [1971] 1997; Klein 1982). Levinson (1983) took up deixis as one of the major themes in pragmatics, and pointed out that it is based on the understanding of not only space but also time, person, context, and social relations through "spatialization" of the concept[4] On the other hand, there have been numerous discourse studies on the shifting of perspectives in the recollection of spatial relations and the results of map tasks (Linde and Labov 1975; Klein 1982, 1983; Brown 1995; Yoshida 2011). For example, Linde and Labov (1975) defined two prominent types of perspectivization, Route and Map, and discussed the correspondence between discourse progression and linguistic forms. Klein (1982, 1983) analyzed the relationship between (mainly) egocentric orientations and geographical factors in route-finding, and pointed out the continuity of perspectives in terms of the "shifted origo."[5]

Levinson (1996a, 1996b, 2003) and his colleagues (Pederson et al. 1998) shed new light on a linguistic relativity hypothesis by focusing on the tripartite typology of FORs and led the spatial cognition research in the 1990s and 2000s. They used a common experimental tool called the Space Kit to realize as natural an environment as possible in the indigenous fieldwork. The authors' basic claims are that different human groups use different spatial frameworks, often with distinctive sets of coordinate systems in both language and cognition. They contended that robust correlations exist between FORs used in language and those used in non-linguistic memory and reasoning and in many aspects of behavior, communication, and culture, which overall suggests a major "Whorfian" effect of language on cognition.

Despite the bewildering terminological inconsistency across disciplines, Levinson (1996b, 2003) suggested capturing approximate commonalities, such that an "egocentric," "viewer-centered," and "2.5D sketch" perspective roughly maps onto the "relative" FOR; an "object-centered," "3D" perspective maps onto the "intrinsic" FOR; and an "environment-centered" perspective corresponds to the "absolute" FOR.[6] To make this model more accessible, his examples in the preface to his 2003 book (specifically sentences (i) to (iii) in Figure 2.1 therein) are used here as a starting point.

First, the sentence in (i) "The cat (1) is behind the truck," is one way of correctly describing the scene. The coordinate system employed here is called the *intrinsic* FOR because the cat's position is identified in terms of the truck's intrinsic back, derived from its default direction of motion. In this FOR, the spatial relation is "binary," or relating two objects/entities (cat and truck) in the immediate context. However, another reading of the sentence is possible if there is the cat (2) on the occluded side of the truck from the viewer's standpoint. The ambiguity comes from another FOR—the *relative*—applied to the spatial expression *behind*. In Levinson's framework, it is distinguished from the intrinsic FOR in that it is characterized by angular specifications computed by the "ternary" relationship among *cat*, *truck*, and *viewer*.[7] In the *absolute* FOR, the referring practice can be simpler because this FOR only requires as an anchor the absolute directions such as "NSEW," "where the sun rises/sets," "uphill/downhill," "upstream/downstream," or any orientation based on fixed and stable geographic features. The relation is thus "binary" between these absolute orientations and the referent. Accordingly, in Figure 2.1, an English speaker could describe the cat's positions with sentences (iii), "The cat (1) is to the east of the truck," and "The cat (2) is to the north of the truck," although such

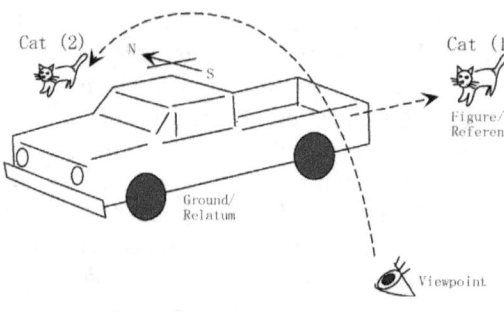

(i) **Intrinsic FOR** (binary relation)
"The cat (1) is *behind* the truck."
(The cat is at the place contiguous with the intrinsic back part of the truck: the coordinate system based on the "truck." Origin: truck.)

(ii) **Relative FOR** (ternary relation)
"The cat (2) is *behind* the truck."
(The cat is on the occluded side of the truck from the standpoint of the viewer, and the truck is between the cat and the speaker: the coordinate system based on the "viewer." Origin: viewer)

(iii) **Absolute FOR** (binary relation)
"The cat (1) is *to the east of* the truck."
"The cat (2) is *to the north of* the truck."
(The coordinate system based on cardinal directions or conventional absolute directions. Origin: truck)

FIGURE 2.1 *"The cat is _____ the truck."*

expressions are highly marked in some societies because they require the speaker to identify compass directions in advance.

Based on this tripartite typology of spatial FORs, Levinson and his colleagues' findings showed that many languages use an "absolute" FOR (e.g., "to the north of the truck" instead of "behind the truck") and that those absolute notions appear as early as topological notions such as "in," "on," and "under" (see also Haun et al. 2006). This is surprising because some researchers (e.g., Pinxten 1976) have proposed that topological notions should be typologically spatial primitives observed in most languages and thus confined to developmentally earlier stages (as clearly articulated in the Piagetian tradition), while absolute notions appear in much later stages. Even more surprising is the fact that spatial lexicons such as "right/left" and "front/back" are fundamentally missing in some languages (e.g., Levinson and Brown 1994). These findings call for a new typology of spatial FORs that adequately covers unfamiliar situations in which angles and directions are specified in different ways from ours (including English- and Japanese-speakers).

2.3.2 Spatial Perspective-taking in Discourse

Although Levinson's notion of FORs (frames of reference) is a "static" etic grid for spatial reference, it can also be a source for a "dynamic" framework to be applied to discourse, with some modifications—i.e., if we conceive it as a series of configurations projected from various emergent vantage points. For this assumption to work, we first need to make a distinction between "spatial frame of reference" (FOR) and "descriptive modes" (DMs) in spatial representations. Since Levinson did not particularly consider this issue, a possible modification of his framework should be proposed for the analysis of discourse data. For that purpose, it is necessary to briefly review some major works that have addressed discourse-related phenomena and how they have treated shifting perspectivization.

The mechanism of spatial perspective-taking has been explored in depth in psychology and linguistics, and is often summarized as the three types of perspective-taking: "route/tour," "gaze," and "survey," as shown in (1) and Table 2.1 (based on Linde and Labov 1975; Ehrich and Koster 1983; Taylor and Tversky 1996).

1   Different descriptive methods (DMs)

   (a) Route: Linde and Labov (1975: 929)

   If you **keep walking** in that same direction, you're **confronted by** two rooms **in front of** you . . . large living room which is about. . . . And on **the right side, straight ahead** of you again, is a dining room which is not too big. . . . .

   (b) Gaze : Ehrich and Koster (1983: 175, English translation from the original Dutch)

   When I come in the door, then I see, **to the left of** me on the wall, a large window with, **in front of** that, a red velvet couch with, **to the left of** that, a wooden couch **Next to** the red couch, in the corner, is an eh large floor lamp. . . . .

   (c) Survey: Taylor and Tversky (1996: 379)

   North of town are the White Mtns. and **east of** town is the White River, which flows **south from** the White Mtns. The stables are **on the south side of** this road, named River Hwy. and across the road **to the north** is the town. . . .

Do the Route/Tour, Gaze, and Survey DMs in Table 2.1 respectively correspond to the three types of FORs, "intrinsic", "relative", and "absolute" (Levinson 2003)? Actually, some critical differences exist between them. For example, the "Route/

Table 2.1 Three perspectives and related notions

	ROUTE (OR TOUR/WALKING)	GAZE	SURVEY
PERSPECTIVE	within, changing	outside (on the eye level), horizontal, fixed	outside (from above), vertical, fixed
RELATIONS	relate objects with respect to the speaker/addressee	relate objects with respect to one another	relate objects in terms of absolute directions
CAN BE SEEN IN ONE VIEW?	No	Yes	Yes
SINGLE ORIGO?	No	Yes	Yes
DESCRIPTIVE TYPE	exploration/navigation	gaze/attention shift	bird's eye view
LEVINSON'S FORs.	Intrinsic (to 'traveling' addressee)	Relative (to viewer/speaker)	Absolute
TERMS OF REF.	LRFB	LRFB	NSEW (UP/DOWN)
PREVIOUS VISUAL INPUT	Necessary	Not necessarily	Not necessarily
REFERENT	person	object or person	object
VERB TYPES	active	stative	stative

Tour" mode adopts a dynamic description method that uses action verbs from the perspective of the moving actors, while Levinson's "intrinsic" FOR describes spatial relations statically based on the orientation inherent in things other than the observing viewer. In addition, although the "Survey" mode assumes the use of an absolute lexicon, it does not posit a correlation with the absolute cognitive style assumed by Levinson's model. In this respect, Levinson's three categories of reference frames are consistent in that they are propositionally defined in terms of "static" and "configurational" spatial relations based on the semantic properties of the lexicon. On the other hand, the styles of perspective-taking in previous studies have characterized the "descriptive modes" (DMs) rather than the features of FOR, rendering the correspondence between them partial and contextual (see Kataoka 2018 for detailed discussion of a finer classification[8]). In short, the concept of FOR is a typological framework based on the Euclidean geometrical and semantic truth-value of a three-dimensional space, while the concept of perspective-taking is defined in terms of the dominant descriptive modes of space, which are based on the perspective of the actor in the (imaginary) space.

One source of confusion regarding these frameworks is that each represents different aspects of spatial descriptions such that Route/Tour perspective is a special case in which Relative FOR is merged with the intrinsic orientation of the object (or actor), and Survey perspective, to (partially but not necessarily) Absolute FOR. Generally speaking, Levinson's "relative reference" corresponds to the "observer-centered perspective," "intrinsic reference" to the "object-centered perspective," and "absolute reference" to the "environment-centered perspective in conventional psycholinguistic parlance. However, an "intrinsic" reference based on the other speaker's (or object's) point of view is often merged with the observer's point of view through what we call "intersubjectification" (or shifted *origo*), representing a "Route/Tour perspective" (Linde and Labov 1975; Taylor and Tversky 1996) and "direct perspective" (Danziger 2010),[9] which is not explicitly formulated in Levinson's classification of FORs. Given this, Levinson's FOR grid does not incorporate intersubjective perspective-taking as a viable type of spatial reference even though intersubjectivity would be the main factor that ensures the achievement of reasoning in dynamic spatial communication.

As previously shown, the FOR grid and DMs are closely related and continuous; however, they are different methods of spatial descriptions, even if they are employed spontaneously and as combined in ongoing spatial discourse. In addition, spatial representations are not limited to verbal descriptions, but can include bodily depictions. In the following, a comprehensive model that can moderate and mediate these differences is proposed for the multimodal analysis of the spatial representations in rock climbing discourse.

2.3.3 Integrating Perspectives Exuded by the Body

To classify the types of perspectivization, the basic parameters considered here are the viewer's "Internal vs. External" linguistic descriptions (Linde and Labov 1975; Levinson 2003) and the 'Character vs. Observer' viewpoints (McNeill 1992) represented in gestures and postures. The rationale for the combination comes from the need to ensure the conceptual and methodological plasticity that can mediate both perspective and corporeal considerations. "Internal vs. External" perspectives in language are major distinctions conceived as extreme ends on a continuum, while "Character vs. Observer" viewpoints are corporeal counterparts of another continuum of perspectivization, both of which are assumed to emerge from the same conceptual source—the "Growth Point Hypothesis" (McNeill 2005). That is, perspectivization is not limited to language, but is also reflected in a variety of bodily representations, making multimodal and interactional consideration essential. In particular, the mechanism of language and gesture production has been the subject of continuous debate (McNeill and Duncan 2000; Kita and Özyürek 2003; De Ruiter 2007), and a point of contention exists around whether the production of representational gestures is influenced by both mental images and structural features of the accompanying speech (Kita's Interface Model), or whether it is a mutually independent process (De Ruiter's Sketch Model).[10] One may stand on either position, however, spatial representations can never be adequately analyzed without taking into consideration both verbal descriptions and corporeal depictions.

Given these theoretical bases, "Internal vs. External" perspectives and "Character vs. Observer" viewpoints can be combined to constitute four basic modes of viewer-centered perspective in a 2 x 2 grid (Table 2.2). These modes will coherently validate

Table 2.2 Viewer-oriented spatial frames of reference reconsidered

	Internal	External
Character	(1) **Character-internal Prs: (Actor's or relatum's VPT):** • Linde and Labov (1975) "tour" • Levelt (1996) "intrinsic" • Ullmer-Ehrich (1982) "walking tour" • Taylor and Tversky (1996) "route" • McNeill (1992) C-VPT • Danziger (2010) "direct" ➢ Levinson's (2003) "intrinsic" is a special case where Origo is replaced by an oriented relatum	(4) **Character-external (Intersubjective) Prs:** • Bredel (2002) "self-positioning *du*" • Kataoka (2004) "merged perspective" • Zlatev (2008) "Joint attention: Third-order mentality" • Parrill (2009) dual viewpoint gestures ➢ Langacker's (1990, 1999) "subjectification" largely captures this phenomenon
Observer	(2) **Observer-internal Prs: (Viewer's VPT):** • Klein (1982) "deictic" • Levelt (1996) "deictic" • Ullmer-Ehrich (1982) "gaze tour" • Taylor and Tversky (1996) "gaze" • McNeill (1992) Inside/outside O-VPT • Levinson (2003) "relative"	(3) **Observer-external Prs (w/ or w/o "absolute" awareness):** • Linde and Labov (1975) "map" • Taylor and Tversky (1996) "survey" • McNeill (1992) Outside O-VPT ➢ Levinson's (2003) "absolute" is a special case where Origo is replaced by a geographically fixed coordinate

previous findings and incorporate what might be called an "intersubjective" perspective in a cogent manner. The following model is a tentative grid of perspectivization based on such awareness (Kataoka 2014, 2018).

The categories marked (1) to (3) in Table 2.2 approximately correspond to the three major types of perspective-taking acknowledged in previous studies, although they are termed differently even in related disciplines (see Levinson, 2003: Ch. 2 for a cross-disciplinary review). The major difference between the current study and those models is our focused attention to the fourth category, or what I call the "Character-external" ("intersubjective") perspective (Table 2.2 (4)). This perspective may present in various combinations and degrees of synthesis. That said, the term "intersubjective perspective" is used in a highly restricted sense here, and is assumed to be one emergent style of a broader notion of intersubjectivity. Figure 2.2 is an illustrated representation of perspectival potentials defined in Table 2.2.

Cases I to III in Figure 2.2 illustrate these possibilities in a visually simplified format and account for the major three types of perspectivization (i.e., the continuum of "C-VPT—Inside O-VPT—Outside O-VPT" to be explained below). These concentric frames indicate a gradual increase in scope and scale as one goes from I to II, and from II to III. The possibilities of perspectivization, however, are not exhaustive, and they may succumb to more expansion. They constitute a multilayered grid in which an active viewer's perspective moves in and out of possible frames of perspective (I⇔II: (IV-a) in Figure 2.2) or II⇔III (IV-b)), or lead to an extreme case in which the Character's internal perspective may be dialectically merged with the Observer's external perspective (I⇔III (IV-c)), a case specifically called the "intersubjective" perspective here. Although theoretically and experientially plausible, such perspectivization is rather rare and not readily mobilized in actual interaction, presumably because speakers/actors have to cross multiple perspectival boundaries.

The reality could be more dynamic and complex. For example, if there are multiple viewers in one region, a result could be another case of "intersubjective" perspective, which requires mutual calibration of where they are in the shared space, whether real or virtual. Such "merged" perspectives would be created between human- and other-oriented entities (such as a car (driver): I⇔I' in Figure 2.2) or between a viewer and a bystander (II⇔II'). The perspectives could also be embedded in multiple layers of displacement (III⇔III')—although there would be a limitation due to the incremental cognitive load. Furthermore, being intersubjective may even concern the same viewer with spatio-temporarily displaced statuses, such as those between his/her selves today and yesterday—in this very sense, narration is inherently an intersubjective practice.

In spontaneous discourse, a process that results in intersubjectivity may be covert, context-embedded, and embodied. As postulated here, spatial perspectives cannot simply be represented by language alone, but are also represented through one's body and/or other entities in the environment—even to the extent that some spatial representations eventually become incongruent. Beyond the surface discrepancies, such perspectives may still attain a higher-order dialectic merger consisting of

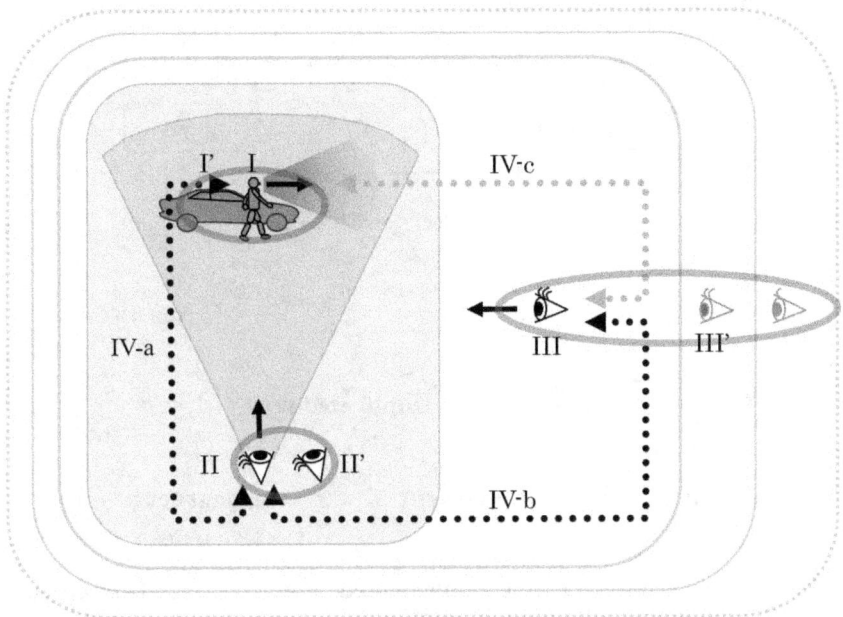

FIGURE 2.2 *Four major types of perspective-taking.*

different realities. Therein lies the importance and need for this micro-analysis of "triadic (bodily) mimesis" (Zlatev 2008) and multimodal semiosis (Goodwin 2003, 2007). For verbal/gestural perspectivization to surface, there could be various possibilities (Figure 2.3).

Perspectivization can surface in the case of (a) language alone and (b) gesture alone ("singular"), and its expression is based only on the content/referent of speech or gesture ("independent"), or, assuming that the Interface Hypothesis is supported, it can surface after being influenced by the other ("fused").

In addition, when speech and gesture co-occur ((c): "duplicated"), the perspectives embedded in both modalities may be "congruent" or "incongruent." In the "congruent" case, words and gestures may "amplify" (e.g., saying "right" and pointing to the right) or "complement" (e.g., saying "this way" and pointing to the right) the described/depicted content. In the case of "incongruence," not only is the semantic content of the utterance "discrepant" with the referent of the gestural depiction (e.g., saying "north" and pointing to the east; see for example Chapter 6, for saying "go" and depicting the "coming" motion), but also the semantic content and bodily representation may intersect, resulting in a "fused" form (e.g., Parrill 2009; Furuyama et al. 2011; Kataoka 2013). These cases would typically correspond to a case of intersubjective perspectivization in which multiple perceptions are dialectically merged and naturalized. However, how these modes of representation are played out in a coordinated way in the ongoing discourse is yet to be fully

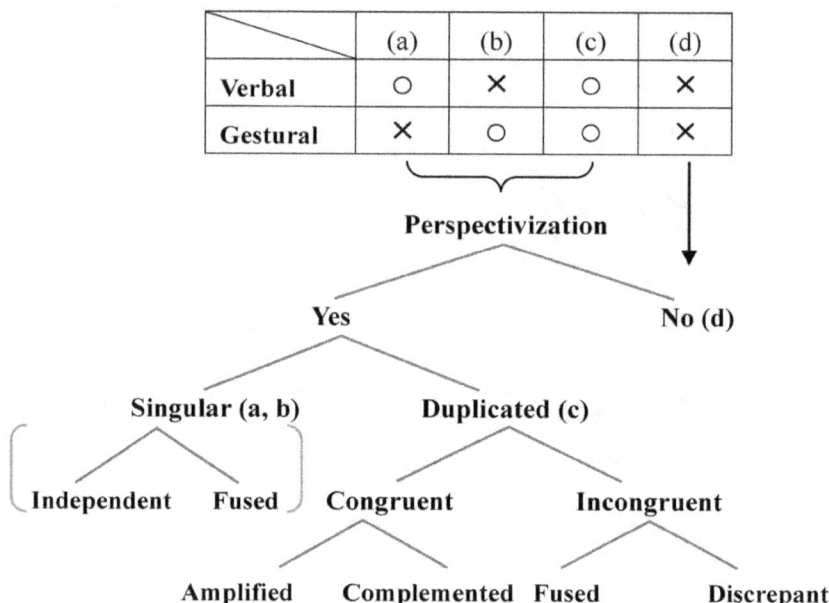

FIGURE 2.3 *Possibilities of verbal/gestural perspectivization.*

examined. Such issues of space and the body are also the main themes of Chapters 5 and 6.

2.4 Gesture and Narration

Following the objectives of this book, multimodal analysis is an essential method in bringing language and the body into the scope of analysis. As background for the analysis, it would be helpful to briefly overview classification of the gesture types and the components of a gesture unit as defined by McNeill (1992, 2005) and Kendon (1990, 2004), who set cornerstones for the present-day gesture studies. The relevance of gesture to narrative is then confirmed based on the findings of Cassell and McNeill (1991) and McNeill (1992).

First, gestures are variably defined in terms of shape, content, and function (e.g., McNeill 1992, 2000). Figure 2.4 shows one such classification of gesture types summarized by Kita (2002: 48). One type of gesture widely acknowledged would be "emblems." Emblems are socially conventionalized and shared in their form and meaning in each community, and include such gestures as "V-sign," "bowing," and "pointing to the nose" (to indicate the self in Japan). In that sense, they have symbolic characteristics similar to words and phrases. There are other types of gestures summarized as "spontaneous gestures" that do not rely on such social conventions and appear mainly with speech (i.e., as co-speech gesture).

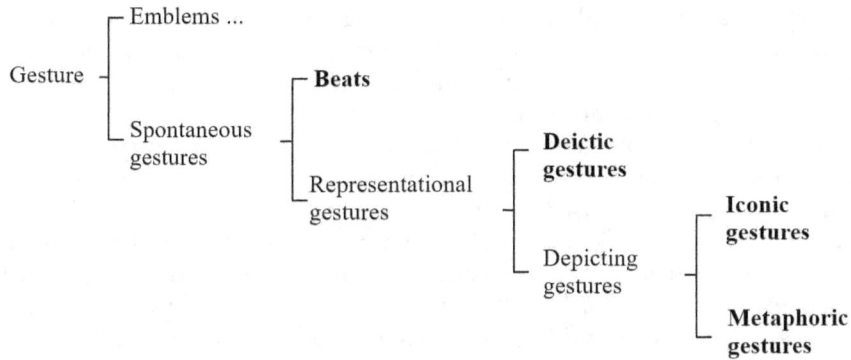

FIGURE 2.4 *Classification of gestures (based on Kita 2002: 48).*

Representational gestures are classified into "deictic gestures," which are used to refer to places and things especially by pointing, and "depicting gestures," which literally depict shapes of objects and images of ideas. Depicting gestures are further divided into "iconic gestures" and "metaphoric gestures." Iconic gestures mainly depict the shape and movement of the referent based on iconicity, while metaphoric gestures describe abstract contents and concepts in a spatialized manner (although the boundary between the two is ambiguous: see Krauss et al. 2000).

According to Kendon (2004), a general gesture forms a "unit" and consists of three major sequential elements: preparation; stroke; and retraction. In addition, there may occasionally appear a "pre-/post-stroke hold" before or after the "stroke" (Figure 2.5). The "nucleus" of this unit is the stroke period (and the post-stroke hold), which expresses the substantial semantic content of the gesture. (The reason why the preparation and withdrawal periods are not included in the nucleus is that the gesture may be prepared but not executed, and that strokes may occur in succession.) Kendon's (2004) transcription system for gesture is also used for some of the following analysis (see the transcription line in Figure 2.5). For holistic analysis bodily signs, it is necessary to include not only fingers and body movements, but also gaze, postures, and bodily organization coordinated among participants. If judged important in a specific context, these bodily features are occasionally included in the analyses and transcribed with specified notations (see the section on transcription conventions in the prelims).

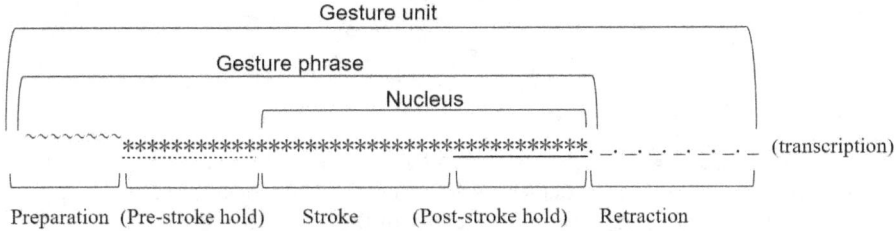

FIGURE 2.5 *Components of a gesture unit.*

More importantly, Cassell and McNeill (1991: see also McNeill 1992) brought new insights to recent narrative research by proposing that certain correlations exist between various aspects of narratives and gesture types. First, they posited three levels of narration—in contrast to, for example, Labov's (seemingly monolithic) narrative model. First, on the narrative level, which Labov prioritized, events are described in chronological order, and experiences and events are narrated mainly through iconic gestures based on the "Observer Viewpoint" (O-VPT) or the "Character Viewpoint" (C-VPT).[11] The meta-narrative level is a layer containing (implicit) references to structural elements of the story such as abstract, complication, peak, denouement, and coda (e.g., "First, of all, . . ." or "this is the most important lesson I learned"), and is said to be often marked by metaphorical and deictic gestures. Finally, on the para-narrative level, the narrator/speaker takes a step back from the "narrated" event and makes explicit the awareness of the hearer/audience who constitute the "narrating" event (e.g., "Oh, by the way, do you have a driver's license?" in a car accident narrative).[12] This level may include no significant gestures except for iconic gestures, but beats may appear throughout all the levels, signaling the shifts between levels (Cassell and McNeill 1991). In sum, Cassell and McNeill assume with this model that a synthetic analysis of speech and synchronized gesture "offers us two coordinated but distinct views of the same underlying processes of thinking/ speaking/ communicating" (ibid: 377).

The narrative main line is pushed forward during complication, which is typically depicted by iconic gestures through C-VPT and/or O-VPT. With regard to gestural perspectives observed there, McNeill posited a graded "distance" (McNeill 1992: 192–3). The examples in Figure 2.6 all depict a spatial movement caused by throwing or jumping (Kataoka 2017).

In Figure 2.6 (a), the narrator depicts a scene in which Character A tries to throw Character B to the opposite ledge. Here, the narrator identifies herself with Character A and demonstrates the "throwing" motion using an iconic gesture based on C-VPT. In Figure 2.6 (b), the narrator depicts the action of characters A and B jumping up and down together as if she were observing the event in the vicinity, most likely based on Inside O-VPT. Finally, in Figure 2.6 (c), she depicts Character A jumping to the other side from a detached and objective point of view, based on Outside O-VPT. These VPTs are assumed to constitute a hierarchy based on the epistemic distance in

 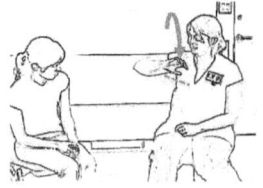 

(a) C-VPT (depicting the situation from the point of view of the characters in the narrative)

(b) Inside O-VPT (depicting the situation from the vicinity of the actor)

(c) Outside O-VPT (depicting the situation objectively from a distance)

FIGURE 2.6 *"Distance" between C-VPT and O-VPT.*

terms of "CVP < Inside O-VPT < Outside O-VPT." Thus, C-VPT is depicted from the most proximal distance such that the narrator's viewpoint is assimilated to that of the character. Also, McNeill (1992) postulates that the distance is proportional to the importance of the depicted event/situation.

For the sake of assuring cross-disciplinary correspondence, it would be conducive to compare the gesture types defined by McNeill (1992) with the FOR grid by Levinson (2003). First, gestures based on C-VPT have a high affinity with the Intrinsic FOR in which the *origo* (the narrator) merges into the intrinsic point of view of the relatum (typically, a character)—i.e., the "Route" perspective (Linde and Labov 1975) and "direct" FOR (Danziger 2010). It is comparable to depicting the scene from the point of view of the narrator's past/future self or of another character. On the other hand, gestures based on O-VPT are roughly comparable to those based on the Relative FOR. This is a way of objectively describing the actions of others or the relations of things in the environment as an observer. Finally, gestures based on the Absolute FOR are typically expressed as "deictic gestures" to geographical locations (Kita 2003, Levinson 2003). Of course, pointing is not necessarily "absolute" and can occur not only to (virtual) objects in the gesture space, but also to the participants in the conversation or to the entity associated with that person/object, such as for pointing to the chair to refer to the person who was sitting there (Haviland 2000). However, unlike the absolute FOR languages such as Guugu Yimithirr and Tenejapa (Haviland 1993; Levinson 2003: Ch. 6), absolute pointing by Japanese speakers rarely occurs in narrative, but when it does, absolute pointing clusters around the orientation of narrative where the spatial setting is usually established (Kataoka 2008). Given these findings, gestures and narration are never separate activities but are mutually motivated and mobilized to make the narrative performance more vivid, credible, and accountable.

2.5 Poetics in/of Performance

Action, as well as utterance, can be "poetic" (Hanks 1989; Bauman and Briggs 1990). As mentioned at the outset, rock climbing activities are systemically repetitive, and the experiences therein can also be conceived and represented in terms of equivalent coordination through language and the body. In general terms, poetry passionately cultivates various figures of speech, rhetorical techniques, and rhythmic/prosodic features, as do climbing talks and narrations.[13] What is called "poetics" here is fundamentally contingent on linguistic poetics advanced by Roman Jakobson (1960, 1966, 1985) and subsequent branches under the rubric of "ethnopoetics" (Hymes 1981, 1996, 2003; Tedlock 1983, 1999; Rothenberg and Rothenberg 1983) and meta-pragmatic poetics (Silverstein 1985, 1997, 2003, 2004; Agha 2007a). Jakobson defined the features of poetics in terms of vertical (paradigmatic) and horizontal (syntagmatic) relations of linguistic elements, as outlined clearly in his oft-quoted statement that "[t]he poetic function projects the principle of equivalence from the axis of selection into the axis of combination" (1960: 358)—here, "equivalence" is a poetic principle analogous to a set of repeated, parallelistic constructions. Since then, poesis in language use has been a major site of (ethno)linguistic investigation, as seen in such subsequent works as Woodbury (1985), Hanks (1989), Tannen (1989), Bauman and Briggs (1990), Friedrich (2001, 2006), Du Bois (2007, 2014), and Kroskrity and Webster (2015). On the other hand, investigation of poetic functions of nonverbal elements in naturally occurring discourse is relatively new (Valli 1993; Farnell 1998), beginning essentially with Cassell and McNeill (1991) and McNeill (1992), and further explored by McNeill (2005) with the notion of "catchment" (see also Kataoka 2009, 2010, 2012a, b). Building on recent endeavors, I take these ideas seriously and expand them to a wider scope, encompassing nonverbal aspects of poetic realization.

At the practical level, poetry is not limited to the products of high culture with which traditional poetry and lyrics are typically associated, as it also encompasses mass culture and even includes obscene, lewd, and profane speech and behavior (Rothenberg and Rothenberg 1983; Bauman 1992; Hill 2005). To be more precise, "poetry" here thrives not only on theme or content but also on actions and concepts that are oriented to a systemic formation that emerges through practice. In this case, it is essential to know what kind of material can be regarded as the "text" of poetic formation in the broad sense. In addition to text that can be represented through propositional, semantico-referential meaning (i.e., "denotational text": Silverstein 1993), an equivalent formation that projects a text-like property, such as a (possibly invisible but recognizable) social relation, is also regarded as "text" in a broader sense (i.e., "interactional text": ibid). Therefore, the elements that make up these texts are not limited to language, but could extend to all semiotic signs perceived to form a particular formation. In the following, the fundamental features of such poetic practice are examined in terms of "repetition" and "parallelism."

2.5.1 Repetition and Parallelism

The phenomenon of repetition and parallelism are common in oral arts all over the world, although they are often not demarcated clearly. In ordinary definitions of the terms, repetition is a rhetorical device that includes the repeated use of the same sounds, words, phrases, clauses, and so forth for emphasis, clarity, amplification, and/or emotional effect; parallelism may or may not include reiteration of such units, but could consist of equivalent or contrastive structures and ideas (Tannen, 1989; Johnstone 1994; Brown 1998). Thus, although the distinction is always rather murky, repetition is more about diction, while parallelism is more about organization (see Kataoka 2012a for detail). In this sense, Jakobson's notions of "equivalence" (Jakobson 1960) and "recurrent returns" (Jakobson 1966) are broader concepts that encompass both phenomena.

First, repetition can be classified into two types based on the time axis: "synchronic repetition" and "diachronic repetition" (Tannen 1989; Howard 2009). Synchronic repetition is achieved locally (i.e., by "text-structurally") by resorting to the semantic cohesion and schematic coherence of utterances (and gestures). On the other hand, diachronic repetition is achieved globally (i.e., "socially, culturally, and historically") by retroactively and proactively linking current discourse to implicit norms and ideologies (Urban 1991; Silverstein and Urban 1996). In particular, in the latter sense, repetition is a resource and asset embedded practically in everyday communication and constitutes a linguistic "habitus" (Bourdieu 1977, 1990) inherent to the community.

Furthermore, two possible forms of participation in repetition are recognized—one achieved individually (by a single speaker/performer) (Rieger 2003), and the other achieved interactionally (by multiple speakers/performers) (Schegloff 1997). These forms of participation characterize different contexts and genres. Repetition has been recognized widely as an individual source of "creativity" in activities such as music, political speech, improvisational theater, and language learning (Sawyer 2002; Alim 2006; Swann and Maybin 2007; Duranti and McCoy 2020). Particularly in everyday speech, repetition also serves interactional functions such as "participatory/ratifying listenership," "humor," "savoring," "evaluation," "(conversational) extension," "initiation of repair," "floor holding," and so forth (Schegloff 1997; Rieger 2003). Given these distinctions, repetition needs to be considered along the spatio-temporal axis of synchronic/diachronic and/or individual/ interactional axes of practice. Repetition in interaction is also the mainstay for "stance-taking." M. Goodwin (1990) called the interlocking repetition of grammatical structures with slight referential shifts "format tying," which occurs frequently in word play and accusation. Du Bois's concept of "resonance" also posits that various interactional stances emerge through "the catalytic activation of affinities across utterances" (Du Bois 2014: 360).

Parallelism is a unit consisting of equivalent structures and concepts, although it does not necessarily include actual repetition of word or utterance because parallelism is not limited to the repetition of semantic content. The importance of parallelism was first advocated by Robert Lowth, Bishop of the Church of England and Oxford Professor of Poetry (Lowth 1778 [cited in Jakobson 1966: 399–400]). Lowth defined three forms of parallelism—the synonymous, antithetic, and synthetic—and argued that these forms are always fused together to give the text its essential beauty and harmonious variety. One of the theories rooted in this tradition is Jakobson's theory of poetics. His theory was also inspired by Russian formalism and the Prague School's approach to poetics in the early twentieth century. For example, Mukařovský (1964 [1932]: 19), one of the leading figures of the Prague School, regarded the function of poetic language as consisting in "the maximum foregrounding of the utterance." Jakobson (1960: 356) took this idea further and argued that the poetic function becomes apparent when it "focuses on the message for its own sake." In this way, the various forms of expression that transcend semantic content become the resources of poetic effect.

However, in Russian poetry theory at the time, a formal analysis based on the independence of the written text was the mainstream, and there was little interest in poetry as social practice. If we apply the theory to naturally occurring discourse, we can include prosodic and syntactic features of speech, accompanying gestures, and even objects in the environment as constituents of oral poetry. These semiotic resources have the potential to participate in an integrative poetic construction by forming parallelism based on equivalence at different levels, such that a certain message is foregrounded as a "figure" in everyday interaction (as "ground") through various semiotic resources/ devices, whether explicit or implicit, and conscious or unconscious. In addition, parallelism stimulates an analogical process of evoking a similar image through association and equivalence between the source and the target. Parallelism is thus a feature inherent in related textual concepts such as "intertextuality" and "polyphony" (Bakhtin 1981), as well as rhetorical devices of "metaphor/ methonymy/ synecdocy" (Lakoff and Johnson 1980; Gavins and Steen 2003), and such social actions as "parody," "pastiche," "simulacrum," "mimetics," and "imitation" (Lempert 2014).

2.5.2 Multimodal Ethnopoetics

We subsequently confirm that multimodal ethnopoetics would make explicit those inherent properties that reside not only in literary text but also in the synthetic use of language-body-environment amalgams (Kataoka 2012a). Ethnopoetics is a movement that was initiated in the 1960s by literary scholars, poets, anthropologists, and folklore researchers such as Jerome Rothenberg, Gary Snyder, Dennis Tedlock, and Dell Hymes. They worked on the ethnopoetics project under the linguistic/anthropological thesis of the time that "all languages and cultures are equally complex and valuable" (Turner 1978), and were primarily concerned with how to interpret and convey culture-specific meanings and aesthetic richness that would be lost in relying solely on Western poetic traditions (Rothenberg and Rothenberg 1983; Rothenberg [1967] 2017). For that purpose, Tedlock (1983) focused on prosodic and tonal features of performance, such as sound length, pitch, and intensity, while Hymes (1981, 1996, 2003) focused more on structural patterns in lexical, morphological, and syntactic forms. Although Tedlock and Hymes were critical of each other's orientation, they shared the common goal of revealing the indigenous, culture-specific values embedded in verbal performance.

In what follows, I specifically summarize the approach called Verse/Stanza Analysis proposed by Dell Hymes (1981, 1996, 2003), who conducted pioneering ethnopoetic analyses of Native American myths and folktales. Building on the thesis, I would propose an updated version called "multimodal ethnopoetics." The basic unit of analysis in Hymes' model is the line, but it is combined to compose larger units through a bottom-up and nested hierarchical structure (Line—Verse—Stanza—Scene—Act). Hymes' approach to ethnopoetics was typically called Verse/Stanza Analysis because of its claim on the cultural significance at the middle range of the hierarchy (i.e., "verse" and "stanza"). After Hymes' model was proposed, scholars such as Gee (1986, 1989) and Chafe (1994) provided findings that contribute to refining the criteria for identifying the basic units of Verse/Stanza Analysis (2) shown below. However, the criteria presented below are not necessarily invariant across (and within) languages, but may vary to some extent depending on the differences in context, genre, purpose, and cultural rhetoric.

2 Units of Verse/Stanza Analysis

<Line>

(a) A line is relatively short and consists of a single pitch curve.[14]
(b) A line is basically an idea unit (Chafe 1980; Hymes, 1996; Gee 1989) or an intonation unit (IU: Chafe 1994), and is ideally comprised of a single clause.[15]

(c) A line is often accompanied by explicit boundary-marking phenomena (hesitations, fillers, pauses, sound prolongations, and other disfluencies).
(d) In written language, where prosodic features are not available, a line is mainly composed of a clause.
(e) In English, "and," "so," "then," "but," or equivalent conjunctions tend to occur at the line-initial/final position. (In Japanese, final particles (*ne, yo, na*, etc.) and *-te* connective serve a similar function (Minami and McCabe 1991)).
(f) Neighboring lines often form a semantic/syntactic parallelism.

<Verse and Stanza>

(a) In a narrative form, the verse is (broadly speaking) a central building block of a sentence-like contour, and may involve more than one line (Hymes 1996: 144).
(b) A new verse is usually demarcated by a preceding, often intonational, period (or a falling contour).[16]
(c) Shifts in temporal and spatial relations may indicate a new verse or a stanza.
(d) Conversational turns are always verses (Hymes 1996).
(e) A series of verbs in the same tense, a chunk of repetitions, or the same topic may indicate a stanza (or a scene).

<Scene and Act>

(a) Drastic change of spatial and temporal relations often mark the change of scenes.
(b) Change of participants often leads to a change of scenes.
(c) A hierarchically higher category of Scenes constitutes an Act.

As shown in the schematic formation of these elements (Figure 2.7), intonation contour (continuous [,] or falling [.]), fillers, and final particles, conjunctions, and lexical/ phrasal/ syntactic constructions are identified in a bottom-up fashion. By taking the boundary features of form and content into consideration, we can figure out lines, verses (a–e), and a stanza (A) as to this segment. Eventually, the whole text can be analyzed following the same steps.

Although Figure 2.7 presupposes an everyday narrative, there are two basic principles in the construction of a traditional (transcribed) text according to Hymes. First, as far as the verse or stanza levels are concerned, speakers of Chinook, Finnish, English, Japanese, and so forth prefer to converge on odd-number relations such as 3 or 5, while many Native American languages and Zuni tend to converge on even-number relations such as 2 or 4 (Hymes 1994: 331). These characteristics are already found not only in the narratives by Japanese preschoolers (Minami and McCabe 1991), but also in TV commercials, instructional settings, and cross-cultural contacts (Kataoka 2012a; Yamaguchi 2012; Kataoka, Takekuro, and Enomoto 2022). However, speakers do not

Stanza	Verse	Line	Text
A	a	1	XXXX XXXXX XX XX XXXX XXX XXXXX,
	b	2	XXXXX XXX XXXXX,
		3	XXXXXX XXXX XXX XXXX.
	c	4	XXXXX XXXXXXX XX XX ,
		5	XXXX XXXXXXXX XX XXXX X.
	d	6	XXXX XXXXXX XXX
	e	7	XX XXX XXXXX
		8	XXX XXXXXX XXXXXX XX

FIGURE 2.7 *Ethnopoetic formation of a narrative text.*

always resort to either one of the principles; they might sometimes make use of both, or even adopt a marked, dispreferred style for "foregrounding" some portions of text depending on the narrative component, levels of organization, or individual narrative styles. In this respect, the key issue in Verse/Stanza Analysis is not only the structural representation per se, but also include covert functions that explicate the mechanisms of power and inequality behind the surface forms (Hymes 1996; Blommaert 2006, 2015). In this sense, poetics is largely an issue of politics (Lempert and Silverstein 2012).

In addition, proposals for expanding the scope of ethnopoetics have been made repeatedly. As Friedrich (2006) pointed out, the field that once developed as "ethno-X" can be re-conceptualized based on its own "poetic" systematics. For example, ethno-semantics investigates conceptual categories based on motivations and worldviews that differ from the Western system of meaning and categorization. Likewise, Briggs (2021), while calling it an analytic leap, proposed that Freud's psychoanalytic philosophy be incorporated into poetics and performance studies, and that not only systematic patterns but also tensions, conflicts, fragments, and emotions that span multiple registers be included in the scope of analysis. Defined this way, ethnopoetics cannot be limited to poetry produced by human intention and creativity using sounds and words, but may cover the entire living environment, ranging from actions to lifestyles and social systems.

One approach intended to include those nonverbal aspects is multimodal ethnopoetics (Kataoka 2009, 2010, 2012a, 2012b). There, not only language and paralanguage but also bodily representations (gesture and posture), patterns of interaction, and manners in which things in the environment are used, are also recognized as semiotic resources for poetic construction. For example, the relationship between bodily representations and poetic features has been widely recognized by sign language researchers (Klima and Bellugi 1983; Valli 1993), but the proposal to place poetic features in the foreground of gesture studies had to wait until recently. McNeill (2003, 2005), for example, showed how certain forms and directions of gestures (as well as the gesture space) are recursively employed within and across discourse in terms of a phenomenon which he calls "catchment." Such recursive gestures enhance the cohesive tie of referents while at the same time allowing us to trace back to the overarching theme that is often overlooked in localized texts. As an exemplar instance, McNeill (2005: 118) describes a gesture made by a subject named Viv after watching an animation titled *Canary Row*, showing that the same referents are indicated by the same hand gesture in the same gesture space, corroborating the cohesion and coherence of the discourse through both speech and gesture.

Given these orientations to nonverbal aspects of poesis, the depth and width of investigation is now critically expanded, providing a renewed potential to cultivating a novel ground of poetic performance. I will examine these poetic phenomena emerging in verbal and nonverbal guises in rock climbing narratives in Chapters 6 and 7.

2.5.3 Metapragmatic Poetics

Another stream of the Jakobsonian poetic tradition on which the present analysis is based is Silverstein's "meta-pragmatic" poetics (Silverstein 1985, 1993, 2004; see also Lempert 2018 and Nakassis 2019 for nonverbal aspects of this idea). First proposed in the mid-1980s under the title "pragmatic 'poetry' of prose" (Silverstein 1985), it was developed to incorporate the poetic organization in the "interactional" text behind the surface "denotational" text (Silverstein 1993, 2004; Agha 2007a). The discourse that Silverstein examined was a scene of "one-upmanship" between two graduate students at the University of Chicago. He described the process of poetic structuring of their value systems that emerged through the formation of deictic expressions ("here/there," "I/you," and "now/then") associated with their academic backgrounds, current fields of study, and "social ranks" in general. This analysis was groundbreaking in that it extended the scope of poetic analysis form phonetic, lexical, and syntactic levels to the underlying social formations being constructed by the participants *in situ* (i.e., as the interactional text). (This data was later reanalyzed by McNeill (2003), providing the impetus for theorizing "catchment" as previously introduced.) This approach places more emphasis on the analysis of socially embedded configurations rather than the semantic content of speech—a tenet that poetic pragmatics mediates "a transcendent structure in exactly the same sense as syntax, but it is developed in realtime through principles that are inherently linear, yet abstract and formal" (Silverstein 1985: 185).

A metapragmatic approach to poetics is clearly articulated in Agha's (2007a: 96–102) exposition of denotational and interactional texts. Agha pointed out that a coherent interactional text lies behind a fragmentary denotational text, saying, "the denotational text is but a fragment of the interactional text" (Agha 2007a: 100). To show that, he reanalyzed an interactional fragment presented in Goodwin and Goodwin (1992). In that scene shown in Analysis (3), Dianne and Clacia give an emotional evaluation of the asparagus pie that Jeff makes. (Below, a, b, and c indicate propositions, the apostrophe—'—indicates the second mention of those propositions. The lower case "R" indicates an identical referent, the asparagus pie.) The double parentheses include the explanations of interactional features.

3   Interactional text (Agha 2007a: 99-101, modified)

1. Dianne: Jeff made en asparagus pie. It $_R$ was s::so[:   goo:d.
   - a_1 b_1
   - ↑ <eye contact with C>   ((lower head))   ((nod, raise eyebrow))

2. Clacia: [I love it $_R$.. Yeah I love that $_R$..
   - c_1 $c_{1'}$
   - ((nod))   ((nod))
   - ....   <avert gaze from D> ↑

3. Dianne: En then jus' the broc-'r the asparagus coming out in spokes. =It$_R$ wz so good.
   - a_2 $b_{1'}$
   - <avert gaze from C> ↑   ((head shakes))

4. Clacia: °(Oh Go:d that $_R$, 'd be fantastic.)
   - b_2
   - <avert gaze from D> ↑

Notice first that Clacia's utterance "I love X" in line 2 is repeated, and that her use of the construction, "X be fantastic" in line 4 shows the cohesion to, and an equivalent repetition of, Dianne's previous utterance, *X be good* in line 3. Furthermore, while Dianne's evaluation is expressed in the past tense, Clacia's evaluation is made in the present and hypothetical tenses, suggesting that it can include a variety of possibilities. More importantly, non-verbal and physical "co-texts" are generated simultaneously in this segment. At the beginning of the utterance, Dianne and Clacia are looking at each other, and in line 1, Dianne says "s::so: goo::d" while enhancing her orientation toward Clacia, simultaneously lowering her head, nodding, and raising her eyebrows. At the same time, Clacia nods her head twice, and the bodily attunement is established. In addition, Dianne makes evaluative comments in lines 1 and 3, as does Clacia in lines 2 and 4, both exhibiting the same interactive contours.

As can be seen from the situation described above, a denotational text is a "figure" or an observable configuration consisting of surface tokens formed by "co-texts" such as linguistic expressions, gestures, eyegaze, posture, and so forth. Under the superficial text lies the interactional text, which is also equivalently and poetically constructed, as summarized in Table 2.3 (Agha 2007a: 99, reproduced with permission)

As shown by Column II in Table 2.3, denotational tokens ("propositions" and "referents") emerge in the metrical (i.e., poetic) structure of propositional acts. This poetic formation serves as a window through which we can detect an interactional text that is being constructed *in situ* by attending to shifting interactional stances, social relationships, and other concurring semiotic cues, or co-texts. Combined with "stances and roles" in Column III and "interpersonal alignments" in Column IV, we finally arrive at the interactional text that emerges in the ongoing communication. As Agha noted, the denotational text is only a fragmentary projection of the interactional text. However, through the mediation of the various "co-texts" (referents, stance, role alignment, cohesion, coherence, *origo* location, bodily representations, and so forth.), the whole picture—the multilayered practice of communication—can be reached.

Table 2.3 Denotational and Interactional Texts (Agha 2007a: 99; reproduced with permission)

		INTERACTIONAL TEXT		
I	II		III	IV
Participants:	DENOTATIONAL TEXT ⇒		Stances and roles ⇒ performed by participants	Interpersonal alignments
	Propositions	Referents		
Dianne	a1 b1	R	D affectively evaluates R	C agrees with
Clacia	c1, c1'	R'	C affectively evaluates R'	D
...				
Dianne	a2 b1'	R	D affectively evaluates R	C agrees with
Clacia	b2	R'	C affectively evaluates R'	D

Given the core concept inherent in these poetic orientations, we can see the danger of trying to read out the intricacies of interaction from only the referential, propositional content in language. Chapters 6 and 7 also address those denotational/ interactional texts constructed by practice.

2.6 Chronotopes in Climbing

The last theoretical background that should be referred to before the analysis is "chronotope" (Bakhtin 1981). Bakhtin's concept of "chronotope" has been widely extended from literature, and applied to art criticism, painting, cinema/documentary, and the empirical study of language use in narratives/conversations, classroom instruction, and therapy, among others. Bakhtin's theory was formulated initially in "Forms of Time and of the Chronotope in the Novel: Notes toward a Historical Poetics" (Bakhtin 1981) and defined as follows:[17]

> In the literary artistic chronotope, spatial and temporal indicators are fused into one carefully thought-out, concrete whole. Time, as it were, thickens, takes on flesh, becomes artistically visible; likewise, space becomes charged and responsive to the movements of time, plot and history. The intersection of axes and fusion of indicators characterizes the artistic chronotope.
>
> BAKHTIN 1981: 84

As this quotation shows, he obviously maintains that time and space cannot be separated from each other in physical and fictional worlds, such that events in plot and history are intrinsically connected. Bakhtin's idea of chronotopes is based on the assumption that narrative texts are "not only composed of a sequence of diegetic events and speech acts, but also—and perhaps even primarily—of the construction of a particular fictional world or Chronotope" (Bemong and Borghart 2010: 4). This idea, as made manifest at the outset of his essay, is said to trace back to Einstein's theory of time-space (time as the fourth dimension of space), though largely as a metaphor.[18] Also, although Bakhtin absorbed Kant's theorem that time and space are central to human mind and the world, he reached a rather conflicting conclusion that they are not "transcendental" but rather "transgredient" and empirical (Holquist 2010).[19]

The ambiguities inherent in Bakhtin's notion of chronotope engendered variable conceptualizations and applications of the idea in literature and cultural studies in general. Currently, many scholars posit that "some chronotopic configuration underlies every kind of narrative, however minimal, including jokes, strip cartoons, fairy tales, animal stories, narrative poetry and the like" (Bemong and Borghart 2010: 10). Likewise, we could assume a diverse array of chronotopic possibilities, including not only literary but also sociolinguistic and linguistic anthropological notions, such as "minor" and "major" chronotopes, "chronotopic motifs," and "chronotopes of whole genres" (Morson and Emerson 1990: 374), "micro-", "local," and "major/dominant" chronotopes (Ladin 1999), "kinship" chronotopes (Agha 2007b), and "local" and "translocal" chronotopes (Blommaert 2015), to name only a few, with each definition designed to address their own emergent issues. Most relevant to my analysis among them is "local" chronotopes (Ladin 1999)[20], which synthetically construct a "major" chronotope. A major chronotope is thus assumed to (1) "control local chronotopes"; (2) "enter into dialogic relations with local chronotopes," (3) "become transsubjective chronotopes that "enter the worlds" of author, performer, and reader" (or audience); and (4) "provide the ground for images of human possibility that also extend dynamically into the worlds of author, performer and reader" (Ladin 1999: 224).

Furthermore, "generic" chronotopes are considered by some to be synonymous with "worldview," and are considered more of a cognitive concept than a narrative feature, influenced by the 1990s' idea of a cognitive turn in narratology. This worldview is relative to each community, and the significance of relativity in the chronotope concept is vividly felt in Bakhtin's writings. It is said that Bakhtin, in theorizing the tenet of chronotopes, was influenced by Lobachevsky's non-Euclidean geometry, which captures space in terms of topological and relativistic perspectives (Holquist 2010). In a similar vein, his notion of "transgredience," which was derived from "transgress" rather than "transcend," is another valuable import to the study of culture in that respect. It is related to what he calls "excess of seeing," and is based on such phenomenon as:

> ... when you and I face each other, I can see things behind your head you do not see, and you can see things behind my head that I cannot see. In other words, the things I cannot see are not outside experience as such, they are merely outside—they transgress—the boundaries of what is available to my sight in a particular moment. If we switch places, that which was invisible to me in my former position comes into sight, and the same happens for you when you do the same thing. Transgredience, then, is the name of a boundary that through interaction (our *changing places*) can be overcome—transgressed—in experience.
>
> HOLQUIST 2010: 30, my emphasis

This is a highly affinitive idea to the phenomenological argument introduced at the outset of this chapter. The following quote from Bakhtin (1990) also represents a cognition view (especially as to "seeing") that is congruent with phenomenological orientations and cognitive scientific tenets as represented in Ingold (2000), Clark (2007), and Chemero (2009): "for cognition, I and the *other*, inasmuch as they are being thought, constitute a relationship that is relative and convertible, since the cognitive *subjectum* (*субъект*) does not occupy any determinate, concrete place in existence" (Bakhtin 1990: 23; original emphasis). Holquist (2010) indicated that Bakhtin's idea precedes Jakobson's notion of "shifter" in that the transportability (or "transgredience" in Bakhtin's parlance) of the *origo* and indeterminacy of referents out of context (as well as the fluidity and the surplus of "seeing"), later developed into, and resonates with, the phenomenological, post-modernistic conception of intersubjectivity and intercorporeality.

As Bakhtin (1981: 243ff) clarified, each chronotope has its own associative features that are loaded with emotions and values—e.g., the chronotope of "the road" evokes "encounter" and different "courses" of life; "the castle" does the same for the feudal era characterized by historical figures, architecture, weapons, etc.; "cafes and salons" are linked to dialogues that reveal the ideas, passions, and philosophies of the characters, and so forth. Each chronotope contains crucial indexes that evoke and stir the reader's imagination and expectations, and "provides the ground essential for the showing-forth, the representability of the events" (1981: 250). The invocation of chronotopes brings about a series of indexical attributions, or what Agha (2007b) referred to collectively as a "chronotopic frame." Through this process, talk in context emerges as a multilayered semiotic complex that reflects the ongoing stance and positioning through various indexicals (see Koven 2012). In this respect, climbers' performance and expertise are also evaluated based on how efficiently the climbers' perceive and behave in the recognizable chronotopic frame.

People tell stories (as authors and narrators) by using two modes of description—the "story" and the "narrative" events in Bakhtin's parlance, which are assumed to belong to separate "chronotopes." In practice, narrators often align these two chronotopes, whether real or imagined, specific or general, by using measures called "cross-chronotope alignment" (Agha 2007b) or "tropical forms of alignment" (Perrino 2005, 2007). Silverstein (2005: 6) re-defined this notion of Bakhtin's as follows: "the temporally (hence, chrono-) and spatially (hence, -tope) particular envelope in the narrated universe of social space-time in which and through which, in emplotment, narrative characters move." He goes on to cite the many instances in which the boundaries of two (or more) chronotopes are unspecified or intentionally blurred, creating situations of "co-eval" alignment (2005: 17–18). In these cases, the two narrative chronotopes (a "narrated" event and a "narrating" event) merge in time and space, so that the "past" and the "present" representations come to converge. As anticipated, one of the most wide-spread strategies of "co-eval," or "cross-chronotope alignment" is the "historical present" in literature and narrative, where narrators shift (and merge) the *origo(s)* so that the tense of "past" events is re-framed as that of "present," that is otherwise assumed to be "past." This notion of merger of "voices" through quotation is pursued further in Chapter 8.

The invocation of a particular chronotope in narratives triggers a constellation of attributions that define the plot (when, what, and where), the actors (who and how), the moral or ethics involved in them, and the possible and anticipated consequences. We thus see such generic types of personas, or "figures of personhood" (Agha 2007a) acted out in particular sociopolitical milieus, mainly through speech filled with "indexicals," or calibrating actions that position speakers/narrators with respect to the here-and-now of the narrating context (Koven 2012, 2016). Further, Blommaert (2015: 110) paraphrased chronotopes as "invokable histories," or "elaborate frames in which time, space, and patterns of agency coincide, create meaning and value, and can be set off against other chronotopes." Chronotopes of such "invokable histories" can also vary in size from small scale (or immediate) settings to large scale (or institutionalized) processes that overarch multiple periods and locations, positioning the speaker/narrator depending on the application of different "scales" (Blommaert 2007, 2015; Carr and Lempert 2016) both synchronically and diachronically.

As previously shown, there have been numerous attempts to apply Bakhtin's notions to spontaneous speech and narrative (e.g., Hill 1985, 1995; Basso 1990). However, the analysis of nonverbal chronotopes is still limited despite the fact that everyday interaction is carried out by language and bodies in the environment (except for a brief mention in McNeill et al. 2015; cf. Rosborough 2016). As Bakhtin stated, the chronotope not only provides the internal structure with a map-like imagery (or "schema"), but it also forms a linkage between the narrative content and the social, cultural, and historical context of the narrative. For example, in climbing narratives, the action, due to its anti-gravitational activity on a vertical plane, always carries an image that an entity which goes up must eventually come down—i.e., to the home position, which may be completed by an unfortunate consequence of falling. In alpine climbing especially, the most important thing is to come down safely, as they say. Such a process of climbing is saturated with distinct perceptions, actions, emotions, and events that form singular "local chronotopes" (Ladin 1999, 2010) along the way to the top (and to the bottom). Their organization may also constitute an upper-level constellation of chronotopes. Chapter 7 in particular focuses on such local-chronotopic aspects of spatial description/ depiction in "near-death" stories.

The discussion in this chapter is an overview of the major analytical models to be relied upon, and possibly modified as necessary, in this book. However, in order to treat various aspects of climbing discourse in depth, not all phenomena can be covered by these models and theories alone. To improve the accuracy of the analysis, I will refer to other concepts and provide supporting explanations where appropriate. With this arsenal of theory at our disposal, we now turn to rock climbing discourse and delve into the vertical space where theories and practices meet for human to be achieved.

3

Rock Climbing as a Site of Embodied Institution

3.1 Introduction

Even if the ultimate goal in rock climbing is to climb a route, the fundamental prerequisite is to climb it *safely*. The skills to ensure this are an important part of the activity and must be mastered fully if participants are not to injure/kill themselves or their partner. In other words, the ability of a climber to "take pro(tection)" for safety and of a belayer to "catch a fall" of a climber is literally a matter of life or death and therefore essential. As long as such actions are carried out efficiently without specific verbal exchanges, I could posit an implicit system that facilitates them. In this chapter, I first investigate how climbing participants, especially belayers, behave to secure safety before, during, and after a climbing partner's fall and examine further the overall mechanism of the multitasking climber–belayer interaction, locating it in institutional discourse.

Leading a route (by a climber) and helping to make an ascent as safe as possible (by a belayer) is a locus of encounter between materiality and communicative protocols (see Goodwin 2007a; Streeck et al. 2011; Matoesian and Gilbert 2018). As Mauss (1973: 75) once claimed, if "man's first and most natural object, and at the same time technical means, is his (sic) body," this perception is sorely felt and duly applied to rock/sport climbing (see Besnier et al. 2018 for other sports). In climbing, the whole body, not just the arms and legs, becomes the instrument for ascending. Ranging from the fingertips jammed in a thin crack or gripped on a micro-hold to the heels, knees, back, and head, all utilized for chimney and wide-crack climbing, different body parts take on specialized functions depending on the technique used for particular rock formations. In addition, climbers need to confront not only the natural environment, but also man-made objects—such as bolts and pitons (called "protections" in climbing)—already placed by previous ascenders to avoid fatal accidents. The only way to be free from such constraints is of course to "free solo."

The self is not necessarily an autonomous entity separated from the environment by a skin; the self, others, and things also communicate with each other through tools in the environment and acquire a unified perception (Hutchins 1995; Ingold 2000; Clark 2006). In climbing as well, the boundary between the body and the instrument is indistinct. Although a climber and a belayer are connected by a rope, that rope is actually an extension of the belayer's arm that is used to stop a fall—that is, a special arm that can be stretched and which supplies enough friction to reduce the impact of a fall. Such remote participation is supported by physical sensation through the rope and as part of the belaying device, a situation similar to teleoperation and online gaming (cf. Mondada 2003; Keating and Sunakawa 2010). Even if the partner is out of sight, the rope that connects them becomes a medium that monitors the movements and perceptions of both parties, like a neuron that sends information to other neurons. This way, climbers and belayers are engaged in an activity that encompasses spatio-temporally displaced communication. In order to deal with such "telecommunication," participants are required to master explicit and implicit climbing skills over a long period of training and practice. I will examine cases where experienced climbers and belayers draw on their expertise in order to protect themselves and their partners, and how the pair manage required activities in climbing.

However, the reality is highly complex and is dependent on a wide range of issues. As the success or failure of belaying can be the difference between a climber surviving a fall or not, tutorial videos and guide books focus on the "do's" and "don'ts" of belaying safety first and foremost. This research focuses on those somatic reactions employed consciously and unconsciously by belayers. Since expertise on both sides of the climbing party is fundamental here, as it is in conversation, the "hearer" and the belayer should be explicitly acknowledged and highlighted.

3.2 Climbing and Belaying from a Discursive Perspective

Extending the scope of communication, I examine shifting and continuous "participation frameworks" (Goffman 1981; M. Goodwin 1997) constructed by rock climbing participants—"shifting/continuous" in the sense that the participants hold the same but expanding framework as the climber moves upward on a vertical or overhanging plane. With this backdrop in mind, I will focus on a covert interaction between a climber and a belayer in "lead" and "top-rope" climbing conducted indoors and outdoors. In addition to a climber's expertise, a belayer's dexterity in handling a rope may determine the success or failure of the climber's achievement—i.e., whether or not s/he can "onsight/flash" or "redpoint" the route, which are better styles for climbing a route than "top-roping" or "hangdogging." Although the belayer's role and skills are easily overlooked in the achievement of a successful climb, they are factors that should be paid closer attention. In other words, leading a route and belaying a climber are two sides of the same coin and closely connected, both literally (by the rope) and metaphorically (in terms of the action sequence that affects each person's perceptions and (re)actions).

It will be subsequently observed that although climbing a route is a collaborative, interactional achievement, it is not generally acknowledged as such. As a realm of social interaction, rock/sport climbing would be an uncultivated but ideal venue where participants' minute bodily coordination is inevitably mobilized and applied to a sequence of actions in order to achieve the best performance. In order to investigate the activity, each participant's actions are subdivided into several steps that need to be coordinated individually and/or collaboratively to secure the overall safety and success of a climb. Bear in mind also that both climber and belayer often shift and adjust their "footing" (Goffman 1981) to mutually align—physically and metaphorically, once more—to achieve a successful outcome overall. It is thus crucial to attend to the interactional subtleties and environmental contingencies emerging *in situ*.

With the exception of solo climbing, the smallest possible climbing party consists of a climber and a belayer, both of whom are expected to be maximally attentive to safeguard against potential dangers such as falling, the misuse of climbing equipment, and poor protections, as well as natural incidents like fallen rocks, weather changes, and the angle of sunlight, among others. Such incidents require rigorous attention from both parties so that "the visible bodies of participants provide systematic, changing displays about relevant action and orientation" (Goodwin 2000: 157). It is these interactional contingencies that I elaborate on and explicate in order to determine the implicit system that I argue is comparable to institutional discourse.

During rock climbing, the primary source of information is often obtained through vision, which plays a crucial role in the discursive achievement of professional and expert work/duties (Goodwin 1994; Heath and Luff 2000; Mondada 2003; Matoesian and Gilbert 2018). Also in rock climbing, the "professional" (or expert) vision and (re-)action are tacitly applied so that they react to both preceding *and* forthcoming actions. For example, when a leading climber stops moving, positions him/herself securely, and reaches a hand toward the rope, that sequence should be interpreted as an attempt to tuck in rope so that it can be clipped into a carabiner for protection. That is, a certain action serves as a harbinger of follow-up events for the immediate participants and their audience. In a context provided by sequential organization, each step in the process constitutes (sub-)actions and ways of seeing and organizing events, both of which are lodged within the practice of rock climbing communities.

Such "expert vision/(re)action" thrives on "ascription" (Levinson 2013; Seuren 2018), as to what should be seen by whom and for what purpose. That is, how do we react to what visual input implicitly tells us should be done? Such "action ascription" in climbing is embedded in types of action, and places specific constraints on the climbing interaction. These restricted forms of actions and reactions show the property of "institutional" discourse defined by Drew and Heritage (1992; also Heritage 2004), in that rock climbing is expected to be goal-orientated and follow a relatively restricted conventional form to which participants make allowable and anticipated contributions while performing the task at hand. Although verbal exchanges occur rarely during climbing, initiating a particular "activity type" (Levinson 1992) projects a proper next action, if not act of speech. Two key concepts that are highly pertinent to this activity type are "conditional relevance" (Schegloff 1968) and "contextualization cues" (Gumperz 1982), both of which rely heavily on the semiotic notion of "indexicality" (Silverstein 1976, 2004). These notions presuppose that a certain utterance or action principally activates and opens up an interpretive frame, or a climbing "script" (cf. Schank and Abelson 1977; D'Andrade 1995) in which whatever happens in adjacency and sequence can be made accountable to the participants.

Drawing on these foundational ideas, I will focus mainly on the skills required of the belayer. In addition to the proper use of appropriate devices, the belaying process specifically requires a belayer to have the ability to make appropriate decisions such as what posture to take, where to stand, and how to react to a climber's moment-by-moment moves (and a fall). Following the psychological notion of "chain complex" (a single chain of dynamic and consecutive links "with meaning carried over from one link to the next": Vygotsky 1878: 116), I would call such a chain of sequentially expected actions the "task complex."

3.3 Data Collection and Method of Analysis

The data for the present analysis are based on a video recording of free climbing activities in outdoor and indoor settings. This portion of data consists of approximately three-and-a-half hours of audiovisual recording, which was captured intermittently from 2020 through 2021 at an indoor climbing facility and a major rock climbing area in mainland Japan (Aichi Prefecture). However, the present analysis deals only with activities that co-occurred with "belaying." To "belay" in climbing includes various techniques such as exerting "tension" on a climbing rope so that in case of a fall, a climber does not tumble too far from where s/he was on the rock/wall. In outdoor settings in particular, poor belaying can prove fatal to climbers, because there are more chances of their hitting a protruding rock, a ledge, or the ground. To avoid such scenarios, a belayer applies friction and tension on the rope with a belaying device. Also, the belayer needs to be cautious about how much rope a climber is given; an appropriate amount needs to be fed out but any excess taken back in. Today, numerous belaying tutorial videos are available online, and information can also be found in rock/sport climbing guide books (e.g., Long 2010). I occasionally refer to them in order to confirm standardized belaying conventions.

Based on this background information, I specifically examine climbing participants' eye-gaze, gestures/postures, use of equipment, and spatial formations at the climbing site. The timing and movement of hands/arms, feet/legs, gaze directions, and the posture of a belayer are crucial in relation with the climber's "multitasking" performance. I thus aim to conduct a multimodal micro-analysis of audio-visual data using ELAN—an annotation software developed by the Max Planck Institute for Psycholinguistics. In the following analyses, separate audiovisual data for Belayer (B) and Climber (C) were synchronized so that it was easier to compare corresponding and interactive moves. The factors I focus on include (a) physical movements of the hand/arm and foot/leg, (b) gaze/vision, (c) equipment use, and (d) posture in relevant environmental conditions.

Starting with the investigation of an overall structure of action, I move on to take an integrated approach to reveal the ways in which action, vision, and other semiotic modalities affect and interact with the spatial formations and vice versa. The affinity of rock climbing to institutional discourse is then closely examined.

3.4 "Leading/top-roping" and "Climbing/belaying"

Belaying is conducted in more or less the same way for "leading" as it is for "top-roping," but the level of caution required is obviously higher for leading. Top-rope climbing is the safest and most convenient style of climbing in indoor and outdoor climbing because the climber is protected by a rope that passes through the anchor system at the top of the climb. The belayer's main task is to take in excess slack on the rope throughout the climb and occasionally catch the climber using a belaying device in the event of a fall, which is usually a short distance. On the other hand, belaying a climber "on lead" requires more experience because it entails finer attunement to the climber's needs/situation and coordination of the rope and the gear. In outdoor climbing, belayers also need to cope with environmental factors such as weather, rock conditions, spatial restrictions, and so forth.

An ordinary starting point for a climb is at the bottom of a wall/rock. The belayer often then moves away from the wall as the climber moves upward, especially when belaying for overhanging routes, in order to gain a wider view of the climb. When lowering the climber at the completion of the climb, the belayer slides the rope out using the belaying device until the climber is lowered onto the ground and is announced to be "off belay."

Because of the technical differences between top-roping and leading, the amount of attention and caution required for belaying would be graded according to the following cline (1). However, it is highly arguable whether "indoor leading" and "outdoor top-roping" requires more belayer attention/caution because the environmental factors and danger levels at play can vary.

(1) Degree of attention/caution required for belaying

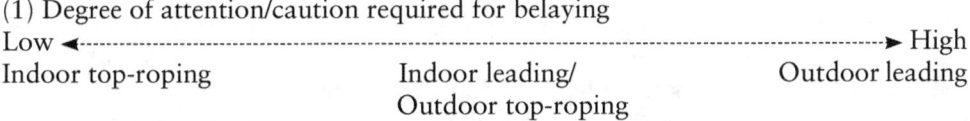

Given this assumption, it seems reasonable to compare "indoor top-roping" with "outdoor leading" for delineating and identifying the organizational features of climbing performance. When top-roping in indoor facilities, it is vital for belayers not to give too much slack on the rope. As long as this system works, major accidents will not usually happen unless the belayer makes a major error.[1] However, belayers have been known to disregard top-rope climbers' safety by looking away or talking on the phone (see the video clip of "The World's Worst Belayer" on YouTube, for example).

In either style of climbing, falling is an inevitable consequence of trial and error in trying to climb as high as possible, or to the end point of a climb. I would argue that: (1) climbing activities are one type of interaction that is based on a particular structural organization comparable to institutional discourse; (2) an expected action by a climber and necessary (re)actions by a belayer require each participant to have the relevant expertise and skills required to conduct the relevant activity.

3.5 Analysis of Climbing and Belaying

Before the analysis, let us first confirm how climbing and belaying are normally conducted. (Those familiar with rock climbing should feel free to skip this section. For technical terms in rock climbing, refer to the glossary.) The ordinary process for

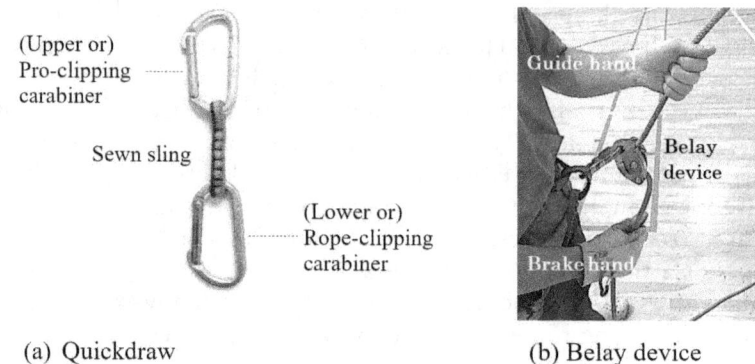

(a) Quickdraw (b) Belay device

FIGURE 3.1 *Climbing gear (quickdraw and belay device).*

a climber to take a pro(tection) is twofold (Figure 3.1 (a)): first, to clip a pro-clipping carabiner on the quickdraw into a bolt (or any kinds of secured pro), and second, to clip rope on the rope-clipping carabiner. In some cases, however, such as on a popular route, quickdraws are already set and free to use after permission is sought (as in our cases).

A belay device is essential for either top-roping or leading. A belayer feeds out or reels in rope through the device as the climber ascends (see Figure 3.1 (b)); in the event of a fall, s/he stops it by holding down the rope with the brake hand. It is imperative that the climber and the belayer have fully mastered the processes of climbing/belaying and share communication protocols, as miscommunication can lead to a serious accident or even death (see, for example, "How to belay" at https://rockandice.com/how-to-climb/how-to-belay/).

The protocol includes simple universal commands that should be confirmed between climber (C) and belayer (B), such as "On belay? (C)"—"Belay on! (B)," and "Off belay. (C)"—"Belay off. (B)" Once a climber starts to ascend, the communication is extremely limited except when the climber wants the belayer to reel out more rope ("Slack!" or *Yurumete!*) or to take in any slack ("Take!" or *Hatte!* ("Tension!")), or especially when the climber is about to fall ("Watch me!" or *Yoroshiku!* ("Please (catch me if I fall)!")). These moments aside, however, both climber and belayer are quite taciturn, concentrating instead on what they can and should do.

3.5.1 Belaying as Institutionalized Practice (1)

3.5.1.1 How a Climb Begins and Ends

Let us now confirm how lead and top-rope climbing starts and concludes. I first look into the communicative protocols/rituals that are shared both overtly and covertly in rock climbing communities. In an activity that runs even the smallest risk of danger, safety measures should be taken as part of a strict routine that demarcates itself from other activities. As in many other types of performances and competitions, rock climbing also has its own standard procedures for securing safety prior to a climb,

EXCERPT 3.1 *Toprope climbing (in a climbing gym)*.

1.	B/C:	((check each other's gear and knots in silence))	
2.	C:	*ikimasu!*	I'm climbing.
3.	B:	>*ii*< *yo.*	Go ahead.
		((4 lines omitted))	
4.	C:	*shiro one-. . shiro ikimasu!*	I'm climbing . . the white (route).
5.	B:	*hai yo*	Got it.
		((2:26 later: B keeps belaying, and C, climbing in silence)	
6.	C:	↑*tensho:n.* ((Lit. "Tension."))	Take!
7.	B:	*hai tensho:n.*	Yeah you are on.
8.	C:	*ja onegai shima:su.*	Then please (lower me).
9.	B:	*hai oroshi ma:su.*	Okay I'm lowering you.
10.		((0:15: B lowers C))	
11.	C:	*arigato: gozai mashita.*	Thanks (for belaying).
12.	B:	*hai otsukare san.*	Sure. Good job.

such as climbers' checking each other's gear, rope knots, and/or route conditions. Once lead or top-rope climbing is underway, a climber and a belayer are expected to focus on their respective tasks: the climber aims to complete the climb with as few "takes" as possible or with a better style than hitherto, while the belayer concentrates on taking in extra rope as climber ascends and, in the event of a fall, minimizing the fall length by efficiently operating the rope with the belay device. Given that the participants share and follow the climbing protocol, conversational exchanges are minimized. Now let us observe how such routine protocols proceed with top-rope and lead climbing (Excerpt 3.1).

As seen in the "initiation" protocol (lines 1–5 in Excerpt 3.1), after B and C check each other's gear and knots, C announces that he will climb the route that is marked with white tape (line 4)—each route in the gym is usually marked by a piece of same-color adhesive tape next to the holds to be used—and B confirms it (line 5). The same sort of fixed protocol is used during the descent. As seen in lines 6–12, very terse announcements and instructions are exchanged but they are clear and there is no miscommunication. I should add that "take" in line 6 could be interpreted in several ways depending on context, but in this case, in practical terms it means "take in extra rope and hold my body with it before you lower me." The response "You are on" (line 7) indicates that the climber is now held securely by the rope, to which C does not explicitly say "lower me," but simply responds with "then please" (line 8). B clearly interprets it to mean "lower me [i.e., the climber]" and complies with that request, as indicated by his next statement—*oroshimasu* ("[I'm] lowering you"; line 9).

Almost the same protocol (with just a slight variation) is used in outdoor lead climbing, as shown below (Excerpt 3.2).

Here again, both B and C check each other's equipment for safety (lines 1–2). After B confirms the route that C is going to climb (lines 3–5), C announces he is

EXCERPT 3.2 *Lead climbing (outdoors).*

1.	C:	*hai ja [one]gai shimasu.*	Okay shall we (check each other)?
2.	B:	[*hai.*] (B and C start checking each other's gear and knots of rope)	Sure.
3.	B:	°*xxxxxx de,*°	(Is it **xxxxxx**,) ((route name))
4.		°*xxxxxx de yokatta ne.*°	(you're gonna climb **xxxxxx**, right?)
5.	C:	*hai.*	Yeah.
6.		*hai=yoroshiku onegai shima:su.*	Okay, I'm ready.
7.	B:	*hai:.*	Climb.
8.	C:	*(i)kima:su.*	Climbing.
		((2:32 later: After climbing to the top))	
9.	C:	*hai ja hatte kudasa:i.*	Okay, take (in rope).
10.	B:	*ha:i!*	Okay.
11.		(3.3) ((B takes in rope))	
12.		*hai okke: de:su.*	Okay, I'm ready.
13.	C:	*hai ja oroshite kudasa:i.*	Okay, lower me.
14.	B:	*ha:i.* ((start lowering C))	I will (lower you).

ready, and they follow the ordinary protocol with the "Climb-Climbing" exchange (lines 7–8). Once C reaches the top of the route, he says *hatte (kudasai)* ("[please] take") to request that he be held by the rope (line 9); B responds with "okay" and then takes in rope (line 11). Here again, a variation of the "Lower me-lowering" exchange (lines 13–14) is performed conventionally and successfully.

Given this sequential organization, a particular set of protocols at the beginning and the end of route climbing is confirmed customarily, as illustrated in Figure 3.2. In order to interpret the figure, we need to follow the temporal sequence starting from the bottom and moving upward along as the climb progresses. During the process, highly stable exchanges between B and C are expected, such that C's intentions/announcements are rigidly met in terms of the climbing procedure with B's acceptance/reception at the beginning and the end, with the middle section filled in with "pro-taking routines" by C (to be examined in the next section). This organization is obviously akin to an ordinary Aristotelian narrative formation, which consists of "beginning—middle—end."

Although the starting/ending protocols are quite rigid, the order of utterances in each "pair set" ("Climbing-Climb" or "Climb-Climbing") could be reversed; the order of the pair sets ("Climbing-Climb" → "Lower-Lowering") must not change, of course.

3.5.1.2 The Middle Section

We have observed above how a climb usually begins and ends, as well as the protocols used. We now look into how a climb proceeds in the middle section, which was

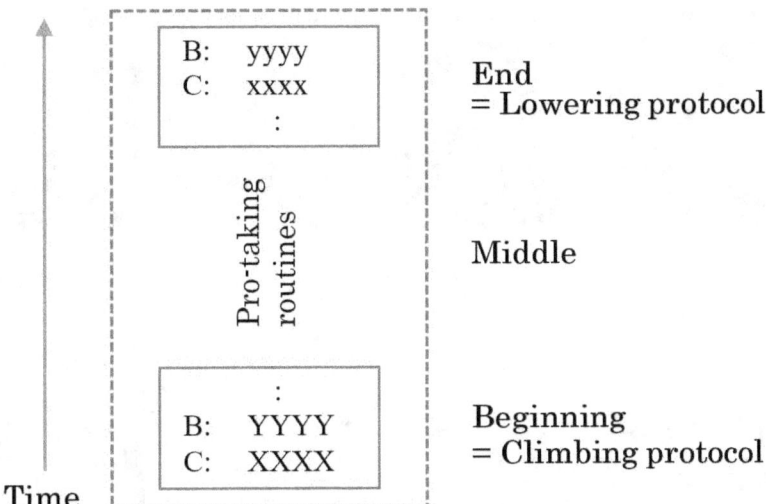

FIGURE 3.2 *Skeletal formation of route climbing.*

simply summarized as "Pro-taking routines" in Figure 3.2. In fact, there is ample motivation to call them "routines" due to the very stable patterns of actions conducted during the phase—i.e., a climber continues to ascend, occasionally clipping his rope into (possibly different types of) pros on the route, while a belayer concurrently feeds out rope. As shown in Figure 3.3 below, belaying techniques (including the correct feed-out posture) are disseminated widely and adhered to as (internationally) standardized forms, as demonstrated by the belayer's stretched-out and tucked-in arms. This posture makes it easier for a belayer to pay out slack so that the climber can clip a rope without difficulty. In all of these cases, however, the techniques simply stress the need to act "quickly" and "appropriately." Although it is obvious that "the quicker the better" is the norm, there are few tutorial videos that depict the minute details of when and how belaying should be conducted (except in slow-motion replay). In the following, I will examine such aspects of the exquisitely expert actions taken by belayers in response to climbers' movements.

Note that, in Figure 3.3, the plates (a)–(d) capture the simultaneous actions of B and C on the time scale. In Figure 3.3 C (a), C, who is a 5.14 climber, is on a 5.13+ route—a short but highly strenuous route in the area, which few climbers have dared to try. The belayer is his wife, and herself an experienced climber. He is now at the beginning of the "crux" (the most challenging point) of the route, trying to take a pro(tection) on the 130-degree phase of the route. We see below that C looks and reaches down to pull the rope before clipping (Figure 3.3 (a)); by that time, B has already fed out enough slack with her "guide hand" (= left hand in this case: Figure 3.3 B (a)) that the rope does not become taut and C can clip easily. At this moment, however, since the next protection is placed at C's eye level, the climber—being aware that not enough rope has yet been pulled up—holds the rope by biting it (Figure 3.3 C (b): not visible from this angle) and tries to pull more rope for clipping (Figure 3.3 C (c)).

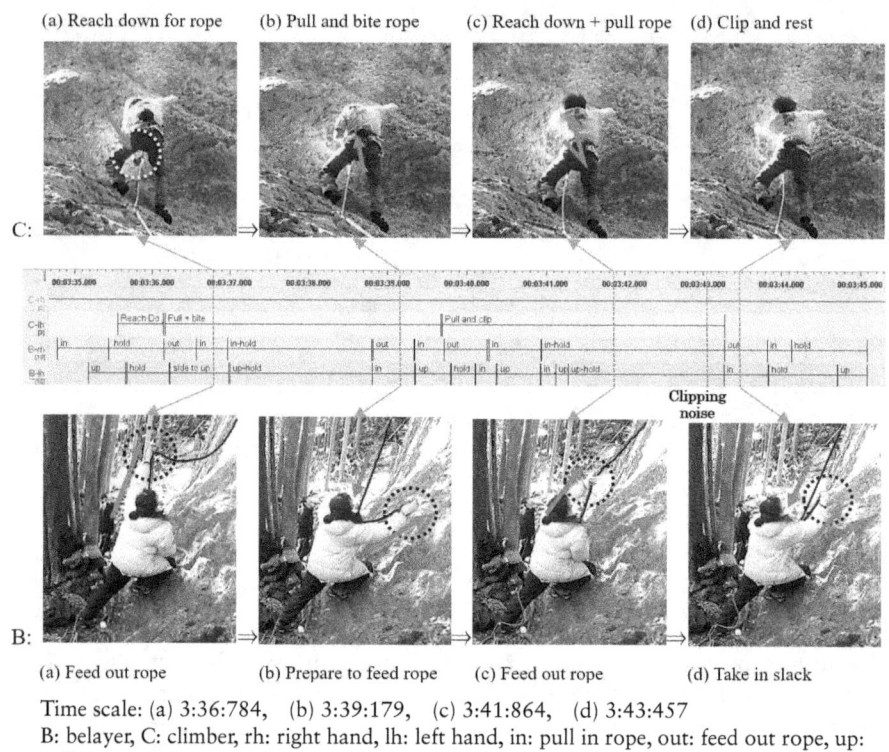

FIGURE 3.3 *Climber–belayer coordination.*

B is also quick to respond to C's action, trying to feed more rope for C by sliding her right hand (=brake hand) outward, at the same time sliding her left hand (=guide hand) downward (Figure 3.3 B (b)), and then pulling the rope with her right hand inward and the left hand upward (Figure 3.3 B (c)). B has made it in time to promptly feed out more slack before C raises his left hand; he can then hold the rope and successfully clip it into the (rope-clipping) carabiner in front of his face (C (c)). As soon as B "hears" the clicking noise (C's clipping a rope at 3:43:050), she instantly takes in slack rope so that C is securely protected in about 200 m (Figure 3.3 B (d)).

The coordination and simultaneous reactions to contingent actions are notable, as shown by the harmonious reaching-up-and-down (re)actions by both participants. Also significant are B's anticipatory actions: Even before the action in Figure 3.3 B/C (a) ensued, B had already slightly reached out her right hand (not shown here) to take in more rope (1.7 seconds before B's taking-in action in B (a)), and made a timely feed of rope in time for C's reaching-down action at C (a). In other words, B (a) is the preparatory action for C (b), B (b) for C (c), and B (c) for C (d), with B (d), the act of taking in slack, serving as the safety measure for minimizing the length of C's potential fall. This step-by-step, minute preparatory action chain constitutes the sequential flow of a "task complex" inherent in every segment of climbing performance, and which builds up to the accomplishment of the climb, whether it is "onsight," "flash," or "redpoint" (see note 1). Climber C had already failed the "onsight/flash" attempt and was aiming for the "redpoint" climb, so he hung onto the rope (after C (d)), took a rest, and finished the route after rehearsing the moves (i.e., by "hangdogging"). This way, most climbers would aim to climb the target route with a better style than "redpoint," because such styles can only be accepted as "leading a route." With this process repeated, climbers aim to improve their highest climbing grade even if doing so involves the risk of falling.

In the following section, I will examine in more detail how a belayer reacts in the event of a fall. The question arises as to whether the belayer should use a "non-dynamic" or "dynamic" belaying style depending on the context of climbing. Although top-rope climbing is not regarded as "leading" a route, I first consider a case of top-roping since non-dynamic belaying is widely used there.

3.5.2 Belaying as Institutionalized Practice (2)

3.5.2.1 Indoor Toprope Climbing: A Case of Non-dynamic Belay

In the following segment, vision and action are crucial to successfully fulfilling the belayer's duties and responsibilities. The scene in Figure 3.4 depicts the crux move in a top-rope climb. As previously mentioned, since top-roping is secured by a rigid anchor point, it qualifies for the "non-dynamic" belay (or "hard catch"), in which the belayer barely moves or, in a more extreme case, takes in slack and squats during the fall (see, for example, the video clip "Dynamic belay technique" at "https://www.youtube.com/watch?v=xOallLz_2Sc" for more detail). This belaying method causes more impact on the anchor, so should be avoided in outdoor lead climbing, but could be used in indoor top-rope climbing.

The belayer shown in Figure 3.4 has had only a few years of climbing experience, but is a frequent visitor to this facility. The movement series depicted is of course continuous and cannot be separated into individual steps in a practical sense, but I managed to pick up on what are assumed to be the significant moments that would explicitly represent the belayer's critical reactions, which occurred approximately within 1,000 milliseconds (1.0 second) after the fall.

Even before C actually falls, B and C were exchanging comments about the next move of sending C's right hand to the red hold (the one in the dotted circle shown in Figure 3.4 C (a). In fact, this move was unanimously regarded as the most technical move on the route. C had already dawdled on the same spot for the last thirteen seconds, and when he was about to take the next action, his right foot, which was jammed in the crack formation of the artificial rock face (the area in the broken rectangular in Figure 3.4 C (a)), suddenly slipped (at 00:53:290) and he started falling (Figure 3.4 C (b)). Although B seems relaxed, he is watching C's struggles intently, bracing himself for a fall by standing with his legs slightly apart (Figure 3.4 B (a)).

It might seem that B did not conspicuously move his body until the moment depicted in Figure 3.4 B (c). However, if we take a closer look at Figure 3.4 B (b), we notice that he had already lifted his left hand upward approximately 200 milliseconds (ms) after C's fall (Figure 3.4 B (b)) and is prepared to pull the rope. At this moment, B is expected to take in rope (if at all possible) to minimize the fall length. Thus, as a

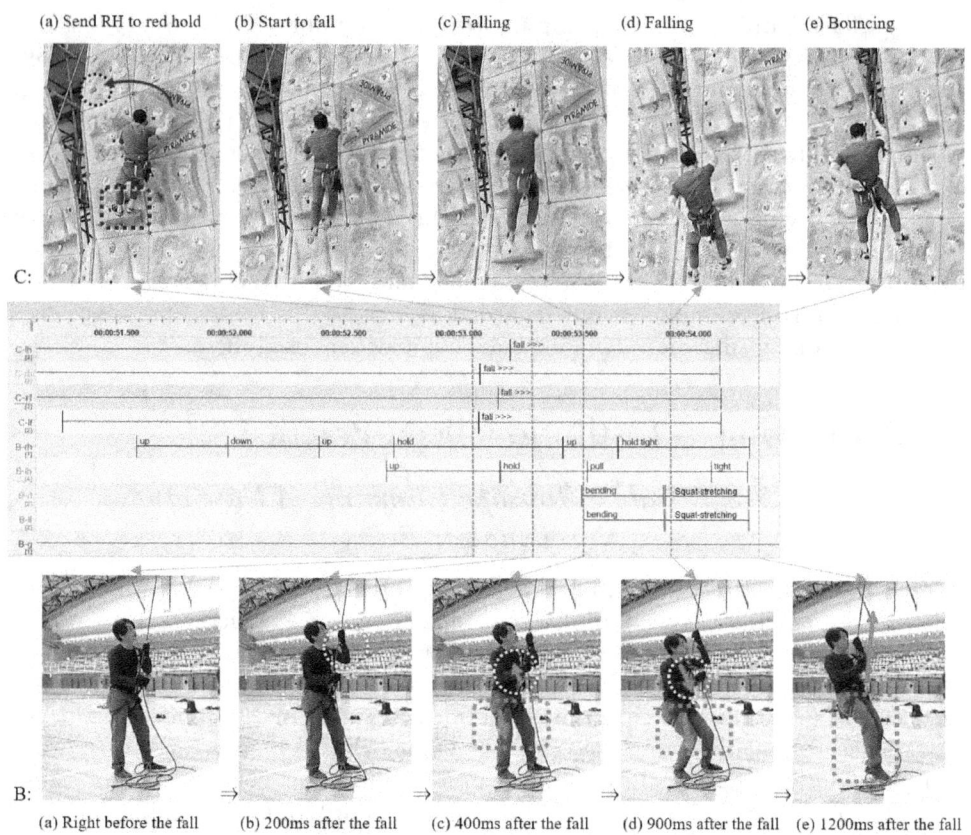

FIGURE 3.4 *Belaying postures.*

counter measure to the fall, B accurately coordinates his actions, taking several factors into consideration. Specifically, B first lifts his left hand upward along the rope (Figure 3.4 B (b)) and then tries to handle the rope with both hands, as can be observed in his raised right hand following his left hand (Figure 3.4 B (c)). At the same time, B also tries to reduce the fall length by bending his knees and starting to squat (B (c)). Further in Figure 3.4 B (d), B executes "textbook" reactions of the non-dynamic belay although they are not totally effective on this occasion. In this case, B tries to lessen the fall length by tightening the brake with his right hand, simultaneously sinking downward to counter-balance the impact of the fall—a typical reaction for a non-dynamic belay. He then lets himself be pulled up by the impact. Given that the fall is a short one, there is little reaction time, but he still somehow tries to take appropriate measures by coordinating his physical actions in a recommended manner.

There are several possible reasons for B's inability to fully implement the countermeasures. First, the rope used in this top-roping activity was a static one (made of woven kevlar fibers) rather than an ordinary climbing rope (made of woven nylon fibers). A kevlar rope is exceptionally durable and strong but exhibits little elongation, which allows less time before the impact of a fall ensues than a dynamic rope. Since all the anchors are well secured in indoor top-rope climbing, B's sudden sinking action is not particularly a problem, but it could have led to a serious consequence in outdoor lead-climbing—the impact of this sudden motion might have exerted impact on the protection, smashed it, and caused a longer (or possible "ground") fall.

As noted above, the basic truism here is "the quicker the better," but our ordinary visual ability precludes us from precisely evaluating the validity of our internal processes. Analyzing video evidence show that B made every effort to stick to the basics, although his physical responses were subtle and restrained (Figure 3.4 B (b)–(d)). He also acted within approximately 200 ms of C falling and completed all the expected measures within 1,000 ms, as is generally expected (but not explicitly articulated) in tutorial videos and textbooks.

3.5.2.2 Outdoor Lead Climbing: A Case of Dynamic Belay

In outdoor lead climbing, some precautions must be executed fully to avoid injury or, in a worst-case scenario, a deadly incident. As a result, a special belaying technique called "dynamic belay" is widely recommended. It is a method in which the belayer does not try to counter-balance the fall momentum on the same spot where he or she is standing, but rather utilizes the movement of his/her own body to reduce impact on the gear, rope, and climber (also called a "soft catch"). (See, for example, "Climb Safe: How to Handle Soft Belaying" at https://www.youtube.com/watch?v=bO1DkxEIavc.)

The next case deals with such a "fall-and-catch" incident in an outdoor lead climb. The climber and a belayer are married, and visit this area frequently. They are expert and skilled climbers with more than ten years of experience: the husband's highest route grade is 5.14 (on the decimal scale) and the wife's is 5.13, both of which fall in the expert range. The following climb was her fourth or fifth "redpoint" attempt (the second attempt on that day) on this overhanging route (graded 5.12c).[2] As shown here (Figure 3.5), she was unable to complete the crux and fell to approximately 2 m from the ground (out of the camera frame). The belayer, on the other hand, quickly reeled in rope and jumped up at the very moment of the fall impact, a subtle but exquisitely coordinated soft-catch sequence.

Figure 3.5 (a) depicts C's unsuccessful lunge attempt and subsequent fall. This crux move (5.12c) at C (a) has bounced many local climbers so far. Before the fall, B was standing still, keenly watching C make the lunge move. In Figure 3.5 C (a), C momentarily pinches a micro hold, but instantly loses her balance and starts falling from rock (Figure 3.5 C (b, c)). Approximately 200 ms after C loses her balance, B promptly slides his left hand upward (Figure 3.5 B (b)) and takes in as much rope as he can with his both hands (B (c)), which takes only about 200 ms. While C is free-falling, B takes further protective action by sliding his left hand along the rope once more to pull in more rope (Figure 3.5 B (d)) while also lending his weight to the pull of the rope, as shown by his bent knees straightening up. As we see from Figure 3.5, these actions take him only another 200 ms.

As C's falling momentum continues to pull B upward, B lets himself lift with the force, jumping slightly (Figure 3.5 B (e)) and floating in the air temporarily (Figure 3.5 B (f)) before finally landing safely on the rock slope (Figure 3.5 B (g)). We notice from Figure 3.5 B (f) that before he lands on the ground, he momentarily looks down

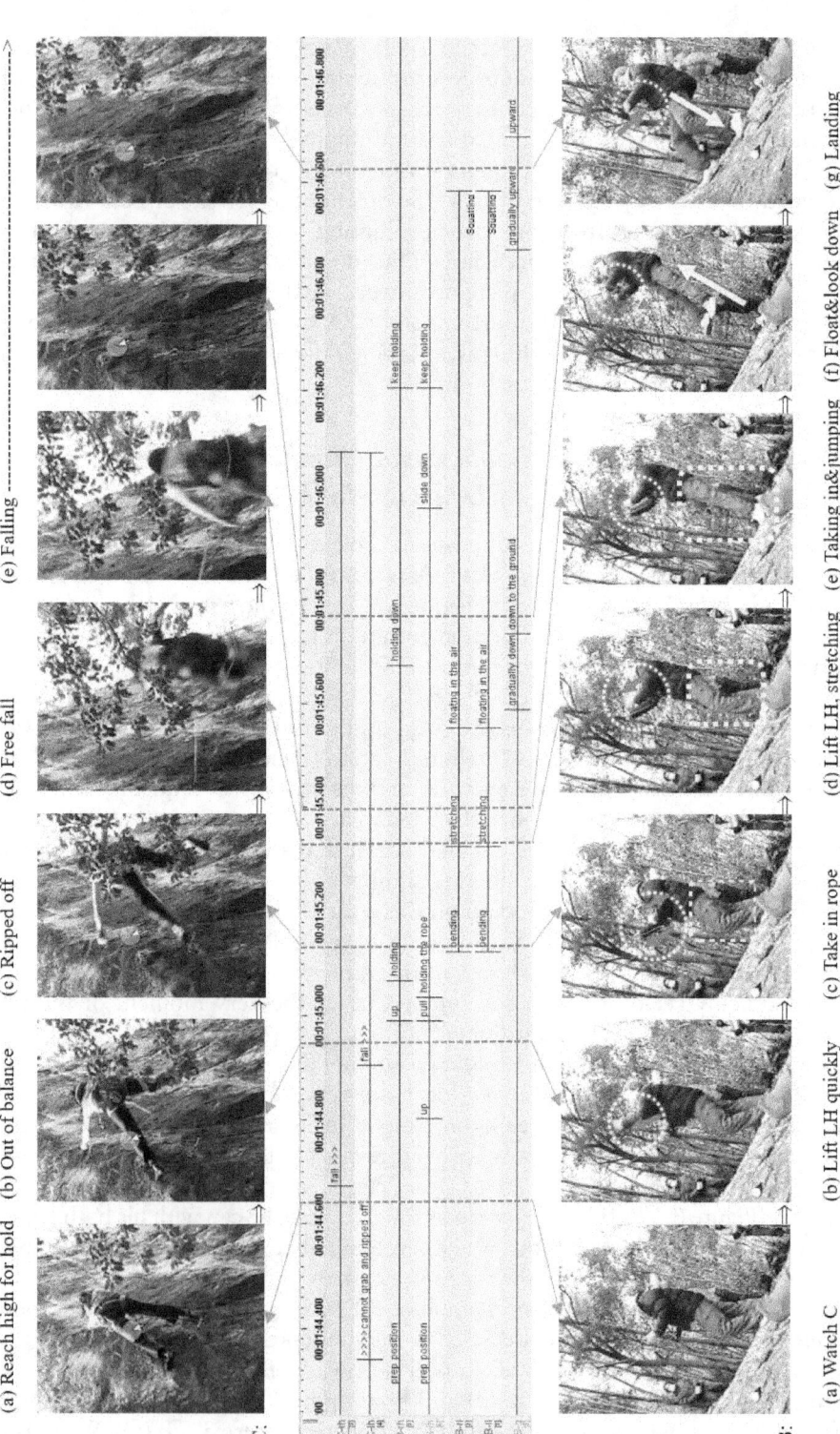

FIGURE 3.5 Belayer's reactions against a fall.

and checks the ground conditions, while also pulling his right hand toward himself so as to not let out more rope (Figure 3.5 (g)). After he lands on the ground, B immediately asks C if she is okay (*daijoubu datta?*), or if she has any injuries, to which C answers, *Daijoubu* ("I'm okay"). This whole sequence of actions, excluding the q&a about C's condition at the end, occurs within just 2.5 seconds, resulting in a well-managed "soft catch."

In the sequence of falling and catching, actions speak louder than words. If we assume that an action is comparable to an utterance in an expected sequence of interaction, each action should project a certain consequence at each moment of execution, indicating to the viewer/perceiver that they need to react accordingly. In our case, C's actions (e.g., to lunge, lose her balance, and fall) inevitably induced B's relevant reactions (e.g., to take in slack, catch the fall, check the landing ground). Since these sets of actions are closely related but individually sequential, they build upon a high level of autonomy as well as the involvement of the concerned party. In other words, once a fall is in motion, the belaying sequence must duly follow, unlike an ordinary conversation that is cancellable. In this sense, we could assume that a covert script exists with specific procedures and mannerisms to be followed by participants, as is often observed in institutional interactions.

3.6 Summary and Discussion

From the abovementioned observations, we notice that C's clipping and B's feeding rope go hand in hand like synchronized dancers, and that B ensures C can clip without any hitches by feeding the right length of rope. A climber and a belayer are tactfully attentive to how they should proceed with top-rope/lead climbing by respectively achieving expected actions and evading possibly negative consequences. Obviously, different roles and expectations are pre-allocated and ascribed to them. This type of task-oriented, largely customized coordination typically exploits a common procedure for the sake of facility and encompasses an interactional protocol akin to "institutional discourse" (Drew and Heritage 1992; Heritage 2004; Levinson 2013). A formal institutional setting postulates that participants are focused on particular tasks (in our case, climbing and belaying), the order of which is fairly rigidly specified, and the type of allowable actions is highly limited and pre-allocated for each, as seen typically in news interviews and gate-keeping encounters at public institutions (Heritage and Greatbatch 1989; Zimmerman 1984, 1992).

In rock climbing, it is anticipated that there is a differential distribution of rights and expertise to participate in the interaction to maximize their verbal/nonverbal performance. A highly prescribed structural organization often exists for achieving institutional tasks, as seen for the "Opening—Request—Interrogative series—Response—Closing" sequence in emergency calls (Zimmerman 1984, 1992). However, our climbing data show that utterance is not an essential part of the performance except for the "ritualistic" components (the initial and final pair sets), which bind and embrace the pro-taking routines (see the left side of Figure 3.6). This is partially because the participation framework often expands as a climber ascends, until it becomes difficult for the party members to communicate easily.

Despite superficial differences in the availability of verbal resources, there surely is a good deal of similarity between emergency discourse and climbing discourse. In a climbing situation, the climber starts from the base of the rock (bottom left of Figure 3.6) after issuing the "initiation" announcement. Once the climber starts, s/he usually takes protections at regular intervals if at all possible. Each pro is taken following a certain sequence of movements, with or without a pre-/post-sequence to the core adjacency pair of actions (as was seen in Figure 3.3). When the end point is reached after repeating the process, the "termination" protocol is executed. We can see from Figure 3.6 that this structure is in principle identical to the institutional discourse in Zimmerman's (1984) analysis of emergency calls to the police station, except that our "action pair" works like a series of "insertion sequences" without the base sequence (lines 2 and 11 on the right side of Figure 3.6). This qualitative and structural affinity suggests that the climbing activity itself operates on the framework of institutional discourse, typically seen in gate-keeping encounters.

One might ask: How, then, is "expert action" relevant in such a framework? The conclusion we reached is surprisingly not novel. The experience-laden prescience gained by every expert through exercise and practice, extends to various aspects of physical coordination ranging from vision, action, and posture, to the perception of surroundings. Such ascribed (re)actions seem to cultivate an activity-oriented scenario that is implicitly and explicitly shared among participants in an activity. To take an ordinary action of "taking a pro" for example, the essential core actions are B's "feeding rope" and C's "clipping rope," both of which could be supplemented by other relevant actions. For instance, before B's feeding rope, C often reaches for rope to clip it into a carabiner, the action of which would serve as a "contextualization cue" for the next action (i.e., "clip a rope"). Likewise, C's clipping rope consequently

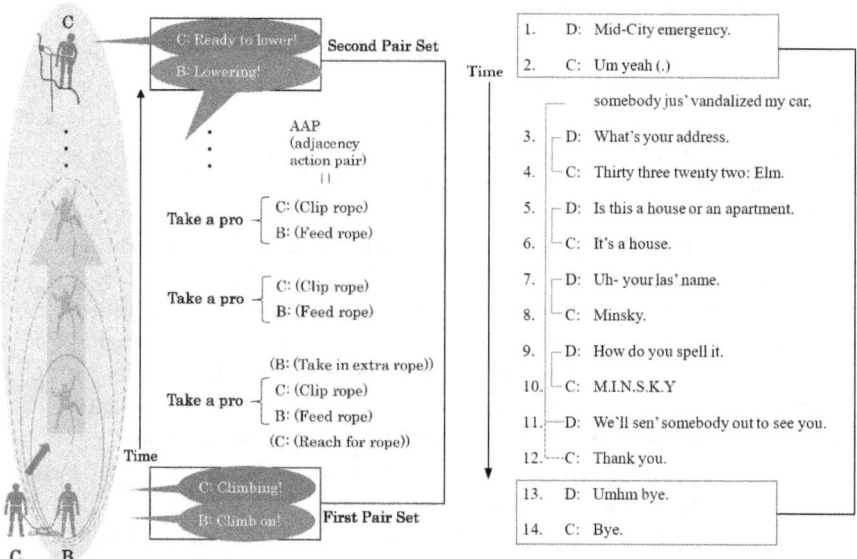

FIGURE 3.6 *Climbing as institutionalized interaction (cf. Zimmerman 1984: 214).*

necessitates B to take in extra slack to minimize the length in case of a fall. These pre-/post-conditions indexically open up a scenario in which a sequence of "taking a pro" actions continues until it completes the necessary procedure, as is the case with an emergency call.

Other issues relevant to ascribed participation include empathic telecommunication. One of the most popular themes among numerous tutorial videos concerns characteristics of the ideal belayer. For example, in "The World's Best Belayer" video (https://www.youtube.com/watch?v=NJHVgkchcbw), the belayer is depicted as one who instantly pre-cognizes possible dangers and takes perfectly pitched precautions in a given climbing context.[3] Notice, however, that this is exactly what most people do in everyday interactions—for example, when you propose an overnight trip next weekend to someone but sense they are going to turn you down, you instinctively make a more acceptable suggestion instead, or even withdraw the notion midway through repairs and reformulations, in order to produce the most comfortable result for the both parties involved. In this sense, it may or may not be a coincidence that according to the data, belayers react to climbers' falls in approximately 200 ms—the average pause length for turn-taking (Stivers et al. 2009).[4] It remains speculative at the moment, but this span of time has been observed widely as a common reaction window for humans in sequential activities that require a prompt reaction.

Also, long-distance communication has been of constant interest since the inception of conversation and multimodal analysis, as typically seen in the analysis of telephone conversation (Sacks et al. 1974), internet gaming (Keating and Mirus 2003), and remote surgery (Mondada 2003)—all activities in which physical distance is mediated and mitigated by technology. Rock climbing falls on a mediated ground between such "telecommunication" and *in-situ* interaction—in rock climbing, the participants are located on vertically staggered levels often in an "aligned" F-formation (Kendon 1990), according to which the participation framework expands by default as the climber moves upward.[5] Still, such a participation framework is stable as long as climber and belayer are connected by a rope—that will set the bounds of the participation framework, but hold each other's actions in check. Whether top-roping or leading, rock climbing is characterized by such an expanding and shrinking participation framework, which serves as common ground for the participants and is governed by a patterned recursivity with an equivalent internal structure of actions.

The main focus of this analysis was to analyze in detail the interaction between the body, the gaze, and the environment, and it was found to be regimented under the purview of verbal and nonverbal schemas shared among participants. Specifically, I observed and analyzed in detail what it constitutes to carefully "watch" the climber and the environment, to deploy one's bodily actions, and to appropriate them in preparation for an emergent incident like a fall. As a result, I found that the specialized skills include visual perception of the climber's movements in context (expert vision), the dexterity to physically manage appropriate actions (expert action), and the precaution paid to the belayer's own safety (expert awareness), all contributing to socializing them to become safety-oriented, proficient climbers.

The key issues I have pursued in this chapter are patterns of institutionalized interaction and implicit ways in which ascribed tasks are tacitly accomplished among rock climbing participants. Interaction with the environment, however, has not been a prominent factor in such cases, although it is not entirely absent. As long as climbing takes place in a specific environment, a fuller picture cannot be obtained without considering the relationship between actors and the immediate physical conditions. Regarding this relationship, notions such as "affordance" and "intersubjectified corporeality" emerge as more pertinent phenomena, which I examine in detail in the following chapters.

4

Affordances in Rock Climbing

4.1 Introduction

4.1.1 Affordances in Learning

Ecological information that can be extracted from the environment depends on the perception and proficiency of actors (Gibson [1979] 2015). Since climbing is an activity in which actors' perception, knowledge, dexterity, and overall proficiency are inextricably linked, Gibson's concept of "affordance" is a highly relevant and useful clue to understanding climbers' actions and subsequent interaction in a particular environment. Gibson's original definition of affordance is controversially simple: "The *affordances* of the environment are what it *offers* the animal, what it *provides* or *furnishes,* either for good or ill" ([1979] 2015: 127). In other words, affordances are properties of the environment and resources that the environment offers any animal, providing opportunities for particular kinds of behavior (Reed 1996). Affordances are relative to animals and thus are both objective and subjective properties, so to speak.

In this sense, a rock wall serves as a "niche" ("*how* an animal lives" (Gibson [1979] 2015: 120) or a set of affordances for a particular animal) for some actors to climb—but not for all. That said, it is often not transparent to novice actors what ecological information they can extract from the environment. Since affordances are animal-relative properties of the environment, someone's affordance may not be others'. Skilled climbers can find a route on a seemingly blank wall, while novice or unskilled climbers cannot. A secure hold or stance, perceived as such by an expert climber, may appear to be a small protrusion or even a blank rock face for a novice climber. Whether or not a climber can complete a route or solve a bouldering problem hinges upon such a precarious balance between climbers' dexterity and affordances from the environment. When such a mutual balance is achieved in the sport-appropriate manner, climbers can anticipate their peak performance and improve their climbing grade.

This notion of affordance is conceptualized differently even among ecological psychologists (see Reed 1996, Chemero 2003, and Rietveld and Kiverstein 2014, for an overview). Building on Gibson's ([1979] 2015) seminal project on "ecological psychology," his followers characterized the features inherent in affordance in terms of "selection pressure" (Reed 1996), "dispotions" (Turvey 1992), and/or "body scale."[1] Along these lines of argument, there are two major acknowledged views on affordance (Chemero 2003): One is the "selectionist" view (e.g., Reed 1996), in which resources in the environment exert selection pressure on animals that causes them to perceive selected resources. This is virtually a biological perspective in that it regards affordances as the driving force to which animals need to conform through evolution by natural selection (Reed 1996). The other is a "dispositional" view (e.g., Turvey 1992) in which affordances are tied more closely to physics than to biology, such that affordances are dispositional properties of the environment and complemented by animals' abilities (or in their parlance, "effectivities"), such as "body scale" in a case of stair-climbing. Considering these differences, I tend to align with Chemero's (2003, 2009) proposal that affordance is about the "relationship" between animals and the environment. In this sense, the "relational" view is a third way that mediates both selectionist (biology-based) and dispositionist (physics-based) positions (cf. Ingold 2018[2]). Chemero (2003: 191) defined affordances as follows: "Affordances are neither properties of the animal alone nor properties of the environment alone. Instead, they are relations between the abilities of an animal and some feature of a situation." In this view, affordances serve as the glue that connects the animal and the environment.

Such a position, which Chemero (2009) and Chemero and Käufer (2015) called a radical empiricist view, is a step toward the integration of the body and the environment. Building on Gibson's and Merleau-Ponty's works, Chemero and Käufer (2015: 61) summarized ecological principles of perception as follows: (1) Perception is direct (perception is not the result of inferences performed on sensor representations, but rather part of the system that includes both the animal and the perceived object.); (2) Perception is for action (the purpose of perception is "to act in it," and action is also for perception or cognition.); (3) Perception is of affordances (the primary objects of perception are affordances. An animal's abilities determine which affordances are available to it.). As implied in this view, as climbers (or any athletes and learners in general) attempt to achieve higher levels of performance, there will be a change in what they perceive as affordances from the environment. As will be shown subsequently, the efficacy of implicit communication between a climber and spectators depends on the level of sensing what is available to them environmentally for the respective tasks in which they are engaged (see also Goodwin 2007a; Mondada 2016). As long as novice climbers attempt to use some features on the climbing wall as possible affordances, they need to enhance their "dexterity" by extending their effectivities. In this sense, affordances from the environment vary from person to person. In climbing, if natural and artificial affordances (e.g., holds and protections to be used) are not readily exploited, climbers may be regarded as taking unnecessary risks or acting recklessly.

Dexterity, according to Bernstein (1996), is not simply a harmony of bodily movements but resides "in finding a motor solution for any situation and in any condition" (1996: 21).[3] Bernstein also stated that "demand for dexterity is not in the movements themselves but in the surrounding conditions" (1996: 23). It must be coordinated *in situ* toward a certain goal (e.g., completing a problem or "onsighting" a route in climbing), because "dexterity will not gain anything from any movements that do not have an objective" (1996: 232). Such activities need to be maximally adapted to the surrounding environment by combining immediate perceptions from the environment with biological endowments. Such contexts are typical of learning and instruction, and offer learners and novices spaces known as "zones of proximal development" (ZPD; Vygotsky 1978) or "fields of promoted action" (FPA; Reed 1996). In other words, ZPDs/FPAs occupy a niche in the environment where "the probability of a developing animal's encountering a given affordance can be markedly raised or lowered by the actions of its caretakers" (Reed and Bril 1996: 439).

The way we perceive the external world is not a fixed mental response, but rather a transformational process by which the body is re-conceived in a given environment during an activity. Building on the points made by Gibson and Merleau-Ponty, Ingold (2000: 262) employed such phenomenological concepts in anthropological investigations and claimed that "the senses exist not as distinct registers whose separate impressions are combined only at higher levels of cognitive processing, but as aspects of functioning of the whole body in movement, brought together in the very action of its involvement in an environment." Perception is an omni-corporeal phenomenon that is always present in climbing. The question here, however, is whether the climbing participant can find a solution to the problem in relation to the given environment (the shape and position of the holds on the rock or wall), and how climbing—or more precisely, "solving a move"—can be accomplished collaboratively by extending the capabilities of an individual climber.

4.1.2 Climbing Styles and Affordance

An expert climber once said to me, *yoikuraimaa wa muubu no hikidashi ga ooi* ("A good climber has many 'drawers' (a metaphor for 'options') of moves." I now believe that this concept is an alternative wording of having the ability to read off/out affordances from the environment and use them to practice whichever skill is required. As would be expected, when undertaking a route for the first time, it is important to be able to assess your own physical condition, the size and shape of holds, and other physical features that may affect your performance. Of course, you don't have to be a particularly good climber to work out which features on the rock can be used as holds: there are often perceptible cues that help you read out affordances. For example, which direction to climb in and the skills you'd need to do that can be deduced from the chalk marks that preceding climbers have left on the wall, the location of bolts nailed in the rock (on bolted routes), and the cracks and crevices where protections can be placed (on natural protection routes).

Still, these cues may not be available permanently, so climbers need to develop a covert capacity, or what could be called the "affordance-reading ability" (ARA), to figure out solution(s) to the problem. This ability is in fact incorporated implicitly into the classification of climbing styles and the degrees of their prestige. As was briefly introduced in Chapter 1, differential prestige has accrued for specific climbing styles (Figures 1.1 and 1.2). Here it is illustrated with a finer distinction of "leading" styles (onsight/flash/redpoint) for bolt-protected climbing (Figure 4.1). This distinction, however, can apply to some traditional free climbing routes (see the dotted line in Figure 4.1).

As far as "leading a route" is concerned, climbers who can "onsight" or "flash" a route are more highly acknowledged. "Onsight" is the most prestigious style of leading because it must be accomplished on the first trial, without resting or falling,

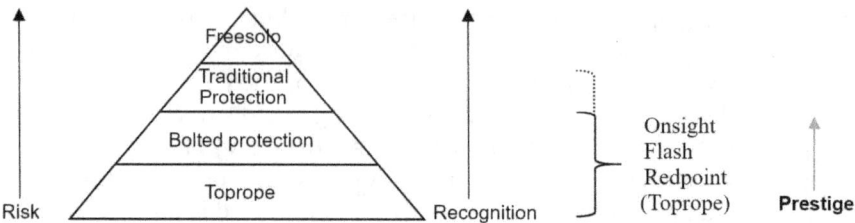

FIGURE 4.1 *Recognition and prestige of climbing styles (reproduction of Figure 1.2).*

and no prior knowledge of the route.[4] "Flash" occupies a slightly lower status, with the only difference being the availability of prior knowledge. Among the styles of leading, "redpoint" is the least esteemed style of leading, but it is the most frequently used, because free climbers usually aim to be a better leader and attempt harder routes than their current highest-achieved grades. Given these conditions, one of the essential requirements of a better leader is an ability to immediately read out available holds (i.e., affordances from the environment) in terms of size, shape, angle, and condition of the rock. In addition, s/he must be able to anticipate and decide on the next immediate moves vis-à-vis their own skills and physical strength, which constitutes a holistic expertise called "dexterity" (Bernstein 1996). Therefore, a climber who is barely able to "redpoint" a route using all their skills is often unable to "flash" (not to mention "onsight") the route. Therefore, the more a climber can read out "affordances" from the environment, the closer the grades between "redpoint" and "flash/onsight" will be. Accordingly, when a climber takes on a route for the first time, it is taboo to offer advice or prior knowledge, no matter how well intentioned, because it deprives the climber of the opportunity to "onsight." Given these criteria, "affordance-reading ability" (ARA) can be regarded as a meta-cognitive skill in which climbers subjectively pick out specific features available for him/herself coupled with his/her own dexterity. Considering the different degrees of recognition/prestige granted to the leading styles, ARA seems to be implicitly integrated into the prestige system of lead climbing as follows (Table 4.1).

As seen in the cline from "onsight" to "top-rope" (Table 4.1), these styles constitute levels of climber dexterity that comprise motor skills and immediate ARA. Needless to say, ARA is an important—indeed, essential—ability required in any style of

Table 4.1 Factors of prestige in climbing styles

Prestige \ Dexterity	Requirements		Occasion/ Condition
	Motor skills/ techniques	Affordance- reading ability	
▲ Onsight	+	+	One-time trial, w/o prior knowledge
Flash	+	+/−	One-time trial, w/ prior knowledge
Redpoint	+	−	Rehearsal allowed
Toprope	(−)	(−)	Practice/ Exercise

climbing, and leading a route or solving a problem is not an assemblage of separate skills but a coordinated activity aimed for dexterous actions in the immediate environment. To confirm this assumption, I will examine two individual cases in which affordances are heavily involved while climbers attempt to solve bouldering problems as efficiently as possible.

4.2 Background and Data

4.2.1 Japanese Vertical Lexicon

The following analysis focuses on how ARA is differentially exerted by climbers on/off the climbing wall. Such differential perceptions are manifested verbally and corporeally through the use of minute differences in Japanese spatial terms. The terms examined in Chapters 4 and 5 consist essentially of a noun phrase with or without a postposition. As English translation equivalents of the Japanese terms show, the latter exhibit grammatically different concepts. In particular, the Japanese coordinate terms *ue/shita* ("up/down") and *mae/ushiro* ("front/back") are morphologically nominals and refer to coordinate directions or regions/parts of an object. However, since they are followed canonically by a (locative) postposition (hereafter "PosP"), they function as adverbial phrases—the PosP may sometimes be dropped (Table 4.2; only *ue* and *mae* are shown as representatives).

As shown in Table 4.2, four notional distinctions are expected of the vertical lexicon *ue* and *mae*, depending on the grammatical construction and context of use (see Heine 1997 for semantic extensions of the spatial lexicon). For example, when

Table 4.2 Spatial concepts of UE/MAE

Ue/Mae (+PosP)	X no ue/mae (+ PosP)		
(a) Direction	(b) Space	(c) Surface	(d) Part
UE			
MAE			

ue is used with the PosP *ni* with an intransitive verb (e.g., *ue/shita ni susumu* ("move up/down")), it encodes an upward "direction" (Table 4.2 (a)); however, when *ue* is used with the reference object X in such a construction as *X no ue/mae* (*no* represents a genitive case), *ue* refers to the associated "space," "surface," or "part" of the object, as in "(above/on/top part of) X" (Table 4.2 (b, c, d)). If interpreted as "direction," the coordinate is based on the three-dimensional grid, while in the three other cases mentioned above, the meaning is based on the dimensions associated with the reference object X. Finer distinctions of spatial relations are made possible depending on the types of PosP and verbs as long as their properties are compatible with the notion of *ue/shita*. Relevant locative PosPs are *de* (area/region), *ni* (direction/destination), *e* (direction/destination), *o* (path), *kara* (source), and *made* (distance), of which the first four are highly relevant to our analysis. The following are typical examples of PosPs used with a verb:

1. *ue e/ni susumu*	"go up(ward)"	[direction]
2. *X no ue (ni ukabu/o tobu)*	"(float/fly) above/over X"	[space]
3. *X no ue (de odoru/ni oku)*	"(dance/put it) on X"	[surface]
4. *X no ue (o motsu)*	"(hold) the upper part of X"	[part]

Treating all of the linking possibilities would go beyond the scope of this analysis. Suffice it to say that we are concerned mainly with these four semantic distinctions.

4.2.2 Data Information

The following snippet of conversation occurred among regular climbers at a well-established climbing gym in Nagoya, a city in Japan's Aichi Prefecture. The gym was one of the oldest in the area (opened in 1993, closed in 2017), and at the time of data collection was home to many of the area's leading climbers. The daily routine at the gym was for several climbers to work together on challenging problems set by skilled climbers and to hone their skills through repeated attempts. Typically (but not necessarily), novice climbers watched expert climbers attempt hard "problems" in an attempt to conquer these problems themselves, occasionally being given guided instruction from experts. One general rule for solving these problems is that although climbers are free to choose their footholds, handholds are strictly designated. The following interaction depicts a typical scene in a "bouldering" session.

Bouldering is a form of free climbing practiced widely both indoors and outdoors. It takes place on a small rock formation (it can be more than 5 meters high) or an artificial wall with removable holds. As such, boulderers do not use a rope for protection. Since the activity requires no particular equipment (except for specialized climbing shoes and a bag of chalk to keep their hands dry and secure a firmer grip), it is a very popular form of sport climbing around the world. Bouldering is also popular because many climbing gyms in Japan are small and cannot afford the facilities for lead climbing.

In what follows, I will consider the process in which the possibilities of encountering a given affordance were identified and scaffolded by experts and experienced climbers. As such, I examine (a) the "side (pull)/under (cling)" move and (b) the "drop knee" technique, which were used as alternative options for solving a specific move on bouldering problems. I focus first on the performance of climbers who tackled the problems named "Polygon" (4.3.1) and on "Too far for shorties" (4.3.2).

4.3 Analysis of Bouldering Moves and Techiniques

The focus in the following analysis is on the use of the vertical lexicon as previously introduced. Due to the polysemous nature of the Japanese spatial term *ue*, an integrated depiction of language, the body, and the environment is required to identify a pursued interpretation *in situ*. Simultaneously, the term allows for semantic extension that relies on a particular communicative context, and thus a discursive and dynamic analysis rather than a static semantic comparison, of spatial categories. The spatial categories of "direction," "space," "surface," and "part" are implicitly and selectively referred to depending on the meaning(s) highlighted. The analytical focus is placed on discourse participants' immediate perception of the affordance available in context and on how they align their conduct and reactions through language and the body.

A crucial commonality among the following activities is the question of how to achieve dynamic equilibrium in the act of climbing, rather than gaining specific skills. For example, stairs afford able-bodied individuals the ability to climb, but a vertical rock/wall does not. If, however, the rock/wall has enough protrusions, it will afford climbing to some humans. In that situation, people will climb it by grabbing those protrusions and raising their limbs alternately, most likely with the "three-point contact" method, which is practiced in conventional rock climbing.[5] Climbers often start with the most naturally affordable move—i.e., holding the upper side of a hold and applying weight along the direction of gravity to move upward. Although many climbers can solve problems with that method, the body scale can occasionally turn out to be an obstacle. One simple solution to that situation is "lunge" (also called "dyno")—that is, jumping upward for the next hold. Thus, climbers, noticing the next hold is beyond reach, often try to solve the move by using the "lunge" or other techniques such as the "undercling" or "drop knee." As will be shown, these moves are not always an instant choice because using them depends on how a certain affordance comes to be perceived and selected in the field of promoted actions.

4.3.1 "Polygon"

The first problem I examine is called the "polygon" (Excerpt 4.1). It is so named because the key hold for the problem—the one held by the climbers' left hand in Figure 4.2—has a polygonal shape. Although it is difficult to see in Figure 4.2, the

(a) G's lunge move (b) K's lunge move

FIGURE 4.2 *Lunge move on "polygon."*

wall is overhanging at 100 degrees. Here, climber G just tried an unsuccessful lunge move (Figure 4.2 (a)). This attempt was still evaluated positively by another climber, K, who later demonstrated how he solved this section with lunge (Figure 4.2 (b)). Notice that their moves are almost identical—a lunge with their left hands pushed downward and right hands extended upward for the next hold (dotted circle) in a "facing" posture. For G, for example, her body's center of gravity (white circle in Figure 4.2 (a)), which used to be in front of the handholds, is now thrust upward with the momentum of the lunge move, although that action turns out to be insufficient.

After G's attempt, another climber M (male), judging that she cannot solve the lunge move, starts suggesting what he thinks of an easier move—undercling (Excerpt 4.1).[6]

EXCERPT 4.1 *"Polygon"*

1	M:	are, <u>shita</u> **andaa** de tot.tara dame desu ka? that, down undercling INS take.COND no.good COP QP 'That one, can't we undercling it?'
2	G:	**an[daa?** undercling '<u>Un</u>dercling?'
3	M:	[ore soo nara-tta-n desu kedo, I so learn.PST.NOM COP though 'That's what I learned, though,'
4		B-san ni. Mr. B DAT 'from Mr. B.'

5	G:	↑_a_ndaa?
		undercling
		'Undercling?'
6	K:	u↑so!
		lie
		'No ↑way!'
7	X:	ikina[ri hidari-te o?
		abruptly left.hand ACC
		'With [(nothing but) the left hand?'
8	M:	[e?
		INJ
		'Huh?'
9	G:	deki-n ze.
		can.NEG FP
		'Can't do it!'
10	M:	hidari-te, e, tashika [soo.
		left.hand INJ, probably so
		'Left hand, I think.'
11	X:	[hidari-te **andaa**?
		left.hand undercling
		'Left hand undercling?'
12	M:	((start demonstrating))
13		ko.o shishoo ni nara-tta °kioku ga°.
		this.way teacher DAT learn.PST memory SB
		'I learned this from my "teacher."'
14	K:	e:: shira-naka-tta.
		eh know.NEG.PST
		'Oh, I didn't know that.'
15	M:	kore o **andaa**-gimini mochi-kaete,
		this ACC undercling-ish hold.change
		'Hold it undercling-ishly like this,'
16		suisuito.
		smoothly
		'and smoothly.' ((M easily grabs the hold))
17	K:	a↑_re;;_!
		that
		'Wow!'

EXCERPT 4.1 *"Polygon"*   continued.

18	M:	*andaa gimini, andaa de °ik-eru°.*
		undercling-ish, undercling INS go.can
		'Like undercling, with undercling, yeah.'

19	X:	*sai- andaa-tte yuu ka, ↑yoko da ne.*
		si- undercling.QM say QP side COP FP
		'Si- it's <u>side</u>pull rather than undercling.'

20	M:	*un yoko: --*
		uhun side
		Uh si::de--'

21	X:	*yoko de, saido de.*
		side INS, sidepull INS
		'It is side, sidepull.'

22	K:	*a: chotto yatte-miyo.*
		Ah a little do.try
		'Okay I will try.'

23		*Sonna-n de todoku-n da.*
		that.way INS reach.NOM COP
		'(I didn't know) we can reach it that way.' ((M jumps off wall.))

24		*ore tonde-ta ze.*
		I jump.PRF FP
		'I've been doing a lunge move.'

To begin, let us review how the audience responded to M's demonstration. Throughout the interaction, M's exposition and performance were greeted with surprise and suspicion by not only G but also climbers K and X, who had already solved the problem. (I also observed that other climbers nearby looked puzzled but did not join the conversation.) In particular, the unexpected nature of M's suggestion is reflected clearly in G's perplexed utterance of "Undercling?" (line 2) and the augmented and high-pitched repeat (line 5). Climber X also asked suspiciously, "With (nothing but) the left hand?" (line 7), followed by G's exclamation of *dekin ze!* ("Can't do it!"; line 9). Notably, she used the final particle *ze*, which is assumed to be an exclusively male usage. Most likely, G spoke in this way to demonstrate her resentment and feelings of abandonment. As soon as M starts demonstrating what he means (line 12), K admits his ignorance of this particular option, saying "Oh, I didn't know that" (line 14); and when M grabbed the hold without jumping, he exclaimed, *a↑re::* ("Wow!"; line 17), which indicates his astonishment at the unexpected effortlessness of M's move. In fact, "undercling" and "sidepull" are frequently used techniques, but this series of utterances shows that it never occurred to them that either would be an effective solution in this case.

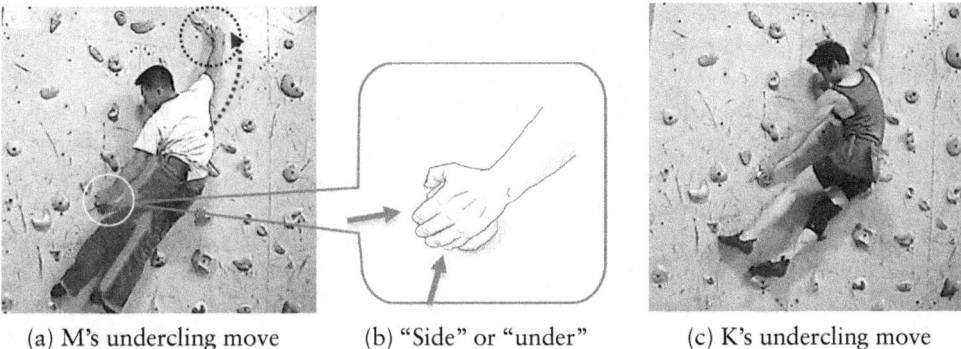

(a) M's undercling move   (b) "Side" or "under"   (c) K's undercling move

FIGURE 4.3 *Undercling move.*

I would like to follow the steps that M took to explain his actions. As seen above, M first revealed that the move was taught to him by another climber (lines 3–4), and then tried to show how effective it was in this context. To demonstrate, M began to climb the wall with the explanation that "I learned this from my teacher. . . ." (line 13); he went on to say "Hold it undercling-ish like this" (line 15), synchronizing the holding action with the demonstrative pronoun "this," which indicates an entity in the proximal region. He grabbed the hold from the underside, and while whispering *suisui* ("smoothly/easily"), he effortlessly reached the next hold that everyone else was struggling to grab (Figure 4.3 (a)). However, it was at this moment that climber X pointed out that M's move was not exactly "undercling" but more like "sidepull," based on his observer status (line 19: Figure 4.3 (b)). To this comment, M returns an ambiguous response, *un* ("uh"; line 20), which serves the function of a temporary "hold" here. However, the following word, "si::de--" trailed off and was left truncated (line 20), which suggests he does not agree with X's judgment. X reiterates the legitimacy of his observation (line 21), but this "side-or-under" issue was not pursued any further because K excitedly jumped into the conversation, making a claim to confirm the validity of this move himself (lines 22–4).

This exchange deserves elaboration in terms of dexterity and affordance because the participants' experiential statuses are different with regard to the move discussed above. As Ingold (2000) stated, the perception of an observer who has not had a direct physical experience cannot achieve the same quality of perception as a participant who has directly had the experience. Here we see a tension between visual and tactile sensoriality concerning the direction of pulling the polygonal hold. For X, who is an observer and has not yet tried the undercling move, it seems reasonable to describe the direction of pulling the hold as *yoko* "side" (line 19, 21) based on his visual perception (the drawing in Figure 4.3 (b)). On the other hand, for M, who is performing the move on the overhanging wall, his tactile perception was more adequately represented by "pulling from below" (i.e., "undercling": lines 15, 18). (This is also consistent with the perception that I gained in my later attempt.) The perception stems partially from the hold that M grabbed: it had a polygonal shape and (unlike a square-shaped hold) allows for variable judgments of the holding direction. Remember that M uttered only a temporary "hold" marker *un* 'uh' but never agreed with X's judgment (line 20). As observed in Figure 4.3 (a), the climber's body leans significantly to the right in order to grab the upper-right hold, and this movement was emulated exactly by K in his later attempt (Figure 4.3 (c)). In this posture, the left hand must maintain the counter vector produced by the right foot, which pushes against the pull of the left hand and resists gravity. Thus, it seems natural that M's action was perceived as being undercling rather than sidepull, which was judged by X's visual but non-tactile perception. In this sense, affordance is "neither an objective property nor a subjective property; or it is both if you like" (Gibson ([1979] 2015: 129). For an actor in this contested environment at least, "undercling" would have been a more accurate phrase that reflects the climber's own perception of the lived space.

As can also be seen in K's utterance, "I've been doing a lunge move" (line 24), he is a climber who solved this problem with a lunge-like move in a facing posture (Figure 4.2 (b)). After M's demonstration, however, K and others were able to grab the next hold with less effort with this undercling move (Figure 4.3 (b)), and they agreed on the efficacy of the move that overrides the body scale constraint. Obviously, there was no change in the abilities of the climbers before and after M's performance—the only difference was that in the field of promoted action, they encountered a given affordance that was not previously selected or shared among some climbers. In other words, they established a new relationship with the given environment, and short climbers encountered a ecological niche that was open to and afforded possible solutions to their problems, eventually establishing a more adaptable relationship with the environment—although G was eventually not able to solve the move on that day.

4.3.2 "Too far for Shorties"

This section looks into the next bouldering problem, "Too Far for Shorties" (Excerpt 4.2). In the following scene, climber C, who had struggled with this problem in a facing position, attempted to solve it using a more sophisticated technique called *kyon* ("drop knee"), a type of "push" techinique with a leg. Here, the angle of the wall is 115 degrees, and the problems are generally more difficult than those on the wall introduced in Excerpt 4.1.

K and Y were not paying attention to C until she started to attempt this problem. When K notices it, he begins to advise C by calling to her by name (line 1 (a)). K knows that C has been working on this problem, but has not yet completed it. He then suggests a *kyon* move as a solution (line 1), and asks if she can use a higher hold for the stance (line 2). Y, who is standing beside K, agrees with the suggestion (line 3), and from then on, K and Y (advanced climbers) start to give instruction together to C. K then advises her to place her right foot "one hold higher" (line 4 (b)), but seeing that C cannot reach the next hold with her current posture, he suggests that she climb back down for a rest (line 5). When C climbs down to a rest position, he points to the target hold with the laser, saying *kore da* ("This is the one"; line 6 (c)). This hold, at her shoulder level, is the one on which she should place her right foot (white dashed circle). As previously mentioned, a Japanese demonstrative prefix "*ko-*" is generally used to refer to a proximal entity. However, K was standing in the "medial/distal" region from the referent (i.e., the hold), for which *so-/a-*demonstartives

AFFORDANCES IN ROCK CLIMBING

EXCERPT 4.2 *"Too far for shorties."*

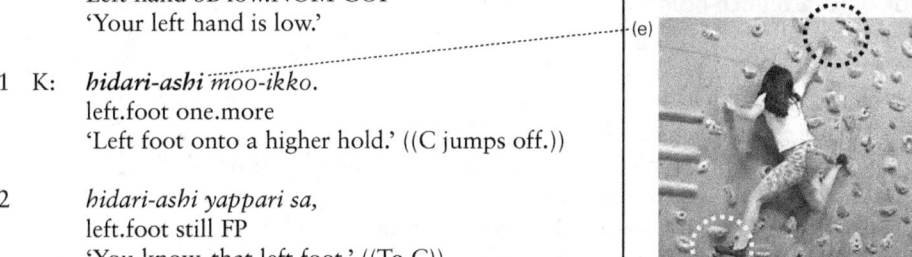

1	K:	*demo C-san **kyon ga ii kamo-shiren.***	(a)
		but Ms. C dropknee SB good may.be	
		'But, Ms. C, you might do better with dropknee.'	
2		*(1.5) mo(o)-hitotsu ue wa?*	
		one.more up TOP	
		(1.5) 'What about one hold higher (for the right foot)?'	
3	Y:	*mo(o)-ikko ue ga ii to omoo.*	
		one.more up SB good COM think	
		'I think one hold higher would be good.'	(b)
4	K:	***moo-ikko ue.***	
		one.more up	
		'One hold higher.'	
5		*(1.2) modose.*	
		redo	
		(1.2) 'Go back down.' ((C backs down and takes a rest))	(c)
6		*(2.8) **kore da.***	
		this COP	
		(2.8) 'This is the one.' ((Indicate with a raser pointer))	
7	Y:	*u:n.*	
		'Uh hu:h.'	
8	K:	*(1.0) de **hidari ashi moo-ikko agete mō ii yone.***	(d)
		and left foot one.more raise also good FP	
		(1.0) 'You could raise your left foot to a higher hold.'	
9	Y:	*un.*	
		'Yeah.'	
10		*hidarite ga hikui-n da.*	
		Left hand SB low.NOM COP	
		'Your left hand is low.'	(e)
11	K:	***hidari-ashi moo-ikko.***	
		left.foot one.more	
		'Left foot onto a higher hold.' ((C jumps off.))	
12		*hidari-ashi yappari sa,*	
		left.foot still FP	
		'You know, that left foot,' ((To C))	

EXCERPT 4.2 *"Too far for shorties."* continued.

```
13        C-san yaru-n dat-tara kore da yo na.
          Ms.C do.NOM COP.COND this COP FP FP
          'if you do it, Ms. C, this is the way.' ((raser-
          pointing to a hold))

14   Y:   an.
          'Ah.'

15        da-ttara todoku-n ja.nai no,
          COP.COND reach.NOM COP.NEG FP
          'If you do it, you can reach it, I guess.'

16   K:   honde[kore de.
          then this INS
          'Then with this,'

17   Y:        [seetai de.
                facing.position INS
                'In a facing posture.' ((this is a wrong
                assessment))

18   K:   ima todoku yone.
          now reach FP
          'you can reach it now, right?'

19   Y:   un.
          'Yeah.'
```

(f) Successful attempt

should conventionally be used. Still, the *ko*-prefixed pronoun is possible because the referent is perceived as being located in his proximal region by pointing to the referent with his laser pointer—i.e. as an object in his ontological *ko*-region. C gives it a glance and starts climbing again, but this time, she uses the hold suggested by K and Y.

Judged by the prosodic features, lines 8–10 are exchanged between K and Y, but not addressed to C, who is now engaged in the crux move of the problem (line 8 (d)). C reaches for the next hold, but is still about twenty centimeters short of the hold (line 11 (e)). Seeing C struggle with the move, K repeats the same suggestion, "Left foot onto a higher hold" (line 11), but she resignedly jumps off the wall. K and Y alternately suggest raising her left foot to one hold higher (lines 12–15) and assure her that she can eventually reach the target hold if she makes two modifications based on the previous comments. As should be obvious by now, the first is to perform the *kyon* on a higher hold (as indicated by a laser-pointer) (lines 2–6). The second is to raise her left foot approximately ten centimeters higher (lines 8, 11, 13, 15), which requires more holding power on her left hand, but provides a better footing for a higher reach for her right hand. Both of these changes, while turning out to be harder, can be made within C's capabilities without too much difficulty. On this occasion, only the first modification was made, which resulted in a failed attempt. However, about five minutes after her rest, C took on the problem again and solved the pending move by correcting the two issues pointed out by K and Y (Excerpt 2 (f)). At that time, she did not receive any instruction from the audience but a cheer before the attempt and applause after it. In other words, K and Y helped her encounter unnoticed affordances and amended her relationship with the environment through these heightened opportunities for adjusting her body's relationship with it.

To sum up, in the case of "sidepull/undercling" (Excerpt 4.1), the center of balance is coordinated by the pushing legs and the pulling arm and by maintaining equilibrium. This means that a part of the limb (in that case, the right arm) was left free to reach the next hold. There, the center of balance is not necessarily the center of the body, although the "three-point contact rule" would usually require them to match. More skilled climbers can anticipate and adapt to situations beyond the default cases. In the case of "drop knee" (Excerpt 4.2), the climber was able to "offset" the pull of gravity by counterbalancing with both feet and her left hand (Excerpt 4.2, line 4 (b)). Also, for conducting a technique like undercling, a climber's perspective would play a more accurate role than that of an observer in terms of providing advice for others climbing on the vertical plane. This, of course, does not reject the utility of perceiving the qualia of actions through an observer's objective perspective. Rather, it is vital to match the appropriate mode of perception to the time and occasion under scrutiny in order to achieve the best possible result for the participant—in this case, climber C.

4.4 Discussion and Conclusion

When ecological psychologists use the phrase "perception is direct," they are referring to the perceptual core of cognitive processes—subsequent perceptions and the situated cognition will then come into play and act around it. The actors' perception and subsequent actions in the environment are key to understanding what really matters for participants in any activity, but specifically here for climbing. In both Excerpts 4.1 and 4.2, there were extensions to the default moves that the normal environment affords to most humans. These extensions were undoubtedly facilitated by the guidance and instruction of experts, who made less experienced actors aware of different options. With this, novice climbers gained opportunities to encounter these alternatives in practice, perform the move, and surmount the challenge successfully.

Given these observations, a series of modifications made in the performance would be illustrated as follows (Figure 4.4). First, Figure 4.4 (a) represents the actions of pulling and holding downward, the vector of which rests on physical protrusions (i.e., holds). These are default moves afforded by the environment, which most humans (and novice climbers) would be able to incorporate into their actions. More experienced climbers in the data solved the problems by using another technique in Figure 4.4 (b) (lunge, dyno), which is an extension of the "pull/hold" action, coupled with squat and leap actions. However, relatively short climbers, who cannot solve the problem with (b) due to their body scale, adopted alternative techniques such as (c) and (d) (sidepull, undercling, drop knee, etc.) that *were* within the range of their

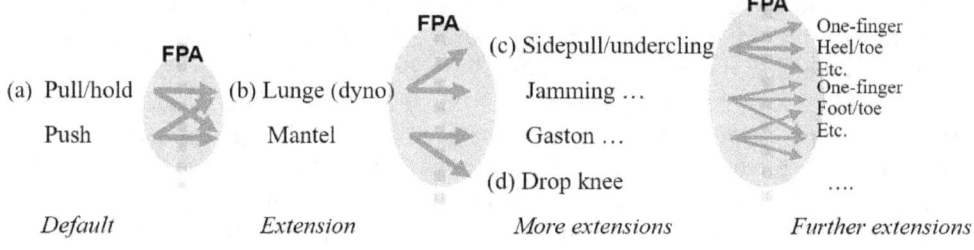

FIGURE 4.4 Flow of extensions.

abilities. Further affordances could well have been facilitated by ARA (affordance-reading ability) as climbers become more dexterous, such that undercling by hand could be replaced by a one-finger undercling, or a foot hook be swapped for one done by a heel or toe. That is what the initial quote about *hikidashi* ("drawer") meant—the availability of other possible means to achieve a certain goal.

More importantly, the flow of extensions for a certain move in (2) does not apply to all climbers. As expected at the outset, efficient climbers have more flexible ARA and can detect and apply higher-level techniques to a problem at first sight. In that sense, the abovementioned order of extensions observed may arguably show a course of development in climbing skills. Although "lunge" (b) and "sidepull" (c) are quite different techiniques, it would be a highly challenging (if intriguing task) to examine whether such a course of development as described here really exists. In other words, whether the options that have been effectivized in this way assure the availability of all the preceding skills such that someone who can afford to achieve "one-finger undercling" (a further extension in (2)) would be able to perform all the techniques on the left along the extension—if not so strictly as on an "implicational" scale (cf. Berlin and Kay 1969; Keenan and Comrie 1977). It is reasonable to think that the climbers' actual abilities did not change dramatically before and after the experts' guidance and/or instruction. What does matter here is whether or not the climbers were given opportunities to perceive the affordances appropriate for each level of expertise and to adjust his or her relationship with the environment in the given context.

A series of observations at this point would represent significant implications for learning. If we take the object of affordances only as those activities afforded to all the members of a species, it precludes the possibility of enhancing perormance and development of those with lesser abilities. There are obviously variations in the adaptability and physical feature of a single species, and "affordances for all" may not be a constructive point of departure, but rather a necessary but insufficient condition. We instead need to pay more heed to diverse cases in which opportunities for affordances are variably secured, especially in learning and instruction in different cultural/communal settings (Vygotsky 1978; Rogoff 1990, 2003). Stair-climbing, for example (Gibson 1979), is feasible for most adults, but rock climbing is not, given that it requires rigorous training to aim higher, both physically and metaphorically. Some activities require effort to discover more affordances as well as to translate them into optimal body movements. In this respect, the perceptibility of affordances is gradual, ranging from overt affordances that are immediately available to the entire animal species, to covert ones that exist only as possibilities that have yet to be effectivized. For creative learning to take place, it will be important to construct a niche that promotes the discovery of such covert affordances. In such a niche, perception is not everything, as a higher-order cognition emerges to address the task at hand as "the cooperative appropriation of affordances" (Reed 1991).

In the same vein, for a niche to serve as a setting for learning, an environment geared toward each actor—what Vygotsky (1978) calls a "zone of proximal development" and Reed (1996), a "field of promoted actions"—is essential. According to Reed's (1996) classification of direct and indirect experiences, climbing is overwhelmingly driven by direct experience that is obtained through the actions of individual agents in the environment. Such an experience is therefore unique to the level of proficiency of each actor and varies according to social and cultural backgrounds. Actors come to be able to conduct "free actions" (ibid.) based on their autonomous skills and through engagement in direct experiences. In the case of bouldering, for example, the boundary between "promoted" actions and "free" actions is not clear. In lead climbing, the daily practice and training environment would correspond largely to the field of promoted actions, whereas onsight/flash attempts typically deserve the field of free actions. Explicitly focusing on human infants, Reed and Bril (1996: 439) stated that "infants will be selectively exposed to only a subset of that niche, to certain selected opportunities for experience and action." This assumption would apply equally to young or novice members of a climbing community. This situation is largely equivalent to "scaffolding" (Bruner 1975, 1983)—the steps taken to "limit, so to speak, those degrees of freedom in the task that the child is not able to control" (Bruner 1975: 12). In our case, novice rock climbers, like children, do not inhabit the complete ecological niche reserved for expert climbers, but only have limited access to a subset of that niche. This selected subset, where climbing moves are negotiated *in situ*, is equivalent to the field of promoted actions for rock climbers. Any problems and routes they attempt to climb beyond their present level of expertise will serve as one such field of actions, which can be expanded by the support of experts.

This chapter focuses on changes in the relationship between the body and the environment as well as on the opportunities necessary for an actor to perceive given affordances. Such a relationship may be immediately established *in situ*, gradually emerge in the "enchronic" time frame (Enfield 2014), or in a larger developmental scale of learning (Rogoff 2003). Regardless of time span, the process is normally mediated by the language of the participants in the lived space. In the next chapter, I will consider another phenomenon that exhibits such an emergence of perception and cognition in the enchronic frame of discursive interaction. The key issue in that discussion also concerns the spatial lexicon *ue/shita* ("up/down"). As was the case with the *yoko/shita* ("side/under") discrepancy in this chapter, the use of *ue/shita* in a certain context exhibits greater incongruence in the selection of expressions and subsequent interactions. These situations are comparable to the third locus of linguistic relativity, now theorized as "collateral effects" (Sidnell and Enfield 2012; Engfield 2015). I closely examine such an effect by focusing on the spatial lexicon representing the vertical axis, which has been regarded as the most incorrigible and "unproblematic" axis of the spatial grid (Levinson 2003).

5

Ue and *Shita* in Horizontal and Vertical Space

5.1 Introduction

In this chapter, I focus on coordinate and topological spatial terms. In Chapter 4, I observed cases in which actors' perceptions of the environment can be directly but differentially represented on horizontal and vertical planes. Here, I will observe how climbing participants intersubjectively and intercorporeally cultivate the vertical space for mutual understanding, and examine how seemingly incongruent spatial expressions can be made sensible in the subsequent re-cognition of the vertical axis. In a place (or "niche") where actors' multiple perceptions are anticipated to maximally adapt to the contested environment, they can emerge as an interdependent and holistic perception. Rock climbing is one such domain, and I investigate phenomena that heavily concern such perceptual mediation by drawing on the works of phenomenological orientations (Merleau-Ponty 1962; Ingold 2000; Ichikawa 2001; Meyers et al. 2017; Hanks et al. 2019).

Here, the notion of "intercorporeality," also described as "carnal intersubjectivity," is the key. Merleau-Ponty used a "hand" metaphor to explain it (alluding to Kant's discussion of "incongruent counterparts"[1]): "My two hands 'coexist' or are 'compresent' because they are one single body's hands. The other person appears through an extension of that compresence; he and I are like organs of one single intercorporeality" (Merleau-Ponty 1964: 175). This notion has been appropriated extensively in the twenty-first century alone and applied to anthropological investigation (Ingold 2000; Csordas 2008; Duranti 2010; Desjarlais and Throop 2011) and discursive, holistic achievements of actions in social contexts (Fuchs 2013; Meyer et al. 2017; Lindstrom et al. 2021). As Meyer et al. (2017) claimed, intersubjectivity/-corporeality is ubiquitously observed not only in cooperative actions, but also in most basic forms of human social interaction including gazing, hugging, kissing, speaking, and in our case, climbing/belaying. The focus of this chapter aligns with that assertion and attempts to delineate the features of, and figure out the relation among, intersubjectivity, embodiment, and corporeal dwelling in the environment.

The basic assumptions in this chapter are two-fold: First, and as ecological psychologists claim, perception of space is direct, so we perceive "up and down" directly as the default axis; and second, the subsequent cognition mediated by language, the body, and the environment come into play to produce the most appropriate outcome for the actors in space. On the vertical plane, climbers directly perceive the "up/down" relationship based on gravity, but while they dwell in the contested space, even the vertical perception can be overridden intersubjectively by embodied cognition. This is also a realm in which "collateral effects" come to affect interactions, as distinct linguistic descriptions induce participants to produce different attendant reactions that must be held accountable and responsible specifically in terms of language.

Using discourse data from rock climbers, I critically reconsider the theoretical frameworks of space in which the dominant value assigned to the vertical space might be overestimated in (European) conceptualizations of space. Thus, I specifically argue that (1) gravity is not always the preferred basis for the linguistic encoding of spatial coordinates, and that (2) it may not be possible to notice this phenomenon without looking into actual language use in contexts where gravity and "intercorporeal" frames of reference compete and collaborate. In these respects, the linguistic coding of verticality may not be a prescribed criterion defined by gravity, but rather an emergent and contextual construct based on indigenous spatial cognition.

5.2 Dominant Doctrines: Egocentricity and Verticality

Concepts of space have always been an important topic in the philosophy of human knowledge and perception, and despite numerous theories on the subject, there is a common consensus that spatial concepts are fundamental building blocks of an epistemological understanding of the world (Eliot 1987; Van Cleve and Frederick 1991). There exist two tacitly assumed doctrines in the Western philosophical tradition concerning human beings' spatial perception: dominance of egocentricity; and over-determination of vertical space. The legacy of egocentrism traditionally goes back to Kantian philosophy, which claims, on the basis of Newtonian "absolute" space, that an egocentric conceptualization of external phenomena in the world is the precursor to other kinds of knowledge.[2] This ego-centrism of spatial cognition is reflected in Kant's early account:

> In physical space, on account of its three dimensions, we can conceive three planes which intersect one another at right angles. Since through the senses we know what is outside us only in so far as it stands in relation to ourselves, it is not surprising that we find in the relation of these intersecting planes to our body the first ground from which to derive the concept of regions in space.
>
> KANT [1768] 1991: 28

Kant (and contemporary cognitive scientists) also assume the primacy of gravity in spatial perception. Prior to his influential work on "incongruent counterparts" (e.g., the right-and left-hand gloves or forms like "_| |_"), Kant is said to have sought to prove that "the very existence of space is due to gravitational force, and that its three-dimensional character is a consequence of the specific manner in which gravity acts" (Kemp Smith [1918] 1991: 43). This dominance of gravity is assumed to be the criterion for defining the vertical and horizontal planes, and it continues to exert an influence on the conceptualization of spatial relations in cognitive science and linguistics.

Over-determination of vertical space is prevalent in the scientific scrutiny of spatial concepts. In linguistics, for example, Fillmore (1982: 36–7) claimed that "(t)he up/down axis is determined by our recognizing the direction of the pull of gravity, and is therefore not to be explained in terms of egocentric or anthropocentric predispositions of language users." Also, in cognitive psychology, Campbell (1993: 75) mentioned that "(o)f course, there is such a thing as the long axis of the body, but that is not the same thing as 'up' and 'down', which continue to be defined in terms of the gravitational field even if one is leaning at an angle." This view is supported by the inequality of spatial cognition in the coordinate system. There is an assumed hierarchy of perceptual stability among the three dimensions in terms of "consistency" and "asymmetry" associated with each dimension: "up/down > front/back > left/right" (Shepard and Hurwitz 1984).[3] Canonically, the vertical dimensions "up/down" are the most stable because they are determined by gravity and do not change orientation even if the deictic center is removed. That is, the vertical dimension is "massively overdetermined and unproblematic" (Levinson 1996b: 373), and the horizontally oriented dimensions "front/back" and "right/left" are more vulnerable. For "front/back" and "left/right," the former dimension is perceptually more salient because the human body is non-symmetrical for "front/back" but symmetrical for "left/right," making the latter dimension more vulnerable to orientational confusion (Shepard and Hurwitz 1984; Logan 1995).[4] These claims seem rational and applicable to canonical settings, but in fact disregard the relativity of lexico-semantic property of vertical notions. They are not attainable given various applications of spatial notions to real-life contexts outside intellectual and/or experimental inquiries.

To begin, the first theorem, the assumed dominance of an egocentric "frame of reference" (FOR: see Chapter 2), appears to be highly contestable. Recent work in cognitive anthropology points to the field's bias toward ethnocentric universalism (Levinson 1996b, 2003; Diessel 2014). For instance, Levinson and Brown (1994) showed that Tenejapan Mayans exhibit a remarkable indifference to right and left, or "incongruent counterparts," a notion that is the source of Kant's assertion for the egocentric basis of spatial perception and his argument against the Leibnizian conception of space as merely a network of relations between material objects. Brown and Levinson (1993) also suggested that spatial language can constrain cognitive categories, but not vice versa. In the Tzeltal, for example, there is a tendency to avoid an egocentric frame of reference and to describe objects "according to their disposition in space" (Brown and Levinson 1993: 66).[5]

Also, developmental and diachronic variability in human spatial cognition is expected. As Piaget proposed, "decentration" of perspective-taking requires maturation, and begins in the concrete operational stage that ranges from ages seven to twelve. In cognitive science, Haun et al. (2006) reported that although infants are born with a spatial cognitive strategy that relies on absolute reference, they converge to the frame of reference that is valued in their own language and culture as they grow up. Moreover, the variation and plasticity in the use of spatial reference frames should not be underestimated. For example, even among Tamil speakers who regularly use the absolute FOR, there is a difference in the preferred use of FORs between urban and rural areas (Pederson 1993), and graded responses are observed among bilingual speakers of Tamil and English (Wilkins, cited in Levinson 2003). In addition, use of the FOR lexicon is adapted differentially to the types of task (Tversky et al. 1999) and is subject to diachronic change (Kataoka and Asahi 2015). These findings have suggested that the cognitive styles reflected upon the use of FORs are not necessarily fixed, and that factors other than language can also be involved.

The second theorem, the over-determination of vertical space, has long been regarded unproblematic and is questioned only rarely. In this sense, Friederici and Levelt's (1990) finding was highly provocative: They discovered that their subjects (astronauts) tended strongly toward egocentric and environment-centered reference frames in spatial term assignment while on Earth, but more toward an egocentric (or viewer-centered) representation in the absence of gravity. Carlson-Radvansky and Irwin (1993: 242), admitted that "on earth, the powerful influence of an environment-centered frame based on gravity most likely dominates, unless the reference object is made salient in some way," and showed clear cases in which the canonical gravitational constraint is overridden in some experimental contexts.[6] The body itself does have a strong tendency to serve as the reference point for gravitational orientation because they canonically match. However, what about an object with no or very little intrinsic orientations? Levelt (1984) and Logan (1995) claimed that reference frames are chosen quite freely when certain frames are made experimentally salient—e.g., by explicit instruction to take such and such a part of an object as "up" (Logan 1995). Tversky (2009: 213) summarized findings in spatial cognition and concluded that "(t)hought is grounded in the world and in the body," thus delineating how spatial thinking can be influenced by embodied and situated cognition in language, action, navigation, gesture, and diagram.

However, empirical investigation of the naturally occurring data is still missing. Judging spatial relations alone in an laboratory could be different from manipulating such relations collaboratively in the natural environment. At least on Earth, individuals' egocentric FOR, with their ordinary vertical axes identified with a "gravity" orientation, is considered the default or dominant system. It is only when subjects are instructed otherwise, or they experience difficulty in (re)constructing the perspective in question, that they begin to rely on other reference frames. I would claim that even such special conditions are not necessary: Only interactional intention, whether explicit or implicit, would suffice, at least in some languages.

Nevertheless, there are few discourse studies focusing on the vertical dimension of spatial descriptions and depictions. One of these rare cases comes from a Map Task study (Brown 1995; Yoshida 2011) that was conducted in a semi-experimental setting where horizontal movements were the main issue. Ochs et al. (1996), Kataoka (1998b), Roth and Lawless (2002) and Murphy (2005, 2012) all studied emergent participation of actors in corresponding (work)spaces that included investigations of spatial descriptions and bodily depictions used in instructional settings. Ochs et al. (1996) focused on how grammar, gesture, and graphic representations mutually interact in physicists' lab meetings, revealing the ways the representations merge different frames of interpretation. Roth and Lawless (2003) investigated gestural depictions in science-related courses such as physics and ecology, showing how instructors incorporate numerous visuals and inscriptions written on a board or projected onto a screen. In all of these studies, some sort of projected axes of *up/down* relations are shown to be manipulated and laminated. However, with the exception of Kataoka (1998b), these authors addressed the projected verticality based on objects such as images, graphs, and screens, but not on the human body. What I will investigate is this lacuna—i.e., the natural usage of vertical terms based on the body axis.

Occasions of increased vertical salience may be limited in ordinary activities, but they do occur naturally in rock climbing. As I will subsequently show, most Japanese rock climbers agree on the acceptability of *ue* ("on/up/above") when describing objects (e.g., rope, bolt, carabiner, their own bodies) in a gravitationally incongruent FOR, suggesting that, at least in Japanese, there can be both canonical and non-canonical vertical dimensions competing for dominance. Consequently, egocentric (not gravity-oriented) verticality may emerge, freed from the gravitational constraint of spatial coordination. Such fluid verticality can be assumed to take on certain characteristics of "trading places" (Duranti 2010) for it to be practically functional in a climbing situation.

In what follows, I consider in detail the variable use of vertical coordinate descriptions/depictions with *ue/shita* (see Table 4.2), and show that even the absolute dimension is vulnerable to intersubjective and intercorporeal adjustments (cf. Merleau-Ponty 1964; Ichikawa 2001; Meyer et al. 2017).

5.3 How Verticality Concerns Culture

One of the major issues since the inception of the Boasian tradition concerns what is called "linguistic relativity"—a tenet which holds that people's perceptions and world views are relative to the language they speak (Boas 1911; cf. Sapir 1921). A well-known example often cited in that line of research is Whorf's "empty" gasoline drums (Whorf 1956). As a fire-prevention engineer, Whorf often observed that accidents occurred when people smoked near a gasoline drum labeled "empty"—a situation that is actually more dangerous because empty gasoline drums are often filled with inflammable vapor. This example shows how the linguistic expression "empty" can evoke an association such as "empty → no gasoline → safe" by exercising a conventionalized reasoning (see Lucy 1992 for a detailed discussion). Although his observation was often criticized as anecdotal and lacking in empirical evidence, it still provides an ample illustration of language's influence on cognition. Provoked by Whorf's contentions, the study of linguistic relativity has been conducted largely on lexical and syntactic classifications, first in anecdotal (e.g., Eskimo snow terminology, the "empty" gasoline drum), and then experimental (e.g., color terminology, noun classification, and spatial frames of reference) manners. However, motivated by an acute awareness of linguistically and culturally relative modes of everyday actions (e.g., Hymes 1966; Hill and Mannheim 1992), researchers have come to pay more attention to the interactional aspects of relativity, focusing on the subsequent behaviors caused by linguistic expressions (Gumperz and Levinson 1996)—similar to a stage of what Levinson (2003: 303) later called "coding after speaking."

An analysis of those different consequences has been largely a central issue in cross-cultural communication. However, this analysis has been re-conceptualized as a third locus of linguistic relativity characterized by "collateral effects" (Sidnell and

Enfield, 2012; Enfield 2015) that typically occur in the "enchronic" (Enfield, 2015) frame of communicative actions. Collateral effects are "side effects of something that was selected as a means to a required end" (Sidnell and Enfield 2012: 313).[7] According to this view, linguistic relativity concerns language, mind, and social reality, and imposes differential, language-specific perlocutionary effects on participants. One method to identify the effect would be through what is called a "next-turn (or action) proof procedure"—by analyzing how an action/utterance is received and/or responded, what is naturalized and/or problematized, and what is omitted and/or added, among others. In line with this assumption, differential interactional consequences are considered in the light of ongoing discussion of spatial description/depiction.

Building on these findings and claims, vertical representations of space are examined in specific contexts. I will closely scrutinize (1) how spatial expressions for the vertical (and horizontal) axes (i.e., *up/down* (and *front/back*)) in life-saving instruction discourse can diverge from the canonical relationship (through conceptual mapping of the canonical orientation), and (2) to what extent such canonical relationships can be re-defined in rock climbing discourse through the axial rotation of the canonical orientation.

5.4 Analysis: Two Cases of Fluid Verticality

The following sections describe a micro-multimodal analysis of the real-life use of vertical expressions. Here, I examine two sides of the same coin of fluid verticality: one extreme occasion in which multiple senses of vertical terms are negotiated and identified for precise interpretation through bodily elaboration (Section 5.4.1), and another extreme occasion in which the climbing environment contextually allows the liquidation of the vertical awareness through participants' intersubjectified corporeality (Section 5.4.2).

5.4.1 *Ue* in Lifesaving Training Session

5.4.1.1 *Data and Informants*

Before analyzing the Japanese spatial lexicon used in rock climbing, I would like to consider the spatial descriptions observed in a lifesaving training session attended by rock climbers because it was an occasion in which fluid verticality was apparently avoided for the purpose of precise interpretation. The training session was organized by a local municipal gymnasium that runs a climbing facility, and it provided an opportunity for participants to learn basic first aid skills in case of a climbing accident. The participants were climbers who regularly practiced on the climbing wall, ranging from beginners to experienced climbers, but with little basic knowledge of first aid. What follows is a scene in which the instructor, K, an employee of the municipal fire department, was explaining hemostasis to the participants with the help of climber S, who was acting as a test subject. After a round of explanations of hemostasis, questions from participants W and M prompted K to explain how to use different methods to stop bleeding, specifically the "compression" method using the hands and the "binding" method using *sankakukin* (a triangular bandage), depending on the location of the injury. Even though this session was targeted at climbers, K's parlance was no different from what was usually offered to non-climbers at standard Japanese first aid information meetings.

5.4.1.2 *The Use of UE and SAKI*

Let us now look into W's question and K's response. The focus here is on K's spatial descriptions and hand gestures along, with the ongoing interaction between the two. The Japanese spatial lexicon is put in a square box, and the "stroke" phases of conspicuous gestures are bolded and depicted in plates (a) to (d) in the transcript (Excerpt 5.1).

EXCERPT 5.1 *Holding.*

K: instructor; W: woman; M: man; S: test subject

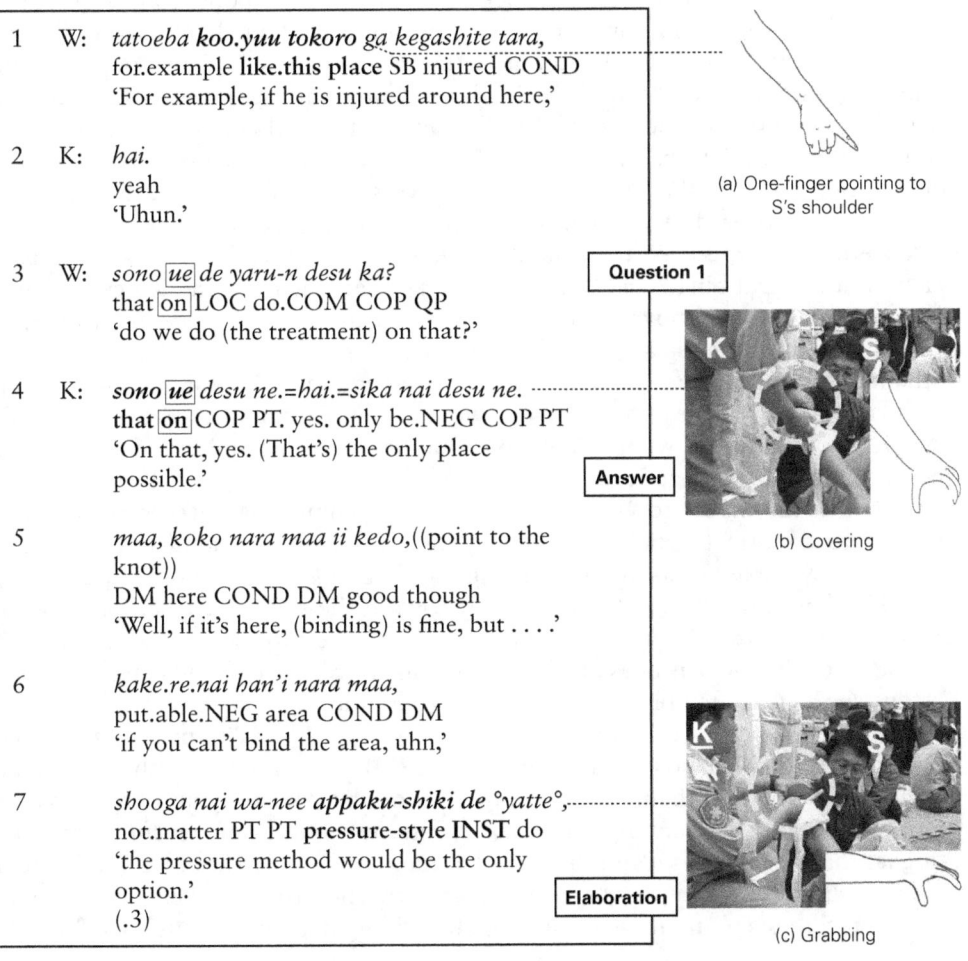

1 W: tatoeba **koo.yuu tokoro** ga kegashite tara,
for.example like.this place SB injured COND
'For example, if he is injured around here,'

(a) One-finger pointing to S's shoulder

2 K: hai.
yeah
'Uhun.'

3 W: sono ue de yaru-n desu ka?
that on LOC do.COM COP QP
'do we do (the treatment) on that?'

Question 1

4 K: sono ue desu ne.=hai.=sika nai desu ne.
that on COP PT. yes. only be.NEG COP PT
'On that, yes. (That's) the only place possible.'

Answer

(b) Covering

5 maa, koko nara maa ii kedo,((point to the knot))
DM here COND DM good though
'Well, if it's here, (binding) is fine, but....'

6 kake.re.nai han'i nara maa,
put.able.NEG area COND DM
'if you can't bind the area, uhn,'

7 shooga nai wa-nee **appaku-shiki** de °yatte°,
not.matter PT PT pressure-style INST do
'the pressure method would be the only option.'
(.3)

Elaboration

(c) Grabbing

EXCERPT 5.1 *Holding* continued.

```
8  W:  (°appaku°) suru shika nai desu ne.
       pressure do only be.NEG COP PT       [Confirmation Q]
       '(The pressure is) the only way
       to do, isn't it?'

9  K:  suru shika nai yonee.=yahari. koofuuni.
       do only NEG PT. still, this way       [Endorsement]
       '(That's) the only way, yeah, like this.'
```

(d) Squeezing

First, in lines 1–3 of this segment, W points with her index finger to S's shoulder area and asks, "If he is injured around here, do we do (the treatment) on that?" Although both the pressure and the binding methods were introduced before this question, it is still unclear whether a pressure or binding method should be applied if someone is bleeding from the shoulder area (line 3). In response to this question, K agrees that she should conduct hemostasis *sono ue* ("on that [wound]"), and covered the area with his left hand (line 4 (b)). Then, in line 5, K also points to the bound part and says that "if it's here, binding is fine," but that "if you can't bind the area, the pressure method would be the only option" (lines 5–7), grabbing S's shoulder with his left hand (line 7 (c)). Following the explanation, W asks a confirmation question (line 8), to which K answers with endorsement, squeezing his shoulder even harder (line 9 (d)). Along this sequence of interaction, the initial action of "covering" is gradually augmented in such a manner as "answer + covering," "elaboration + grabbing," and "endorsement + squeezing." W's and K's expressions of *sono ue* ("[on/over/above] that"; (lines 3–4) are apparently vague in meaning as to whether it specifies "space," "surface," or "part" (see Table 4.2). However, in line with the abovementioned gestures, the expressions gradually narrow down from "surface" to "part" meaning (i.e., the wound) by K's manner of holding. This interpretation is exactly what W anticipated in her question, and was duly reflected upon K's responses and gestures.

As soon as the answer to W is completed in line 9, climber M starts asking another question to confirm the point of binding for an imaginary would (Excerpt 5.2). In line 10, M first points to the bandage and says *kizuguchi yori* ""[than] the wound"), then slides his right hand slightly toward the shoulder, synchronizing the gesture with his utterance *ue* (line 10 (a)). From this gesture, we can posit that M's intended meaning of *ue* is not "on" but rather "up(ward)," which indicates direction. K stops short in contemplation after uttering *ue* (line 11), which is overlapped by M's utterance including a repeated demonstrative *kono* ("this"; line 12), with each of which M makes a poking gesture (line 12 (b)). M continues with *kono tome yorimo (ue)* ("[higher] than this knot") to indicate the starting point of the directed motion, while K, overlapping with M, repeats M's phrase *kizuguchi yorimo ue* ("higher than the wound", and slides his left hand toward S's shoulder (line 13 (c)). Evidently, lines 10–13 represent heavy cross-turn and cross-speaker repetitions in order to facilitate common understanding. K's sliding hand gesture in line 13 tacitly

EXCERPT 5.2 *Sliding.*

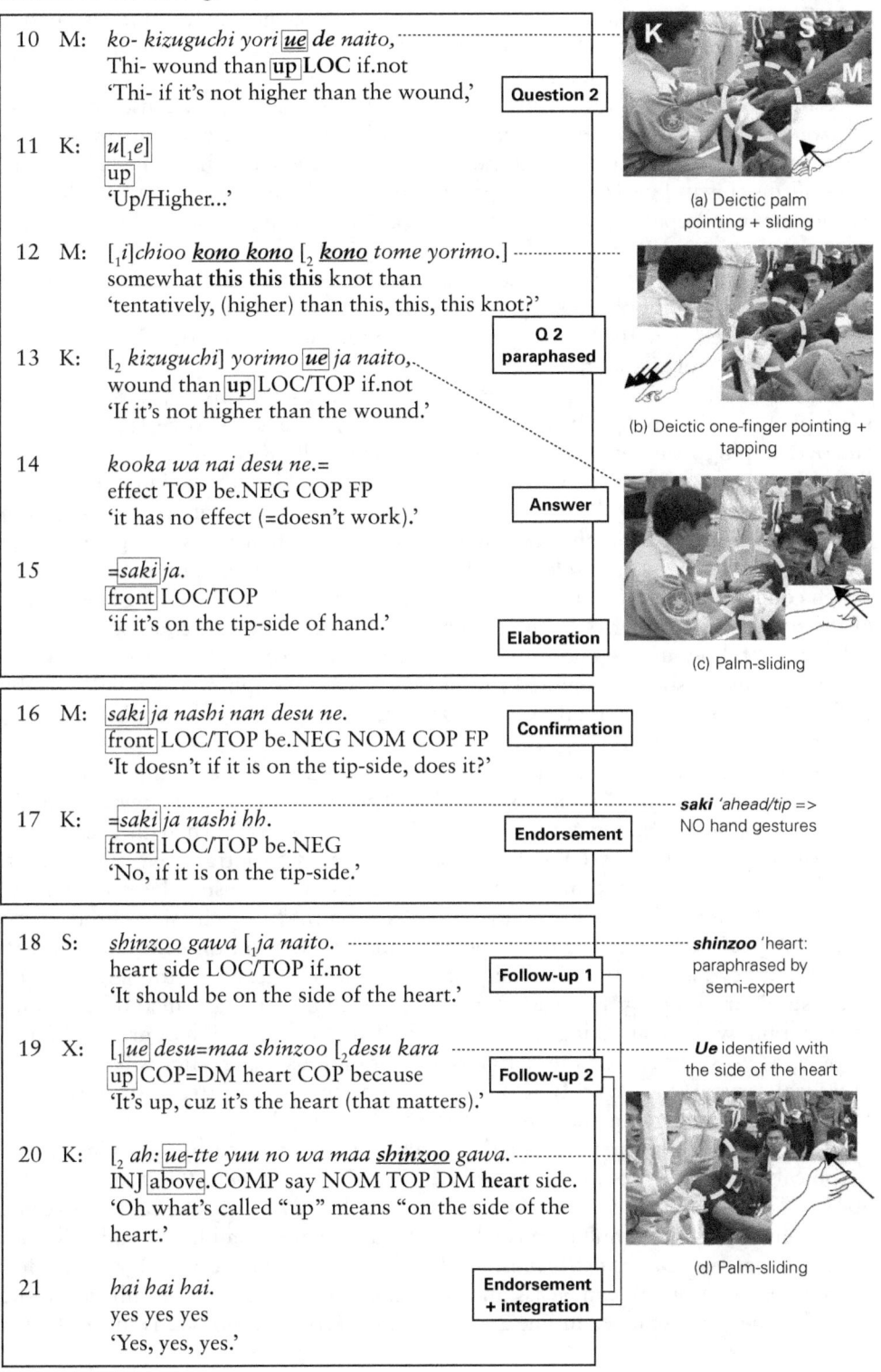

10 M: ko- kizuguchi yori ue de naito,
        Thi- wound than up LOC if.not
        'Thi- if it's not higher than the wound,'   — Question 2

11 K: u[₁e]
        up
        'Up/Higher...'   (a) Deictic palm pointing + sliding

12 M: [₁i]chioo **kono kono** [₂ **kono** tome yorimo.]
        somewhat **this this this** knot than
        'tentatively, (higher) than this, this, this knot?'   — Q 2 paraphrased

13 K: [₂ *kizuguchi*] yorimo ue ja naito,
        wound than up LOC/TOP if.not
        'If it's not higher than the wound.'   (b) Deictic one-finger pointing + tapping

14   kooka wa nai desu ne.=
        effect TOP be.NEG COP FP
        'it has no effect (=doesn't work).'   — Answer

15   =*saki* ja.
        front LOC/TOP
        'if it's on the tip-side of hand.'   — Elaboration

                                                    (c) Palm-sliding

16 M: *saki* ja nashi nan desu ne.
        front LOC/TOP be.NEG NOM COP FP   — Confirmation
        'It doesn't if it is on the tip-side, does it?'

17 K: =*saki* ja nashi hh.   ---- **saki** 'ahead/tip =>
        front LOC/TOP be.NEG   — Endorsement   NO hand gestures
        'No, if it is on the tip-side.'

18 S: **shinzoo** gawa [₁ja naito.   ---- **shinzoo** 'heart:
        heart side LOC/TOP if.not   — Follow-up 1   paraphrased by
        'It should be on the side of the heart.'   semi-expert

19 X: [₁ue desu=maa shinzoo [₂desu kara   ---- **Ue** identified with
        up COP=DM heart COP because   — Follow-up 2   the side of the heart
        'It's up, cuz it's the heart (that matters).'

20 K: [₂ ah: ue-tte yuu no wa maa **shinzoo** gawa.
        INJ above.COMP say NOM TOP DM **heart** side.
        'Oh what's called "up" means "on the side of the heart.'

                                                    (d) Palm-sliding

21   hai hai hai.   — Endorsement
        yes yes yes   + integration
        'Yes, yes, yes.'

shows his understanding that M's use of *ue* is intended to mean "direction" along S's arm. Given these observations, these uses of *ue* are not the canonical *ue* as defined along the vertical axis of the upright body, but rather those based on the horizontally projected axis of S's extended arm.

K then introduces, presumably to elaborate on the projected use of *ue*, the horizontal axis using the term *saki* ("ahead/front"; line 15), and affirms that the treatment should be conducted on the other side of the hand (vis-à-vis the wound). M confirms this in line 16 with a repetition that combines lines 14 and 15; K gives endorsement by repeating *saki ja nashi* ("No, if it's on the tip-side"; line 17). This sequence (lines 15–17) is again characterized by the heavy cross-turn, cross-speaker repetitions. Through these processes, the participants seem to corroborate mutual understanding, thereby crossing the boundaries of different spatial axes and perspectives between the vertical and horizontal, as well as the canonical and projected planes of spatial descriptions.

Notably, S, the guinea pig, who has remained silent until this point, supplements K's explanation by saying, "It should be on the side of the heart" (line 18). Following and overlapping with this, someone X in the audience also confirms the interpretation (line 19). K, too, overlaps with this utterance, acknowledging the validity of equating *ue* with "the side of the heart" (line 20). In line 20, K then utters a "realization marker" (Heritage 1984), *ah:*, revealing that he realizes that *ue* can be paraphrased more appropriately by "the side of the heart." Next comes a mitigation marker, *maa*, which could be interpreted as a self-defensive excuse against not having been aware of the relationship hitherto. In these segments, "confirmation → endorsement" and voluntary "follow-up → endorsement" occurred consecutively to secure mutual understanding. It should be noted that it was K who paraphrased *ue* with *saki* by shifting back to the horizontal axis (line 15) and acting as a stickler to the canonical use of the spatial lexicon.

After these spatial relations are agreed upon, K goes on to make a final remark on this "pressure-or-binding" issue (Excerpt 5.3). The key terms here are *ageru* ("raise") and *sagaru* ("lower"), the former of which is a transitive verb with a causative construction—"CAUSE [x GO-UP]"—and the latter is an intransitive counterpart. These verbs are semantic counterparts, which are also written using the same Chinese characters for *ue* and *shita*. In Excerpt 5.3, based on the "*ue* = the side of the heart" relationship, K returns to the main theme of his explanation on hemostasis. Up to this point, they have been discussing first aid providers' means of stopping bleeding ("pressure" or "binding"), but M starts referring to an auxiliary method based on the natural law that "anything with mass is pulled in the direction of gravity." Thus, it comes as no surprise that the spatial representation used hereafter is based on the canonical vertical axis. Possibly, K, as a lecturer/instructor, tried to avoid unnecessary ambiguity by conforming and returning to the default axis.

In Excerpt 5.3, the previous axial projection is normalized by returning to the canonical vertical relation. First, in line 22, K says *ager-eru nara* ("if you can pull it up") and claims that the affected part should be held *shinzoo yori ue* ("above the heart"; line 23) while simultaneously lifting S's arm higher than his shoulder. K goes on to say that *kanzen ni sagatte masu node* ("since [it's] totally down"), which defies literal interpretation but can be assumed to mean "since the heart is totally below the wound." The next sentence in line 26, *age-yatteru hitsuyoo mo nai*, is most likely a

EXCERPT 5.3 *Raising and lowering.*

```
22  K:  de naokatsu ager-eru nara ((slowly lifts up
        S's hand))
        and besides raise.can COND
        'And in addition, if you can pull it up,'

23      ma shinzoo yori ue °tte yuu koto;°
        DM heart than above COMP.say thing
        'I would say it should be above (higher than) the
        heart.'

24  ?:  m:m.
        uhum
        Uhum.=

25  K:  =ma kore kanzen ni (.2) sagat-te masu node:,
        ((hand on S's arm))
        DM this perfectly down.COP because
        'Well, since this is totally down,'

26      maa kore age-yatteru hitsuyoo mo nai-to
        DM this raise.give need too not.exist.COMP
        iyaa-nai-n da kedo:. ((pulls down S's arm))
        say.no.NOM COP but
        'so you actually don't have to pull it up in this
        case,'

27      (1.2) shimeta baai.
        squeezed case
        'when you squeeze.'
```

Elaboration/Axial projection normalized

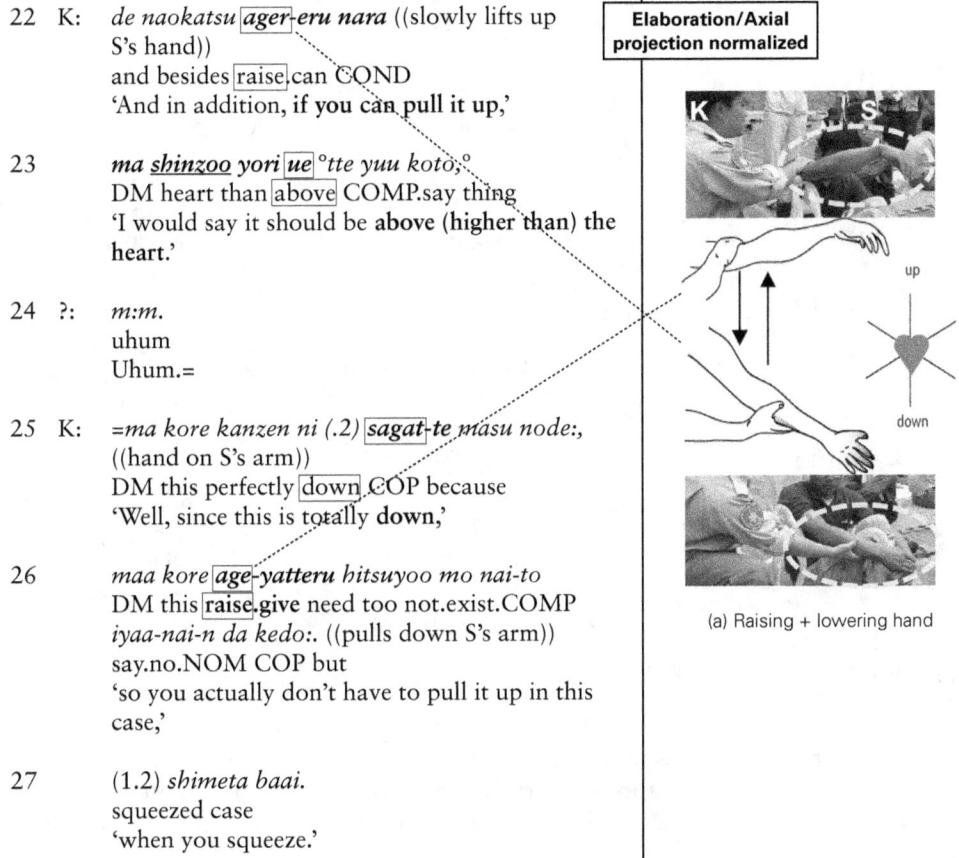

(a) Raising + lowering hand

speech error for *agete-yaru hitsuyoo mo nai* ("you don't have to pull it up"). If we follow these interpretations, the series of utterances in lines 25–6 would make the most sense as "since the heart is totally below the wound in this case, you don't have to pull up the hand (to enhance hemostasis)." In addition, after the utterance in line 27, M opens the triangular bandage held in his hand and moves on to a new topic—bandage usage.

Figure 5.1 is a diagrammatic representation of the spatial axis transitions described. First, the directional concept of *ue* based on gravity is the one perceived and acknowledged directly as the default axis by the participants (left side of Figure 5.1). In our case, however, such an assumption has been rendered ambiguous by W's use of *ue* as "surface/part" (upper right part of Figure 5.1) to indicate the imagined wound on S's shoulder. Further semantic extension was applied by M, who used *ue* based on a horizontally projected vertical axis. This semantic extension was mitigated temporarily by K's introduction of *saki* ("ahead/front"), which is based on the real horizontal axis, but when *ue* is identified with the side of the heart, this

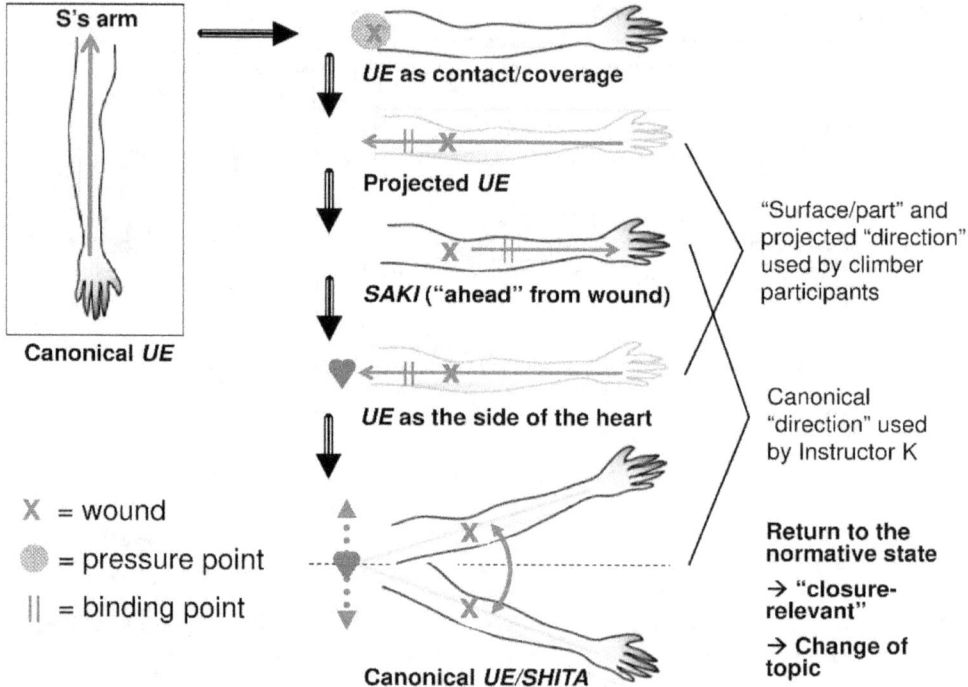

FIGURE 5.1 *Axial shifts and projections.*

"pressure or binding" issue is resolved by K's demonstration of the "up/down" movement based on the canonical axis. K's utterance possibly indicates a return to the normative vertical axis and implies closure-relevance, motivating the shift to the next topic.

There seems to be a tension here between a centripetal (=canonical) and centrifugal (=projected) use of *ue*, as well as between the instructor and participants. Below this superficial tug-of-war lies a highly systematic distinction of spatial concepts through bodily management. As shown in Figure 5.2, this series of utterances is characterized by an alternating process of deviating from and returning to the canonical vertical axis, which seems to contribute to the closure-relevance of the abovementioned topic. Whether intended or not, it is no coincidence that this chain of axial shifts is appropriated to negotiate mutual understanding of pressure/binding points.

As shown in Figure 5.2, the organizational consistency of participants' hand gestures is highly palpable. At the outset of the exchange, *ue* is used in the "on/over" sense, accompanied by a series of K's "holding" actions and gradually augmented by "covering," "grabbing," and "squeezing" gestures. M's use of *ue* is accompanied by his sliding gestures along the projected vertical axis, to which K also responded with a sliding gesture. Then, after a temporary return to the canonical *saki/ato* ("ahead-back") relation, *ue* is used with the canonical "above/below" meaning. K's raising and lowering S's arm represents the canonical verticality with the heart as the reference point. The visual support by these hand gestures plays a crucial role in differentiating in detail the spatial notions variably encoded in *ue/shita* because, as

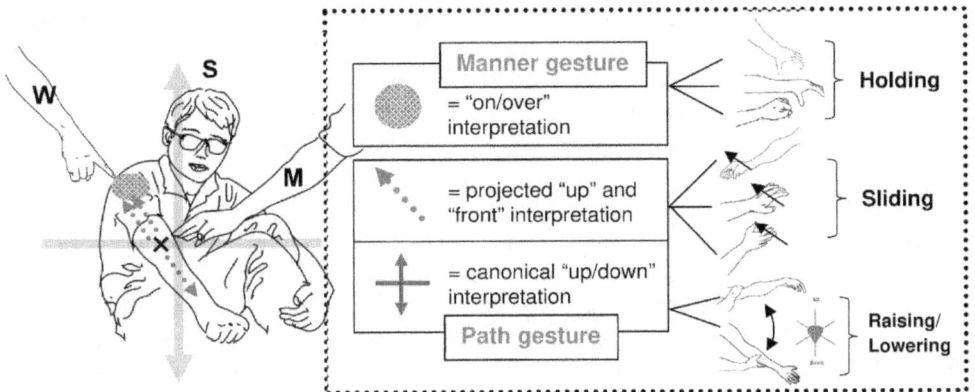

FIGURE 5.2 *Pointing, manner, and path gestures in the negotiation of meaning.*

shown above, the visible bodies of the participants provided systematic displays of relevant actions (see Goodwin 2000, 2017). The distinction is also made by manner and path gestures (Figure 5.2), which are two basic elements for spatial description/ depiction (Talmy 1983). It is evident from these observations that the distinct spatial axes are precisely differentiated by "manner" and "path" gestures that delineate "direction/ space/ surface/ part" meanings.

Japanese people make ordinary use of these "up/down" relations based on both the canonical and non-canonical projected axes. For example, when having our hair shampooed at a barbershop or hair salon (Figure 5.3), the expression used by the hairdresser to ask the customer to move closer to the wash basin is, in my experience, almost always something like *Moo sukoshi **ue** ni onegai shimasu* ("Move upward a little, please"). While it is also possible to say "Move over here," this deictic expression

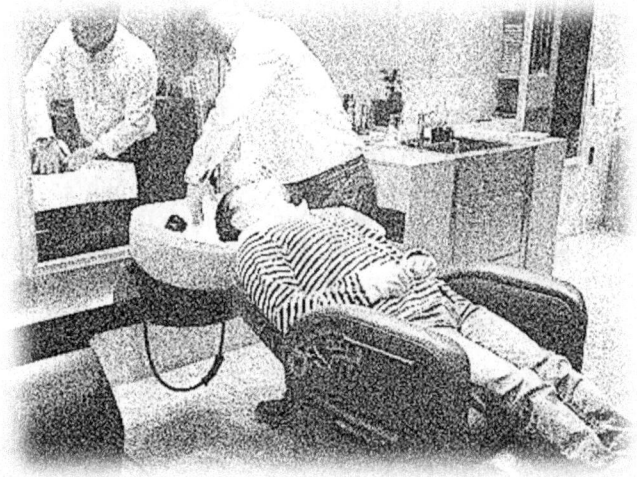

FIGURE 5.3 *'Move upward."*

can be used only when the hairdresser is near the basin on the side of the customer's head. That is, the *ue* expression is a more versatile option because it concerns the physical axis of the actor only and is less context dependent as long as we accept fluid verticality. This sort of projected use of the vertical dimension is not only common but feasible, appropriate, and/or effective even at the expense of the canonical verticality.

What can we glean from the abovementioned observations? As mentioned in Chapter 4, the Japanese spatial lexicon *ue/shita* can be variably interpreted for "direction," "space," "surface," and "part" depending on a following PosP (postposition), which can often be omitted. In this sense, the Japanese spatial lexicon is underspecified compared to, say, the English prepositions and adverbials such as *up/down, above/below,* and *over/under.* This property allows for a variety of interpretations and induces discourse participants to identify finer distinctions through language-specific reasoning, with or without the assistance of gestures. It remains arguable whether, for example, English speakers would equally feel required to go through the same trouble in clarifying the differences between "on," "over," "up," and "above," all of which are compressed into Japanese *ue*-phrases. Although not pursued in this section, these cross-linguistic differences in spatial categories would possibly motivate language-specific inferences and reasoning, leading to particular subsequent reactions or "collateral effects" (Sidnell and Enfield 2012; Enfield 2015).

As Bühler ([1934] 1982) pointed out, humans exhibit numerous bodily coordinates based on the body, the head, arms, hands, and so forth, among which the bodily axis is the most stable. It still remains to be examined whether a more stable axis than the arm (here, the body) would succumb to the same process in a more gravity-laden context than that seen in this section. In the next section, it will be further argued that, based on observations of actual climbing situations, the Japanese absolute spatial lexicon induces what is called a "coding after speaking" process (Levinson 2003) and an interactional "collateral effect."

5.4.2 Avoiding "Back Clipping" in Lead Climbing

The vertical space is a contested area of perception and cognition where language and culture meet. The main issue here is a degree of habituation and acceptance of the usage of vertical lexicon—an arguable but noticeable index of a linguistic relativity effect. Climbers should feel gravity equally regardless of the language they speak. However, when an object or event is perceived and processed through each language, even gravity-defined verticality can be affected through the interaction with the environment. Such dynamic processes cannot be addressed fully by ordinary experimental methods. Examining actual discourse phenomena is a reasonable and resourceful approach to considering collateral effects that emerge in ongoing communication.

5.4.2.1 Dada and Climbing Equipment in Focus

In what follows, I focus mainly on climbing instructions, which are usually given by expert climbers to novice climbers in order to teach climbing skills and comment on route conditions. Such instructions thus provide rich research resources for studying

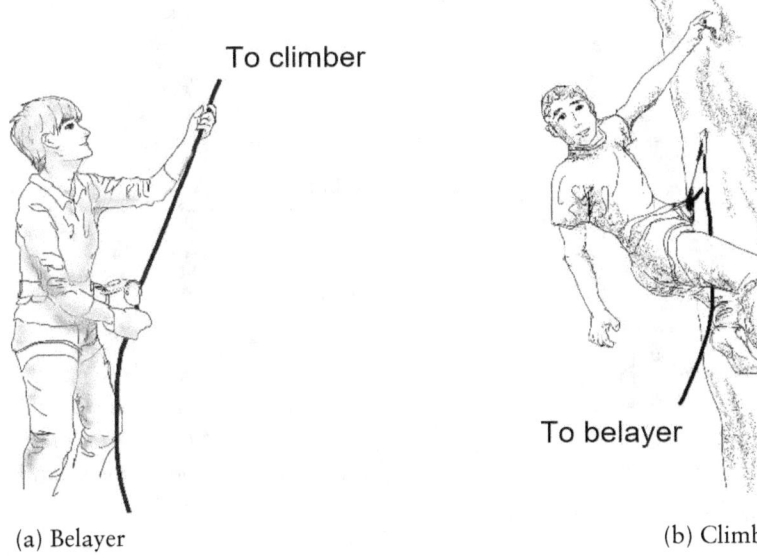

(a) Belayer   (b) Climber

FIGURE 5.4 *Situation of instruction-giving.*

body-movement descriptions, topological/coordinate features, and the human–tool–environment interface on the vertical plane. Figure 5.4 illustrates participants' postures in which the following exchange was heard. Although I have only the audio data, the visual representations were created based on my memos and fieldnotes.

Before we proceed to the analysis, it would be helpful to know about the tool/equipment referred to in the data. Tool use, or materiality in general, is crucial in many sports and occupations. It has attracted attention from researchers of social interaction (Heath and Luff 2000; Goodwin 2000, 2007a; Carr 2010) because expertise in tool use is inherently interactional in that "it involves the participation of objects, producers, and consumers of knowledge" (Carr 2010: 18). Here, the analysis concerns two specific pieces of climbing equipment: a rope and a carabiner. A rope is essential in stopping a climber from falling a long distance (unless you are a free/solo climber) and in minimizing the fall impact. Should a fall occur, the belayer's expertise is crucial when it comes to their making appropriate decisions about where to stand, what posture to take, and how to react to a climber's moment-by-moment moves, as well as about adjusting the device in order to minimize the fall distance (see Chapter 3).

Another indispensable tool for climbers is a carabiner, on which I elaborate in more detail below; some knowledge of its function is vital to understanding the following discussion. A carabiner is assumed to have intrinsic and canonical directions as a physical object. In order to clip it into a bolt or other pro(tection)s, it is normally held as shown in Figure 5.5 (a), which is the case with a pro-clipping carabiner of a quickdraw (a sewn sling with carabiners). The rope-clipping carabiner, on the other hand, is usually turned upside down to facilitate the action of clipping it to a rope (Figure 5.5 (b)). This operation makes it difficult to identify which part

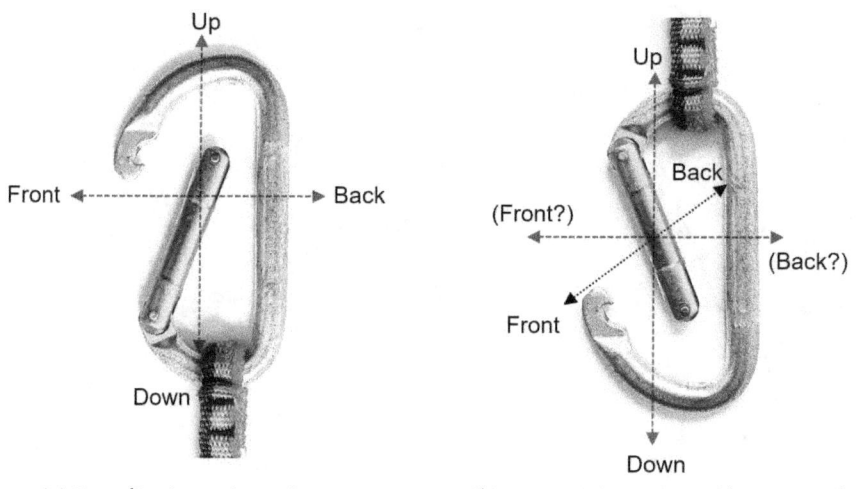

(a) Pro-clipping orientation (b) In-use orientation of lower carabiner

FIGURE 5.5 *Orientations of carabiner.*

of a carabiner is oriented to which direction. However, climbers would generally agree that the spatial term assignment for the rope-clipping carabiner is not based on the intrinsic orientation of a carabiner, but on the user's personal frame of reference. Thus, the typical "front" of a carabiner is the side facing the climber (as in Figure 5.5 (b)), rather than the part intrinsically defined when upright (as in Figure 5.5 (a)). The phenomenon I consider here, back-clipping, is so called because it represents a situation in which a rope goes through "to the back" of the carabiner.

An expected, correct way of clipping is shown in Figure 5.6 (a). Back clipping (Figure 5.6 (b)) is a wrong and dangerous way of clipping a rope into a carabiner because were a climber to fall, the rope could unclip. In Japanese, that situation is called *gyaku kurippu* ("reversed clipping"), which renders the direction of the rope ambiguous and emphasizes instead the invalidity of the action.

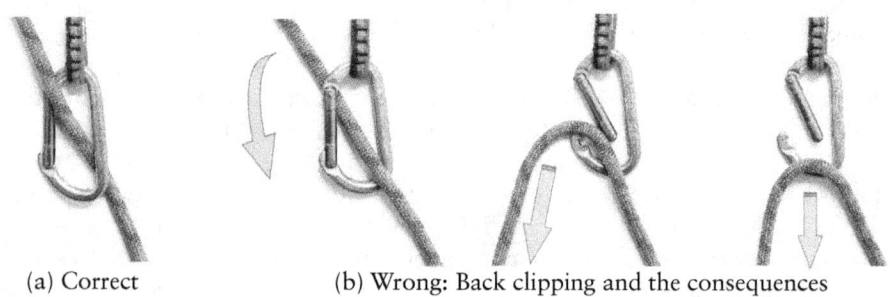

(a) Correct (b) Wrong: Back clipping and the consequences

FIGURE 5.6 *Correct and wrong ways of clipping a rope.*

5.4.2.2 *Use of* ue *and* Shita *on the Vertical Plane*

The critical issue in this section concerns the use of the vertical expressions *ue* ("up/above") and *shita* ("down/below"). Canonically, it is the direction of gravity, not the orientation of the body, that defines the vertical axis (Fillmore 1982b; Campbell 1993). No matter how widely this view is shared among participants, however, the actual use of language and the movement of the body in a given environment can defy the assumption. As the following example shows, these expressions can be used non-canonically to demonstrate what *gyaku kurippu* ("back clipping") is and how it should be avoided. Specifically, an expert's leaning back and a novice's stepping back serves as an initial step to the axial projection and invites a novice to participate in a contested space where the canonical vertical axis is overridden, eventually provoking an intersubjectified vertical dimension.

Let us first review the sequence at issue (Excerpt 5.4). The route that climber Y starts climbing is an over-hanging 5.11c route—one of the most popular routes in the area. Here Y climbs up to the second bolt and briefly explains where a belayer should stand (lines 1–4). Y then moves up to the third bolt, takes the self-belay by connecting the bolt and his harness with a quick-draw, and begins to demonstrate to the belayer (a novice climber in the same alpine club) what "back-clipping" is like (line 6 and onward). The spatial expressions in focus are both canonical and non-canonical uses of spatial relations, and are put in a square in the transcript. Also, the *jibun* phrases are bolded and for later reference. The detailed gloss of these will be given later.

EXCERPT 5.4 *Whole Sequence*

	Sp	Japanese transcript	English translation
1	Y:	*dakara ma* shita *de yatteru no ga ii desu ne, furare nai kara.*	So it's better to do that right below me cuz you won't be pulled around (when I fall).
2		(2.0) *de,* (2.0), *maa, shibaraku yasunde, ikimasu to ieba,*	(2.0) And, (2.0) well, if a climber takes a rest and says, "I'm climbing,"
3		*ikimasu to ieba, zairu o yurumete kudasai.*	if s/he says "I'm climbing," you give it a slack.
4		(1.5) *soo desu ne.*	(1.5) That's right. ((Y starts climbing))
5		(18.0) *doo?*	(18.0) How are you doing? ((Y takes a self-belay on a bolt))
6		(3.0) *de, mokkai karuku harigimi ni.*	(3.0) And, take (in rope) a little bit again.
7		*de san pin me guraiikuto, moo, ochitemo gurando shinainde,*	And if s/he goes past the third bolt or so, s/he won't take a ground fall.
8		*mizurai desho,* ue *o,*	Now it's hard to look up,
9		[*kubi ga itaku natte kite*]	[cuz your neck starts to hurt, right?
10	B:	[*e e e e e e e e*]	[Yeah, yeah, yeah, yeah.
11	Y:	*ni-sanpo* sagatte *mo iim desu yo.*	You could take a few steps backward.
12		(1.0) ushiro *no hoo de.*	(1.0) (Belay me) at the back there.

EXCERPT 5.4 *Whole Sequence* continued.

13		*sonna kanji desu nee.*	That's the way.
			<One turn omitted>
14	Y:	*sore de kore, muki . . . ko, zairu no tooshi kata nansu kedomo,*	And this, the direction, I mean, as to how to clip a rope,
15		*jibun ga noboruhoo ga, ko, iwa yori* ue, kotchi gawa *ni muku yoo ni surun desu.*	make sure that **self**'s rope is upper than (= above) the rock, or comes to this side.
16		(2.0) *wakkari masu?*	(2.0) Do you understand?
17		(1.8) *kore o ne,*	(1.8) I mean, this one,
18		(1.8) *kore ga gyaku nandesu.*	(1.8) this one is reversed.
19		*jibun no noboru hoo ga* shita *desu yone.*	The direction of **self**'s rope comes down, right?
20	B:	(1.7) *ee ee ee.*	(1.7) Yeah yeah yeah.
21	Y:	*kore yatchauto,* (2.2) *ko, nobotteki masu yone, kotchi kara.*	If you do this, (2.2) when you keep climbing this way,
22	B:	*hai hai hai hai.*	Yes yes yes yes.
23	Y:	*de ochita baaini, ko,ko hazureru koto ga arun'desu yone,*	and if you fall, the rope can clip itself out (of the carabiner), you know,
24		*jibun no zairu ga* shita *dattara.*	if **self**'s rope is below (the carabiner).
25		(3.8) *ko,* <u>*gyaku-kurippu*</u> *tuun desu kedomo,*	(3.8) This is what is called "back clipping."
26		(2.0) *kore ga gyaku kurippu no jootai ne,*	(2.0) This is what back clipping is like.
27		*. . .jibun no zairu ga, kanarazu* ue *muki ne,*	See, **self**'s rope must always go upward.
28	B:	*hm hm.*	Hm hm.
29	Y:	*de kore de nobottette ochiruto,*	If you keep climbing this way and fall,
30		(0.5) *hazurerun desu.*	(0.5) the rope can clip itself out.
31		(1.5) *Wakari masu?*	(1.5) Do you understand?
32		(2.0) *kore ga tadashii kurippu no hoohoo.*	(2.0) This should be the way to do.
33		(1.2) *kore dattara ochitemo daijoobu nansu.*	(1.2) This will work all right even if you fall.
34		(1.5) *Wakkan'nai'su ka?*	(1.5) Are you not understanding this?
35		(2.2) *maa iisu wa.*	(2.2) Okay, don't bother.
36	B:	*nanto naku* (.2) *dakara* (.3) *hh*	Sort of, (.2) I mean, (.3) hh ((smile)).
37	Y:	*koo, jibun ga noboru hoo ga* shita-*muki dattara, ochita toki ni hazureru to.*	You know, if **self**'s direction of climbing is downward, the rope can clip out when you fall.
38		(4.5) *ja ikimasu ne.*	(4.5) Okay, I start climbing again.

As far as the transcript shows, the main addressee (novice climber) keeps responding with "continuers" (back channels) and exhibits his understanding, although he seems to be somewhat confused at the end. Still, none of the five climbers gathered around asks Y any questions about his instructions. Our main focus is on how the rope and the lower carabiner are related through the use of spatial expressions. In Excerpt 5.5, what I determine as the breakthrough into performance starts in line 14, so the text is further divided into the Pre-sequence (Excerpt 5.5 (1): lines 1–13) and the Main sequence (Excerpt 5.5 (2): lines 14–38), with the gloss for close examination. In the Main sequence in particular, the set phrase *jibun* + *ue/shita* "self'" + "up/down" is used five times.

EXCERPT 5.5 *Pre-/Main-Sequence*

(1) Pre-sequence (lines 1-13):
(a) Line 1: *shita*
   dakara ma-shita de yatteru no ga ii desu ne, furare-nai kara.
   so right.below LOC doing GEN SUB good COP FP, swung.NEG because
   'so, it's better to do that (belaying) **right below** me, cuz you won't be pulled around.'

(b) Line 8: *ue*
   mizurai deshoo, ue o, kubi ga itaku natte-kite.
   hard.to.see COP, up ACC, neck NOM hurt become.come
   'Now it's hard to look **up** (at me), cuz your neck starts to hurt, right?'

(c) Line 11: *sagaru* 'step back'
   ni-sanpo sagat-temo ii-n desu yo.
   2-3.steps go.down.CONJ good.NOM COP FP
   'So (you) could take a few steps **backward**.'

(d) Line 12: *ushiro* 'back'
   ushiro no hoo de.
   back GEN direction LOC
   '(Belay me) **at the back** there.'

(2) Main sequence (lines 14-38):
(a) Line 15: *jibun* + *ue*
   ***jibun** ga noboru hoo ga iwa yori **ue**, kotchi-gawa ni muku-yooni suru-n desu.*
   self SB climb direction SB rock than up, this.side DR facing.manner do.NOM COP
   'Make sure that **self**'s rope is **upper** than (=above) the rock, or comes to **this side**.'

(b) Line 19: *jibun* + *shita*
   ***jibun** no noboru hoo ga **shita** desu yone.*
   self GEN climb direction SB down COP FP
   'The direction of **self**'s rope comes **down**, right?'

(c) Line 24: *jibun* + *shita*
   de ochita baaini, ko- koo hazureru koto ga aru-n desu yone,
   and fall in.case thi- this.way slip.out event SB be.NOM COP FP
      ***jibun** no zairu ga **shita** dat-tara.*
      self GEN rope SB down/below COP.COND

EXCERPT 5.5 *Pre-/Main-Sequence* continued.

'And if you fall, the rope can clip itself out (of the carabiner), you know, if self's rope is **below** (the carabiner).'

(d) Line 27: *jibun + ue*
*jibun no zairu ga, kanarazu **ue-muki** ne.*
self GEN rope SB, always upward-oriented FP
'See, self's rope must always go **upward**.'

(e) Line 37: *jibun + shita*
*koo, **jibun** ga noboru hoo ga **shita-muki** dat-tara,*
this.way, self SB climb direction SB down-oriented COP.COND
    ochita tokini hazureru to.
    fall when clip.out COMP
'You know, if **self**'s direction of climbing is **downward**, the rope can clip out when you fall.'

I will consider the main sequence first and then return to the pre-sequence, which I believe contributes to the foreshadowing of a gradual progression into the climber's "intersubjectified" vertical space. Even more simplified correspondences are given in Table 5.1, in which only the *ue/shita* usage in the main sequence is summarized in terms of the "If X is Y, then Z" format.

First, let us take a closer look at how the speaker (climber) tries to distinguish between *ue* and *shita* of the related objects. As we see in Table 5.1, his use of *ue* ("up") is consistently described as correct, and *shita* ("down") as incorrect, that is, "back clipping." In both cases, the rope tied to the climber goes up, the other end goes down to the belayer (Figure 5.4), and thus the canonical interpretation does not apply here. One possible interpretation is that this spatial term *ue* is a translation equivalent for the English word "on," which represents a topological concept such as "contact" and "attachment," as seen in "on the wall." If this is the case, such use of

Table 5.1 If X is Y, then Z

X: *Jibun*-phrase	Y: Coordinate term	Z: Result
(a) *jibun ga noboru hoo* 'self's direction of climbing'	*ue* 'up(ward)'	Correct
(b) *jibun no noboru hoo* 'self's direction of climbing'	*shita* 'down(ward)'	Back clipping
(c) *jibun no zairu* 'self's rope'	*shita* 'down/below'	Back clipping
(d) *jibun no zairu* 'self's rope'	*ue-muki* 'upward'	Correct
(e) *jibun ga noboru hoo* 'self's direction of climbing'	*shita-muki* 'downward'	Back clipping

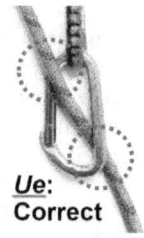

Ue:
Correct

Shita:
Back clipping

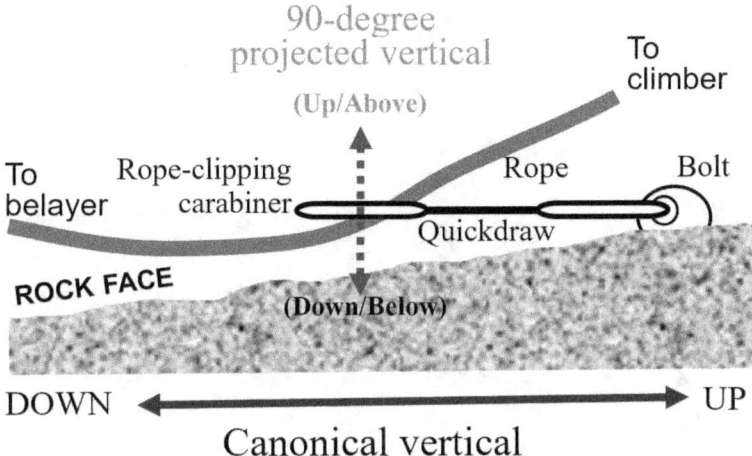

FIGURE 5.7 *Side view of quickdraw in projected vertical space.*

ue is doubly ambiguous and inefficient communicatively because there are two points of contact for the rope and the carabiner (right side of Table 5.1). Given this, all the cases should have been described with *ue*, but not with *shita*. Notice also that none of the instances accompanies a locative particle, which makes the semantic distinctions even vaguer. Therefore, the series of *ue* vs. *shita* contrasts must refer to some other relationship(s) between the rope and the carabiner.

The only consistent interpretation of this *ue/shita* relationship would be as follows: (1) the flat extension of the lower carabiner on a quickdraw is seen as parallel to the vertical plane (Figure 5.7); and (2) although the carabiner is dangling vertically from a bolt hanger nailed into the overhanging rock, the relationship between the rope ("figure") and the carabiner ("ground") is rotated schematically 90 degrees from the canonical vertical axis along the climber's sagittal axis. Only in this virtual space can we understand why the rope must go "up" from the carabiner in order to be properly clipped in.

The question now would be: What has motivated the shift—the climber's body axis, or the scheme of verticality regarding rope and carabiner? Both conceptualizations are possible, but I assume that a more empirical factor, the body's axis, has likely facilitated it. One might suspect that it is the other way around, given that the verticality schema pre-exists as a shared image and is conceptually manipulable. Rather, the activation of the projected verticality is a contextual consequence that the bodily axial shift triggered. Let us now look into the process of activation.

5.4.2.3 *Process Toward Intersubjectified Corporeality*

Several factors contribute to creating this projected virtual space. I classify these according to three types of motivation—perceptual, linguistic, and interactional—although the distinctions between them are interconnected. Perceptual environment is the first factor I consider here, and the intersubjectified body axes of the climber and the belayer may contribute to the new FOR projection depicted in Figure 5.8. Here, bolts and quickdraws provide artificial affordances to the climber for clipping a rope to

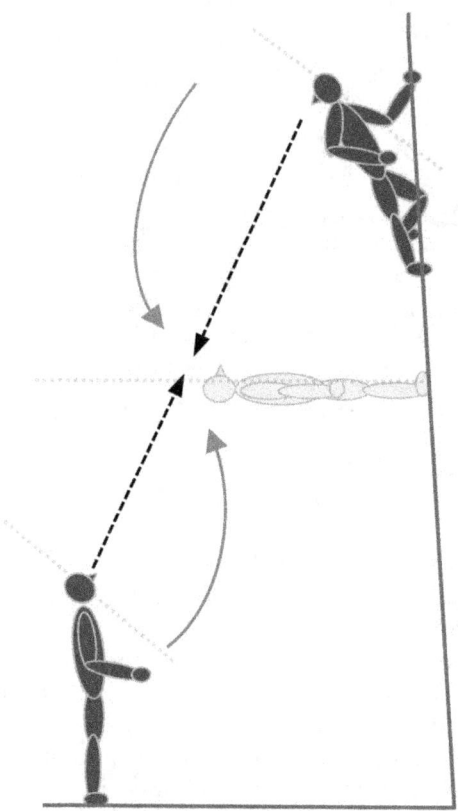

FIGURE 5.8 *Bodily axis rotation in the environment.*

ensure their safety. In order to provide instructions on avoiding back clipping, the climber leaned back, twisted his body, and looked down at the belayer; the belayer looked up at the climber and listened to his explanation (Figure 5.8). In this situation, the canonical line of sight, which is normally perpendicular to the body axis and parallel to the horizontal ground, is rotated sagitally along with the climber's body axis. As a result of these adjustments, both the climber's and belayer's body axes approach the fully intersubjectified body axis in the 90-degree-projected coordinate system.

Note also that the speaker starts the Main sequence with *iwa yori ue* ("above the rock") (Excerpt 5.5 (2a)), which makes no sense if we take it literally. In the present context, he is obviously talking about the relationship between the rope and the carabiner. I could thus assume that *iwa* ("rock") is a metaphorical analogue for (the flat extension of) the lower carabiner (see Figure 5.7), which is dangling roughly parallel to the rock face and fused with the vertical plane. This identification of the tool with the environement would have prompted the emergence of the intersubjectified vertical axis (Figure 5.8). However, since the lower carabiner on a quickdraw is easily manipulable, a possibility still exists that the flat extension could have tilted toward the true horizontal plane by the climber. Given that the climber constantly mentions *iwa* rather than *karabina* throughouthis utterances, this rules out the possibility that he actually manipulated the carabiner horizontally so that its flat extension would correspond to the horizontal plane. Finally, the phenomenon observed here should thus occur in the perceptually proximate region. In this instructional setting, the anomalous *ue/shita* expressions would make sense only when the climber is near the lower carabiner. It would be unimaginable for a belayer standing at the base of a route to refer to the rope and the carabiner using the vertical coordinate terms *ue/shita*. In fact, the initial perception gained by the climber seems canonical, but the intercorporeal process gradually affects the linguistic descriptions of the spatial perception, to which I now turn.

I next consider the linguistic choices for instruction. Spatial axial projection may not have been achieved solely through visual and bodily perceptions; the climber's step-by-step lexical selection for constructing an intersubjectified, intercorporeal FOR may also have contributed to it. Such socialization into a projected axis seems to have been facilitated by the schematic mapping of the body-ground relation on the horizontal plane (diagramatically, "i̲") onto the vertical plane ("•—|"), for which "i̲" and "•—" represent the canonical and the intersubjectified body axis, respectively. Obviously, the latter body axis is non-canonical because the body axis on the vertical plane is normally parallel to the surface of wall (i.e., "i|": see the "climibing situation" in Figure 1.1). Table 5.2 exhibits such an accommodation process from the pre-sequence through the main sequence.

Notice that the climber never uses *mae/ushiro* ("front/back") *Kotchi-gawa/atchi-gawa* ("this side/that side") is another option, but he uses it only once (Table 5.2: Main sequence (a)). Instead, he prefers to use *ue/shita* throughout the sequence. One notable element that facilitated the process seems to be the Japanese spatial motion verb *sagaru* ("go down"; Table 5.2: Pre-sequence (c)). This verb can be used for both vertical and horizontal space without reference to the gravitational force. Originally, the term refers to a gravitationally defined downward motion; however, this movement became associated with the up–down alignment of the social hierarchy, which was further metaphorized to refer to interpersonal relations in the canonical encounter. Thus, we get at least three types of *sagaru* (3): *sagaru$_1$*, "to go down," as in *(shita ni) sagaru*, "to go down vertically"; *sagaru$_2$*, "to go back," as in *(ushiro ni) sagaru*, "to step back," and; *sagaru$_3$* "to take oneself out of the scene," as in *omeome hiki-sagaru*, "to withdraw in shame."[8]

The verb *sagaru$_2$*, "step back"—a phenomenon similar to the English expression, "go down the street" (Shepard and Hurwitz 1984), appears in the pre-sequence just before the series of *jibun* expressions (Table 5.2: Pre-sequence (c)), and seems to serve as a bridge to the Main sequence. The spatial schema "i̲" is the one activated by the phrase *sagaru* ("step back(ward)") and *ushiro* ("back"; Pre-sequence (c, d)), and is shared by the belayer on the horizontal plane. This spatial schema of *sagaru$_2$* (i̲) could have schematically "primed" the prospective intersubjectified axis (•—|), preserving the same figure–ground relation. In the Main sequence (Table 5.2), the climber rotates the schema as evidenced by the use of *ue*, which is used to describe the 90-degree rotated space (i.e., '•—|'). In fact, the climber could have used other expressions with the same propositional value and more naturalness instead of *ue*, such as *kotchi-gawa* ("this side"), *temae* ("in front"), *karabina no mae* ("in front of the carabiner"), *jibun no hoo* ("towards the self"), and so forth, all of which represent deictic or coordinate relationships defined on the canonical axis. The climber obviously did not opt for any of these alternatives. By maintaining the schematic

Table 5.2 Accommodation to intersubjectified corporeality

Pre-sequence		\ Intersubjectification Process	
a)	*ma-shita*= (right below)	*canonical* vertical	(i↓)
b)	*ue*=above	*canonical* vertical	(i↓)
c)	*sagaru*= (step back)	*canonical* horizontal	(i̱)
d)	*ushiro*=back	*canonical* horizontal	(i̱)
Main sequence		\	
a)	*jibun=ue* (self=**up**)	*projected* vertical introduced	(•—|)
	kotchi-gawa 'this side'	return to the *canonical deictic*	(i̱)
b)	*jibun=shita* (self=**down**)	*projected* vertical re-introduced	(•—|)
c)	*jibun=shita* (self=**down/below**)	*projected* vertical presumed	(•—|)
d)	*jibun=ue-muki* (self=**upward**)	*projected* vertical maintained	(•—|)
e)	*jibun=shita-muki* (self=**downward**)	*projected* vertical maintained	(•—|)

equivalence between 'i̱' and '•—|,' the gravitational constraint imposed on the vertical FOR is neutralized, and the semantic content of the spatial term is also "bleached." The worlds thus blended are what Fauconnier (1994) termed "cross-world identification," such that the horizontal and vertical planes are qualitatively merged and blended by preserving the essential schema.

Spatial nouns categorize the world and classify it into distinct concepts (Levinson 2003), and semantic distinctions made in one's language project a network of indigenous inferences. Moreover, different levels of category boundaries in Japanese have been repeatedly raised (e.g., Ikegami 1981; Tanaka 1987). According to Ikegami (1981, 1996), in English, action verbs and countable nouns are prototypes for conceptualizing events and things. English speakers thus tend to perceive events and things as "individual entities" with clear boundaries. In Japanese, on the other hand, "state" verbs and uncountable nouns are prototypes, and Japanese speakers tend to perceive events and things as a "continuum" that lacks clear boundaries. In other words, the English mode of perception of the external world prefers to take individual entities out of an event and focus on them, using the "Agent + Transitive Verb" construction to express the "Subject DO something" schema. In Japanese, however, things and actions tend to lose their independence, to be buried within the whole event or situation, and to be described as "(Experiencer/Patient +) Intransitive verb" using the "Situation BECOME" schema.[9] Such incomplete boundedness seems to inhere in Japanese (spatial) nouns, allowing leeway even for semantically obstinate concepts (e.g., verticality) to flirt with context. The phenomena observed in this chapter obviously reflect the latter tendencies.

A final factor I consider is interactional attunement. It also seems to have contributed, though covertly, to the reinforcement of schematic projection triggered by the shift of bodily axes. Table 5.2 clearly shows how this intersubjectification process is achieved gradually through the climber's lexical selection and transitions into the projected verticality, to which the hearer succinctly adapts. In the first *jibun-ue* pair in Table 5.2 (Main sequence (a)), the climber seems to be aware that he needs to take into consideration the belayer's perspective, which is inevitably constrained by the canonical horizontal plane. It is probably due to this awareness that the speaker attempts to remedy his excessive intersubjectivity by temporarily retreating to the belayer's horizontal axis. His statement *kotchi gawa* ("this side"), a paraphrase of *ue* in the Main sequence (a) supports this assumption. Since both the climber and the belayer are on the same side of the reference object—the carabiner—"this side" represents not only his egocentric (or "relative") realm but also the belayer's and therefore is a safer choice. Also, when the climber utters the sentence, he is looking down and talking to him as if to induce him to share his perspective. Thus, a radical shift that the projected *jibun-ue* schema (•—|) brought about was temporarily mitigated by *kotchi-gawa* ("this side"). This is a less radical change than the use of *ue*, and retains the same (non-projected) status as *sagaru*$_2$ (i) in Table 5.2 (Pre-sequence (c, d)). As of the second attempt (Main sequence (b–e)), the climber seems to have determined that the belayer aligned himself appropriately with the projected verticality (•—|), and continued to use the same intersubjectified axis until the end of the series of exchanges. He also received positive responses from the belayer during his explanation.

In addition, while all the spatial expressions in the Pre-sequence describe the belayer's spatial positions and movement, the uses of *ue/shita* in the Main sequence are always accompanied by the word *jibun* ("self"). The word is non-specific with respect to the referent, as can be seen from the English gloss: it can variably mean "I," "you," "generic YOU," or almost any person with whom one can contextually identify. This underspecificity of *jibun* may have motivated the intersubjectifying process. The climber could have used other self-referential expressions such as *watashi/ore/boku* ("I/me), but all come with socio-indexical values (Silverstein 1976, 2004): formal and polite, if not distancing, for *watashi*; coarse and masculine for *ore*; and young or childlike for *boku*. It is difficult to find a perfect self-referential term for a young male adult like this climber. The climber and the belayer are acquaintances but not yet close friends in the club, so using *ore* would sound harsh or over-familiar. *Watashi* is too formal for a recreational activity like this, while *boku* is not appropriate for an expert—a status assumed to represent some sort of authority—since *boku* can suggest an inferior status. Therefore, the word *jibun* would have been the safest option. This vague referentiality can facilitate an empathic and intersubjective perspective, especially because the novice belayer will soon learn to lead a route as a climber.

Is this a temporary accommodation or socialization? It seems to be possibly the latter. Every actor can be socialized into a particular way of seeing, conducting, and encoding experience within a certain range acceptable in each community (Cohn 1987) based on an observation that "whatever you say may be used as evidence of what you are choosing not to say" (Enfield 2015: 217; cf. Grice 1989). Likewise, the verticality observed here is the result of what the participants chose to accept as reality. We can assume from their "fashions of speaking" (Whorf 1956) that verticality thus conceived would not be so "absolute" nor "over-determined" but could be context-sensitive. That said, there seem to be different degrees to which each language is allowed to diverge from the gravitational dominance. As long as the world is categorized through language, and in order for language to serve as a communicative means, speakers of each language will have to live with those covert constraints. Although the absolute axis is canonically defined by the gravitational orientation, it can be re-cognized interactionally through the participants' intersubjectified corporeality, according to which differential collateral effects will ensue.

It would be easy to shrug off those phenomena as insignificant and trivial, but we can readily think of situations in which such effects can lead to critical misunderstandings and fatal accidents, without bringing up Whorf's (1956) anecdote on "empty" gasoline drums. Rather, given an assumption that the linguistic items/structures thereby selected inevitably exert different consequential effects in the subsequent social interaction (Sidnell and Enfield 2012), the point here is not simply of the lexical association as in Whorf's "gasoline drum" but of the cultural inference that the use of those items has caused. The fact that our informants' linguistic and bodily actions were perfectly communicative indicates that they are acknowledged (by)products of the means to achieve a required goal. In fact, Climber Y's use of vertical terms were never problematized by other climbers, and it suggests that such use of spatial terms is a widely accepted practice as part of the activity, and possibly an interactional consequence of socialization into the community.

The (Kantian) notion of "up" and "down" derives from the perception of gravity, which primarily sets the spatial frame of reference. In this sense, gravity acts equally on everyone everywhere on earth, and the spatial frame of reference is fixed such that gravity-based verticality is the default state. In other words, the spatial grid (based on gravity) is Ground, and an object (or an agent) in the environment is perceived as Figure within the space. At the same time, however, a different mode of perception is possible. As shown in this analysis, the perception of gravity can be contextually overridden, and the individually constructed "up-down" relationship takes priority in the field of experience. That is, the subjective verticality derived from immediate experience is foregrounded, and the gravity-free "up–down" relationship is assigned according to the body schema that matches the context. By immersing oneself in the contested space, the human body becomes the primary battle ground for re-creating the spatial axes without dependence on gravity. Here, two different orientations are in competition: one is to identify the objects according to spatial relations based on gravity, and the other is to grasp spatial relations along the body axis based on immediate experience. This kind of "field dependence" would be a cognitive style common to all human beings, but to varying degrees. Cultural/linguistic differences in the degree of leeway seem to be in order through a cognitive style that is conventionalized in language.

5.5 Conclusion: Intersubjective/intercorporeal Merger

Perspective-taking and language use are inextricably linked in lived cognition, and it is in this critical domain that linguistically mediated spatial cognition develops its maximum adaptability or resilience to the variable encoding of space. The observations made here suggest a continuum of verticality regarding the contextual sensitivity and conformity to gravity. It seems possible that languages vary to the extent that they allow this kind of intersubjectified perception even in the use of vertical lexicon. Seen in this light, the value placed on the vertical dimension may have been overestimated in conceptual frameworks of space.

A series of phenomena I have examined represents the feature of what Vygotsky (1978) calls a "chain complex" (a chain of dynamic and consecutive meanings), and is explicitly characterized by the following statement concerning the relation between thought and word:

> The relation of thought to word is not a thing but a process, a continual movement back and forth from thought to word and from word to thought. . . . Every thought tends to connect something with something else, to establish a relation between things. Every thought moves, grows and develops, fulfills a function, solves a problem. This flow of thought occurs as an inner movement through a series of planes. An analysis of the interaction of thought and word must begin with an investigation of the different phases and planes a thought traverses before it is embodied in words.
>
> VYGOTSKY 1986: 218

In light of this, Pinxten's (1976) claim may be correct in assuming that topological relations such as 'on' are epistemic universals in the sense that they are consistently observed across languages, whereas more coordinate/Euclidean concepts tend to exhibit cultural variation when incorporated into the lexicon of language. The question is the degree of loyalty to such concepts. In our case, for example, Japanese *ue* can represent both topological concepts "on" and "over" (as "surface" and "part" interpretations) and a coordinate concept such as "up" and "above" (as "direction" and "space" interpretations) depending on how it is combined with a PosP and/or a verb. The degree of encoding those concepts varies cross-linguistically, which inevitably induces differential recognition of conceptual boundaries.

This idea has been confirmed by Levinson and his colleagues as to the horizontal space—e.g., languages such as Hausa (Hill 1982), Tamil (Pederson 1995), English, Japanese, and others (Pederson et al. 1998) seem to allow different manners and degrees of coordinate transformation in the canonical encounter. Similarly, the vertical axis may not be as inflexible as claimed by cognitive psychologists, but may be constructed more freely within the speaker's cognitive elbow room allowed by each language. Almost certainly, gravity is the dominant factor in defining the vertical axis, but the potential ease and difficulty of staying in or moving out of the frame may vary across languages, as may the sensitivity to, and the constraint of, gravity in a spatial lexical assignment. Such differences in the normative context would engender variable collateral effects, one of which would be the negotiability of verticality.

Here, the total bodily experience is key to understanding the phenomena I observed. Following a phenomenological tradition, Merleau-Ponty (1962) argued that the body is the site of myriad sensory experiences (including rational "reflection" itself as an experience) that come into play and create the amalgam of our perceptions of the world. Humans interact internally and externally with the environment, binding body and mind through reciprocal transactions. Therefore, spatial perception is always re-contextualized and constitutes a basis for subsequent extensions of the lived space. Of particular relevance to the present discussion is his argument that the body is not "a collection of adjacent organs but a synergic system, all of the functions of which are exercised and linked together in the general action of being in the world" (Merleau-Ponty 1962: 234). That way, the body becomes "the fabric into which all objects are woven" (Merleau-Ponty 1962: 235).[10] These ideas have also been extended and widely applied to cognitive and social sciences by such authors as Varela et al. (1991), Ingold (2000), Chemero (2009), and Meyer et al. (2017), to name just a few. Valera et al. (1991) sought a middle ground in which mind and body can be mediated through what they call "structural coupling" and "mindful (i.e., mind-body-mediated) reflection" (Varela et al. 1991: 27), and claimed that "sensory and motor processes, perception and action, are fundamentally inseparable in lived cognition" (Varela et al. 1991: 173). Ingold (2000) also made a similar claim that "(l)ooking, listening and touching, therefore, are not separate activities, they are just different facets of the same activity: that of the whole organism in its environment" (Ingold 2000: 261). He specifically referred to "looking," "listening," and "touching," but as long as other senses are involved, "feeling" gravity with the whole body is also part of the system, just as the climbers attempted to offer the most facilitative descriptions/depictions by integrating visual, aural, and tactile perceptions. It is this mind–body–environment-aligned activity that I have observed in this chapter.

With few exceptions, vertical space has been examined very rarely from experiential perspectives in language studies, let alone through actual interaction and conversational exchanges. We now see that, contrary to what has always been assumed, vertical space can be re-interpreted through direct perception of gravity and subsequent cognitive processes. Obviously, some people in the world can live happily with such "under-determined" fluid verticality, and it can only be known by actually residing in it. In the next chapter, I consider another case of such intersubjectified and intercorporeal spatial construction achieved through collaborative wayfinding.

6

The Body and Deictic Verbs of Motion in Imaginary Space

6.1 Introduction

The previous chapter investigated the process of intersubjective and intercorporeal integration of vertical and horizontal axes between two participants. This chapter looks into the more complex process of participants' integration of fragmented spatial perceptions into a holistic mental map through collaborative wayfinding. Through the analysis, it will be argued that intersubjectified corporeality is a key factor in explicating the complex use of semiotic resources such as language, gaze, gesture, and environmental affordances. Along with the argument, the two seemingly unrelated issues—intersubjectivity and poetics—are theoretically united to reveal the interactional alignment in a climbing talk.

The following sections specifically investigate two sets of multi-layered, micro/macro-levels interaction. First, as a primordial site for discursive investigation of intersubjectivity and corporeality, we examine a micro-interactional phenomenon in which the body in space was exquisitely exploited in the discussion of a climbing accident. We seek to investigate intersubjective phenomena seeping through spatial descriptions/depictions by applying four basic types of spatial perspectives (Chapter 2.3.3) and examine the process by which mutual understanding interactionally emerges through "trading places" (Duranti 2010). Specifically, it will be shown that participants' gesticulations are efficiently differentiated in terms of types of perspectives that are mediated by "egocentric/allocentric" frames of reference (Levinson 2003) and "Character/Observer Viewpoints" (C-VPT/O-VPT: McNeill 1992) in which iconic gestures and deictic gestures (pointing) are major resources for spatial depictions. As Trafton et al. (2006) have shown, gestures are more likely to occur with speeches that express (1) geometric relations, and (2) spatial transformations, and the latter is correlated more strongly with gesturing. In particular, what is found crucial is what I call the "intersubjective" perspective—an essentially "merged but detached" perspective with the viewer's perception floating away from the *origo* (center of cognition) and around the scene at issue. Based on the analysis in this chapter, it is emphasized that intersubjectified corporeality is a major factor that facilitates the current spatial construction.

Second, by carefully examining referential and non-referential aspects of indexicals, a more macro-level "interactional text" (Silverstein 1985, 2004) is confirmed to emerge *in situ* in terms of "poetic" (Jakobson 1960) formations of text. The interactional text, much like mental imagery, immanently underlies the "denotational" (semantico-referential) text and characteristically emerges through a valued alignment of deictic tokens. The use of deixis in naturally occurring discourse has been regarded as the battlefield of what is denotationally represented and connotatively presupposed/created (Silverstein 1976). It has been claimed repeatedly that even the spatio-temporal deixis is inevitably meshed with interpersonal configurations created among discourse participants (Hanks 1990, 1992; Haviland 1996, 2000; Silverstein 1985, 1993; Enfield 2003; and Wortham 2003, to name only a few). In other words, the surface indexical configuration, here realized as a poetic alignment of deictics, may inexorably subsume some social orders and inequalities that have been formulated tacitly in ongoing discourse. Based on the analysis of these phenomena, it is claimed that intersubjectivity literally stems from "trading places," and is simultaneously reflected upon deictic shifts in the collaborative wayfinding.

6.2 Theoretical Background

It is widely acknowledged that the development of human sociality is essentially constructed by fully fledged human interaction (Enfield and Levinson 2006). Among others, fundamental preconditions for the process are phenomenological concepts of intersubjectivity and intercorporeality (Merleau-Ponty 1962; see also Ingold 2000; Lusthaus (2003); Duranti 2009, 2010; and Meyer et al. 2017). According to Meyer et al. (2017), intercorporeality is considered to serve fundamental functions in human social interaction and typically achieved through joint attention and taking the perspective of others in cooperative and collaborative situations. Such awareness has triggered a reconsideration of the Western scientific tradition that has mainly addressed actor-oriented cognitive abilities (see also Ichikawa 2001 on *mi-wake* "corporal division" and Hanks et al. 2019 on the theory of *ba(sho)* ("place")), such that the focus of analysis has shifted to collaborative achievement and shared cognition with others (Tomasello 2008; Frank and Trevarthen 2012). Our assumption here is that this mutual meta-awareness of others' minds should be achieved not simply on linguistic levels but also through "co-operative" actions (Goodwin 2017). Specifically, what we will subsequently observe is a kind of "collaborative imagining" (Murphy 2005) by rock climbers in that they refine the configuration of an imaginary route through gestures and other semiotic resources. This chapter thus seeks for an interdisciplinary venue in which these notions are incorporated into a unified approach to language, the body, and the environment.

Among linguistic interests in this vein, the focus has been placed on the spatiality of grammar and language use (e.g., Langacker 1987; Fauconnier and Sweetser 1996; Dancygier 2011). In particular, intersubjectivity and embodiment have been widely acknowledged among linguists as a major motivation in promoting the grammaticalization of mutual epistemic stances (Traugott 1995), as typically addressed by "the question how linguistic syntagma may shift towards the expression of meanings of which the hearer is an essential part" (Davidse et al. 2010). However, interdisciplinary attempts to bridge the gap with related fields such as linguistics, discourse analysis, and gesture studies are still in a developing stage despite the significant awareness of, and expressed calls for, collaboration with related disciplines (e.g., Kristiansen and Dirven 2008; Cienki 2016). This chapter is one such attempt to present an integrated analysis of *ba* ("place/space/context"), intersubjectivity/corporeality, and discursive practice.

Linguistic expressions and bodily depictions of spatial relations in collaborative wayfinding are highly relevant to the following analysis. We will concentrate on the use of the deictic verbs of motion (DVMs) *iku/kuru* ("go/come"), and the spatial coordinate terms *migi/hidari* ("right/left") because they encode and index partial but crucial features of the *origo* (origin of cognition) and the spatial configuration in the making. In linguistic theories of deixis (e.g., Fillmore [1971] 1997; Ohye 1975; Koizumi 1990 for Japanese), the *origo* of deictic expressions is judged based on the acceptability judgment of constructed sentences, and it is assumed to be quite freely and instantly transposable depending on the speaker's intention. In actual interaction, however, the locus of the *origo* may not be as flexible as is assumed as it is literally "down-to-earth" and constrained by epistemic and experiential variables related to the context. Also, the shift of the *origo* is often gradual and sometimes needs to be negotiated interactionally among participants. In this chapter, this shift will be examined in terms of how discursive consequences emanating from such constraints exhibit the need for mutual calibration.

Spatial expressions in context are contingent upon the viewer's positioning in relation to the surrounding environment, and they evoke certain spatial configurations and motion events. Such configurations induce systematic and schematic extensions of case frame structures, metaphorical expressions, and linguistic constructions (e.g., Fillmore 1982a; Lakoff 1987; Levinson and Wilkins 2006). In linguistic spatial analyses, for example, locative semantic roles are usually represented by SOURCE, PATH, and GOAL (Fillmore [1971] 1997, 1982b), often along with a less-accurate candidate, DIRECTION (e.g., Lakoff 1987: 275; Jackendoff 1983: 168). To specify these semantic categories of space, one needs to identify the viewer's *origo* or "home base" (Fillmore [1971] 1997) because its positioning affects the features of a motion event such that the motion from a "source" could be at the same time a motion toward a "goal," depending upon which end of the segment the viewer happens to be more affiliated with. Therefore, the notion of *origo* can be presupposed and achieved adequately by the use of deixis and the choice of COME and GO.[1]

Before the analysis, it is necessary to review and compare some fundamental features of Japanese DVMs with their English counterparts: *kuru* ("come") and *iku* ("go") vs. *come* and *go*, respectively. Basic features of these verbs have been discussed intensively in Fillmore ([1971] 1997), Gathercole (1978), Morita (1977), Matsumoto (1996), and Sawada (2016) among others. What we need here is a conceptual formulation that can be adapted efficiently to the current data and analysis. In some languages, COME does not allow deictic projection as widely as it does in English. The use of COME to represent motion to the hearer's location, which is generally available in English, is extremely restricted in languages like Japanese, Spanish, and arguably Thai and Mandarin (Gathercole 1978). In these languages, COME always encodes the motion to "me," not to "you." Thus, the response to "come here" is not "I'm coming" but "I'm going"—*ima iki masu* in Japanese (and *Voy* in Spanish); hence the asterisk in the "accompaniment" situation in (1).[2]

1   a. *Anata to isshoni {ittemo/*kitemo} ii desu ka?*
       'Can I (Sp) {go/*come} with you (Hr)?'
    b. *Watashi to issho ni {ko(ra)re/ike} masu ka?*
       'Can you (Hr) {come/go} with me (Sp)?'

Thus, the schematic representation for COME and GO in Japanese (and in English for comparison) can be shown as follows (Figure 6.1).³

A covert assumption here is that however seemingly physically grounded a spatio-temporal deixis may be, it leaves a trace that reaches the underlying social values embraced, disseminated, and re-created among discourse participants in a particular "indexical ground" (Hanks 1992). One such exemplar element is the "deictic verbs of motion" (hereafter DVMs) such as "go/come" and "give/take," which often embed value-laden information about the speaker and the addressee vis-à-vis the source and the goal of motion, which are variably empathized with (Kuno and Kaburaki 1977; Radden 1996). In this sense, the indexical ground signified by these verbs is essentially "sociocentric" (Hanks 1992; Bennardo 2009). In addition, the maintenance, shift, and creation of the indexical ground may not necessarily be random but rather systematic and "poetic" in the sense of Jakobson (1960). As will be shown subsequently, both denotational and interactional texts are coordinated to form perceptually and socially metricalized patterns in ongoing interaction.

Another highly noticeable type of deixis in our data is "pointing." For example, Levinson and his colleagues investigated the indigenous use of pointing gestures (Levinson 2003, Ch. 6; Kita 2003a; Enfield 2014) and claimed that distinct pointing behaviors are a reflection of two major "frame of reference" (FOR) types—i.e., the "relative" (egocentric) or the "absolute" (allocentric) FOR (see also Haviland 1993, 2000). For example, Japanese speakers' default gestures are largely "relative" and thus "egocentric" in nature. They are mostly small and are enacted in front of the individual (utilizing an imagined, flat "2-D scratch pad" with shallow depth; McNeill 1992). Also, pointing gestures made by Japanese speakers are usually associated with gaze and normally accompanied by a turning of the trunk when referring to an object behind them (Levinson 2003, Kita 2003a).⁴ Although there are no "absolute/allocentric" pointings observed in the current data, various types of "egocentric" pointing still give us a glimpse into covert intersubjective processes (however, see Kita 2003b and Kataoka 2011 for Japanese speakers' "absolute" pointing in route instruction).

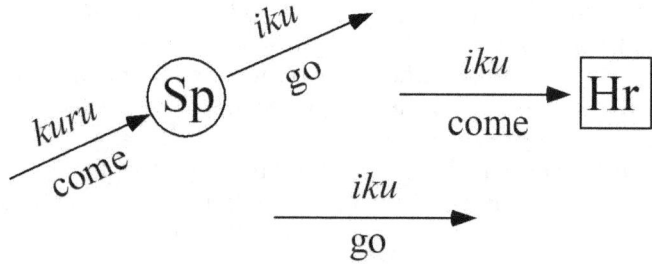

FIGURE 6.1 *Default use for COME and GO: Japanese and English.*

6.3 Data and Informants

In our data, certain spatial expressions are shown to appear at the crucial moment of mutual understanding in wayfinding and also seem to accompany layered manipulations of language and the body. Wayfinding heavily concerns how people formulate places to identify where they are with multimodal resources of particular indexical values (Schegloff 1972; Goodwin 2007b; Kataoka 2005, 2009, 2010; Sicoli 2016, 2020). In order to focus on these aspects of deixis, recurrent usages of Japanese *iku* ("go") and *kur-u* ("come") are examined specifically in the following wayfinding discourse. It will be argued that these DVMs (deictic verbs of motion) immanently index differential epistemological understandings that codify both denotational and interactional values of the socio-cognitive space.

The data referred to come from the discussion that spontaneously developed among nine Japanese rock climbers. The discussion occurred in the base camp tent where all of the participants in the climbs (eight climbers) and a newcomer to the base camp gathered for dinner and lasted about twenty minutes, excluding the meal time that interrupted the discussion. The discussion concentrated on the cause of the twenty-meter fall that one of the climbers experienced unexpectedly on the Matsukoo (hereafter, M) Route on the Center Face of Peak 4 (Figure 6.2).[5] (Fortunately, she suffered no major injuries—only several bruises.) For such an accident not to be repeated, the climbers attempted to identify the location of the fall, but faced

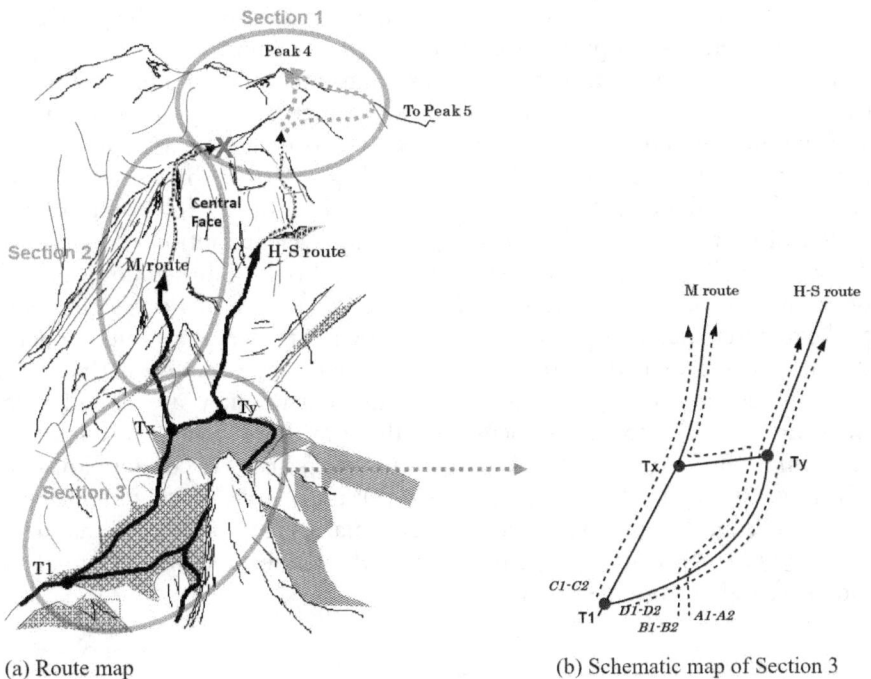

(a) Route map (b) Schematic map of Section 3

FIGURE 6.2 *M Route and H-S Route on Central Face of Peak 4.*

enormous difficulty, mainly because what they thought to be M Route turned out to be wrong, or a variation of the original route at best. Thus, the participants voluntarily provided specific information from their limited spatial experience and finally concluded that the accident location must be around the point marked "X" in Section 1 in Figure 6.2 (a).[6] The discussion consisted of a tripartite macrostructure about the M Route, the Hoojoo-Shin'mura (hereafter, H-S) Routes, and related locations. Divided into three major sections, it respectively concerns the identification of the fall point vis-à-vis Peak 4 (Section 1), the correct line of the M Route (Section 2), and the correct starting point of the M Route (Section 3).

It would be helpful to illustrate the participants' experiential differences as to the climbs because such differences are heavily contingent on the following analysis. Eight rock climbers (four pairs of two) embarked on two routes on the Central Face of Peak 4 (Figure 6.2 (a)): four members (two parties of two) on the M Route, and the other four (two parties of two) on the H-S Route. However, their trails to embark on these routes were all different (Figure 6.2 (b)). Two parties, A1-A2 and B1-B2, climbed up a gully and merged into the middle section of the trail leading from Terrace 1 (T1) to Terrace Y (hereinafter, Ty).[7] The A1-A2 party then climbed the H-S Route, whereas the B1-B2 party traversed left from Ty to a lower ledge, which we tentatively call Tx, and climbed a false M Route (to avoid confusion, I nevertheless call this line the M Route). A short while later, the C1-C2 and D1-D2 parties embarked on the M and H-S routes, respectively: the D1-D2 party reached Ty via T1, while the C1-C2 party reached the base of the M Route (Tx) via T1. C2 is the person who had a serious fall (as noted, of approximately twenty meters) during the climb. There was one more participant in the discussion—IM, who had just arrived at the base camp that day. IM, a climbing expert who wrote a chapter of the guidebook on this climbing area, did not participate in any of these climbs.

As will be shown in the transcription, although the utterances inevitably include numerous false starts, repetitions, overlaps, and concurring speeches, they are tentatively modified into what are similar to "extended clauses" (Chafe 1987). This way, I respectively obtained 105, 329, and 143 clauses for the three sections—or 577 clauses in all. Of these, 109 clauses included DVMs. In the following analysis, a limited set of spatial terms are in focus: specifically, deictic motion verbs *iku* ("go") and *kuru* ("come"), and the coordinate terms *migi* ("right") and *hidari* ("left"), and deictic terms *kotchi* ("here") and *atchi* ("there"). These terms reveal the ways in which the maintenance, shift, and merger of participants' vantage points are achieved collaboratively and extended creatively *in situ*. Here, my criterion is that as far as *ik-u* and *kur-u* encode any kind of spatial movement, they are included in the following analysis. The tokens in focus are either the "bare" forms of *ik-u* and *kur-u* or the "compound" forms in the present (PRS) and past (PST) conjugations—*(V-te)(i)k-u* (PRS)/*(V-te)(i)t-ta* (PST) ("go/went –ing") and *(V-te) kur-u* (PRS)/*(V-te) ki-ta* (PST) ("come/came –ing").[8] However, an aspectual usage (underlined) as in *kare o suki ni natte kita* ("I have <u>come to</u> like him") which does not encode actual spatial motion, is excluded from the analysis.

6.4 Analysis of Intersubjectified Corporeality and Poetic Formation of Spatial Construction

In this section, it will be confirmed that distinct types of verbal and gestural representations are employed differentially depending on participants' experiential levels of understanding. At the same time, we look into a converging process in which "trading places" (Duranti 2010), both literally and metaphorically, takes place on multiple levels of spatial descriptions and depictions. The key issues here are, first, to examine how the spontaneous and systematic use of deictic and coordinate terms motivates the spatial understanding, especially at the heuristic moment of determining the holistic picture of recalled scenes. It is at this moment that intersubjectified corporeality is relied upon heavily (6.3.1). Second, it will also be confirmed that space, body, and environment are coordinated in terms not only of the denotational text constructed by deictic tokens, but also of the interactional text emanating from it *in situ* (6.3.2).

6.4.1 Wayfinding Through Individual and Collaborative Perspectives

In what follows, we examine (1) IM's verbal and gestural practice, which is consistently based on the "Observer-external" perspective; (2) A1's verbal and gestural practice, which barely succeeded in shifting the "Observer-internal" to the "Character-internal" perspective; and finally (3) B1's spontaneous (and A1's subsequent) shift from the "Character-internal" to the "Intersubjective" perspective made available in the language-body-environment nexus. The following excerpts come from Sections 2, 1, and 3 in Figure 6.2, respectively. The analysis concerns the exquisite spatial configuration in which the perspective cohesion is corroborated by the choice and shift of DVMs—a strategy not explicitly considered in the conceptualization of "cohesion" (Halliday and Hasan 1976).

We first confirm IM's persistent use of the "Observer-external" (and occasionally, "Observer-internal") perspective, which pushes forward an objective and individual spatial description. It is readily known from IM's gestural performance that he employs different modes of spatial descriptions and depictions from other participants. Let us first look at a typical case of his co-speech gestures.[9] The transcription of gesture is based on Kendon's (2004) system (see Transcription keys). Unfortunately, the visual quality of the plates is quite low because the data was recorded in a dimly lit tent after sunset.

In Excerpt 6-1, Plates (a)–(d), IM illustrates carefully how climbers usually proceed on the M Route (see Figure 6.2 (a)), which has the overhang section in the third pitch (line 12 (c)). Here, he clearly employs a wide-range, Observer-external perspective that holds the whole spatial scene in scope as viewed from afar and above. Considering the fact that the length of "one pitch" is about forty meters,[10] we can easily imagine the actual scale that IM's gesture depicts. (Notice that Excerpt 6.1

114　　　　　　　　LANGUAGE AND BODY IN PLACE AND SPACE

EXCERPT 6.1 *IM's perspective gestures.*

1　IM:　*Sore o ne*
　　　　~~~~~~~
　　　　'On that route,'

2　　　*ni pitchi gurai wa agaranto ikan no.*
　　　　* * * * */* * * * *-.-.-.-.-.-.-.-.-.-.-|
　　　　'you have to climb up about two pitches, you know.'

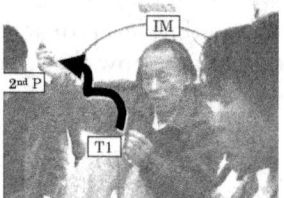
(a) 'Two pitches'

3　B1:　*e?*
　　　　'What?'

4　IM:　(1.0) *Ano..ma- mawarikonde.*
　　　　~~* * * * * * * * */* * * * * * * * * ((slow repetition of (a)))
　　　　'I mean, tur- after you turn around.'

5　X:　*aa::n?* ((response of incomprehension))
　　　　'W- wha::t?'

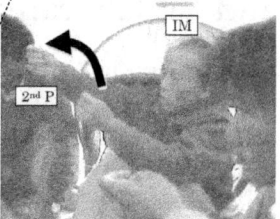
(b) 'two pitches, you know'

6　IM:　*wan-*
　　　　* * * * ((quick repetition of (a)))
　　　　'One-'

7　　　*ni pitchi ne.*
　　　　* * * * * * * * *| ((nodding and raising LH to RH))
　　　　'Two pitches, you know.'

8　　　*ni pitchi itte,*
　　　　* * * * * * * * * ((gesture of "1 pitch" by RH))
　　　　'You go two pitches,'

((3 lines deleted due to disfluencies))

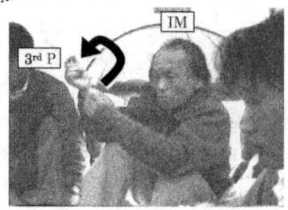
(c) 'the third pitch is...'

12　　(0.5) *nnn mi- san pitchi me ga,*
　　　　* * * * * * * * * *|* * * * * * * * * * *| ((quick and small ark))
　　　　'uhhn th- the third pitch is,'

13　　*ano:::*
　　　　* * * * *
　　　　'you know,'

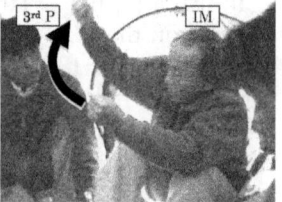
(d) 'the overhang section'

14　　(1.8) *yoosuruni hangutai ni naru wake,*
　　　　* *-.-.-.|
　　　　((repair of (c)))
　　　　'what is called the overhang section.'

15　C1:　*nn::?* ((response of incomprehension))
　　　　'Huh:::n?'

THE BODY AND DEICTIC VERBS OF MOTION IN IMAGINARY SPACE 115

(d) is an actional repair of Excerpt 6.1 (c).) As is evident from IM's gestures (a)–(d) here and elsewhere, he consistently employs a large-scale, Observer-external perspective through language and the body, and this descriptive style never changed throughout the discussion.

The perspective he takes is also connected to his choice of DVMs such that he constantly opted to use *iku* ("go"), which may encode a non-deictic, objective spatial movement. Up to that point, no one else has relied upon such uses of iconic gesture or *iku* in referring to the virtual space under construction—nor have they specifically referred to the segments/nodes of pitches illustrated in Figure 6.2. Also, no confirming responses are heard from the other participants, indicating that they do not yet share a spatial imagery of the scene. However, when the spatial information accumulates to a certain amount, other participants also start to comment on the mental image under collaborative construction. It is not hard to imagine that IM's perspective, due to its map-like, bird's-eye-view characteristics, serves as a clue to help create a holistic picture in the participants' minds. However, at this stage—at which IM's spatial imagery is not shared fully—his spatial descriptions do not appeal to other members, who must rely only on their experience-based perspectives.

In Excerpt 6.2.1, we can observe different perspectives used by A1 in an initial phase of the discussion—specifically a shift from the Observer-internal to the Character-internal perspective. It is covertly indexed by the choice of DVMs and coordinate terms for the "up/down" relation, but are overtly gesticulated by a synthetic type of gesture or what may be called "deiconic" (deictic + iconic) gestures.[11]

At the outset, A1 makes extensive comments about the trail he took to get to Peak 4, where he waited for other members to catch up (Figure 6.2). The shift of the *origo* from the base camp, where this discussion is occurring, to the (envisioned) Peak 4 was a tacit one and never explicitly articulated. At the outset, A1 depicted Peak 4 while uttering *yon hoo no* ("of Peak 4"; line 2), making a "holding" gesture with both hands as if to metaphorically indicate something solid (line 2 (a)). This "Peak-4 gesture" is abandoned instantly and replaced by his deiconic gesture, based on the view from Peak 4. During the one-second pause in line 3, A1 raised his right hand, the gesture of which serves as "preparation" for the upcoming gestures. In fact, when he actually mentions *go hoo gawa* ("on the side of Peak 5"; line 3), he slides his hand to his left (toward Peak 5), at the same time turning his gaze to his right (line 3 (b)). The target of the gaze is the starting point of the rock band that he will depict next.

EXCERPT 6.2.1 *A1's perspective gestures (1).*

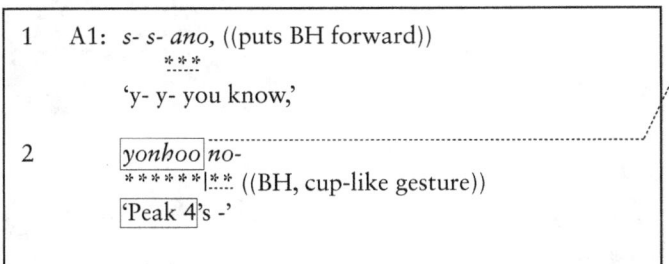

EXCERPT 6.2.1 *A1's perspective gestures (1)* continued.

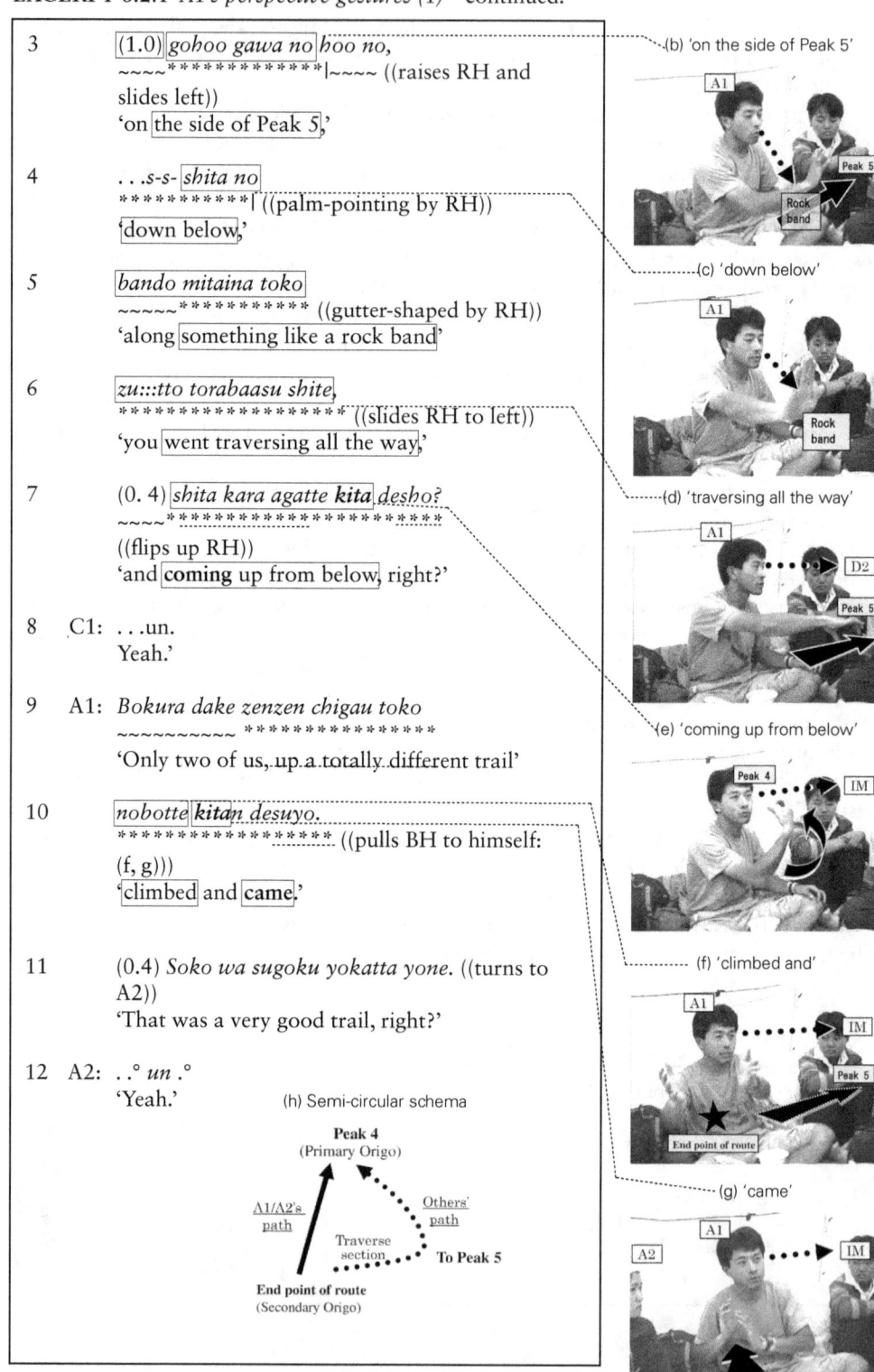

3   (1.0) gohoo gawa no hoo no,
    ~~~~**************|~~~~ ((raises RH and slides left))
    'on the side of Peak 5,'

4   ...s-s- shita no
    ***********| ((palm-pointing by RH))
    'down below,'

5   bando mitaina toko
    ~~~~~********** ((gutter-shaped by RH))
    'along something like a rock band'

6   zu:::tto torabaasu shite,
    ******************* ((slides RH to left))
    'you went traversing all the way,'

7   (0.4) shita kara agatte kita desho?
    ~~~~****************
    ((flips up RH))
    'and coming up from below, right?'

8   C1: ...un.
         'Yeah.'

9   A1: Bokura dake zenzen chigau toko
         ~~~~~~~~~~ ****************
         'Only two of us, up a totally different trail'

10 nobotte kitan desuyo.
    *****************---- ((pulls BH to himself: (f, g)))
    'climbed and came.'

11 (0.4) Soko wa sugoku yokatta yone. ((turns to A2))
    'That was a very good trail, right?'

12 A2: ..° un .°
         'Yeah.'

(h) Semi-circular schema

Peak 4
(Primary Origo)

A1/A2's path   Others' path
                Traverse
                section   To Peak 5

End point of route
(Secondary Origo)

- (b) 'on the side of Peak 5'
- (c) 'down below'
- (d) 'traversing all the way'
- (e) 'coming up from below'
- (f) 'climbed and'
- (g) 'came'

A1 then started depicting a narrow rock band (line 4), first uttering *shita no* ("down there") and explaining the location with his right hand stretched out forward (line 4 (c)). While uttering *bando mitaina toko* ("something like a rock band"; line 5), his gaze was briefly turned to the left (Peak 5) and finally to D2, who he knows actually treaded on the path near Peak 5. He then slides his right hand to the left while he utters *zu::tto torabaasu* ("traversing all the way"; line 6 (d)), and brings it up to his face (center of cognition, or Peak 4 in this case) with the expression *agatte kita* ("coming up"; line 7 (e)). At that moment, his gaze is turned toward IM for confirmation, probably because IM is an expert climber and currently the most reliable source of information on the area under discussion.

A1 wants to emphasize that the trail he and A2 (his partner on the climb) took to Peak 4 was much safer and more comfortable than the one taken by the other members. He uses adverbial emphasizers *dake* ("only") and *zenzen* ("totally"; line 9) in order to stress the difference. A1 then depicts the endpoint of the route with both hands on his right (the "star" sign in line 10 (f)), which is further to the right from the starting point of the rock band depicted in line 6 (d), consecutively pulling his hands toward himself (line 10 (g)). This endpoint, combined with the previous trail (Excerpt 6.2.1 (a)–(e)), completes the semi-circle configuration of the actual environment (Excerpt 6.2.1 (h)).

Once A1 finishes depicting the semi-circular configuration to get to Peak 4, he talks to A2 to confirm his interpretation (lines 11–12). However, the following conversation shows an interesting twist of the perspective shifts in the face of IM's inquiry (Excerpt 6.2.2).

EXCERPT 6.2.2 *A1's perspective gestures (2).*

```
12   A2:   ° un .°
            'Yeah.'

13   A1:   Nannimo fuan naku,
            'Without any worry,'

14         (1.0) moo zairu toite,
            ~~~~ ************
            'without a rope,'

15         taka taka taka taka taka taka kimochi yoku=        (i) 'like trot trot trot trot . . .'
            **************************-.-.-.-.  ((climbing
            gesture))
            'like trot trot trot trot trot trot,'

16   IM:   =Iya dakara ne--=
            'So you know--,'

17   A1:   =n- katai iwa o [nobotte kuru (kanji).]
            'we came climbing up on rigid rock.'

18   IM:   [Nani ato no,]
            'You mean, after the climb,'
```

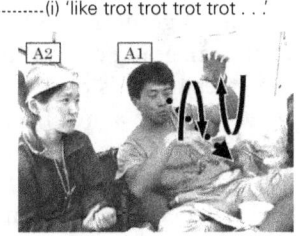

EXCERPT 6.2.2 *A1's perspective gestures (2).* continued

```
19      shuuryooten no hanashi?
        'talking about the endpoint of the route?'

20  A1: Shuuryooten made agatte (i)ku ho-
        (j) 'to the end of route/Peak 4'
        ************************************ ((LH
        pointing))
        '(That's) where we go/climb up to the end of route-'

21      yonhoo no choojoo made agaru ho-
        ******************************************
        'where we climb up to Peak 4-'

22      agatte (i)ku mitchi desu.
        *******************-.-.-.
        'the trail we go/climb up on (to Peak 4).'
```

(j) to the end of route/Peal 4

In line 14, A1's gestures suddenly switch to the one based on the Character-internal VPT so as to precisely depict his own actions (lines 14–15 (i)). His "climbing" gesture is accompanied by the onomatopoetic repetitions, *taka taka taka taka taka taka* ("trot trot trot trot trot trot"), both of which elaborate on the agility and ease of their actions as well as the validity of trail choice. Seeing A1's descriptions/depictions, IM must have noticed something different. Preempting with a discourse marker *nani* ("you mean"; literally "what") and the truncated phrase *ato no* ("after the-"), he raises a suspicion about A1's current *origo* by asking "are you talking about the end point of the route?" (line 19). This question is ambiguous because IM's phrase *shuuryooten* ("endpoint") in this case can mean both "the endpoint of H-S route" and possibly Peak 4. To this question, A1 avoids answering in a Yes/No format, but reformulates his response as *shuuryooten made agatte(i)ku hoo* ("climbing up to the endpoint"), stretching his left arm upward with his gaze directed to IM (line 20 (j)). He notices the incongruence between his gesture and utterance right away and self-repairs his utterance, not gesture, as *yon hoo no choojoo made agaru ho-* ("(the direction) going up to Peak 4"), which is further repaired as *agatte(i)ku michi desu* ("the trail going up to Peak 4"). This phrase, *made agatte(i)ku* ("going up to"), clearly indicates that his *origo* no longer resides at Peak 4 because the locative case marker *made* ("as far as to") can only encode the "approach to/arrival at" the destination. His bodily representation also attests to this interpretation. His left hand, stretched out and upward, evidently depicts the viewing direction based on his Character-internal perspective from the endpoint of the H-S Route (secondary *origo*). Still, throughout this sequence, the final destination is invariably set at Peak 4 (primary *origo*), and the spatial coherence is established and maintained at Peak 4 in support of the centripetal schema, embodied by the synthetic, "deiconic" (i.e., "deictic + iconic") gestures. Overall, we can identify parallel, centripetal shifts toward the *origo* in terms of several layers of language, gesture, gaze, posture, and imagery.

Given all this, it is evident that the spatial embodiments are not necessarily motivated individually, but also activated interactionally. The following excerpt further reveals that spatial perspective-taking can emerge in somatically more complex manners to the extent of being collaboratively extended and even creatively invented.

6.4.2 Wayfinding Through Intersubjectified Corporeality

In this section, we examine more complex processes that lead to intersubjective understanding at the heuristic moment of a holistic spatial construction. To begin, we focus on the utterances by one climber who turned out to be a "transgressor" due to his dual identities, derived from different experiential statuses. That climber, B1, can be differentiated epistemologically from the other participants in that he was the sole participant who had climbed the M Route previously and also on this occasion. Arguably, though, owing to his dual statuses in the sense that he could combine different perspectives based on his past and present experiences, he comes to grasp the whole picture more quickly than the other participants. Consequently, his utterances help elicit subsequent understanding among the participants through the "intersubjective" perspective he presented. His perspective is not readily shared, but turns out to incorporate multiple perspectives not specified by the three types of perspective-taking observed in Section 6.3.1 (see Table 2.2 (1) to (3)). Let us first look into the route discussion that leads to the heuristic moment when the participants realize the spatial relations of landmarks (Excerpt 6.3.1).

EXCERPT 6.3.1 *B1's perspective gestures (1).*

1	M:	[*Wan-pitchi nobotta*] *tokoro kara ne,* 'After you climbed one pitch,'
2		*ookii terasu atta ra?* ************** 'there was a big terrace (Tx), right?'
3	All:	*Hai hai, arimashita.* 'Yes, yes there was.'
4	?:	*Un atta.* ((agreeing voices)) 'Yeah, there was.'
5	IM:	*Sokkara nee,* 'From there,'
6		*mi*[₁ *gi e*] *za::tto* [₂ *torabaasu shite-(i)kun da.* *******************-.-.-.-. 'you **go** traversing all the way to the **right**.'
7	B1:	[₁ **Migi e--**] 'To the **right**--'

EXCERPT 6.3.1 *B1's perspective gestures (1)* continued.

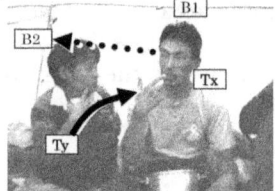
(a) 'the opposite way we went'

8   [₂ <u>Ah:</u>, yappari soo da.
    'Yes! That's what I thought.'

9   [₃bokura ga **itta** no to gyaku. ((To B2))
    ~~~~~************ ((pulls RH))
    'That's the opposite way we went.'

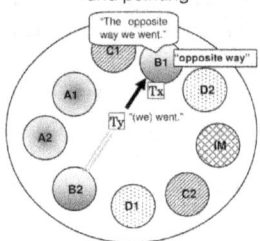
(b) Overview of the scene and pointing

10 A2: [₃ E dooyuu [₄ koto?
    'Huh? What does that mean?'

11 D1 san tachi –
    'D1's party-'

12 IM: [₄ **Migi** e da::tto torabaasu shite[₅ (i)ku.
    '**Go** traversing further to the **right**, OK.'

13 D2: [₅ A: soo desu ka.
    'Oh, it that right?'

14 D1: Un un un =
    'Yeah, yeah, yeah='

(c) '(where) we'

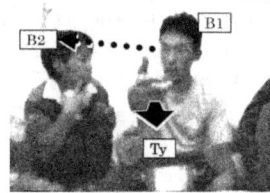

15 B1: =Bokura ga saa, ((To B2))
    |~~~~~ ((RH, pointed forward))
    '=You remember (the point) where we'

16 **hidari** ni [₆ toraba**a**su shita jan.
    ********************** ((pulls it back))
    'traversed to the **left**?'

(d) 'traversed to the left'

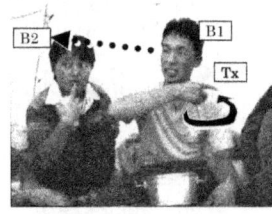

17 B2: [₆ A: a:. ((To B1))
    'Yeah yeah.'

18 B1: [₇ Are o **migi** ni ikutte yuu.]
    ~~******************-.-.-. ((points forward))
    'We need to **go right** on that (trail)!'

(e) 'we need to go right'

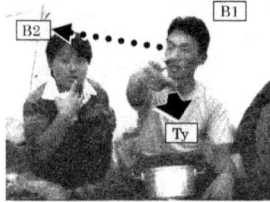

19 B2: [₇<A t t c h i>gawa kara **ku**]ru kara wa-
    'Oh, because we **come** from the other side'

20 machigaeru no ka.
    'we make mistakes!'

(f) Overview of the scene

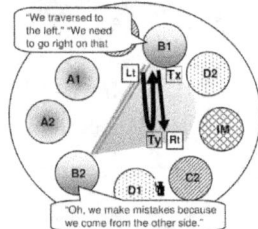

IM initiates this portion, which B1 then elaborates. The fact that B1 is the first to realize the overall configuration becomes manifest in line 7, where he utters *migi e* ("to the right"), overlaps and echoes IM's utterance in line 6. Then, overlapping further with IM, B1 says "that's what I thought" (line 8), confirming to himself that his speculation was correct. In this discussion, the participants are following IM's imaginary (and arguably "authentic") path up to Tx (see Figure 6.2 (b)). Thus, the temporary *origo* shared among the participants at this point is set at Tx (lines 1–4). The main speakers here are B1 and B2, who climbed the M Route starting from Ty through Tx and onward (Figure 6.2 (b)). Thus, with regard to this segment, the statement "the opposite way [to the one] we went" (line 9) indicates the spatial movement from "Tx to Ty." If we examine B1's hand gesture closely, we see that he stretches his arm to B2 at *bokura ga* ("we") and retracts it at *itta* ("went")—an emblem interpreted conventionally in Japan as referring to himself or "come" (line 9 (a)). Since the shared temporary *origo* is Tx, this hand gesture translates into the movement from Ty (= B2) to Tx (= B1) (Excerpt 6.3.1 (b)). Because B2 does not yet share the same spatial configuration as B1's at that point (B2's fully heuristic moment must wait until line 19), B1 probably assumes it to be more comprehensible to temporarily situate B2 at Ty, from which they traversed to Tx in the climb.

However, this retracting gesture (indicating a "coming" movement and self-reference) obviously contradicts the propositional meaning of *itta* ("went"), which is a phenomenon of what may be called the "mind–body split," or the utterance–gesture mismatch. Moreover, through B1's consecutive gestures, the spatial configuration envisioned by B1 changes shape gradually as the discussion progresses. In line 15, B1's gesticulations develop to the next stage by relocating Ty in front of B2 and conceptualizing them as equivalent. We can assume this is the case because at that moment he stretches his right arm toward the camera operated by D1, the researcher (line 15 (c)), not toward B2 (as the case in line 9 (a)). B1 then mentions to B2, "you remember where we traversed to the left" (lines 15–16), retracting his right arm to himself again and depicting the path they took from Ty to Tx (line 16 (d)). He elaborates on the same path again in line 18, but in the opposite direction from Tx to Ty, as seen in "we need to go right on that trail" (line 18 (e)). Notice that a different starting point is employed here, but the current *origo*, Tx, is maintained with a schema like "Tx ⇆" in terms of "traverse to the left" and "go right." From these gesticulations, we see that B1 tries to share his schema by projecting it in front of B2 (Excerpt 6.3.1 (f)). Plate (f) shows that B1's pointing direction is "to the right" viewed from B2's seating position, and thus B1's retracting gesture in Plate (d) represents a movement "to the left (Lt)," or "Ty to Tx."

Provided with B1's reformulations of space, B2 excitedly exclaims *Aa!* indicating that it was a heuristic revelation to him. He then self-assures that *atchi-gawa kara kuru kara machigaeru noka* ("[we] make mistakes because [we] come from the other side"; line 19), via which he identifies himself with B1's temporary *origo* at Tx, as is evidenced by his use of *atchi-gawa kara* ("from over there") and *kuru* ("come"). Although the distal deictic root "a-" in *atchi* originally refers to an object equidistant from both the speaker and the listener, it also indexes a shared memory or common knowledge among discourse participants (Kuno 1973). Since B1 and B2 are the only pair that passed this portion of the trail/route (from Ty to Tx) (see Figure 6.2 (b)), this fact legitimizes him to say *atchi-gawa kara kuru* ("come from the other side") to represent the movement. In addition, the final particle *noka* (*no* + *ka*) represents a belated (and regretful) realization of the missteps taken so far, confirming what is right and wrong (or left) with the spatial configuration that is finally shared. Through "trading places" like this, B1 and B2 successfully achieve a dialectical merger by diverting into two selves, or the "mind–body split," to draw on a widely used phrasing. Obviously, it is not simply a split but a merger, which eventually serves to prompt the grounding and creation of a shifted *origo*.

In effect, the process does not stop there. What is more interesting is A1's subsequent gesticulations, prompted by B1 and B2's verbal, gestural, and place exchanges. Their intersubjective perspective is now picked up by A1, who appropriates it ingeniously to his advantage (Excerpts 6.3.2). Among other participants in the tent, A1 seems to have more trouble figuring out the overall configuration of the scene—he does not utter a word even though he actually turns out to be the most loquacious participant. However, in line 20, A1 claps his hands (an emblem of sudden awareness in Japan), abruptly exclaiming, *A!* ("Oh!"), and uttered *gya-* ("opposi-"), which is truncated before completion (line 21 (g)). The reason for the truncation is still speculative, but he may have wanted to avoid the confusion with B2's preceding use of *gyaku* ("opposite") because B2's *gyaku* (Tx ← Ty) and A1's *gyaku* (Tx → Ty) indicate contradictory directions at this moment.

After the truncation, A1 quickly repairs it as *kotchi* ("this way"), with a hand gesture pointing to the space in front of B1 (line 21 (h), (i)), only to abandon it once more. We see from his use of the *ko-* deictic root and pointing gesture that A1 tries to ride into the imaginary space previously constructed by B1 (compare Excerpt 6.3.1 (f) and Excerpt 6.3.2 (i)). However, the phrase that A1 finally selects both circumvents the risk of confusion and guarantees his experiential basis. In line 23, A1 tries to somehow specify the trail (between Tx and Ty) by referring to *asoko no ban-(do)* ("that rock ban(d)"). As is evident from the use of the distal *a-*deictic (indexing shared knowledge) in *asoko*, his referential field switches from B1's space (referred to by the proximal "*ko-*" deixis) to A1's virtual space (referred to by the distal "*a-*" deixis) by setting up Ty and the rock band in front of him (Excerpt 6.3.2 (n)). Here, the spatial parallelism exists between "B2's and B1's seating positions" and "Ty and Tx" ("B2 : B1 :: Ty : Tx"). This schema is more grounded physically and available publicly, so A1 starts to manipulate it for his own purposes.

A1 pushes his hands forward to B2 (i.e., the imaginary "Ty": line 23 (j)), setting B2 as the starting point of the following slide gesture toward B1 (imaginary "Tx") and embodying their spatial movement from Ty to Tx with both hands (line 24 (k)). In addition, A1 makes a holding gesture with his palms upward, and the shape could encode his delicate consideration toward B1 and B2. First, pointing with a palm upward is a polite form of finger-pointing in Japan, and thus this represents politeness toward B1, who is a senior member in the club. Second, both B1 and B2 move along the path together, and this fact is represented by the two-handed sliding gesture that follows. Remember that A1 previously used a two-handed gesture to represent the action conducted by "plural" significant actors (A1 and A2).

Whether he consciously managed it or not, A1's final comments are highly strategic because he eventually succeeds in snatching the current *origo* (Tx) from B1 and shifting it to the next (Ty), where he is assumed to reside. First, building on

THE BODY AND DEICTIC VERBS OF MOTION IN IMAGINARY SPACE   123

EXCERPT 6.3.2 *A1's perspective gestures (3)*.

```
20  A1:  A!
         **  ((clap hands))
         Oh!

21       Gya- kottchi-
         ****|*****  ((pointing))
         'Oppos- This way-'

22       A, jaa nani,
         -.-.-.-.-.|~~~  ((pull BH to his chest))
         'Oh, you mean,'

23       asoko no ban-
         ******-.-.-.|  ((BH pushing))
         'that rock ban-'

24       Semai ban- bando mitaina toko o
         ~~~~*******************|  ((BH slide))
         'narrow ban- along something like a rock band'

25       gyaku kara kurun da.
         ~~~~*******|-.-.((RH pulling))
         'we must come from the other side.'

26  B2:  Un un.
         'Yeah yeah.'

27  A1:  ((A1 turns to B2))
```

(g) 'Oppos-'

(h) 'this way'

(i) A1's place deictic embodiment (abandoned)

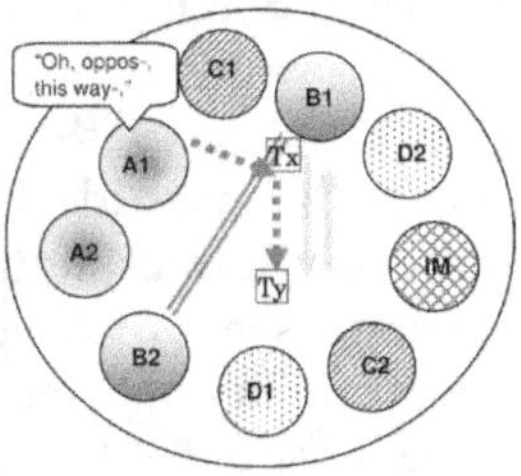

(j) 'that (rock ban-)' 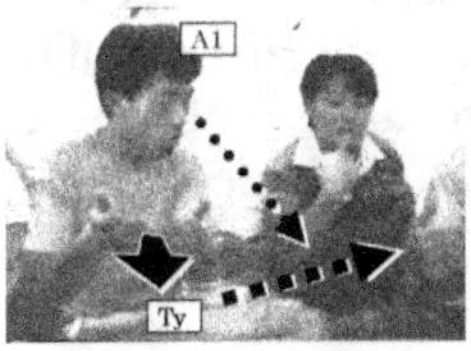   (k) 'like a rock band' 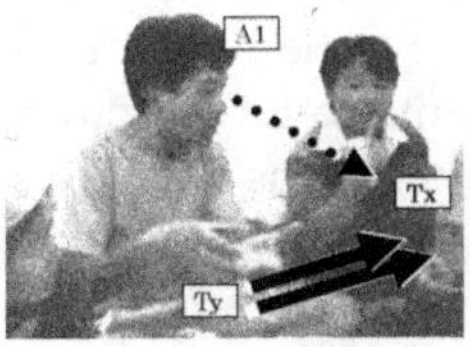   (l) 'from the other side' 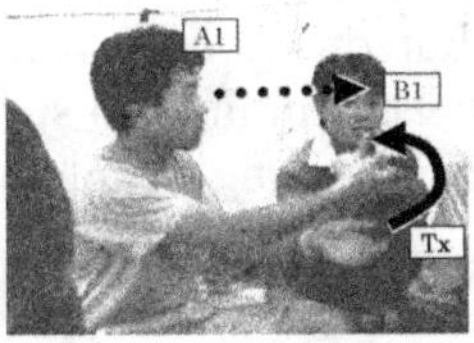   (m) 'come'

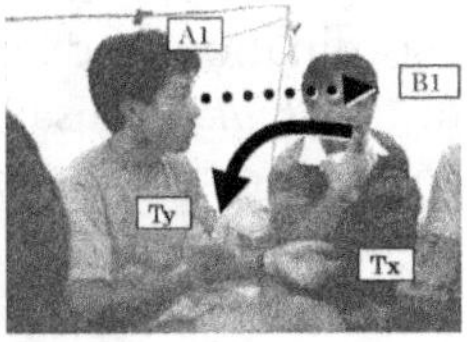

(n) Sequence of A1's performance

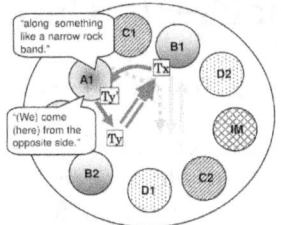

multiple repairs of *bando* ("rock band") in lines 23 and 24, he reiterates it as *semai bando mitaina toko* ("something like a narrow rock band"), and finally re-introduces *gyaku* ("opposite"; line 25 (l)), saying *gyaku kara* ("from the opposite side") with his left hand left beside B1 (i.e., Tx) and his right hand pulled to himself (a new *origo*, or Ty) with *kuru* ("come"; line 25 (m)). This way, the originally contradicting directions represented by *gyaku* is now compromised to make sense. This pulling gesture co-occurs with the DMV *kuru*, which serves to authenticate A1 (at Ty) as the new *origo*. Now, with the nodes Tx and Ty connected through the process, all the participants seem to comprehend the holistic picture of the scene, and A1 ultimately controls the following discussion.

As was initially theorized by Bühler (1982 [1934]), any "oriented" entity, including a human body, has the potential to project multiple coordinates with which a certain angular specification becomes available. For example, human body parts—head (face), hand, torso, foot, etc.—may possibly project a coordinate system (RLFB or up/down) based respectively on their intrinsic orientations, and some body parts may even allow rotation, lamination, or bending of the coordinate. In the abovementioned case, we may then ask: Which body part served as the basis for the coordinate expression that B1 employed? As can be postulated from the previous observations, it seems to be the speakers' torso-based coordinate that contributed to the spatial-configuration calibration (see also Schegloff, 1998 on "body torque"), as is the case with this circular "F-Formation" (Kendon 1990) in a multiparty interaction.

To sum up, with respect to the abovementioned cases, their intersubjective perspective was made available only by the participants' being there at that time, with bodily orientations in that particular formation and environment. For the shared goal of making sense of their experience-based perspectives, intersubjectivity presupposes "the possibility of being in the place where the Other is" (Duranti 2010: 1), and it may not necessarily be the "effect" or "product" of interactional intentions. However, real interaction poses a question to an extreme version of such intellectual extension devoid of the body and environmental affordances in place. Given this, intersubjectivity in an interaction provides us with a focalized porthole into the workings of the embodied coordination of distributed cognitions. At the same time, the systematic applicability of the *iku/kuru* usage is not limited to such micro-level interaction as seen above—it could also serve as an underlying template that spans a longer stretch of interaction.

6.5 Poetic Construction of Denotational and Interactional Texts Through Deixis

6.5.1 Denotational Meaning of Japanese DVMs

In this section, I present a synthetic account of (1) denotational patterning encoded by *iku* and *kuru*, the distribution of which serves to indexically construct a multi-segment poetic structure; and (2) an interactional patterning of social inequality reflected by the choice and the tense forms of DVMs. The point of this section is to see how the discursive interaction in discussing the cause of a "fall" accident converged "centripetally" on IM's authoritative perspective through the use of deictics and perspective shifts lodged on the conspicuous landmarks on the route. In effect, the experientially differentiated perspectives of the participants became adjusted to those of the expert through heuristic revelations of expert knowledge and interactionally emergent social relationships.

It should be noted here again that when the speaker is the agent of *kuru*, as is the case with our data, the use of *kuru* strongly indexes the speaker's arrival or perception at Goal (see Figure 6.1). It further connotes the first-hand experience of being/getting there regardless of the hearer's presence or absence in the scene. In contrast, the motion represented by *iku* could be either the speaker's departure from Source, arrival at Goal, or progress along Path; as a result, its indexical value cannot be determined. In this respect, we could assume that the indexical potential for encoding the notion of *origo* is higher for *kuru* than for *iku*. In English, however, the use of *come* with the first-person singular subject still under-specifies whether the territory indicated by *come* is the speaker's or the hearer's, which represents a lower indexical value about the *origo*.[12]

Given this background, it is expected that the effect of using such DVMs exhibits certain semiotic values and can be captured in terms of both "denotational" and "interactional" texts (Silverstein 1985, 1993, 2004). It is denotational in that by binding the speaker's perspectives to salient vantage points, the verbs may serve as indexical cohesion devices and topic boundary markers. Such a DVM is also interactional in the sense that it covertly projects the underlying social order and evolving human relations in the collaborative effort of imagery-building. Based on these observations, I claim that the use of COME and GO in the present text is coordinated in a highly systematic way in terms of a "poetic" structure even in this multiparty, heavily overlapped discourse.

6.5.2 Denotational- and Interactional-text Construction

The following excerpt (Excerpt 6.4) focuses on the salient landmarks concerning Section 3 in Figure 6.2, and is a longer, but partially simplified, version of Excerpts 6.3.1 and 6.3.2. This part of the discussion occurs at the final stage of the search and leads to the "discovery" of the holistic spatial organization of the landmarks. The schematic map of the scene is reproduced in Figure 6.3. The thick dotted line marked by "IM" indicates what he claims to be the original trail to reach the starting point of the M and H-S Routes, unlike those taken by the current participants (except C1 and C2).

EXCERPT 6.4 *Heuristic moment*

1)	IM:	*Iya, hajime wa nee,*	IM:	Well, at the beginning, we
2)		*yasashii rijji dakara-tte,*		wonder if we should use a rope
3)		*zairu tsukeyoo ka dooshiyoo*		cuz it's an easy ridge. That's
4)		*ka-tte yuu gurai no tokoro o,*		where we **go** climbing (to take
5)		*koo nobotte **iku** wake ne.*		on M Route).
6)	C1:	*M:::m.*	C1:	Uh:::n.

EXCERPT 6.4 *Heuristic moment*   continued.

7)	A1:	E::hehe?	A1:	Wha::t?
8)	IM:	Ano, T1 kara.	IM:	I mean, from T1.
9)	B1:	M::m.	B1:	Hmmm.
10)		Wakaru wakaru.		I understand, I understand.
11)		Kyoo, [kyoo **kita-**		That's where (we/you) **came-**,
12)		nobotta toko.] ((to C1))		((to C1)) you climbed today.
13)	C1:	[Kyoo watashira ga **kita**,]	C1:	It is the route where we ((to C2))
14)		iki kaketa tokoro?		came--,started to **go**?
15)	C2:	Ah::, asoko ka!	C2:	I see, there!?
16)	B1:	[XXX de **itta** tokoro]	B1:	That's where you **went** xxx.
17)	A1:	[Do- do- do- doko doko	A1:	Wh- wh- wh- where where where
18)		doko doko?]		where?
19)	D1:	[aa aa aa.]	D1:	Oh, oh, oh. ((nodding))
20)	C2:	Watashira ga **nobottetta**	C2:	The trail(/ridge) we ((to C1))
21)		[tokoro.]		**went** climbing, you know.
22)	B1:	[Soo soo] soo soo.	B1:	Yeah, yeah, yeah, yeah.
23)	A2:	[Henna hoo] kara	A2:	I know you guys **came** out from
24)		dete **kita** ne.		a strange place.
25)	B1:	Soo soo soo.	B1:	Yeah, yeah, yeah.
26)	B2:	Ah: [soo soo soo.]	B2:	Oh, yeah, yeah, yeah.
27)	C2:	[Watashira ga] nobotte **kita**	C2:	That's the trail on the ridge,
28)		henna rijji mitaina [toko].		along which we **came** climbing.
29)	IM:	[Honde] are ga, horekara--	IM:	And, that is, then--
30)	D2:	[Are ga:,] wanpitchime-tte koto?	D2:	Is THAT the first pitch, you mean?
31)	C2:	[Are ga wanpitchime] nanda.	C2:	That is the first pitch, yes.
32)	B2:	[Un soo soo soo.]	B2:	Hm, yeah, yeah, yeah.
33)		[Are ga wan pitchi-me.]		That is the first pitch.
34)	IM:	[Wan-pitchi nobotta] tokoro kara	IM:	After you climbed one pitch,
35)		ne, ookii terasu atta ra?		there was a big terrace, right?
36)	A1:	Hai hai. Arimashita.	A1:	Yes, yes there was.
37)	IM:	Sokkara nee, mi[gie] za::tto	IM:	From there you **go** traversing
38)		torabaasu shite**kun** da.		all the way to the right.
39)	B1:	[Migi e]	B1:	To the right.
40)	B1:	Ah: yappari soo da.	B1:	Yes! That's what I thought.
41)		Bokura ga--,		You know, we--
42)	IM:	Migi e daaa-tto torabaasu shite(i) **ku**.	IM:	**Go** traversing further to the right, OK.
43)	B2:	Ah: ah:	B2:	I see I see.
44)	D1:	Un un.	D1:	Uhuh uhuh.
45)	B1:	Bokura ga saa, ((to B2))	B1:	You remember where we ((toB2))
46)		hidari ni torabaasu shita jan.		traversed to the left?
47)		[Are o migi ni **iku**.]		We need to **go** right on that trail!

48)	B2:	[Atchi-gawa kara] **kuru** kara,	B2:	Oh, we make mistakes because we
49)		machigaeru no ka.		**come** from the other side!
50)	A1:	Ah:, gya- kotchi- a- ja	A1:	Oh, the opposi- this way,
51)		nani, asoko no semai ban-		you mean, we should **come** from
52)		bando mitaina toko o,		the opposite side on that narrow
53)		gyaku kara **kuru**'nda.		rock band, right?
54)	A1:	Demo ne, boku ga ima yutteru no	A1:	But what I am talking about now
55)		wa ne, kono hangu nan desu.		is this overhang. ((open a map))
56)		Hoojoo-shinmura wa, kono hangu		Hoojoo-Shinmura Route runs on
57)		no kotchi-gawa o tootteru desho.		this side of this overhang.
58)		Sore wane sonna murishite		That (route) isn't so unnatural,
59)		konna fuu ni **itte** nain desu yo.		and doesn't **go** like this.
60)		Kekkoo sunao ni		So if you/we **go** straight up
61)		pyuuu-tto **agatte(i)ku** to,		naturally (along this line), you
62)		koko ni **kuru**-n desu yo.		**come** here, you know.
63)	C1:	Soo soo. **Kuru kuru**.	C1:	Yeah, yeah. We **come**, we **come**.

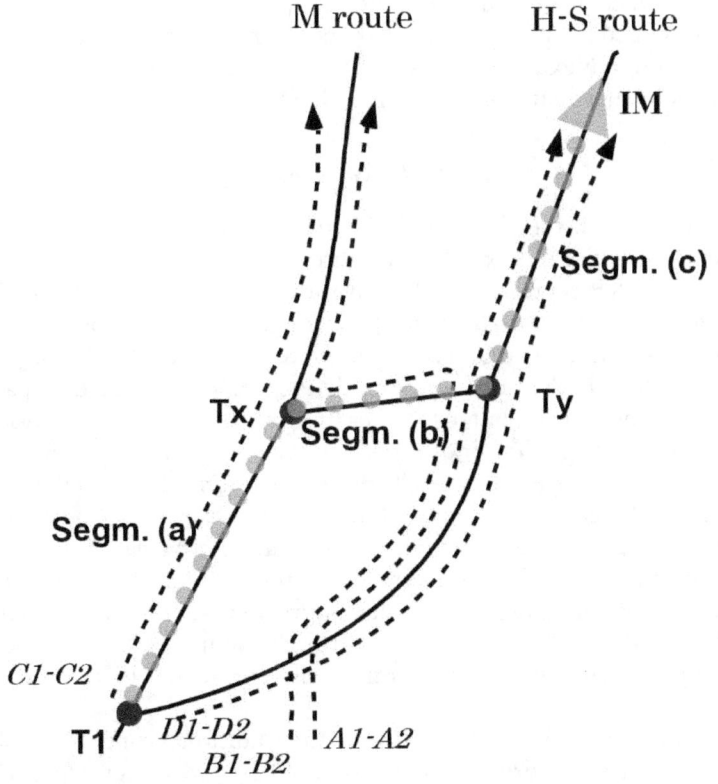

FIGURE 6.3 *Schematic map of the approach trails in Section 3.*

A general sequence of the climbers' discussion is as follows: The trigger for the heuristic moments is first given by IM, whose comments on the first pitch of M Route was questioned by other participants (lines 6–7). At that point, only B1 gives an affirmative response to IM's comments (line 10). B1's supportive comment in lines 11–12 helps C2 figure out the puzzling spatial relationships, and C2 offers a similarly constructive comment in lines 15, 20–1, 27–8, and 31. By line 33, most of the participants vaguely grasp the holistic picture of the scene, which lays the groundwork for a heuristic moment among the participants. The portion until here corresponds to Segment (a) in Figure 6.3.

Building on C2's explanations and IM's further comments (lines 34–5, 37–8), everyone in the discussion further determines the original line from which the H-S Route embarked, and the geographic relationships between Tx and Ty by line 53. This portion corresponds to Segment (b), which we examined in Section 6.3.2. Although A1 did understand the spatial relationships, he still poses a question about the authenticity of the M Route indicated by IM, by pointing out the route's discrepant spatial relation to the H-S Route (lines 54–62). His comments, however, are not addressed after B1's response in line 63. This portion (lines 54–63) stands for Segment (c).

Let us now examine the use of Japanese DVMs in more detail. The participants used them more frequently here than in other portions of the text, probably for the purpose of identifying and relating the geographic landmarks in their mental maps-in-the-making. Once grounded in a mental map, these landmarks could be utilized as pivots onto which the participants could hook their emergent vantage points with these motion verbs. Next, we look into the participants' spatial descriptions with respect to which participants uttered which DVMs.

6.5.2.1 Segment (a)

Segment (a) deals with the progression from T1 to Tx. Table 1 shows the phrases, including spatio-temporal deixis, DVMs, and relevant features. The fourth and fifth columns from the left represent the locative notions related to a respective DVM—S(ource), P(ath), G(oal), and D(irection), although each clause does not necessarily include explicit locative expressions. Also, the treatment of the notion Path is quite broad here. I include in the category not only the elements denoted by path locatives (e.g., "on/along (the trail)"), but also other phrases that refer to a portion of path or describe its features (e.g., "the trail on which we went climbing"). As noted above, *kuru* always connotes "speaker('s territory)-as-goal," and thus is deictic and strongly indexes Goal, whereas *iku* usually (but not necessarily) encodes orientational connotation such as "speaker('s territory)-as-source." *Iku* can equally represent a neutral motion that is neither from nor toward the speaker's/hearer's territories, and thus it may or may not be deictic or index Source. First, I summarize what portions of the trails are "denoted" or "indexed" through the use of DVMs. The right-most column in Table 2 refers to the temporal deixis represented by the *-ru/-ta* (roughly, PRS/PST) forms.

In (1) of Table 6.2, IM started to delineate the traditional route from T1 to Tx. His current deictic center was firmly established at T1 by the Source expression *T1 kara* ("from T1"; line 8), preceded by the "departure" and "short-range" path motion encoded by the compound expression *nobot-te ik-u* ("go climbing"; line 5). In addition, IM cannot legitimately use the *–ta* (PST) form (*it-ta* ("went") and *ki-ta* ("came")) as others do, because he did not participate in the specific climb referred to here. Thus, he instead used *iku* ("go") in the *–ru* form (PRS), and by choosing to use the form, he seemed to assume the status of an outsider (and an expert), who could act as an omniscient observer from a "nomic" (Silverstein 1993) perspective.

On the other hand, other members actually participated in the climb on that particular day and are confined to their experiential status. For (2) and (3) in Table 6.1, the situation is a little more complicated. B1, who is talking to C1, his wife, first uses *ki-ta* ("came"; line 11), but corrects it immediately with *nobot-ta* ("climbed"). Because Tx is not yet identified and shared conceptually, B1 may have felt it premature to conceptually finalize the segment with the goal-indexing verb *kur-u* ("come") at that moment. The same phenomenon is observed in (3). This was C1's overlapping

Table 6.1 Sequence of iku/kuru *across Participants in Section (a).*
Keys: E.g., "1/5" = "Token #/Line #": Spkr = speaker: H-T = Haimatsu Terrace; S(ource), G(oal), D(irection), P(ath); loc. = locative; Denoted = 'explicitly elaborated (by locative and relevant expressions)'; Indexed = 'covertly and associatively connoted by DVMs'

#/Line: Spkr	Segment (a): <T1 – Tx>	Notes	Iku (+ loc.)	Kuru (+ loc.)	ru/ta form
(1) 5,8 : IM	*nobot-te ik-u* ... *T1 kara* (S) 'go climbing ... from T1'	S denoted	S = T1	--	*ru*
(2) 11: B1	*kyoo ki-ta, nobot-ta* (paraphrased) *toko* 'where (= the trail on which) (you) came, climbed today'	G attempted but paraphrased	--	(G)	*ta*
(3) 13: C1	*kyoo watashira ga ki-ta, iki kake-ta* (paraphrased) *tokoro* 'where (= the trail on which) we (C2 & C1) came, started to go today'	P denoted, G attempted but abandoned	P	(G)	*ta*
(4) 16: B1	*it-ta tokoro* 'where you went'; presumably describing C1 and C2's Path on T1-Tx.	P (betw. T1 & Tx) denoted	(P)	--	*ta*
(5) 20: C2	*watashira ga nobot-te(i)t-ta tokoro* '(the place/trail) where we went climbing'	P (betw. T1 & Tx) denoted	P	--	*ta*
(6) 23: A2	*henna hoo kara de-te ki-ta* '(you) came out from a strange place'	S denoted, Entry into Sp's perception	--	S (≠ T1) G (≠ Tx)	*ta*
(7) 27: C2	*watashira ga nobot-te ki-ta henna rijji* 'something like a ridge along which we came climbing (to Tx)'	P denoted, Tx as G indexed	--	P G = Tx	*ta*

response to B1's statement. C1 first uses *ki-ta* ("came", but abandoned it instantly, and repairs it with *ik-i kake-ta* ("started to go"). Again, this switch indicates a re-setting of her vantage point onto T1 rather than onto Tx[13], presumably because she was not yet certain if the portion under discussion corresponds to the trail she actually climbed. Given these observations, B1's and C1's switch to the neutral or less indexical terms "climbed" and "went" seems to be motivated by the premature construction of Tx as Goal.

At this moment, it is difficult to identify the location referred to in *it-ta tokoro* ("where you went") in (4), but it seems to indicate the path from T1 to Tx. Moreover, in (5), C2, the climbing partner of C1, clearly refers to the intermediate path between T1 and Tx, as is indicated by the motion compound *(nobot-te) it-ta* ("went [climbing]"). However, this consistency of the deictic center is suddenly violated by A2, who reaches Ty, and goes on the H-S Route with A1. Given the abovementioned observation, one may wonder why A2 is able to use *ki-ta* ("came") despite the fact that she never reaches Tx. In fact, however, *kuru* ("come") does not necessarily indicate the reaching motion to Goal/Speaker, but can simply indicate the entry into the speaker's perceptual domain. Since A2 was at Ty when C2 and C1 popped out on the ridge near Tx, her compound phrase *de-te ki-ta* ("came out"; 6) properly describes C2's/C1's unexpected entry into her perceptual (precisely, visual) domain observed from Ty. With A2's confirmatory comment, C2 is more confident of her mental map and feels justified using *ki-ta* (7).

Thus far, the schematic motion constructed by the participants is clearly linear. Its movement, with or without denoting and/or indexing elements, was deconstructed and elaborated systematically by the alternations of *iku/kuru* phrases in such a way that the earlier phase of the motion was depicted spontaneously by *iku* and the latter phase by *kuru*, with no specific cues for the shift. As will be shown, not only is the DVM distribution systematic, but the tensal shift also seems to rely on a different mechanism that is now emerging to reflect the asymmetric relationship between IM and the other participants.

6.5.2.2 Segment (b)

This Segment (b) was the focus of multimodal analysis of the previous section. By line 34, the trail T1–Tx was identified to be the first pitch of the M Route. The next question is how to embark on the M and H-S Routes from Tx. IM continues to describe the next motion rightward, again with the *–ru* form as he did in Segment (a): *migi e za::tto torabaasu shi-te ik-u* ("go traversing all the way to the right") (Table 6.2 (1)). This explanation translates into the spatial motion from Tx to Ty. Notice first that IM explicitly mentions the source, *wan pitchi nobot-ta tokoro kara* ("from where you climbed one pitch (i.e., Tx)"), then paraphrased it to *sok-kara* ("from there"). IM corroborates the induced shift with the repeated utterance *Migi e da::tto torabaasu shite(i)ku* ("go traversing further to the right") ((2): line 42).

For B1, the next user of *iku* (3), this movement (Tx => Ty) was the opposite of his actual progression—he traversed from Ty to Tx. Because the current deictic center is Tx, B1 follows the current orientation denoted by IM by situating his *origo* at Tx. We have already seen in the previous section that this process leading to the heuristic moment was achieved meticulously through intersubjectified corporeality by

Table 6.2 Sequence of **iku/kuru** *across Participants in Section (b).*

#/Line: Spkr	Section (b): <Tx – Ty>	Notes	Iku (+ loc.)	Kuru (+ loc.)	ru/ta form
(1) 34, 35, 37, 38: IM	*wan pitchi nobotta tokoro kara* (S) ... *sok-kara* (S) *migi e* (D)... *torabaasu shi-te(i)k-u* 'from where you climbed one pitch, from there, go traversing to the right'	S, D denoted	S = Tx, D	--	*ru*
(2) 42: IM	*migi e* (D) ... *torabaasu shi-te(i)k-u* 'go traversing to the right'	D denoted	D	--	*ru*
(3) 47: B1	*are o* (P) *migi ni* (D) *ik-u* 'go right there (on the trail)'	D, P denoted	D, P	--	*ru*
(4) 48: B2	*atchi-gawa kara* (S) *ku-ru* 'come from the other side'	(S denoted) (G indexed)	--	(S = Ty) (G = Tx)	*ru*
(5) 52-53: A1	*bando mitaina toko o* (P) *gyaku kara* (S) *ku-ru* 'come (to Ty) from the opposite side on that trail like a rock band'	S, P denoted, G indexed	--	S (= Tx) P G = Ty	*ru*

switching the vantage points from Tx and Ty among multiple participants (IM, B1, B2, and A1). In this segment also, we can confirm a systematic sequence in which the earlier phase of the motion was invariably described by *iku* and the latter phase by *kuru*, without any specific cues.

Notably, there is another type of convergence emerging in terms of "tense" in this segment. Below, it is shown that the choice of tenses is an implicit means of constructing the "interactional" text in this collaborative wayfinding. Remember that back in Segment (a), the participants (except for IM) rely wholly on the *–ta* form to describe the spatial motion. However, after the heuristic moment, the participants acknowledge IM's spatial imagery as authentic and use it as the template for the spatial imagery building. This is when they all switched to the *–ru* form in Segment (b). In other words, they switch their stance from their experience-based distal perspective *then-and-there* (the *-ta* form) to the IM's expert, "nomic" perspective associated with the *-ru* form. This shift toward IM's authority indexes a temporal—in addition to spatial—alignment with the deictic center, and it covertly reveals the interactional text in the making in this particular indexical ground.

In this sense, the following Segment (c) exhibits an interesting twist, or a slight deviation from the current discussion, but it also supports our assumption about the asymmetric use of DVMs.

6.5.2.3 Segment (c)

At this moment, A1 still seems a little confused and indeterminate about the general spatial configuration. He suddenly opens up a route map (line 54), holds it up, and starts questioning the presumed location of Haimatsu Terrace (H-T) (from line 54),

Table 6.3 Sequence of **iku/kuru** across Participants in Segment (c).

#/Line: Spkr	Segment (c): <Ty – Haimatsu-T >	Notes	Iku (+ loc.)	Kuru (+ loc.)	ru/ta form
(1) 59: A1	*konna fuu ni **it-te** nai* '(that) doesn't go like this'	S, D, P gestured	(S, D, P)	--	*ru*
(2) 61: A1	*sunao ni pyuuu-tto agat-te(i)k-u* 'you/we go straight up and fast (along this line)'	D, P gestured	(D, P)	--	*ru*
(3) 62: A1	*koko ni* (G) ***ku-ru*** '(we) come here'	G gestured, denoted, and indexed	--	G G = H-T	*ru*
(4) 63: B1	***ku-ru, ku-ru*** '(we) come, (we) come'	G indexed	--	G = H-T	*ru*

saying "(that) doesn't go like this" (Table 6.3 (1)) and "(you/we) go straight up (along this line)" (Table 6.4 (2)). Although the source of movement is not denoted, it is supplemented instantly by his finger-pointing gesture onto the map and the sliding gesture from Ty to H-T in the map—i.e., source, direction, path, and goal are all gesticulated in order.

Here again, *iku*s precede and *kuru*s follow. The final set of *kurus* are anchored at the end of the first pitch of H-S Route. The first was uttered by A1 (Table 6.3 (3)), and it is then echoed twice by B1 (Table 6.3 (4)), who had climbed H-S Route several years before. B1 acknowledges A1's statement with the duplication *kuru kuru* ("we are coming (there), we are coming (there)") in the *-ru* form, indicating again that this is a shared interpretation and a widely accepted fact. Given B1's previous experience, it would be possible to see his use of the *-ru* form (present tense) as motivated by a (pseudo-)expert status similar to IM's.

Going back to A1's abrupt move to take the floor in line 54, I suspect that another social and interactional motivation is lurking behind it—presumably, A1's resistance against the imposition of the "authentic" view of IM, who pre-determinatively acts as a "ritual" leader of the discussion. Although A1 is not as experienced as IM, he is one of the most energetic members and the leader of the present expedition. His authority is now being threatened by IM's presence, and it seemed to me he struggles to somehow resume his control throughout the discussion—as can be seen from his verbosity around the end of Segment (b) and onward. In fact, he jumps in and snatches the turn at the outset of Segment (c) with supportive material (a route map) for suppressing IM's authority. Actually, after the participants agree that the route map itself is incorrect and inappropriate to use, A1 declares the adjourning of the discussion and a recess for sleep, exerting his authority that has now been restored.

In addition, taking an overview of the sequential flow of turn allocation in this discussion, we notice an implicit parallel between the participants' experiential status and the opportunities of utterances. Table 6.4 shows the different experiential

Table 6.4 Different experiential status as to spatial segments.
* Those in parentheses are novices or a participant observer (D1); IM (bold), B1 (bold Italic), and D1 have climbed the routes before.
** B1 and C1 uttered kuru at the early stage, but abandoned it.

Place/path	Experiencer on nodes/segments	Users of *iku* 'go'	Users of *kuru* 'come'	Users of *migi/hidari* 'right/left'
Segment (a)				
Source: T1	C1, C2 *(D1,) (D2)	**IM**	---	
Path: T1-Tx	C1, C2	C1, C2, *B1*, **IM**	C2	
Goal: Tx	C1, C2, B1, B2	---	**[C1, *B1*] C2, B2	
Segment (b)				
Source: Tx	C1, C2, B1, B2	*B1*, **IM**	B2	*B1*, **IM**
Path: Tx-Ty	B1, B2	*B1*, **IM**	---	*B1*
Goal: Ty	A1, B1, B2, (A2, D1, D2,)	---	<u>A1</u>	
Segment (c)				
Source: Ty	A1, B1, B2, (A2, D1, D2)	<u>A1</u> (by gesture)	---	
Path: Ty~H-T	A1, (A2, D1, D2)	<u>A1</u>	---	
Goal: H-T	A1, (A2, D1, D2)	---	<u>A1</u>, *B1*	

statuses of the climb participants. We can easily confirm from the table that the speakers who used the DMVs "come/go" and the coordinate terms "right/left" are limited strictly to those who actually passed the segments of the routes under discussion ("Experiencer" column in Table 6.4). I hasten to add that B1 and IM should be exempt from the restriction: Both climbers can duly envision a large-scale spatial image based on their previous experience of climbing these routes, and thus they may legitimately and more confidently comment on any segments. At least with respect to the present data, the use of DMVs, coordinate terms, and the corresponding gestural performance seems to be aligned along these experiential parameters. One might claim that any team members should be able to make comments and/or suggestions without an experiential basis, but that was not the case in this discussion.

To summarize the shifts of spatial and temporal deixis used through this sequence, we could detect multiple layers of texts activated through the use of *iku* and *kuru*. First, the denotational "poetic" text (Figure 6.4 (1)) was constituted by an equivalent formation through repeated patterns of "going and coming." Second, the interactional text emerged through differential alignments in terms of authority and perceived social power through the tense shift (Figure 6.4 (2)). Especially after the "heuristic moment" onward, these two levels are subtly integrated through the conversion of individual and authentic perceptions by maintaining the poetic recursion, while concurrently merging into IM's authoritative nomic perspective.

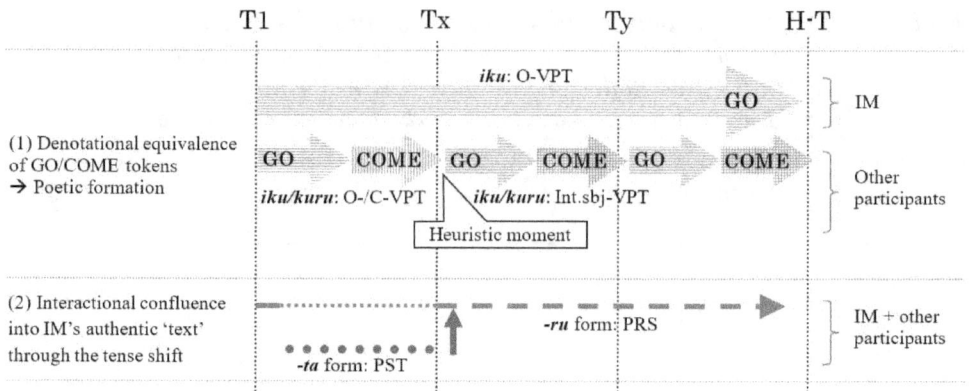

FIGURE 6.4 *Synthetic view of denotational and interactional texts.*

Previous linguistic studies on deixis and coordinate terms have implicitly assumed that "putting oneself in others' shoes" should be a pan-human ability and would be assured automatically and instantly through the mental process. Thus, these studies rarely addressed variable or unequal realizations of perspective-taking reflected upon language and the body. This study suggests instead that spatial perspectivization is not monolithic—it is at least partially experience-dependent and context-embedded, as well as a mutual/collaborative achievement rather than a natural endowment. In our data, a distinct experiential basis does matter, serving as a "certificate" via which a participant can participate confidently in spatial encoding and decoding as a qualified speaker.

6.6 Conclusion

In this chapter, by focusing on rock climbers' discussion of a "fall" accident that one of the parties encountered, we analyzed a micro-process in which the spatial descriptions/depictions from particular vantage points became focused and integrated *in situ* through collaborative wayfinding. Firstly, it was confirmed that the deployment of verbal and gestural features was differentiated cooperatively in terms of the "internal/external" perspectives mediated with "Character/Observer" VTPs. Specifically, the transfer of the *origo* and the subsequent mutual understanding were efficiently achieved by integrating the dispersed cognition of the participants through the process of "trading places" (Duranti 2010). Such a practice is obviously not an exclusive feat by rock climbers but rather an everyday practice of language users.

We identified four types of perspective-taking at the outset (Table 2.2). These types do not have equal status, but they can reveal contextual and cultural diversity in practice. At least, an extreme case of what we call an "intersubjective" perspective was made available only by particular participants who avidly negotiated for it. If intersubjectivity is a precondition to objectivity, it was no coincidence that particular participants (IM and B1), who were able to objectively envision the holistic picture from their previous experiences, took the initiator/coordinator roles of the intersubjective perspective-taking. Such an integrated perspective was not a "given" in our case but instead a construct wrought through the "triadic (bodily) mimesis" (Zlatev 2008), which was obviously another mode of *mi-wake* ("corporal division"; Ichikawa 2001: see Chapter 2) that we observed in Chapter 5, but on a horizontal plane here.

At a deeper level of understanding, however, not only the inter-subjectivity/-corporeality between individuals but also a shared sense of *ba* ("place/space/context") (Hanks et al. 2019; Shimizu 1998)—such as a habituated pattern of "going/coming" (and "leaving/arriving"), vertical and horizontal planes, schematic configurations of the narrated/narrating scenes, and so forth— need to be presupposed to interpret the phenomena we observed. In other words, the sharing of subjectivity and corporeality is not enough, but rather the sharing of situational awareness of *ba* is essential, as was postulated at the outset (Chapter 2). The tokens used for collaborative wayfinding were semiotic representations of "the secondary Ba," which presupposes the (partial) sharing of, and mediates (partial) representations of, "the primary Ba." In previous (mostly linguistic and philosophical) investigations, the speaker has been conveniently assumed to take others' perspectives quite freely by transposing the *origo* via intersubjectivity. While this might be true on the individual level, discourse participants need to share a sense of being in the contested space (or *ba*) in order to entertain the privilege of collaborative participation because the inequality of perspective-taking inheres at the discursive level of practice. In this very sense, an empirical treatment of language, the body, and the environment should be pursued rigorously to clarify what mode of perspective management may (or may not) happen naturally and instantly.

Second, naturally occurring interaction thrives on multiple levels of the semiotic import. One such distinction is of the denotational and interactional texts. On the denotational level of DVMs, there appears to be a highly consistent pattern in which *iku* tokens were used in the earlier phase of the segment and *kuru* tokens in the later phase, with both types distributed in a highly systemic way and aligned through conceptual "equivalence" (Jakobson 1960). More precisely, *iku* and *kuru* exhibited a salient time–space iconicity in discourse and functioned as a covert topic-boundary marker in such a way that the mental scanning of bounded trails began with Source/Path-denoting *iku* and ended with the Goal-indexing *kuru*. In this sense, *kuru* ("come") may serve as a covert "agreement" marker and evoke an epistemological conversion of the participants due to its centripetal progression to the deictic center. Also, *kuru* (and *iku* to a lesser degree) could be characterized as a covert "cohesion" device (Halliday and Hasan 1976) mobilized by the participants' collaborative shift and convergence of perspectives. The use of *iku/kuru* is thus based on the immanent poetics, which are not necessarily measured out in transparent poetic organization like feet, lines, verses, or other formally metricalized chunks, but rather are formulated by conceptually segmentable nodes and regions in the shared mental map. It is also shown that social configurations can be created tacitly and immanently through the participants' orderly convergence onto the expert's tense use in interaction. To be more specific, combined with the tensal shift of the *ru/ta* forms, the differential social order comes to be gradually legitimated through the forms and the distribution of DVMs. In this respect, although the conventional view of DVMs is principally true, it is overly semanticized because in actual discourse, the use of *iku* and *kuru* can be more efficiently captured in terms of the speaker's experiential basis and interactional status.

All these phenomena point to the importance of investigating the sequential vicissitudes of perspective maintenance and shift in discourse. More importantly in the situation presented in this chapter, they are organized systematically not only by the denotational poetic text, but also by the interactional text emerging *in situ*. In the next chapter, we will delve further into other cases of ongoing poetic formations of denotational and (inter)actional texts. The approaches taken to tackle the issue are "ethnopoetic" and "chronotopic" analyses of spatial configurations in the narration of near-death events.

7

Poetic Construction of Vertical Space and Chronotopic Analysis of "Fall" Experiences

7.1 Introduction

The main focus of this chapter is the possible interface between poetic and chronotopic configurations in narrative, and concerns the kind of linguistic and physical links realized through them. Specifically, I examine how the retelling of a nearly fatal rock-climbing event is related closely to "ethnopoetic" formations and "chronotopic" construction of epistemological values, and confirm that an involved narration can be represented in terms of highly poetic patterns in coordination with bodily actions and spatial imagery. Spatial transitions in narration have received considerable attention since the inception of discourse analysis as a criterion of the structural boundaries in narrative (Grimes 1972; Payne 1984; Longacre 1996; Hymes 1981, 1996; Keating 2015). For example, in Hymesian Verse/Stanza Analysis, transitions in time and space are major indicators of new verses or stanzas (or even scenes). Building on the contention of these precursors, I will show that the poetic construction of chronotopes is well motivated in climbing talks due to the place-specific encoding of experiences.

Chronotope (Bakhtin 1981), etymologically "time-space," is a notion that refers to the inherent inseparability of temporal and spatial relationships that are realized and fused into a coherent whole. As such, any images that have been socio-historically constructed through discourse are always regarded as chronotopic, and they define emergent genres and textual distinctiveness (Blommaert 2015, also De Fina and Perrino 2020). A typical example by Bakhtin is a chronotope of "the road," which evokes "encounter" and different "courses" of life. Such temporally and spatially created signs (or indexes, when realized as epitomized constructs) serve as an ideologized asset shared in each community. Along this vein, another example would be Basso's (1990) discussion of Western Apache place names, which reveal "the moral teachings of their history." The ambiguities inherent in Bakhtin's notion of chronotope led to variable conceptualizations the idea to accommodate different scales and phenomena, ranging from "minor" and "major" chronotopes (Morson and Emerson 1990), "micro," "minor/local," and "major/dominant" chronotopes (Ladin 1999,

2010), "kinship" chronotopes (Agha 2007b), and to "local" and "translocal" chronotopes (Blommaert 2015), among many others. According to Ladin (1999: 225–7), chronotopic relations are concatenated in a simple sequence, with the earlier chronotope replaced by the later version, and are constituted in dialectical relationships among (local) chronotopes, which may be paradoxical, compounded, and/or overlapping with each other. They can be contained in other chronotopes and thus are formed in hierarchical relationships. As such, the concept of the chronotope has been extended from literature, cinema, art criticism, and generally to the empirical study of language use (Perrino 2015; Blommaert and De Fina 2017).

Narration of climbing experiences exhibits a particular chronotopic configuration that is differentiated from those on the horizontal plane in terms of precarious positions and the acute awareness of gravity. A style called alpine climbing necessarily evokes specific chronotopic values among climbers owing to its activities conducted in the natural environment—e.g., temperature, altitude, weather, and rock formations, all of which may cause unexpected consequences. As such, a fatal and/or massive fall experience in mountains necessarily evokes particular affects owing to its emotional significance. Furthermore, the images embraced by rock/alpine climbers project ordinary narrative temporality (e.g., Labov and Waletzky 1967; Fleischman 1990) as well as a singular spatio-temporal iconicity due to the inherent activities such as "climbing/descending" and "leaving from/arriving at home base," both of which can emerge in an (ethno)poetic formation meshed with the narrator's cultural background and social relationships (Chapters 3 and 6: cf. Hymes 1981; Tedlock 1983; Kroskrity and Webster 2015).

Relying on such an interdependent coordination between chronotopic and poetic configurations, distinct narrative components are marked by the choice and switch of spatial descriptions and bodily depictions. It has been pointed out that vantage-point shifts in the topological structure are not haphazard, but rather mobilized collaboratively along with and across chronotopes (Basso 1990; De Fina and Perrino 2020; cf. Payne 1984). In the climbing and falling narratives under discussion, the speaker typically moved into the "co-eval" (Silverstein 2005; Perrino 2011) mode at the narrative's point of culmination. In other words, specific narrative components are highlighted and demarcated by particular verbal/nonverbal features that serve an indexical function comparable to the historical present (cf. Wolfson 1978; Schiffrin 1981; Sakita 2002) and the "indirect free style" of narration (or "free indirect speech" in Leech and Short [1981] 2007),[1] which "use the very locutions of the character to narrate what the character thinks, does, says still from the perspective of a narrator" (Silverstein 2005: 14).

The first distinction we must make is that between a narrated event and a narrating event (Perrino 2011; De Fina and Perrino 2020). A narrated event belongs to the past while the narrating event to the present, and in that sense, they belong to separate chronotopes, often marked by different deictic elements such as demonstratives, tense, and pronouns. In this vein, distinctive actions in ascending/climbing and descending/falling seem to belong to separate, and possibly "local," chronotopes owing to their experiential significance characterized by these actions. Such local chronotopes can be generated by the tension between contradictory forces even within a unit of verbal/nonverbal representations smaller than a sentence (Ladin 1999, 2010).

Despite these seemingly clear differences, there are many cases in which the two or more chronotopes do not have clear boundaries or are deliberately (or unconsciously) blurred. Some of these cases give rise to situations of what Silverstein (2005) calls "co-eval" alignment, in which those distinct chronotopes overlap spatio-temporarily. In such cases, the "past" and the "present" (or even the "imaginary") come to converge not only through verbal but also bodily representations. As articulated by Perrino (2007, 2015), one of the best-known strategies of co-eval cross-chronotope alignment is the "historical present" of narrative, where narrators shift into non-past deixis for events that are conceived of as past.

This case is one comprehensible instance that aligns separate chronotopes between the narrated event and narrating event. In the following, I examine how distinctive chronotopes constructed by the "narrated/narrating" and the "imagined/imagining" interface could also be achieved through bodily representations. Specifically, in one of the case analyses, the narrator's iconic gestures, occurring abundantly in Complication and Result/Coda, meta-discursively depict the events and actions before and after his massive fall in such a way that he perceives it as an omniscient observer, incorporating and coordinating cross-chronotopic configurations. I would take some types of gestures as a harbinger to the "breakthrough into performance" (Hymes 1966) because it often marks the beginning of the cross-chronotopic merger between "here-and-now" and "then-and-there" through his "constructed" performance (cf. Tannen 1989).

Discursive construction of the narrated world can be achieved not only through language, but also bodily representations (cf. McNeill et al. 2015; Rosborough 2016; Kataoka 2020). What is highly relevant to this analysis is McNeill's proposal that three different narrative levels (narrative, metanarrative, and paranarrative) are connected closely with particular gesture types such as iconic, deictic, and metaphorical gestures (see also Koven 2001, 2012 for similar distinctions of narrative levels). Under this assumption, different modes of gestural representations in the recalled scene could be recognized as indexes of distinct chronotopes that may not be noticeably demarcated by surface denotational features. Based on these observations, I will argue that climbing narrative is realized through local, embodied chronotopes that eventually constitute a major, vertical chronotope.

7.2 Targets and Methods of Analysis

In this chapter, I employ the ethnopoetic Verse/Stanza analysis (Hymes 1981, 1996, 2003) and findings from gesture studies (McNeill 1992, 2005) and combine them to help identify chronotopic configurations. Unlike Tedlock's (1983) emphasis on tonal performance, such as sound length, pitch, and intensity, Hymes (1981, 1996, 2003) focused more on structural patterns in lexical, morphological, and syntactic language forms. In this approach, the narrative text is first segmented into "lines" (1, 2, 3, . . .) according to combined intonation units, and then grouped into "verses" (a b, c, . . .), "stanzas" (A, B, C, . . .), and "scenes" (i, ii, iii, . . .) based on his criteria that lines are subsumed under verses, which constitute a stanza. Stanzas are further grouped and correlated according to rhetorical components of narrative. They also exploit lexical and syntactic features through culture-specific patterns and recurrence. It will be shown that with the exception of a couple of sections, the following Japanese texts largely conform to the oral patterns of threes (and fives), as previously confirmed in several studies (Minami and McCabe 1991; Masuda 1999; Kataoka 2009, 2010).[2]

To provide a general picture first, I briefly go over the focus items and the cues for segmentation (see also Chapter 2). What are found useful for identifying the constitutive units on the verse and stanza levels are generally "repetitions," "lexical ties," "oppositions," and "parallelism." On the line level, the narrators mainly rely on conjunctions such as *hoide/honde/soide* ("and/then"), as well as "time" (*hoshitara*, then"), *-no toki ni* ("at the moment of"), "space" (*-no tokoro de*, "at the place of"), and "causal" (*dakara*, "therefore" and *(-da) monde*, "because") connectives in their utterances. Also prominent are the use of discourse markers *ano(o)*, *sono(o)*, *e(e)*, and disfluencies, all of which indicate the speaker's inability to readily articulate what is in his/her mind owing to some psychological, social, or interactional constraint. These markers are assumed to serve "regulatory" functions and demarcate the cognitive boundary of utterances (Chafe 1994).

The connectives usually occur at both the beginning and the end of a line. Hesitation markers usually occur at the beginning. Also, some connectives such as *honde* and *dakara* tend to mark a new verse or stanza. Another type of line-marker includes final particles such as *ne*, *yo*, and *sa* (see Minami and McCabe 1991) and arguably *wake* and *n'da*.[3] Final particles are ordinarily seen as emotive arbitrators for interpersonal relationships. The command of these particles is an important repertoire of interaction skills, and they also represent a regulatory function in ongoing discourse. Here those connectives and particles are used to decode the speaker's affective orientation toward an event, which encapsulates a developing "idea unit" (i.e., line) in narration. Finally, a new verse may also start at the appearance, or inclusion, of mimetic expressions. Such expressions are almost always uttered with a heavy stress in the data, elaborating on the semantic and emotive information of a motion event with iconic gestures (Kita 1997; see also Dingemanse 2013 for a strong coupling between ideophones and iconic gestures in narratives in Siwu, Ghana).

Given that one motion event corresponds to one idea unit, paying attention to gestural co-occurrence with utterance (co-speech gestures) would be reasonable. As to the criteria for defining bodily representations in discourse, I found McNeill's (1992, 2005) classifications of gesture types and gestural perspectives highly useful. Above all, the suggestion that there are correlative relations between aspects of narration and gesture types (McNeill 1992) has brought new insights to recent narrative research. First, McNeill (1992) posited three levels of narrative in contrast to Labov's (seemingly) mono-stratal model (see Chapter 2 for a detailed exposition of gesture types). In the "narrative level," which Labov prioritized, events are described fundamentally but not necessarily in chronological order, and experiences and events are narrated mainly through iconic gestures based on the "Observer Viewpoint" (inside/outside-O-VPT) or the "Character Viewpoint" (C-VPT). The "meta-narrative level" is the level that refers to the structural components of the narrative (e.g., "First of all. . ." or "This is the end") rather than the chronological order of narrated content. This level corresponds to "abstract," "orientation," and "coda" in the Labovian model, and is assumed to be marked by "metaphorical" and "deictic" gestures. Finally, the "para-narrative level" concerns an interactional frame in which the narrator, stepping out of the narrated event, pays attention to the ongoing communication (e.g., "By the way, how old are you?" uttered in a narrative about binge drinking). No significant gestures have been noted in this level, but it is posited that "beat" and "deictic gesture" (pointing) may appear throughout all levels (McNeill 1992).

One phenomenon that holds gestural and discursive features in scope is the concept of "catchment" (McNeill 2005). Catchment refers to the recursive use of certain gestures across discourse, and it is assumed that the similarity of the underlying visual and spatial imagery makes it possible to trace back to underlying themes that are often overlooked in localized texts. Therefore, a catchment in discourse is expected to reveal hidden thematic coherence and provide a key to clarifying the mechanism of discursive cohesion. Also, highly relevant to our chronotopic interest is the use of onomatopoeia. Onomatopoeia can be thought of as one emergent form of chronotopic values in that it foregrounds distinct auditory, visual, and kinesthetic "qualia" (Harkness 2015). Owing to the perceptual proximity, onomatopoeia not only indicates that a speaker assumes a narrator role, but also triggers Character Viewpoint (C-VPT) because it evokes people's perceptual and experiential associations.

7.3 Analysis of Two Near-death Narratives by Japanese Climbers

In this section, we address two narratives told by Japanese alpine climbers. I closely examine the narratives by identifying ethnopoetic formations and corresponding bodily representations, both of which are mobilized to encode distinct chronotopic values. In this sense, an overt "denotational text" (Silverstein 1993) and a covert epistemic formation are corporeally coordinated to elaborate on local chronotopes of spatial scenes. In the following two narratives, the narrators relay their past climbing experiences to an interviewer. In this sense, they fall into the category of a canonical "big" story (Bamberg 2007; Georgakopoulou 2008), in which the "character" in the narrative, the "observer" of the scene, and the the narrator all overlap. Still, I assume a need remains to separate them so as to read out chronotopic representations accurately.

Because the following narratives are largely conversational, they include several "turn" exchanges, which are detached from the narrative main line. In a traditional narrative analysis, interactional elements have rarely been included in the narrative structuring because they are assumed to be irrelevant to the narrative content itself. However, prompted by conversation-analytic interest in the interactional relevance of narration, Hymes (1996) also proposed that conversational turns be treated as verses—a criterion which I also follow in this chapter. Palpably, the following narratives are not unilateral, but are accomplished collaboratively by interweaving reactive tokens and commentaries. These elements include not only exchanges consisting of typical adjacency pairs such as "Question-Answer (Q-A)," but also of various sets of "Initiation–Response–Evaluation (IRE)" chains (Mehan 1979), which occur frequently in educational and instructive settings. Following this, when considering the structural profile of the narratives, conversational chains such as "Question (by interviewer)–Answer (by narrator)–Comment (by interviewer)," with or without the final element, are also regarded as a subset of the IRE format. Those elements initiated by the interviewer K are written in the transcription as "<<K: >>." When producing transcriptions, I employed for the most part Du Bois et al's (1993) discourse transcription system, relying partially on the notations used in Conversation Analysis (Jefferson 2004).

7.3.1 Climber T on Cho Oyu: Falling into a Crevasse

7.3.1.1 Denotational Text Analysis

The first narrative to be examined is that of a renowned alpinist, who had an unexpected fall into a crevasse on his training expedition to Cho Oyu (8,188 m) in the Himalayas.[4] A crevasse can be massive and very deep, but in this case, he was fortunate to not fall too far and able to climb back up safely to the glacier's surface. In reality, he had a relatively narrow escape but told the story as if it were funny.

As mentioned previously, the following retelling outlines one of the climber's own past experiences, so is rather canonical from a narrative point of view. However, given the concept of gradient chronotopes, a seemingly single consistent narrative could be deconstructed and characterized in detail as the one comprising (local) chronotopes constructed by the narrator's physical gestures, including gaze and postures. I argue that it is a necessary step towards exploring the narrator's perception and representation of different realities within and outside the narrated scene. Thus, we look first into an overt level of narration that converges on an ethnopoetic formation and then focus on a covert level of coordination based on a multimodal chronotopic analysis.

In Excerpt 7.1, bounding features such as discourse markers (DM), conjunctions (CON), final particles (FP), and laughter are marked by gray shade in the transcripts, while onomatopoeias and quotations of utterance/thought are put in squares.

EXCERPT 7.1 *Falling in a crevasse at Cho Oyu.*

Ver.	St.		Line
Scene i: Abstract			
	I	<<K: *nadare igai dewa nai desu ka?*>>	
		<<'Are there anything else other than avalanches?'>>	
A	R/a	*kurebasu buchi-ochita-tte no wa ari-mashi-ta kedo.*	
		'(There was an incident that) I fell into a crevasse, but'	
		<<K: *buchi-ochite, demo-* [. . .>>	
		<<'You fell, but [. . .'>>	
	b	[*kore wa un ga yokat-ta.* ((external eval.))	
		'I was lucky in this case.'	

EXCERPT 7.1 *Falling in a crevasse at Cho Oyu*   continued.

	E	<<K: *un.*>> <<'Uhun.'>>	5

Scene ii: Orientation

A   a   *e: Cho Oyu nobori-itta toki-ni:*
'Uh: when I went to climb Cho Oyu,'

       b   *ano: C (1.5) 2 kana,*
'Ah:, at C2, I guess,'
    C2 made hayameni tsuite,
'I arrived early at C2.'

       c   *ma atakku no toki-de*
'Well it was the time of attack (of ascent),'

B   a   *de are wa jun'noo ga mokuteki no yama datta kara,*   10
'and the goal of the climb was to acclimatize ourselves,'
<<K: *un.*>>
<<'Ahun.'>>

       b   *koodoo wa sugoku raku de,*
'so the activities were very easy.'

       c   *san jikan gurai koodoo sureba ichinichi no koodoo wa owari to.*
'After about three hours of walk, the day's activities were over.'
<<K: *ha:n.*>>
<<'Ah:n.'>>

C   a   *de, sherupa ni niage mo shite-moratte,*   15
'We had Sherpas do all the transport,'
<<K: *u::n.*>>
<<'Hmm.'>>

       b   *de okyakusama taiguu de noboru dake datta kara,*
'and we were treated like guests, and all we did was climb.'
<<K: *n.* @>>
<<'Hm.' ((laugh)) >>

       c   *sugoi raku datta'nda kedo,* ((external eval.))
'So it was really easy.'

Scene iii: Complication~Orientation (suspense)

A   a   *de C2 ni tsuite,*   20
'and then we got to C2,'

       b   *moo chotto jun'noo-koodo shite okoo kana* to omotte,
'and I thought "I will do some acclimatization,"'

       c   *noo zairu de,*
'without (protection by) rope,'
    chotto ue made hyoko-hyoko-to shamen nobotte,
'I unsteadily climbed up a slope a little bit,'
<<K: *mh:m.*>>
<<'Uh huh.'>>

    Peak

B   a   *saisho koo naname ni nobotteta'nda kedo,*   25
'At first I climbed diagonally like this.'
<<K: *un.*>>
<<'Uhuh.'>>

EXCERPT 7.1 *Falling in a crevasse at Cho Oyu* continued.

	b	kudari wa massugu ikya hayaiya-tte kanji de,
		'but I thought, "it's faster if I go down straight,"'
	c	tento kara hon'no hyaku meetoru guraino tokoro de,
		'and it was only about 100 meters above the tent (at C2),'
	d	toko-toko-tto kudari hajime-tara,
		'so I started to descend steadily,'
	e	ikinari don to kurebasu o fumi-nuite, 30
		'and I suddenly stepped through a crevasse like "boom."'
		<<K: ↑he:>>
		<<'Wow.'>>

Orientation (Suspense)

C	a	kurebasu ga ano: yuki de kakuretete,
		'The crevasse was hidden by the snow.'
		<<K: a::n.>>
		<<'I seeee.'>>
	b	hidwun kurebasu ni natte-ta mon'da kara,
		'It was a hidden crevasse,'
	c	shamen de, 35
		'and on the slope.'

Scene iv: Result 1/Coda

A	a	nde, sokode
		'and then I...'
		ni meetaa gurai pon-to okkochita no kana.
		'fell down like "pomg" about two meters, I guess.'
	b	kedo tochuu ni iwadana ga atte,
		'But there was a ledge,'
	c	soko ni pa-tto tateta mon'da kara,
		'and I was quickly able to stand on it.'
		<<K: u:n.>> 40
		<<'hmmm.'>>
	d	dakedo shita mitara araa-tte kanji de. @@@@
		'But when I looked down, I was like "Wow!"' ((laugh))
		<<K: horaa moo->>
		<<'Oh that was-'>>
	e	yabak-[atta. ((external eval.))
		'It was a narrow [escape.'
	I	<<K: [hontoni un ga yok-atta.>>
		<<'You were really lucky.'>>
	R	un yabai-tte yuu. @@@ ((external eval.)) 45
		'Yeah totally a narrow escape.' ((laugh))

Scene v: Result 2/Coda

A	a	de maa pikkeru motte-ta kara,
		'and, you know, I had ice axes,'
	b	hieee-tte XXXX nobotte-
		'so I climbed crazily like "Yipes!"'
		haidashite. ((repair))
		'and crawled out,'
	c	de yuki-mamirede haidashitara=
		'and when I crawled out covered in snow,'

EXCERPT 7.1 *Falling in a crevasse at Cho Oyu*   continued.

	d	=min'na geragera waratte-tan' dakedo. @@@ 'everyone was guffawing at me.' ((laugh))	50
	I	<<K: @@ waratte-(rare)reba ii kedo ne::>> <<((laugh)) 'Lucky it was a laughing matter.'>>	
	e/R	=un are wa hijooni (0.5) kowa-katta. ✪✪✪ ((external eval.)) '=yeah I was very ... scared.' ((nods 3 times))	
	E	<<K: hu::n.>> <<'Hmmm.'>>	
	I	<K: moo shita su-....n nani mo nai kuu[doo d-atta?>> <<'It was a hollow space with nothing down below?'>>	
	R	[un nani mo nai, 'Yeah there was nothing,' nani mo nai-cchuu. 'nothing below.'	55

Addendum (Result 1'/Coda)

(A)	a	ma cho- kekkoo dekoboko wa atta kara, 'Well, the surface was a litt- pretty uneven, so'	
	b	dokka ni hikkakat-ta kamo shin'nai kedo, 'I may have gotten stuck somewhere, but'	

	c	ichiban ii tokoro de chanto,
		'precisely at the best spot,'
		  maa konna bando ga atte
		  'there was this band, and'
			60

	d	soko ni pon-tte yuu kanji de nokkat-ta kara, 'I fell on it like "pomg."' <<K: hu::n,>> <<'hmm'>>	
	e	are wa un ga yok-atta. ((external eval.)) 'I was so lucky.'	
	f	de maa hijooni yabai are deshita ne. ((external eval.)) 'And it was really a narrow escape.'	

As previously shown (Bright 1984; Fabb 2002; Kataoka 2009, 2010), the structure of Verse and Stanza in Hymesian ethnopoetic analysis is largely compatible with the boundaries of such narrative components as those defined in the Labov's model.[5] In order to doubly check the validity of ethnopoetic formations, I refer to both the Hymesian bottom–up approach and Labovian top–down methods. The narrative components thus classified are also shown in the Profile (Table 7.1).

Prompted by K's question, the narrative begins with the IRE (Initiation–Response–Evaluation) format that provides the rationale for the narrative, with which Abstract interlocks. This part, though brief, can be considered as Scene i because it sketches out the "bare bones" of the story that will be elaborated in the main narration. Scene ii consists of three stanzas, A–C, each of which contains three verses (abc), making up a fractal structure of tripled triplets. The particle *-(da)kedo* at the end of Scene ii, Stanza C (hereafter, abbreviated as "Stanza ii-C") is a conjunction that generally leads a subordinate clause, but in colloquial Japanese speech it is often used as an

Table 7.1 Profile of Crevasse-falling Narrative

Scene	Stanza	Verse	Features	Line	Narr. Component
		IR	Q-A	1, 2, 5	—
i	A	ab	Summary of narrative content	2, 4	Abstract
ii	A	abc	DM: e:, ano:, ma, CON: -te, -kara, FP: kana, toki 'time/when'	6-9	Orientation
	B	abc	CON: -kara, -de, -to.	10, 12-13	
	C	abc	CON: de, de, -te, kara, kedo.	15, 17, 19	
iii	A	abc	CON: de,-de, -te, start gesturing (O-VPT), quotation, mimetic	20-23	Complication ~ Orientation
	B	abcde	No initial CONs, higher proportion of "proximal" gestures, quotation, mimetics,	25, 27-30	(suspense~ Peak)
	C	abc	No initial CONs, Explanation of "hidden crevasse" in free clauses, separate gestures	32, 34-35	Orientation
iv	A	abcde	CON: nde, kedo, Proximal gestures, quotation, mimetics, laughter, ext. eval. at the end	36-39, 41, 43	Result 1/Coda
		IR	Assessment-acceptance	44-45	
v	A	abcde	Proximal gestures, quotation, mimetics, laughter, ext.eval. at the end	46-50, 52	Result 2/Coda
		IRE, IR	Comment-endorsement, Q-A	51, 52-56	
(vi)	(A)	abcdef	DM: ma(a), Elicited by K's Q, CON: de, DM: maa, Repeated ext.,eval. as Coda, use of ne	57-61, 63-64	(Addendum): Result 1'/ Coda

iisashi expression ("insubordination"), and the main clause is often omitted, as in this case.

Scene iii also consists of three stanzas, A–C, which respectively consist of the verse structure of 3–5–3. Although Scene iii begins with the conjunction *de*, no DMs or conjunctions are used at the beginning of the lines. The lack of these elements creates tension and a sense of urgency especially because this narrator use these elements so liberally at other times. (Notably, the narrator, who eschewed hand gestures until Stanza ii-C, started to use them frequently from Scene iii, as will be explained in the next section.) Also, Stanza iii-B corresponds to Peak, and only this stanza is told over five verses in Scene iii, which contributes to the strengthening of the suspense up to that point. In addition, although the fact of "stepping through a (hidden) crevasse" (which anticipates a serious consequence) is mentioned, its consequence is left untold. In the following Stanza iii-C, the result is also not mentioned, but instead an explanation is inserted as Orientation about why the crevasse was not seen, which further prolongs and enhances the suspense.

In particular, Scene iii and iv abundantly include mimetics. Onomatopoeia is used in Stanza iii-A to describe the awkward climbing action up the slope (*hyokohyoko*), and in Stanza iii-B he narrator describes the scene of walking down the slope by quoting his own thought, *kudari wa massugu ikya hayaiya* ("it would be faster to go straight down"). Following this quotation, the onomatopoeic *tokotoko*, which indicates a steady gait, and *don*, which indicates a sudden impact (of falling), are used consecutively. With these mimetics, the actions of "climbing and descending" and "walking and falling" are clearly contrasted and differentiated. K, the listener, also gives appropriate evaluations at the boundaries of Stanza iii-A and iii-B (lines 24, 31), which indicates that the participants tacitly recognize the narrative components and enhance their structure through appropriate actions.

Finally, in Scene iv, Result 1 is told. Although it is clear that the narrator T did not die, it is hard to imagine that he fell into a crevasse without any ominous consequences. In this case, he was caught miraculously by a ledge on the way down the crevasse and able to survive. The sense of urgency in Stanza iv-A is not as strong as it was in Stanza iii-B, because the beginning of each line is demarcated by conjunctions such as *nde*, *kedo*, and *dakedo*, which were entirely absent Stanza iii-B. However, there are some evaluative devices here to maintain the suspense that was heightened in Stanza iii-C. First, as seen in Peak (Stanza iii-B), the onomatopoeic expressions (underlined) *pon-to okkochita* (line 37) and *pa-tto tateta* (line 39) appear twice, and then the quotation of self-speech (or thought), *araa-tte kanji de* ("it was like 'wow!'"; line 41), occurs, accompanied by laughter, to describe his astonishment at the infinite space below his feet. Stanza iv-A then concludes with the external evaluative utterance *yabakatta* ("it was a really narrow escape"; line 43). This structure of "onomatopoeia + self-quotation" is exactly the one used in Stanza iii-B, and we can see that they are repeated renditions of the same formation.

K also responds to the result in an excited but evaluative manner, and anticipates the upcoming conclusion by repeating and replacing the subject "I" with "you" as shown by "you were really lucky" (line 44). The narrator responds to K's evaluation ("initiation" in the IRE format) by repeating the expression *yabai* (as "response") with laughter, which indicates his relief that he narrowly escaped death. However, this fall incident is not over completely because the narrator is still in the crevasse. In Scene v (Result 2), the narrator continues to describes how he hurriedly crawled out of the crevasse with his ice axes, using the self-quote *hiee-tte* 'like "Yipes!"' and the onomatopoeic *geragera*, which represents the guffawing of the other team members. Although onomatopoeia is used only once in Stanza v-A, this is the third time that the "onomatopoeia + self-quotation" pair is repeated. This pair occurs only in the Peak–Result section, serving as a means of "internal evaluation" (Labov 1972) through repetition of the equivalent construction.

As we have seen, the narrator tends to end the turn with an *iisashi* ("insubordination") phrase. Here again, the word *dakedo* in line 50 strongly suggests closure, followed by an evaluative token of laughter, to which K immediately adds: "Lucky it was a laughing matter." The narrator's speech in line 52, however, does not exactly react to K's comment in terms of content, although he superficially does so by saying *un* 'yeah' at the beginning. Rather, the following utterance *kowakatta* ("I was scared"; line 52) is not a response to K's comment, but should be interpreted as Verse e, which concludes Stanza v-A. Understood in this way, it is noteworthy that the evaluation *kowakatta* ("I was scared"), 'I was scared', occurs in the same position as the external evaluation *yabakatta* ("it was a narrow escape") in Stanza iv-A (line 43), clearly indicating that the consecutive Results 1 and 2 consist of the repetition of the equivalent structures. In addition, Stanza iv-A and v-A are both accompanied by laughter, which affects the perception of negative evaluations, *kowakatta* and *yabakatta*, in those stanzas. In particular, in Verse e of Stanza v-A, the narrator nods three times (❂❂❂), which embodies acknowledgement and projects further closure relevance. As shown in (1), we can see that the pair "onomatopoeia(s) + quotation of self-thought/inner voice" occurs in every stanza after a Complication. Obviously, Stanza iii-C does qualify for the category because it is an inserted "orientation," and is narrated in "free" clauses, not in "narrative" clauses.

(1) Equivalence across stanza

Scene iii
    Stanza A   onomatopoeia + quotation of self-thought
    Stanza B   onomatopoeias + quotation of self-thought
Scene iv
    Stanza A   onomatopoeias + quotation of inner voice
Scene v
    Stanza A   onomatopoeia + quotation of inner voice

Given these observations, it seems that there was no problem in ending this narrative with Stanza v-A. However, in line 54, in which K tries to confirm T's situation in the crevasse by asking 'It was a hollow space with nothing down below?' (line 54), the following segment appears as an addendum to Result 1, which we tentatively call Stanza vi-(A) for convenience (Table 7.1). It arose from the interactional need to respond to K's question; the fact that the verse structure of Stanza vi-A is clearly different from other stanzas also supports this assumption. Here, although the narrator comments on a hypothetical situation in Verse a and b, almost the same content as Stanza iv-A (Result 1) is repeated in Verse c-g (hence, Result 1). The description of the fall including the same onomatopoeia *pon* is also given in Verse e, and the same evaluations *un ga yokatta* ("I was so lucky"; line 63) and *yabai* ("a narrow escape"; line 64) are repeated in both Verses f and g.

The case examined here is not a story that has been told repeatedly and therefore become conventionalized, unlike the case with the Chinookan tales or myths that Hymes investigated. Although the data were collected in a semi-structured interview interlaced by interactional elements such as continuers, repairs, adjacency pairs, and IRE units, it was still possible to identify ethnopoetic patterns in T's narrative that underlie and retreat following the odd-number cultural template.

7.3.1.2 Multimodal Analysis of Covert Chronotopic Text in T's Narrative

The preceding section presented an ethnopoetic analysis based on the semantic content of the transcriptions. In the following, I examine how interactional elements that cultivate gestures and bodily representations (gaze and body posture) are linked to the poetic construction of the narrative and contribute to the creation of differentiated local chronotopes in narrative. Through Scene (i) and (ii), which are Abstract and Orientation(s) of this narrative, no gestures are used at all, whereas from Scene (iii) and onward, highly frequent and detailed physical depictions are employed. Thus, in what follows, we focus on Scene (iii) through Scene (v).

Here again, the key concepts referred to are the classification of Observer Viewpoints (outside-/inside-O-VPT) and Character Viewpoint (C-VPT). These classifications are combined analytically with the ethnopoetic formation to show how distinct spatial scenes are chronotopically embodied according to different perspectives. However, gestures are continuous and integrated, making it difficult to break down the whole narration into moment-by-moment frames, so I basically extract the stroke phrase of co-speech gestures most relevant to the narration. Those stroke phases are bolded and shown in a plate when necessary. Let us now follow T's exposition leading up to the fall scene (Excerpt 7.2).

EXCERPT 7.2 *(Scene iii: Complication~Orientation (suspense))*.

Complication
A a *de C2 ni **tsuite**,* ·········(a)   20
'and then we **got to** C2,'

b *moo chotto jun'noo-koodo shite okoo kana to omotte,*
'and I thought "I will do some acclimatization,"'

c *noo zairu de,*
'without (protection by) rope,'
*chotto ue made **hyoko-hyoko-to shamen nobotte**,* ·········(b)
'I **unsteadily climbed up a slope** a little bit,'
<<K: *mh:m.*>>
<<'Uh huh.'>>

Complication (~Peak)
B a *saisho koo **naname ni nobotteta'n dakedo**,*   25
'At first I **climbed diagonally** like this.'
<<K: *un.*>>   (c)
<<'Uhuh.'>>

b *kudari wa massugu ikya hayaiya-tte kanji de,*
'but I thought, "It's faster if I go down straight,"'

c *tento kara hon'no **hyaku meetoru guraino tokoro de**,*

150   LANGUAGE AND BODY IN PLACE AND SPACE

EXCERPT 7.2 *(Scene iii: Complication~Orientation (suspense))*. continued.

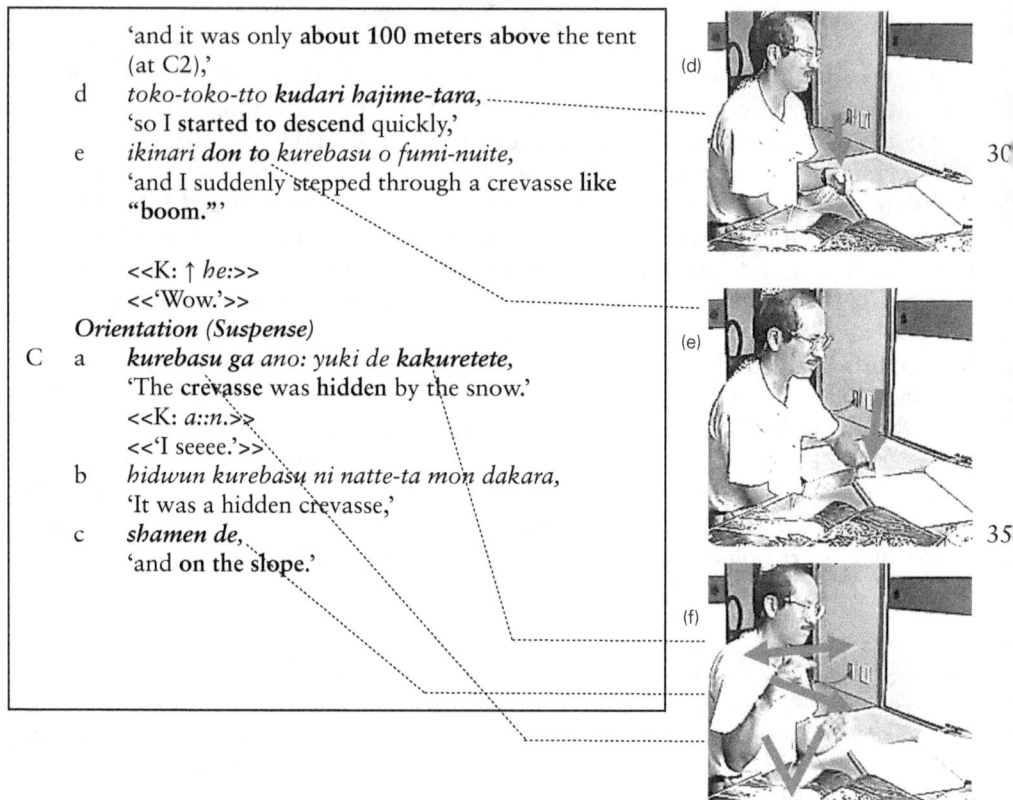

      'and it was only **about 100 meters above** the tent (at C2),'
d   *toko-toko-tto **kudari hajime-tara**,*
      'so I **started to descend** quickly,'
e   *ikinari **don to** kurebasu o fumi-nuite,*
      'and I suddenly stepped through a crevasse **like "boom."**'

    <<K: ↑ he:>>
    <<'Wow.'>>
    Orientation (Suspense)
C a *kurebasu ga ano: yuki de **kakuretete**,*
      'The **crevasse** was **hidden** by the snow.'
    <<K: a::n.>>
    <<'I seeee.'>>
  b *hidwun kurebasu ni natte-ta mon dakara,*
      'It was a hidden crevasse,'
  c *shamen de,*
      'and **on the slope**.'

First, in Stanza iii-A, Camp 2 is set up in front of the body by the left hand (line 20 (a)), and the act of climbing up the rocky slope for acclimatization is described by imagining a "large space" in front of the narrator. This assumption can be confirmed by the fact that the environment surrounding Camp 2, which should comprise glaciers, moraines, and ridges, was set up by the narrator's O-VPTs. Recycling the expression in line 23, his experience of falling into a crevasse, which can be regarded as the peak of this narrative, is then described in detail from line 25 in Stanza iii-B. First, T once again describes how he climbed up the slope with the same O-VPT (lines 23, 25 (b)) and then, in line 27, he describes his psychological state by quoting his inner thought, "It's faster if I go down straight," which may have induced his following gestures. In fact, in line 28, when he utters *hyakumeetoru gurai no tokoro* ("about 100 meters [above C2]"), he turns his body to the left, and mimes looking down from somewhere above (line 28 (c)). This posture indicates that it was performed by transferring the *origo* (locus of perception) from the narrating event in the "here and now" to the narrated event in the story, and assimilating his point of view with that of the character (his past self) through a C-VPT gesture—i.e., in a "co-eval" mode, in which the past and the present merge as in the historical present. The change from O-VPT to C-VPT is subtle but essential in terms of the following features. In line 29, he starts to describe the descending action by stating *tokotoko to kudari hajimetara* ("so I started to descend steadily"), with the downward movement of the left hand (line 29 (d)). This gesture is conducted right in front of his body, but not from the C-VPT, so I consider it as the one conducted in inside-O-VPT. In line 30, the last line of Stanza iii-B, he then describes his unexpected fall into the crevasse with the onomatopoeic phrase *don* ("boom"), along with an even larger falling movement by his left hand (line 30 (e)). This physical illustration depicts the fall from the perspective of the person who fell into the crevasse and can also be regarded as an inside-O-VPT gesture. This way, Stanza iii-B, which describes this potentially fatal fall, accounts for Peak in the narrative. As mentioned above, this stanza, which is rich in quotations and onomatopoeia as well as C-VPT and inside-O-VPT gestures that represent the internal/proximal perspectives of the character, increases the degree of immersion (involvement), and creates the excitement and vividness leading up to Peak.

The subsequent Stanza iii-C is a segment that can be regarded as another "orientation," providing a background explanation that deviates temporarily from the plot line. Specifically, this part is told in "free clauses" (Labov 1972) with T's iconic gestures depicting an ordinary formation of "hidden crevasse" (line 32 (f)). Although it does not contribute to the development of the narrative plot itself, it provides crucial information on why the unexpected fall in Stanza iii-B occurred. In line 32, he utters *kurebasu ga* ("crevasse was") and makes a "V"-shape (information not delivered verbally) with his both hands. He then makes a sweeping gesture repeatedly with his right hand while uttering *kakuretete* ("covered"; line 32) and incrementally adds *shamen de* ("on the slope") with a slanting gesture to the left with his right hand (line 35 (f)). Line 35 consists of a phrase and thus does not qualify as a principal verse, but because it refers to the slope rather than the crevasse itself, I assume it constitutes a separate (if minor) verse. These O-VPT gestures depict exactly how a hidden crevasse might be invisible to climbers, emphasizing the "nomic" (Silverstein 1993) value rather than the narrator's own experience.

In Stanza iv-A (Result 1/Coda), the gestural perspective then switches again to a proximal, character-affiliated mode that comprises inside-O-VPT and C-VPT (Excerpt 7.3). Two onomatopoeic expressions—*ponto okkochita* ("fell down like 'pomg'"; line 37) and *patto tateta* ("quickly able to stand"; line 39) were enacted from inside-O-VPT, depicting the falling movements from the proximal perspective (lines 37 (g) and 39 (h)). The consequent action—his looking down to his right, to the hollow space under his feet (line 41)—is depicted with C-VPT in tandem with his own inner verbal expression *araa* ("wow"; line 41 (i)). Notice that his viewpoint merges that of the character for this action, representing the "co-eval" mode of narration as he did in Stanza iii-B (line 28), which seems to foreshadow this final consequence. T conducts these "looking down" gestures when he is at the highest point on the slope (line 28 (c)) and the lowest point in the crevasse (line 41 (i)), possibly contrasting the extremes of the up–down relation in terms of the "looking down to the left" and "looking down to the right" gestures—although he may have actually looked down to the left from above and to the right in the crevasse. These differentiated bodily representations, whether intentional or unintentional, real or fictional, contribute to (re)creating distinct perceptions and experiences for spatial scenes in terms of poetically constructed formations and perspectively differentiated gestures that help construct distinct chronotopic values.

EXCERPT 7.3 *(Scene iv: Result 1/Coda).*

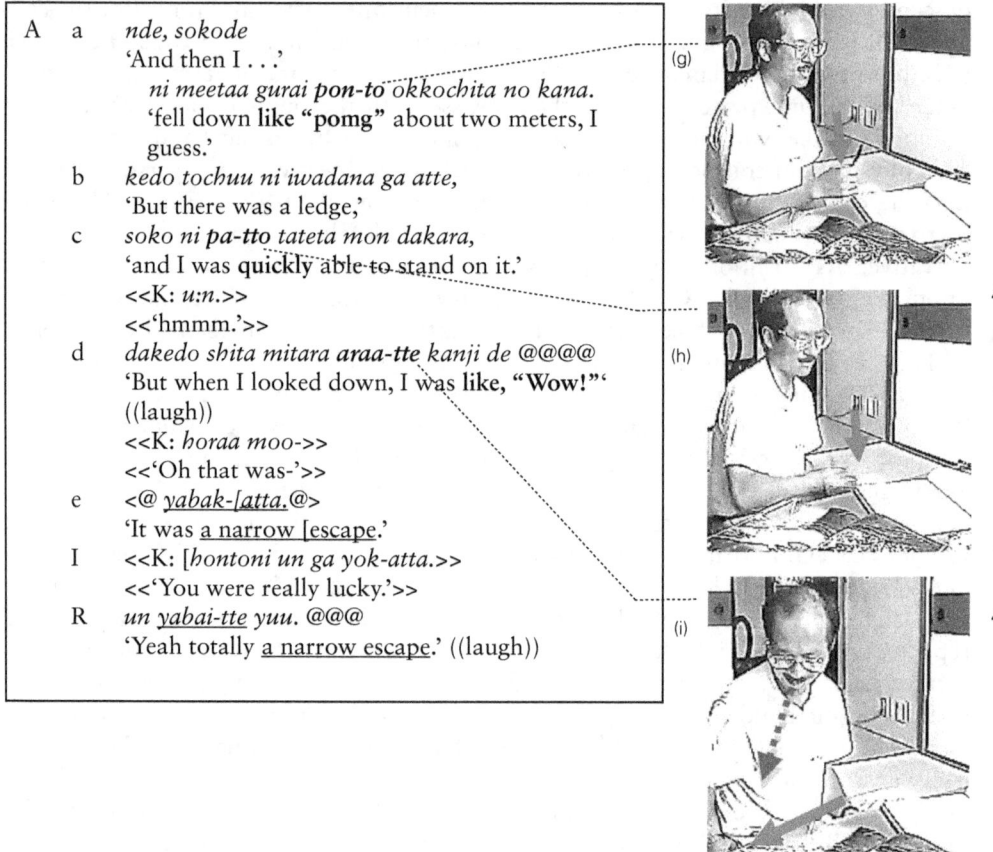

A	a	*nde, sokode*
		'And then I . . .'
		ni meetaa gurai **pon-to** *okkochita no kana.*
		'fell down like "**pomg**" about two meters, I guess.'
	b	*kedo tochuu ni iwadana ga atte,*
		'But there was a ledge,'
	c	*soko ni* **pa-tto** *tateta mon dakara,*
		'and I was **quickly** able to stand on it.'
		<<K: *u:n.*>>
		<<'hmmm.'>>
	d	*dakedo shita mitara* **araa-tte** *kanji de* @@@@
		'But when I looked down, I was like, "**Wow!**"'
		((laugh))
		<<K: *horaa moo-*>>
		<<'Oh that was-'>>
	e	<@ *yabak-[atta.*@>
		'It was a narrow [escape.'
I		<<K: [*hontoni un ga yok-atta.*>>
		<<'You were really lucky.'>>
R		*un yabai-tte yuu.* @@@
		'Yeah totally a narrow escape.' ((laugh))

In Stanza v-A (Result 2/ Coda: Excerpt 7.4), the denouement, the narrator's gestural depictions are limited to two particular scenes: one for the (char)actor's climbing action using the ice axes (line 47), and the other for his looking down at other members who were guffawing at his faux-pas (line 50). I should emphasize that this final scene is depicted only by C-VPTs. The speaker describes the former situation using the exclamation *hieeee* ("yikes!") to express his emotions while also making the iconic gesture of wielding ice axes (line 46 (j)). This axe-wielding gesture is the only C-VPT besides the looking-down gesture. Also, another looking-down gesture from the slope (line 50 (k)) onto which he climbs back up from the crevasse, is coordinated to the same side (i.e., to the left) as that in line 28 (Plate (c)). This type of gesture serves as a "catchment" (McNeill 2005) and contributes to buttressing the thematic coherence and correspondence between seemingly isolated events. We now see that these C-VPT gestures merge the here-and-now of the narrating event and there-and-then of the narrated event, serving the equivalent function as the "co-eval" representation typical of historical present and (free) indirect speech. Of course, this statement does not mean that ephemeral local

EXCERPT 7.4 *(Scene v: Result 2/Coda).*

A	a	*de maa pikkeru motte-ta kara,*
		'and, you know, I had ice axes,'
	b	***hieee-tte XXXX nobotte-***
		'so I climbed crazily like "Yipes!"'
		haidashite.
		'and crawled out.'
	c	*de yuki-mamirede haidashitara=*
		'And when I crawled out covered in snow,'
	d	*=min'na **geragera** waratte-tan' dakedo.* @@@
		'everyone was **guffawing** at me.' ((laugh))
	I	<<K: @@ *waratte-(rare)reba ii kedo nee*=>>
		((laugh)) 'Lucky it was a laughing matter.'
	e/R	=<@ *un are wa hijooni (0.5)* <u>*kowa-katta*</u>.@> ❁❁❁
		'=yeah I was very ... <u>scared</u>.' ((nods 3 times))
	E	<<K: *hu::n.*>>
		<<'Hmmm.'>>
	I	<<K: *moo shita su- ...n nani mo nai kuu*[*doo d-atta?*>>
		<<'It was a hollow space with nothing down below?'>>
	R	[*un nani mo nai.*
		'[Yeah, there was nothing.'

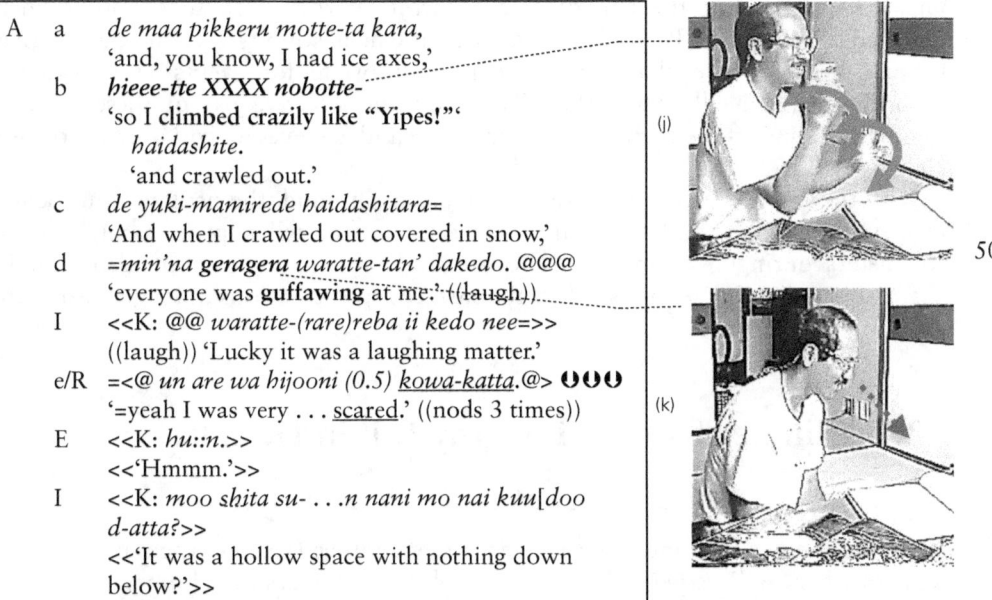

(j)

50

(k)

55

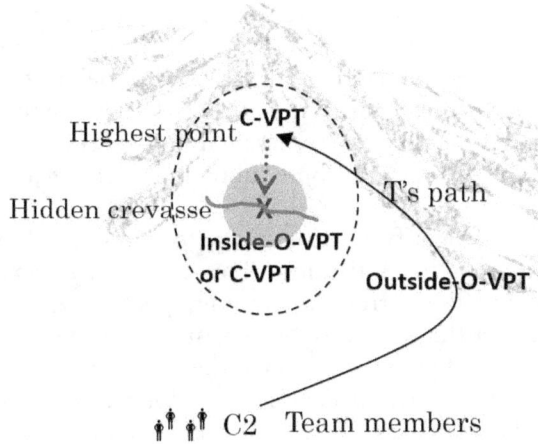

FIGURE 7.1 *Spatial configuration and gestural perspectives.*

chronotopes will not be recognized if the data do not involve bodily depictions (see Ladin 1999, 2010). Rather, we can use those depictions to identify precisely embedded chronotopes that cannot be readily discerned by verbal descriptions alone. Based on this discussion, Figure 7.1 shows the transition of perspectival gestures in T's narrative along the story plot.

As can be seen here, the depiction of the large space in Orientation is done by outside-O-VPT, while the climax of the narrative from Peak to Result is finely managed by inside-O-VPT to C-VPT, a series of which exhibits a shorter perspectival distance because "the character voice is appropriate for events of the greater importance" (McNeill 1992: 193). This way, the selective use of these gestures eventually enhances the realism of the narrative and achieves a vivid description as a whole.

With the above observations and assumptions in mind, the next section focuses on a more extensive fall scene in which the narrator fell approximately twenty-five meters during his climb. It is longer and more complex, but also exhibits systematic underlying features below the surface representations of language and the body.

7.3.2 Climber S on an Lengthy Fall in Hodaka

7.3.2.1 Denotational Text Analysis

In this section, we look into a narrative told by another Japanese rock mountaineer, M, about his "fall" experience. He is a well-known Japanese climber who made several first (winter) ascents on the Hodaka Mountains in Japan's Northern Alps. Here he talks about a precipitous fall he endured because of a loose rock on one of the traditional routes on Mt. Maehotaka. His narrative is constructed by occasionally disregarding the chronological order but in repeated laminations of crucial scenes, as observed in the "overlay" formation (Grimes 1972). For example, the fall narrative outlined below is characterized by the repetition of specific elements, abrupt transitions between spaces, and timeline reversals. It recursively moves through a series of spaces, filling the whole spatial scene rather than delineating a chain of events in chronological order—the default assumption in Labov's model. It will also be argued that the narrator's physical representations reflect distinct epistemic stances in perspective-taking, which contribute subtly to the emergence of distinct local chronotopes.

As in the case of Section 7.3.1, I first identify an ethnopoetic formation, followed by a multimodal chronotopic analysis of narration. For clarity, the spatial configuration of the fall situation and the corresponding ethnopoetic scenes and stanzas are illustrated in Figure 7.2. In the text, Y is M's partner (and the belayer here), in front of whom the narrator fell downward through the air.

As reflected in Excerpt 7.5 below, this narrator devises much longer verses than the narrator discussed earlier. The basic principle is that a verse corresponds to a clause or a sentence-like construction no matter how many lines the utterance spans. This narrator frequently constructs a single verse spanning several lines by employing modified phrases and subordinate clauses with disfluencies and/or repairs. The same is true for line segmentation based on the intonation unit; lines come out relatively longer in M's narrative. He also relies on the extensive use of discourse markers

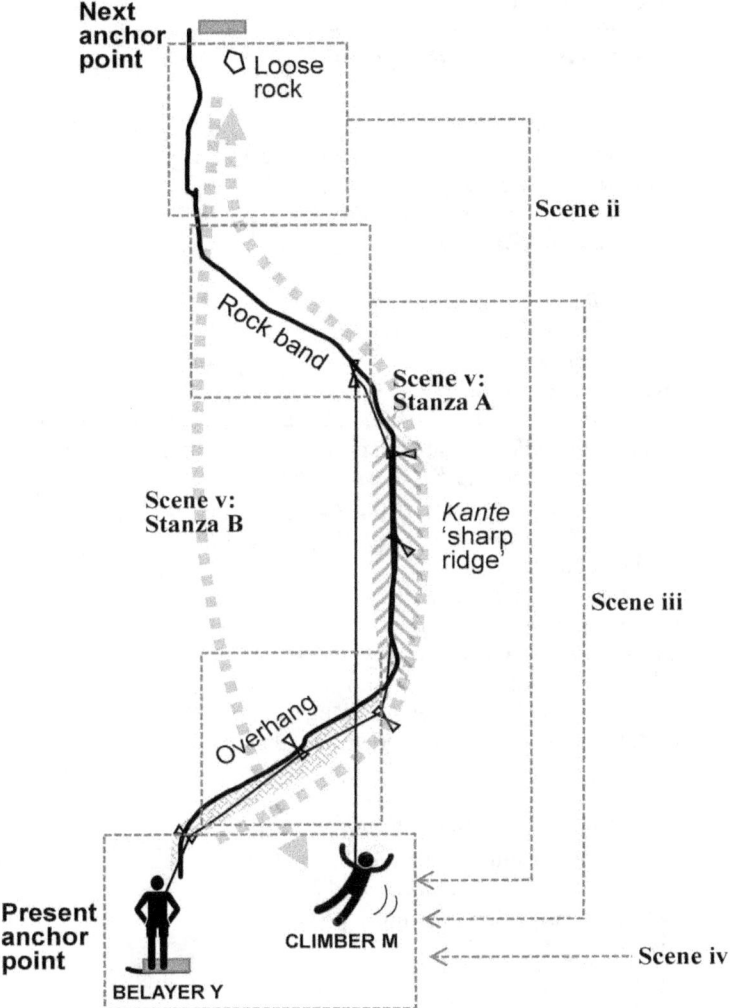

FIGURE 7.2 *Correspondence between rhetorical components and places.*

(*anoo, sonoo, ee*: DM), conjunctions and conjunctive particles (*honde, sorede, -te, -de*: CONJ), final particles (*ne, sa, yo*: FP), and phrases for specific times and places (*toki ni/ tokoro de* ("at the time/place of")). Due to the his prolific use of these elements, the boundary between line and verse is recognized relatively easily.[6] As in the previous section, these boundary markers are shaded in gray, and onomatopoeia and quotations appear in squares.

EXCERPT 7.5 *Massive fall at Mae-Hodaka*

Scene i : Abstract 1 (including clarification questions)

Stanza	Verse	Text
A	a	*ato wa maa nee*

'well, as for others (= critical experiences),'
    are wa shinu koto wa naka- ((restart))
    'although that was not so bad as –'
        nakattan dakedomo
        'near-death, though,'
            jibun ga nobottete:
            'in my climbing experiences,'

      b   *anoo...reino anoo*   5
            'weell, you knooow,'
            e:: yonpoo no toonanpeki no shimizu RCC ruuto-tte yuunka naa.
            'ah:n, I wonder if it's Shimizu RCC Route on SE face of Peak 4?'
            <<K: *ah: haa haa haa haa [haa haa hai.]*>>
            <<'oh:, yeah, yeah, yeah, yeah, yeah, yeah, yes.'>>
            [*asoko no nee*].
            'there, you know,'
                natsu ni itta toki ni,
                'when I went in summer,'

      c   *anoo: rokkotsu kossetsu shitan da nee.*   10
            'uh:n, I had broken ribs, you know.
      I   <<K: *a sonnano mo attan desu ka?*>>
            <<'Oh, did you have an accident like that?'>>
      R   *un.*
            'yeah.'
            ano: Y-kun to issho ni nobotta toki ni ne.
            'well, when I climbed with Mr. Y, you know.'
      I   <<K: *e sore fuyu ja nakattan desu ka?*>>
            <<'Wait, wasn't that in winter?'>>
      R   *iya iya.*   15
            'no no.'
                sore ja naku te sono mae.
                'not that, before that one.'
      E   <<K: *ah:::*>>
            <<'Okay.'>>

(B)   a   *tsumari...anoo*
            'that is, uh:n,'
                sore wa sono setsujokusen ni itta wake de atte
                'that was when we went to take a second chance,'
      b   *sonoo fuyu ni iku yotei mo atta monde,*   20
            'I mean, we had a plan to go there in winter,'
      c   *ichido anoo nobottokoo-chuu koto de nobottan dawa nee.*
            'so we decided we should climb it before that, you know.'
            <<K: *mmn.*>>
            <<'Uhun.'>>

Scene ii: Complication 1~Peak 1~Result 1

A   a   *hoshitara sono toki ni,*
            'then, at that time,'

EXCERPT 7.5 *Massive fall at Mae-Hodaka*   continued.

		boku ga toppu de nobotteta toki ni	
		'when I was leading the route,'	
	b	*konna ookina iwa ga . . .koyatte . . .*	25
		'a huge rock like this, this way,'	
	c	*anoo (2.1) sawatta dakede koo ochi- ochitekitan-* @@@@[@@@]	
		'uh:n, just by touching it, (it) came off li- like this.' ((laugh))	
		<<K: [*asoko*] *nara arisoo desu nee.*>>	
		<<'That could happen there.'>>	
		sawatta dekede ochitekita monde saa	
		'cuz it came off just by touching it,'	
	d	*hoide issho ni ochichatta wake nee.*	
		'so I fell with it, you know.'	
	e	*honde ano chuuburarin ni natte.*	30
		'then, uhn, I hung in the air.'	

Scene iii: Orientation~Complication 2~Result 2

A	a	*eeto anotoki wa nee*	
		'well, at that time,'	
		tochuu ga nee . . .	
		'cuz it was the section,'	
		anoo anmari haaken ga uten toko da monde,	
		'uh:n, where I couldn't nail any pitons,'	
	b	*da::to nagaku,*	
		'because, for a veeeerry long distance,'	
		anoo . . .e::: chuukanshiten o torazuni o--	35
		'you know, ah:::n, without taking protections,'	
		are shitotta monde	
		'I was running out, so,'	
	c	*sootoo ochite nee*	
		'I fell quite a long distance.'	
		20 meetaa chikaku ochitan<@ja naika naa @>@@@.	
		'I guess I had about a 20-meter fall.' ((laugh))	
		<<K: *Ah::n.*>>	
		<<'oh:::.'>>	
	d	*honde. . .anoo*	40
		'then, you know,'	
		hangu no shita de kakuhoshiteiru Y-kun no sugu mae ni	
		'right in front of Y, who was belaying me under the overhang,'	
	e	<@ *buwa::nto burasagattan da.* @>	
		'I fell hanging like a pendulum.'	

Scene iv: Result 3

A	a	*hoide [soide]. . .ano,*	
		'then then, . . . well,'	
		<<K: [*ja*]-->>	
		<< 'then --'>>	
		koko. . .ano. . .nante yuunka naa. . .	45
		'this, I mean, how should I put it.' ((Exhale))	
		are:. .joohanshin--	
		'the upper body--' ((truncated))	

EXCERPT 7.5 *Massive fall at Mae-Hodaka*   continued.

		ue gawa no ano roopu ga--	
		'the upper side where the rope--' ((truncated))	
		ano: haanesu no ue mo tsuketeta monde,	
		'uh::n, I was wearing a chest harness, too, so'	
		<<K: *ah:::*>>	
		<< 'Okay.'>>	
	b	[*ba::n to*] *hippararete*	50
		'I was caught ((by the rope)) very hard,'	
	c	*rokkotsu otchattan dawa ne.*	
		'and I got my ribs broken, you know.'	
	I	<<K: *ah: sono shokku de.*>>	
		<<'oh, because of the impact.'>>	
	R	*un.*	
		'yeah.'	
	I	<<K: *a jaa hoka no. . .iwa jitai niyoru kega wa nakattan desu* [*ka*]?>>	
		<<'oh so, you didn't get hurt due to the fall itself?'>>	
	R	[*hm.*]	55
		'right.'	
	E	<<K: *ah::.*>>	
		<< 'I see.'>>	
	R	*datte. .kuuchuu ochitetta dake da monde.*	
		'cuz I just fell through the air,'	
		choodo hangu no ue kara ochite kita monde saa.	
		'I just fell from above the overhang, you know.'	

Scene v: *Complication 3~Result 4~Coda*

A	a	*ha- hangu koshite koo itte*	
		'ov- I went past the overhang like this,'	
	b	*kante itte*	60
		'and went along the ridge,'	
	c	*bandotorabaasu shiteru to*[*ki tot*]*te,*	
		'and got my protection when I was traversing the rock band.'	
		<<K: [*h::m.*]>>	
		<<'uhun.'>>	
	d	*moo* <@ *shuuryo--* @>	
		'almost over --' ((truncated))	
		kakushinbu wa owari to yuu tokoro no temae no tokoro de saa	
		'where I was almost through the crux, before the end of it,'	
	e	*ano bando. .agatteru. .tochuu de*	65
		'while I was going up along the rock band,'	
	f	*sooyuu koto ga okottan dawa nee.*	
		'that incident just happened, you know.'	
B	a	*honde* buwa:::n to *ochita monde,*	
		'and, cuz I had a massive fall like a pendulum,'	
		bando no-. . .bando no kono tokoro wa. ((increment))	
		'the rock band-, over this rock band.'	
	b	*hotondo nan'nimo shiten ga tottarahen monde saa*	
		'and I had almost no pros along the rock band, you know,'	
	c	*honde moo* buwa::to *ochite,.*	70
		'then, just fell like a pendulum,'	

EXCERPT 7.5 *Massive fall at Mae-Hodaka* continued.

		choodo sono...hangutai: o koshita tokoro da monde ((increment))	
		'cuz it was just where I passed the overhang,'	
	d	*hangu no shita made ochitetchatta wake.*	
		'I fell way down below the overhang, you know.'	
	e	*honde nannimo ataranakattan da.*	
		'and that's why I didn't hit anything.'	
	I	<<K: *aa jaa kaette hangu [shite]ta no ga yokattan desu ne.*>>	
		<<'oh so you were okay because it was the overhang instead.>>	
	R	[*Un.*]	75
		'Yeah.'	
C	a	*dakara hangu shiteru tokoro no hoo ga*	
		'so, if it's an overhanging section,'	
		anoo: e:: iwa ni gekitotsu shite	
		'uhn, such a thing as hitting on a rock'	
		shinu-tte yuu yoona koto ga naikara nee.	
		'and getting killed won't happen, you know,'	
		aruiwa ke- sonshoo o ukeru. ((increment))	
		'or getting hurt.'	
	b	*dakara...(H)...ima no dakara:*	80
		'so, the current (area), I mean,'	
		anoo onishi mitaina tokoro @@@ no hoo ga nee,	
		'at a place like Onishi*, you know,'	
		<<K: *Anzen desu ne.*>>	
		<<'safe, isn't it?>>	
	c	*zettai anzen nan'da yo.*	
		'it's absolutely much safer.'	

* *Onishi* 'Demon Rock' is a free climbing area at *Horai* in Aichi Prefecture. It is nationally famous for its overhanging faces and roofs with high-grade routes.

Shown below is the profile of the ethnopoetic formation of the text (Table 7.2). It is evident that, with the exceptions of two sections, this Japanese text basically conforms to the oral patterns of threes and fives. Scene i consists only of Stanza A, which comprises an Abstract of the narrator's experience of breaking his ribs. From the outset, we see that M's utterances include numerous disfluencies such as repairs, truncations, and hesitations, which serve as boundary markers of lines, in addition to DMs and final particles. At the same time, the rest of the verses, except for line 10, consist of relatively long lines of four (lines 1–4, 5–9). Immediately after that, K asks a question to confirm the difference from his similar previous climb and the supplementary explanation is inserted in the IRE format (lines 11–17). The explanation in lines 18–21, although I did not include them in the components of this narrative, possibly constitute a stanza consisting of three verses (Stanza (B)), serving as Orientation that provides background information of the narrative yet to be delivered.

Scene ii also consists only of Stanza A, and can be seen as the first rendition of Complication. As shown in Figure 7.2, the actual sequence of the fall narrative is as follows: (1) M climbed up the overhang and along a rock band; (2) he fell off the wall after grasping a loose rock near the end of pitch; and (3) landed at the starting

Table 7.2 Profile of "Massive Fall" Narrative

Scene	Stanza	Verse	Features	Line	Narr. Component
i	A	abc	anoo, e:, -naa, -nee, -dakedo, -te, -toki ni	1-10	Abstract
		IRE	Q-A anoo, ne, e	11-17	—
	(B)	abc	tsumari, anoo, sonoo, -monde, -te, -nee	18-21	(Orientation)
ii	A	abcde	anoo, eeto, hoshitara, honde, -naa, -da, laughter, pivot verse	23-30	Complication 1/ Peak 1/ Result 1
iii	A	abcde	eeto, anoo, e:, honde, -naa, -nee, -da, -monde, laughter, pivot verse onomatopoeia	31-42	Orientation/ Complication 2/ Result 2
iv	A	abc	anoo, hoide, soide, -te, -naa, -ne, -da	43-51	Result 3
		IRE	Confirmation-endorsement, Q-A monde, saa,	52-58	—
v	A	abcdef	-te, -tokoro de, -tochuu de, -saa	59-66	Complication 3
	B	abcde	honde, monde, -saa, -da, onomatopoeia	67-73	Result 4
		IR	Confirmation-endorsement	74-75	—
	C	abc	dakara, anoo, -nee/-da + yo	76-83	Coda

point where his partner was belaying him. Scene ii repeats describing (2) and (3), while Scene iii focuses on (1) and (3) once again. In the first half of Scene ii, the narration starts at the moment of the fall, while the second half explains its consequences in chronological order—i.e., he fell a long way and eventually was suspended in midair. Although the connection between the content of Scene ii (a fall) and Abstract in Scene i (broken ribs) is tenuous at the moment, we can speculate that M's broken ribs would have been a result of the long fall. As in the previous scene, Stanza A in Scene ii (hereafter, Stanza ii-A) is also rich in linguistic markers that facilitate the division of text into lines; conjunctions (*hoshitara, hoide, honde*), conjunctive particles and phrases (*-te, -toki ni*), and final particles (*sa* and *ne*).

There are two additional points that should be made here. First, Verse b (line 25) does not contain a predicate and thus does not seem to satisfy the requirements to qualify as a verse. However, as will be discussed subsequently in the multimodal analysis, the iconic gesture and gaze made while uttering *konna ookina iwa* (line 25), as well as those made immediately afterwards while saying *sawatta dakede* (line 26), are qualitatively different in size, shape, and direction. Thus I interpret them as utterances based on different perceptions (or cognitive units), and separated them into different verses. Second, a relatively long pause (2.1 seconds) occurred in line 26, suggesting a distinct line unit. In fact, in lines 26 and 28, almost the same expression is repeated as a "repair", and thus I treated them together as Verse c. A similar phenomenon was pointed out by Hymes (1981: 231) for Hiram Smith's text in which the middle section between the onset and the outcome plays an interlocking function as a pivot. Here, Verse a–c and Verse c–e are connected at Verse c and consequently emerge as a structure consisting of an odd number of overlapping units, as "3 + 3 = 5."

In Scene iii, the story of the fall narrated in Scene ii is recounted with modifications. As mentioned above, the first half of Scene iii describes the rock band section, and the second half, the consequence of the fall. Notice that, in Stanza iii-A, the same event is paraphrased in detail in Verse c, which, here again, seems to play the role of a pivot connecting the first and the second halves of the stanza. In line 37, the narrator says *sootoo ochite* ("fell quite a long distance"), which is paraphrased further in line 38 as *20 meetaa chikaku ochita* ("fell about 20 meters"). In particular, in the second half, M's point of view shifts to, and merges with, that of his partner, Y, embodying multiple characters' perspectives. These minute details of the scene, as will be examined further in the multimodal analysis, are acknowledged widely as indexes of a narrative's climax (Longacre 1996).

To summarize the above observations, the overall plot in Scene ii and Scene iii can be outlined as follows (2). In each scene, Verse c consists of repeated renditions and serves as a pivot, which divides the first half (upper part of the route) and the second half (lower part of the route) of the narrated contents. At the same time, the pivots in these Stanzas are contrasted in terms of the onset (touching a loose rock) and the outcome (fell about 20 meters), forming both equivalent and contrastive poetic structures.

(2) Equivalence and contrast (1)

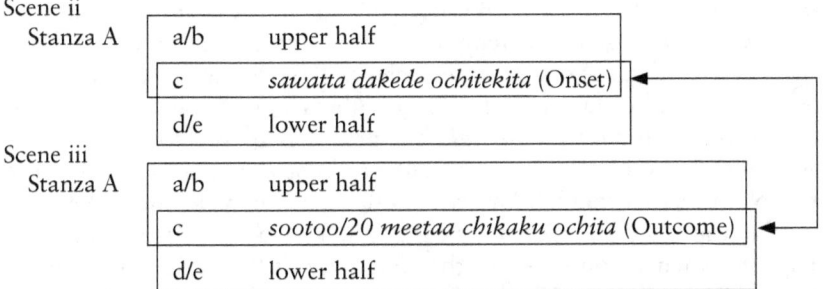

Stanza iv-A delineates the condition of the fallen climber (Result 3). The narrator manages to utter a sentence through five lines of disfluent fragments and truncations. He finally states in line 48 that he was wearing a chest harness that caused his upper body to be pulled so hard by the fall impact that his ribs were broken. Unlike Scenes ii and iii, this part of the story is very concise except for Verse a, which is filled with disfluencies. Furthermore, the use of the onomatopoeia *ba::nto* ("bang"; representing the impact of the pull of rope) in Verse b also highlights the peculiarity of this ending because a normal expectation would be that the injury is usually caused by the contact or crash with a rock wall. This incongruence with expectation seems to have motivated further narration, as we will see in Scene v. In addition to this observation, onomatopoeia is known to occur abundantly in Japanese narratives, but is also coordinated to appear alongside iconic gestures at moments of high emotion (Kita 1997).

In terms of the entire narrative structure, it seems as if the preceding events were supplemental incidents that led up to this Result 3 (the rib fracture mentioned in Abstract). In other words, the suspense on the run-up to Result 3 is prolonged by the preceding incidents (although it is arguable whether proper suspense was maintained here), and the denouement is presented abruptly so that the significance of Result 3 (Scene iv) looms large through the contrast. According to this interpretation, we could possibly think of the organization of "Scene ii, iii, iv" as "Scene ii: Stanza A, B, C". However, because Scenes ii, iii, and iv separately describe distinct facets of the fall incident (Figure 7.2), they are judged to form different scenes rather than stanzas.

After Result 3 follows a clarification question by the interviewer, K, M matter-of-factly confirms that there was no injury other than the rib fractures with the IRE format (lines 52–8). The narrator then begins to reiterate the progress of the climb from the overhang section (line 59), thus starting another round of the fall narrative (Scene v). Following Scene ii and iii, Scene v is the third exposition of the fall scene. Stanza v-A recapitulates in five verses the climber's actions before the loose rock tumbled. Here, no disfluencies are observed, and the process is described objectively, mainly by the conjunctive particle *-te*, which delineates the temporal sequence. Whereas in the latter half of the stanza, more spatial descriptions (*tokoro* ("place"), *temae* ("[in] front"), and possibly *tochuu* ("along/during")) and interpersonal attention (the emotive final particles *sa* and *ne*) come into play. From the beginning of Stanza v-B, which describes the fall scene, the story then is told in a five-verse structure, with the conjunction *honde* repeated three times at regular intervals (in Verses a, c, e), as well as the conjunctive particle *-monde* and boundary markers (*-sa*, *-wake*, and *-da*) repeated three times, respectively. It is noteworthy that the onomatopoeia *buwa::(n)to* is used repeatedly in Verses a and c. In addition, Verses a and b refer to the rock band, and Verses c and d refer to the overhang, whereas Verse e describes the result: "I didn't hit anything." In combination, the sequential set of "*honde* → *buwa::(n)to* → *monde* → *sa/wake*" contributes to the construction of contrast and homology between the two spaces. Overall, the momentary event of the fall is elaborated extensively through Stanza v-B as if to ensure the iconicity between the length of explanation and the distance of the fall. This unusual sluggishness is even more conspicuous when compared to the simplicity of the fall descriptions in Scene ii (line 29) and Scene iii (lines 37–8). Put another way, we can posit a discursive motivation to expand the momentary event to fit the structure of this stanza that consists of a culturally preferred five verses. Given all this, Scene v can be seen as complementary content induced by K's clarification question (line 54), to which M responds painstakingly by going through another round of the fall narrative.

Finally, Stanza v-C, which begins without disfluencies, shows a simple structure consisting of Verse a, b, and c. The rationale for this formation is the combination of common boundary markers: the conjunction *dakara*, the DM *ano(o)*, and the final particle *ne(e)*, which demarcate Verse a and b. Verse c concludes with the copula *da*, which represents a definitive statement, followed by the final particle *yo*, which emphasizes the speech act content addressed to the hearer. Given this, the combination of *da* and *yo* indicates M's intention to complete the narrative at this point, with Stanza C given as a lesson from "the consequences of falling through the air," or as Coda to Scene v (but obviously not to the whole narrative).

The equivalence between the last two stanzas in Scene v is particularly striking. From the above observations, we can see the following pattern of equivalence and contrast (3).

(3) Equivalence and contrast (2)

Scene v

Stanza A	a/b/c	-te + -te + -te, -toki (temporal/objective)	
	d/e	tokoro, temae, (tochuu,) -saa, -nee (spatial/interpersonal)	
Stanza B	a/b	honde + buwa::nto + -monde × 2	+ -sa
	c/d	honde + buwa::to + -monde	+ -wake
	e	honde	+ -da
Stanza C	a	dakara + anoo	+ -nee
	b	dakara × 2 + anoo	+ -nee
	c		+ -da+-yo

From the arrangement of these elements, we can posit the existence of a narrative style that is oriented to, and preferred by, the speaker (and his community). Evidently, the elements used in this narrative are based on a formation that converges on an odd-number structure at the verse and stanza levels. These are higher levels than the line or moraic organizations, with which the traditional Japanese poetry cultivates odd-number structures.[7] As Hymes (1981, 1996) contended, the verse and stanza levels are the locus where cultural characteristics can be typically and conspicuously observed. This fact points to an anticipated attitude for us that Japanese, or any other language, should be considered from multiple levels and aspects of organization to fully appreciate indigenous aesthetic achievements. To follow this approach, we still need to address nonverbal aspects of narration and how they can help construct affect-laden spaces in the narrated world, which we examine in the next section.

7.3.2.2 Multimodal Analysis of Covert Chronotopic Text in M's Narrative

In what follows, we will look into M's bodily depictions of the spatial sequence, especially in terms of how the spatial perspectives are reflected upon those representations. Here again, we focus on the classification of Observer Viewpoints (outside-O-VPT and inside-O-VPT) and Character Viewpoint (C-VPT). As in Section 7.3.1, the stroke phase of a gesture is bolded (and shown in a plate when necessary). Let us first examine Scene ii, where M's bodily depictions start to appear (Excerpt 7.6).

The first thing M does is to show the size of the rock that caused the fall, by saying "such a huge rock like this" with both hands outstretched (line 25 (a)). At this point, his gaze is directed to K, which indicates that his *origo* is not yet merged with the perspective of the character (i.e., his past self) and objectively depicts the size of the rock in the inside-O-VPT. However, in line 26, after the hesitation marker *anoo* ("uh:n"), and a pause of 2.1 seconds, the shape of his gesture and his gaze direction change. When he says, *sawatta dakede* ("just by touching it"; line 26), he looks upward (line 26 (b)), depicting the manner of holding up a rock and how the rock was coming loose (line 26 (c)). That is, in order to recount the critical moment, M assimilates into the character and reiterates the scene through C-VPT. The laughter that follows foreshadows that this unexpected, scary incident does not lead to serious

EXCERPT 7.6 *(Scene ii: Complication 1~Peak 1~Result 1)*.

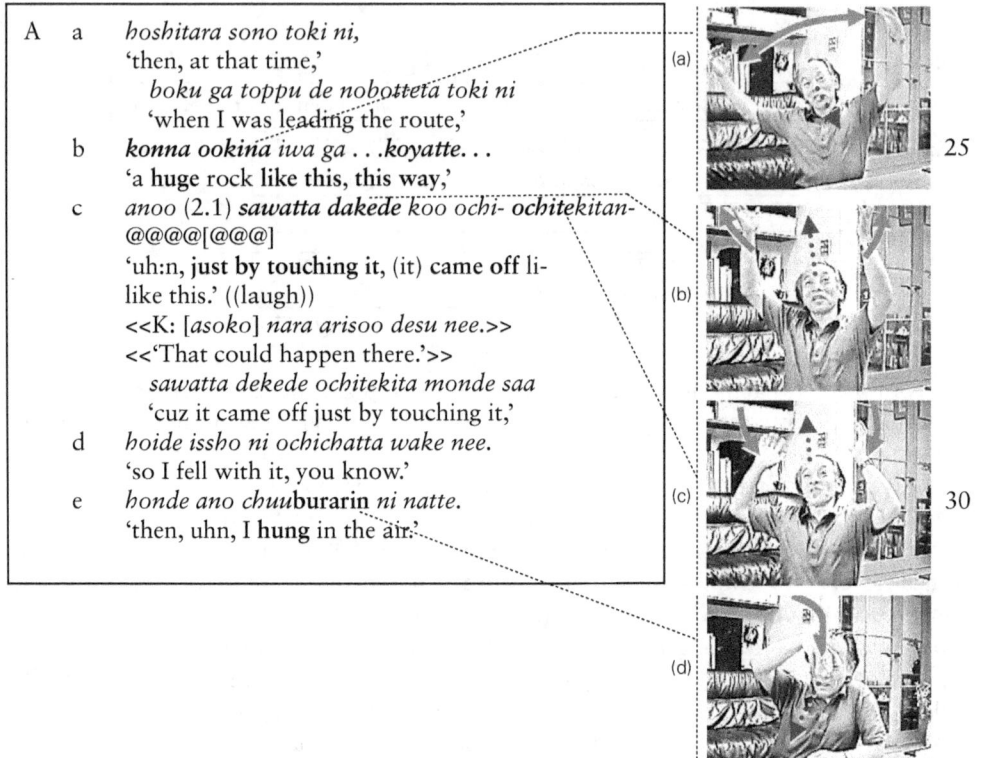

A   a   *hoshitara sono toki ni,*
       'then, at that time,'
       boku ga toppu de nobotteta toki ni
       'when I was leading the route,'
  b   **konna ookina** *iwa ga . . .koyatte. . .*
       '**a huge rock** like this, this way,'
  c   *anoo* (2.1) ***sawatta dakede** koo ochi- ochitekitan-*
       @@@@[@@@]
       'uh:n, **just by touching it**, (it) came off li-
       like this.' ((laugh))
       <<K: [*asoko*] *nara arisoo desu nee.*>>
       <<'That could happen there.'>>
       sawatta dekede ochitekita monde saa
       'cuz it came off just by touching it,'
  d   *hoide issho ni ochichatta wake nee.*
       'so I fell with it, you know.'
  e   *honde ano chuu**burarin** ni natte.*
       'then, uhn, I **hung** in the air.'

consequences. K laughs along with him, and agrees that "that could happen there" (line 27) because he knows the route described by M.

In the last line of Stanza ii-A, M then mimics a shape similar to that of an upside-down cup with his right hand and lowers it from the upper to the middle gesture space along the trajectory of the fall (which was 20 m in reality; line 30 (d)). This gesture is performed in front of his body with an outside-O-VPT gesture with the utterance "I hung in the air" (line 30) with his gaze directed to K. All of these shifts in physical representation indicate that the mode of perceiving the event quickly changed from "inside-O-VPT" through "C-VPT" to "outside-O-VPT," embodying the zooming in and out of the critical moment. It is no coincidence that he skipped the depiction of the fall itself because it spans only a matter of seconds, and he could not have exercised any agency during it. In other words, the lack of agency and perception from the actor seems to have induced the shift, which separates local chronotopes before and after the fall.

After the depiction of the fall, he suddenly switches back to the moment before it, and launches Scene iii. Here he follows the path of climb from the middle section—the "rock band" (Excerpt 7.7).

In Scene iii, he starts to provide background information (i.e., Orientation) without any noticeable gestures (even for the onomatopoeic expression in line 34)

VERTICAL SPACE AND "FALL" EXPERIENCES   165

from lines 31–6. However, after M utters the phrase *honde ano::* ("then, well"; a conjunctive + DM in line 40), he emphasizes the distance of the fall by referring to the partner who was belaying him at the bottom of the pitch. Remember that he had almost reached the next anchor point when he fell. What is significant here is the quick switch of local chronotopes with his finger-pointing. First, he looks down and points downward with his right finger (line 41 (e)), saying *hangu no shita* ("under the overhang"), which specifies the location of his partner Y. He says *kakuho shiteru* ("(be) belaying"), while moving his right hand further down. Next, while saying *Y-kun no* ("of Mr. Y"), he quickly points to his own nose (self-referring gesture in Japan), indicating that M is now behaving as Mr. Y (line 41 (f)). This phrase is then followed by *sugu mae ni* ("right in front"), at which M puts his right hand out in front of him (line 41 (g)). Finally, uttering the mimetic phrase *buwa::nto (burasagatta)*)"[fell hanging] like a pendulum"), he further stretches his right arm forward from Y's perspective. Obviously, however, Mr. Y did not make this gesture himself while belaying—it is M's constructed performance as the narrator, building upon, and riding into Y's visual sensation in the co-eval mode.

EXCERPT 7.7 *(Scene iii: Orientation~Complication 2~Result 2).*

A	a	*eeto anotoki wa nee*	
		'well, at that time,'	(e)
		tochuu ga nee...	
		'cuz it was the section,'	
		anoo anmari haaken ga uten toko da monde,	
		'uh:n, where I couldn't nail any pitons,'	
	b	*da::to nagaku,*	
		'because, veeeerry long,'	
		anoo...e::: chuukanshiten o torazuni o--	35
		'you know, ah:::n, without taking protections,'	(f)
		are shitotta monde	
		'I was running out, so,'	
	c	*sootoo ochite nee*	
		'I fell quite a long distance.'	
		20 meetaa chikaku ochitan<@ja naika naa	
		@>@@@.	
		'I guess I had about a 20-meter fall.' ((laugh))	(g)
		<<K: *Ah::n.*>>	
		<<'oh::.'>>	
	d	*honde...anoo*	40
		'then, you know,'	
		hangu no shita de kakuhoshiteru Y-kun no	
		sugu mae ni	(h)
		'under the overhang, right in front of Y who was belaying me'	
	e	<@ *buwa::nto burasagattan da.* @>	
		'I fell hanging like a pendulum.'	

In this second exposition of the fall scene, the same event ends up being depicted through C-VPT after M imaginatively assimilated into Y's perspective. As is clear now, this series of gestures tells us that the locus of perception has shifted drastically within these two lines, from above the overhang to below it, and finally into Y's. The whole process occurred in just four seconds of interaction in rapid and precise succession, a phenomenon that cannot be revealed without looking into the subtle changes of both verbal descriptions and gestural depictions.

As abovementioned, Scene v is different from Scenes ii, iii, and iv in that it does not narrate about fragments of the scene, but about a continuous flow from the beginning of the climb to the end state after the fall (Excerpt 7.8). In this sense, this version of the fall narrative is complete and canonical in that it follows the chronological and logical sequence based on the actor's experience. Still, it encompasses multiple chronotopic configurations in his performance.

In scene v, M once again depicts how he went over the overhang, climbed the arête, and traversed the rock band with outside-O-VPT gestures (lines 59–64 (i–l)) as shown by the minutely differentiated angles of his right hand. At the same time, the direction of his gaze is coordinated with the movement, indicating that his perspective is based at the bottom of the route. This may (or may not) be Y's C-VPT at the (present) anchor point because I know from experience that the belayer cannot see the climber once he or she has moved over the overhang section. Given these facts, we can infer that M's experience-based, imaginary perspectives are instantly merged in this performance such that he simultaneously assimilates with Y's (or omniscient observer's) visual perception, and intersubjectively and intercorporeally realize them in the narrating event. Such a perception is no one's, as it straddles in and out of someone's or something's, or even omniscient and omnipotent god's perspectives. It is as if multisensory (and extra-sensory) perceptions emerged through the use of perspective-laden gestures that integrate multiple (imaginary) participants in the co-eval mode.

In Stanza v-B, Verse a, M then turns his gaze forward and depicts the massive fall with the right hand (line 67 (m)), saying *buwa::n to ochita* ("fell like a pendulum"; line 67). I assume this and the next gesture (line 68 (n)) occur at the turning point of the chronotopes, or as the pivot between Stanza v-A and B, because a shift to a new chronotopic stance is underway. When he refers back to the rock band (line 68 (n)), he raises his right hand to the upper-left direction to depict the rock band (as he did in line 61), but his gaze is turned downward and maintained until the end of line 70, as if he is observing the scene from above. Now, the locus of his perspective has floated from the anchor point and is located somewhere above in the air. M's utterance in line 70, *buwaanto ochite* ("fell like a pendulum"), is an almost verbatim repeat of line 67. However, we see that it is not exactly a repetition of the first rendition because M looks down while uttering *buwaanto ochite*, and lets his right hand fall down even lower—so low that it almost touches the table. In other words, even though he is describing the same situation verbally, the gestures he uses to depict the path and manner of the event are clearly based on different perceptual stances (and chronotopes). Given this, we can postulate that the narrative is partially based on his own experience and partially on others' experience, as if their perspectives are merged and free to move around the fall scene, cultivating the omniscient "God's view" in the co-eval mode.

EXCERPT 7.8 *(Scene v: Complication 3~Result 4~Coda).*

A	a	*ha- hangu* **koshite** *koo itte*
		'ov- I went **past** the overhang like this,'
	b	*kante* ***itte***
		'and **went along** the ridge,' (i) 60
	c	***bando torabaasu shiteru** to[ki tot]te,*
		'and **got** my protection when I was **traversing the rock band**.'
		<<K: [*h::m.*]>>
		<<'uhun.'>>
	d	*moo <@ shuuryo-- @>* (j)
		'almost over --' ((truncated))
		*kakushinbu wa **owari** to yuu tokoro no temae no tokoro de saa*
		'where I was almost **through** the crux, before the end of it,'
		ano bando. .agatteru. .tochuu de, 65
		'while I was going up along that rock band,' (k)
	e	*sooyuu koto ga okottan dawa nee.*
		'that incident just happened, you know.'
B	a	*honde **buwa::nto** ochita monde*
		'and, cuz I had a massive fall **like a pendulum**,'
		bando no-. . .bando no kono tokoro wa.
		'the rock band-, over this rock band.'
	b	*hotondo nan'nimo shiten ga tottarahen monde saa*
		'cuz I had almost no pros along the rock band, you know,' (l)
	c	*honde moo **buwa::to** ochite,* 70
		'then, just fell **like a pendulum**,'
		choodo sono. . .hangutai: o koshita tokoro damonde
		'right at the-, cuz it was where I passed the overhang,' (m)
	d	*hangu no shita made ochitechatta wake.*
		'I fell way down below the overhang, you know.'
	e	*honde nannimo ataranakattan da.*
		'and that's why I didn't hit anything.'
	(i)	<<K: *aa jaa kaette hangu [shite]ta no ga yokattan desu ne.*>>
		<<'oh so, it was good because that was the overhang instead.>> (n)
	(r)	*Un.* 75
		'Yeah.'

(o)

7.4 Conclusion

So far, we have observed that climbing narrative is realized through local, embodied chronotopes that eventually constitute a major, vertical chronotope. Based on the observation, I highlighted the "ethnopoetic" and "chronotopic" interfaces in terms of verbal and nonverbal resources. Although they are intermeshed and difficult to discuss separately, I will raise a few issues for each to refine these concepts. As far as the ethnopoetics formations in Sections 7.3.1 and 7.3.2 are concerned, T and M employ different narrative styles on the "line" level, but converge on higher levels of "verse" and "stanza." T's narrative is relatively short, listing events in chronological order, and the overall structure of the narrative is more effectively captured on the stanza level. Whereas M's narrative is independent of "scenes" or "stanzas" and repeatedly recounts a single event with modifications and supplements. Thus, it is verse, rather than stanza or scene, which serves as a conspicuous indicator of the ethnopoetic organization. Even with these two examples, it is difficult to single out the most significant level of poetic formation in Japanese, as Hymes' own analysis also shows some fluctuation and uncertainty in these respects. Thus, we should expect some fluidity in individual styles and context-dependency of the criteria rather than those anticipated at the outset (Chapter 2). However, even at less-conscious levels such as verse and stanza, culture-specific preference was evidently observed, endorsing Hymes' initial contention.

A highly notable feature of these narratives is what Silverstein calls "co-eval" (cross-chronotopic) alignments. Silverstein (2005: 12–13) presents as varieties of interdiscursivity a grid of "axes of 'evals'" consisting of type-token and source-target combinatory possibilities. One such variety of "co-eval-ness" is the "indirect free style" of narration (or "free indirect speech" in Leech and Short 2007: see also Chapter 8) and "historical present" (De Fina 2007). Likewise, in our case, such co-eval-ness was realized not only in terms of the denotational text, but also of the physical representations accompanying the narration (cf. McNeill, Levy, and Duncan 2015). Such intersubjectified performance was realized through C-VPTs in a series of embodied depictions of "local chronotopes" (Ladin 1999, 2010). The narrators' iconic gestures meta-discursively point to the ways in which they perceive the time-space and merge the evaluated stances toward the scenes and objects in narration through the local-chronotopically differentiated embodiments. In particular, such proximal gestures as inside-O-VPT and C-VPT seem to trigger the "breakthrough into performance" (Hymes 1966) with the value and affect-laden mode of perspectivization.

These differences in ethnopoetic and chronotopic formations could be related to linguistic encoding of spatial experience and information. As mentioned above, Japanese is found to frequently cultivate mimetics with iconic gestures (Kita 1997; cf. Dingemanse 2013),[8] and tends to realize the "path" and the "manner" information in separate segments of gesture rather than combining them into one as in English (Kita and Özyürek 2003).[9] As such, I posit that the tendency to assimilate into a character's perspective and depict it with C-VPT is likely to increase by incorporating the more action-oriented "manner" information. On the other hand, I assume that the "path" information, which mainly represents the direction of spatial movement, is more likely to be described with O-VPT. In addition, there could be language-specific differences in the above tendency. For example, it was found that, when comparing O-VPTs and C-VPTs used in English and Japanese narratives, Japanese speakers tended to use more C-VPT and inside-O-VPT gestures in depicting the characters' actions in the story, and the degree of empathy and immersion in the characters increased as they approached the climax, rather than in other parts of the narrative (Kataoka 2017).[10] In light of these findings, it is possible that typological differences in "lexicalization patterns" (Talmy 1983) may produce gradient tendencies to realize certain aspects of the narrated event, which would contribute to constructing distinct chronotopes.

In Chapter 8, we will address another type of the "recapitulated" event and mainly examine "quotations" in gossip as a means of reinforcing alpine climbers' ethics and sharing an idealized mental model within the community of practice, both of which constitute a potential socio-cultural text hidden behind a denotational text.

8

Views from Mountaineer Ethics and Deviations

8.1 Introduction

Gossip is an inherent part of climbing—people talk about how so-and-so succeeded or failed in climbing a 5.14 route, what area is being developed and/or opened, when and where so-and-so was injured/killed, and so forth. Gossip is mundane talk about other people who are not present at the scene and often centers around aspects of the character, appearance, or personality of those absent in a less than charitable way. Gossipers tend to focus on the way in which others' characteristics, behaviors, situations, or attributes differ from theirs—usually in a critical way. Here, I focus on mountain climbers' gossip and examine how it was made sense of and accountable in light of their community norms and common outlook, particularly concerning a deadly accident on a winter mountain.

Although there is no one-to-one correspondence of the term "gossip" between cultures (cf. Haviland 1977), it is roughly comparable to the Japanese words *uwasabanashi* ("rumors"), *shuumon* ("ugly news"), *waruguchi* ("bad-mouthing"), and *kageguchi* ("backbiting"), all of which are associated with a sense of secrecy. In this chapter, I examine a phenomenon that includes all of these phrases, and which evolved into an extremely radicalized form—i.e., insults and slander. It started from what is called *zatsudan* ("casual and idle talk") in Japanese (Murata and Ide 2016; cf. Coupland 2003), and escalated into a heated discussion mixed with hearsay and individual observations about a climber who was involved in a lethal accident. In that sense, it is located on a continuum of several genres of talk, which consists of "orienting frameworks, interpretive proceedings, and sets of expectations" (Hanks 1987), exhibiting open-endedness and negotiability (Bauman 1986). Similar to our case, despite the seeming easy-goingness of gossip, certain orientations can gradually be underscored and fostered through interactions among participants who invest in each other's value judgments and ethical comments.

8.2 Types and Features of Gossip

While studies of folklore and discourse have traditionally treated gossip as a separate genre, much discussion exists about its connection to other genres, mainly inspired by discourse-centered approaches to culture (Bauman 1992). According to Brenneis (1992), for example, the study of gossip focuses not only on the content, but also on four themes that have converged in the process of research: (1) the character of a social activity; (2) the moral elements regarding a gossiper, a gossiped-about, and the participants themselves; (3) an aesthetic and expressive aspect with its focus on formal and structural features; and (4) the significance of social interaction on a micro level. Although it is sometimes difficult to distinguish between these categories, I would like to briefly outline the representative studies and the connection between them to clarify key concepts for the present analysis.

First, in terms of a "social activity," gossip is regarded as one of the fundamental human communication activities, and its purpose is to build ties through solidarity (Malinowski 1926; Dunbar 1996, 2004). Gossip is mundane but fundamental in that it can occur anywhere in everyday talk and anywhere in the world, serving as lubricant for human relations. According to Dunbar's evolutionary biological point of view, for example, as social groups become larger, it becomes more difficult to maintain physical contact with all members. Gossiping acts as a substitute for such contact and serves as "social grooming" to repair diluted human relationships. Humans exchange information and sentiment through that form of grooming, maintaining and strengthening ties among community members. Such a feature, conventionally called "phatic communion" (Malinowski 1926), is common not only in gossip but also in small talk and conversational joke-telling (Jefferson 1978; Norrick 2000; Holmes 2005). Human sociality lies at the heart of social norms and developing group solidarity, and it can be projected, created, and disrupted by gossip as well. Gossip may also have malicious intentions aimed at promoting selfish interests (Tierney 2009), and in this sense can be regarded as a highly "political" activity to regulate human relations (Besnier 2009) and exploited as a powerful tool in the arsenal of the oppressed, or the "arts of resistance" (Scott 2008). As this chapter shows, gossip often leads to more gossip and evokes more radicalized content, exposing the narrator, the listener, and all involved to various dangers. For this reason, it has been warned that gossip is "a three-pronged tongue" as a form of "discreet indiscretion" (Bergmann 1993).

Second, gossip is saturated with moral awareness, which reflects upon the speaker him/herself. The speaker's own ethical values are projected recursively through reasoning and an evaluation of the actions of a targeted third party who often deviates from the normalcy and decency of the speaker's community. Depending on the degree to which these evaluations are accepted by other participants, they contribute to the strengthening (or weakening) of the group's ethical values and highlighting of the speaker's own moral position. As such, gossip becomes a medium via which different stances, viewpoints, and ideologies can be represented by adopting different narrative "voices" (Bakhtin 1981; see also Basso 1990, Hill 1995, Keane 2011). In Basso (1996), for example, various "place names" in Cibecue Apache conversations are shown to be used metonymically as moral lessons or as a "topological gossip" (Lewis 1976; see also Rumsey and Weiner 2000), evoking historical events and people involved there as well as the dangers associated with them. Also, as shown in Hill's (1995) analysis of Don Gabriel's narrative of his son's tragic death, the most dramatic breakdown in fluency concerned the language of business and profit, exhibiting a refusal to a capitalist ideology, while the passages about his son's death were narrated in the most poetic voice, imbued with elegiac elegance. As this case shows, the styles and voices in narrative implicitly represent the emergent status of the inner self and a hidden ideology.

Third, as an aesthetic/expressive art, gossipers often employ formalized repertoires and techniques to attract attention and convince the audience. For example, gossip encompasses the stylistic features that make it recognized (and communicated) as gossip. As in other oral traditions, gossip co-occurs with a variety of speech acts, including humor, satire, irony, envy, rancor, slander, and admonition, among others. These acts are not used independently or exclusively but rather integrally to achieve the act of "gossiping." Among the Nukulaelae people of Polynesia, gossip narrators use "zero anaphora" to wrap important information in ambiguous phrases and elicit a repair chain from the audience (Besnier 1989), thereby incorporating the audience as "co-authors" of the gossip (cf. Duranti and Brenneis 1986). In addition, a complex quotation format—"he said, she said"—is often used in the gossip of African-American girls (Goodwin 1990), while among high school girls in Northwest England, "tag questions" (both standard and nonstandard forms such as "weren't she?" and "aren't they?") are often used to describe and evaluate others critically (Moore and Podesva 2009). Brenneis ([1987] 1996) also pointed out that the gossip of the Fiji Indians has the function of creating an integrated harmony, embodying an egalitarian society through the use of repetition and rhythm that resonates comfortably to the ears of local people. The accumulation and customization of structural awareness of these activities eventually lead to (co-)constructing and sharing what are called "cultural models" (D'Andrade and Strauss 1992). Holland and Quinn (1987: 4) defined cultural models as "presupposed and predetermined models of the world that are widely shared by members of a society and that play a significant role in understanding the environment and their behavior in it." This shared perception is roughly equivalent to the concept conventionally called "schema" (D'Andrade 1992), and as a socially conceived schema, it can frame the performativity of gossip concerning who can gossip about who, what, when, and where.

Finally, gossip is not without social significance (Haviland 1977), as it serves as a crucial aspect of social interaction. One such aspect is language socialization, which helps members of each community acquire the verbal/ nonverbal skills and semiotic resources available and necessary for the society (Goodwin 1990; Evaldsson 2002; Goodwin and Kyratzis 2007). Also, gossip, as well as small talk, is an everyday activity, but because of its mundanity, speakers use a variety of means to pique their listeners' attention and keep them involved (Fine 1986), whether intentional or not. One such means is what is called "constructed dialogue" (cf. Tannen 1989), used for various purposes such as to highlight the point of talking, promote camaraderie and solidarity, and legitimize derogatory comments, to name a few. For example, Mohammad and Vásquez (2015) focused on a single extended gossip episode, and examined how gossip unfolds over time by inviting evaluative commentary through constructed dialogue that serves as "interactional bait." Thus, gossip is not necessarily a fixed genre, as it might undergo transformation in accordance with the ongoing talk. All of this points to the significance of gossip as an interactional achievement.

Given these observations, gossip is a highly contestable but suitable venue to inquire into the meaning and significance of ongoing events. As such, gossip works as a distinct but transformable genre of narration, exhibiting chimera-like features.

In the following, by analyzing the development of an idle talk into blame and slander, I attempt to reveal the process of interactional constructions of how and what mountain/alpine climbers should be as a responsible member of society.

8.3 Data and Method of Analysis

In what follows, I focus on a series of recursive accusations that evolved from gossiping and developed into defamatory discourse. The analyzed data consisted of gossip among six participants: three regular guests to a mountain lodge (K, W, and N), the manager of the lodge and his wife (M and T), and the researcher (R) who used to be a regular guest there. At the time of data collection, K, W, M, and T are in their fifties, and N in his early forties. The gossip started when the topic of the conversation shifted from the guests' mountaineering experiences to a fatal accident that occurred the previous winter in the Japanese Northern Alps, during the time of data collection.

The gossip targets are J (a third party who was not present) and S (a victim of the accident). J is a male alpine guide based in the research area, and S (deceased) was an experienced female climber who had climbed Gasherbrum II (8,035 m) in the Himalayas and Mt. McKinley (6,191 m) in North America. S allegedly fell into a steep valley when she was downclimbing an icy and rocky slope at night. J and S were tied to each other with a rope when the accident occurred and reportedly, J secured her with the rope from above and left the scene.

The conversation, including the following excerpts, started in a pleasant and friendly atmosphere and lasted for more than three hours (as part of a casual get-together). This chapter focuses on a 45-minute segment in the conversation about the present topic. (1) is a summary of those who took part in the gossip session and others named in it.

1 Participants and third parties

<Participants in the gossip>

K (m):   Experienced alpinist, leader of a Himalayan expedition and numerous domestic climbs
W (f):   Experienced climber, K's ex-wife
N (m):   Experienced mountain guide, member of a Himalayan expedition
M (m):   Co-Manager/owner of the mountain lodge
T (f):   Wife of M and co-manager of the mountain lodge
R (m):   Researcher

<Third party characters in the gossip>

J (m):   Experienced mountain guide
S (f):   Experienced alpinist practicing domestic and overseas climbs (deceased).

In the following segments, I attempt to specifically identify the participants' strategies that were used to hold J responsible for the accident, and confirm how these strategies were achieved by reporting in a number of ways the voices and actions of themselves and others. Thus, before the analysis, it would be helpful to review the categories of "reported speech" and the Japanese markers of "quotation" employed here (Du Bois 1986; Leech and Short [1981] 2007; Kamada 2000; Yamaguchi 2009). One of the most inclusive models of reported speech would be Du Bois' (1986) proposal of a hierarchy of ritual speech, which includes not only quotations but also other speech phenomena such as mimicry, impersonations, and trances. His model also incorporates the notion of "transfer of control," which, based on degrees of indexicality, constitutes a broader scope of reported speech. His notion of "personal presence" delineates the types of experience encoded in language, and is helpful in fine-tuning the experiential status of the speaker, to which I refer in passing. In this analysis, I also need to focus on degrees of "constructedness" and levels of speaker control in the reported speech.

Also highly compatible with our purposes is the model proposed by Leech and Short ([1981] 2007). Although their classification was based on English literary texts, it could also be applicable to other languages including Japanese (see also Kamada 2000). In their model, reported speech constitutes a cline of speech presentation from the more bound to the freer end (Figure 8.1), consisting of "free direct speech" (FDS), "direct speech" (DS), "free indirect speech" (FIS), "indirect speech" (IS), "narrative report of speech acts" (NRSA), and "narrative report of action" (NRA).[1] These salient types could be identified according to the speaker's control, or the "levels of (speaker) intervention."

Although these are just representative modes of reported speech, they provide a useful resource for the analysis. According to the cline in Figure 8.1, for example, the utterance "I'll come back here to see you again tomorrow" could be reported/represented in a number of ways (especially as to FIS, NRSA, and NRA) (see left side of Table 8.1: Leech and Short 1981: Ch. 10). Kamada (2000) also examined types of Japanese quotations from a pragmatic perspective and basically confirmed a similar cline, which I employ for the following analysis of climbing discourse. On the right-hand side are rough equivalents of Japanese representations (my translations).

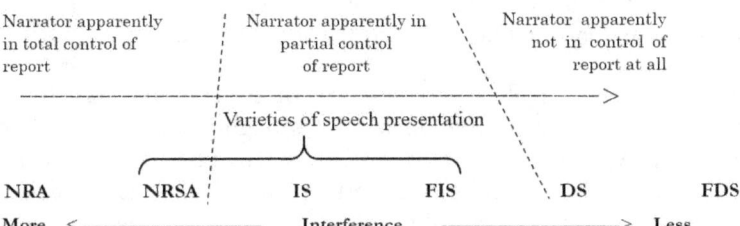

FIGURE 8.1 *Cline of "interference" in reporting (Leech and Short 2007: 260; reproduced with permission).*

Notes: FDS: free direct speech DS: direct speech
FIS: free indirect speech IS: indirect speech
NRSA: narrative report of speech acts NRA: narrative report of action

Table 8.1 Types of quotation in English and Japanese.

Q-type	English	Japanese
FDS:	(He said) "I'll come back here to see you again tomorrow."	*"Ashita mata kimi ni ai-ni kokoni kuru yo" (to kare wa itta).*
DS:	He said, "I'll come back here to see you again tomorrow."	*"Ashita mata kimi ni ai-ni kokoni kuru yo" to kare wa itta.*
FIS:	He would return (/come back) there to see her again tomorrow (/the following day).	*Ashita (/yokujitsu) mata kanojo ni ai-ni kare wa soko ni modoru (tsumori da).*
IS:	He said that he would return there to see her the following day.	*Yokujitsu mata kanojo ni ai-ni soko ni modoru to kare wa itta.*
NRSA:	He promised his return./ He committed himself to another meeting.	*Kare wa modotte-kuru to yakusoku shita.*
NRA:	(He muttered the sentence.)	*(Kare wa tsubuyaita.)*

In the case of Japanese, reported speech is mainly introduced by linguistic markers such as *-to, -tte, -nante, -to(ka), mitaina,* and *-gurai* (Kamada 2000; cf. Yamaguchi 2009). These markers may be optional when a sentence includes onomatopoeic expressions, as in *Kare wa noronoro-to aruita* ("he walked slowly"), where *noronoro* is the adverbial onomatopoeic word representing the manner of a reported action, and "*-to*" is the quotation marker. However, even when these markers are used, the judgment of a reporting style is not so straightforward, exhibiting a gradual difference in the reproducibility and "constructed-ness" (Tannen 1989) of the reported/quoted content. For example, Kamada's (2000) examples include:

(2) *Kono su-miso   no guai   ga wakara-nee*   -tte *yuu'-n da yo.*
    This vinegared-miso POS condition SB judge-NEG (VLG) QT   say-COP PT
    "(My wife says) she can't judge the taste of this vinegared miso." (Kamada 2000: 53)
(3) *Osamu-san, Jefurii ga boku ni mo mikan   choodai*-tte *yuuteru wa-yo.*
    Osamu-PT   Jeffrey SB me   to also orange   give.me-QT   saying PT-PT
    "Hey Osamu, Jeffrey [dog] says, 'give me the oranges'." (Kamada 2000: 60)

Examples (2) and (3) show that the reported content may be modified by incorporating the speaker's judgment and imagination. In (2), which would presumably be a typical construct of IS, the content of the subordinate clause (the utterance by the speaker's wife) was reported through the male speaker's parlance, as shown by the vulgarized form of the predicate, *wakara-nee* (judge-NEG (VLG)). Since his wife would not have used the form verbatim, this vulgarized version must be attributed to his own modification. Also, since Japanese is one of those "pro-drop" languages, the subject pronoun of the subordinate clause is elided here, but it still can be retrievable from the co-text. Example (3) is a more obvious case. Because Jeffrey is a dog and could not have said "give me the oranges," this represents the female speaker's interpretation of the dog's intention/feeling. (We know it is an utterance by a female speaker from the duplicated final particles *wa-yo*, the set of which is dominantly used by women.) Here again, the dog's imaginary utterance is marked by the *-tte* complementizer as in (3), and the quoted clause *boku ni mo mikan choodai* ("give me the oranges") smacks of DS especially because the phrase *choodai* ("give [me]") represents a dialogic setting where "space/person deixis" is typically concerned.

These examples clearly show that a phenomenon called reporting (and more specifically, quoting) is often achieved through performative modifications, and that the accuracy of utterance is a distinctive issue. This is the reason why some scholars have preferred to call it "constructed dialogue" or "represented speech" (Tannen 1989; Banfield 1993), because what matters here is rather "effectiveness" than "accuracy" in reproduction. Since accuracy mainly concerns "denotation," while effectiveness concentrates on "interaction," they need to be investigated separately (Silverstein 1993; Agha 2007a, Ch. 1). Based on these observations, my approach to the present data basically follows Kamada's (2000) and Yamaguchi's (2009) discourse analytic frameworks, which characterize Japanese quotations as *shinayaka* ("flexible"), compared to English quotations as *meiseki* ("logical"; Yamaguchi 2009). Thus, the distinction between "direct" and "indirect" quotation is secondary in Japanese, and is controlled not only by syntactic phenomena but also by a perspectival configuration of the participants' psychological attachment to the target under discussion. In some cases, I relied on a pragmatic interpretation of the context to identify reporting types.

In fact, reported speech is part of deictic management and related closely to the concept of "denotational indexical" (Agha 2007a) in that the positioning of the *origo* indexes the speaker's footing on the "here-and-now" vis-à-vis the "there-and-then." Referring back to Figure 8.1, FDS, which conveys the utterance verbatim, shows the highest "iconicity," with the *origo* transferred from the time-space of "here and now" to "there-and-then." On the other hand, the highly controlled citation forms toward the left end of the hierarchy are mainly realized by syntactic operations such as "subordination/ conjunction," "embedding" of a clause—i.e., with heavier "construction" or "speaker interference/control." Accordingly, the model in Figure 8.1 provides us with a promising point of departure for further investigation of deictic management of climbers' identities and ethics in gossip. Still missing, however, is the focused attention to the "interactional" configuration that emerges through the denotational content of quotation/ reporting. We will return to this issue after confirming several strategic metaphors employed by the discourse participants. In the last section, I will then show that the coordination and distribution of "reporting" styles are an indicator of their epistemic stance and evaluative footing in the interactional setting (Goffman 1981; Jaffe 2009).

8.4 Analysis of Gossip About a Fatal Accident

The greatest responsibility one must bear as a human being is for errors that might threaten someone else's life; the ultimate penalty for such transgressions is to atone for them with one's own life. Even in the absence of a third party, telling others that someone has caused the death of another person entails a social risk for both the teller and the third party being told. As such, I will examine a case in which gossip participants, confronted with the death of a close friend, tell how and to what extent the responsibility for S's death is attributed to J (the deceased's climbing partner). Specifically, in this particular gossip, the participants (except the researcher) question the validity of J's reactions to S's accident and countermeasures he took for S's safety at the time of it. In what follows, I analyze the gossip in term of denotational (1), cultural (2), and interactional (3) levels of discursive formation: (1) the use of "conceptual metaphors" (Lakoff and Johnson 1980; Kövecses 2002) related to the human psyche and pathology; (2) the "Cultural Model" (D'Andrade and Strauss 1992) shared among the participants (i.e., the climbers' community); and finally (3) the social formation constructed by the accumulated representation of epistemic and experiential stances (cf. Goffman 1981 and Jaffe 2009).

8.4.1 Conceptual Metaphors

8.4.1.1 Infantilization

The first case to be examined is the insult made in metaphorical terms about J's developmental inferiority in the eyes of those present. Although there are cultural differences in what kind of behavior is considered mature, given children's underdeveloped mental and physical capabilities, an utterance that characterizes an adult as a child ordinarily serves as criticism and insult. In Japanese society, the term *gaki*—literally "hungry devil"—is used as a derogatory epithet for a child, roughly meaning "brat" or "son of a bitch." It is also used as a metaphor for a person with little experience, poor intellect and discretion, or a bad demeanor, i.e., as an instance of a conceptual metaphor IMMATURITY IS CHILD.

In the following Excerpt 8.1, K describes the behaviors of J, who allegedly abandoned the accident victim, as those of an irresponsible *gaki*. This and other relevant terms are also underlined. Prior to the utterance of Excerpt 8.1, the gossip participants expressed their strong suspicion about J's behaviors at the time of the accident. It is known that after his partner (S) slipped off an icy, rocky ridge, J secured her with a rope. Determining that he could not rescue her alone, J left the scene and returned to the tent of some acquaintances who happened to be camped in the nearby area. (Before the accident happened, S and J had met them and chatted over a cup of coffee.) There, J spent the night in a somewhat delirious mental state, watched over by his friends. Since the accident occurred on a winter mountain in the Japanese Northern Alps, leaving his injured partner out in the open overnight would instantly mean her death, but J did not provide any details in his report as to why he left her without proper treatment. The report was judged by the community members to be inadequate and insufficient at best, but J volunteered no further information despite repeated requests from various quarters. This background explains the statement in line 15.

Here, J does not literally put on a *futon* (thick bedquilt; lines 6, 8), but *futon* serves as a metaphor for a comfortable night in a tent where one does not freeze. In other words, the underlying image is that of a lazy child who is reluctant to get out of bed on a cold morning—a metaphor for J's lack of urgency in going to S's aid. In fact, the same metaphor is repeatedly used in other portions (Excerpt 8.2).

EXCERPT 8.1 Gaki *'brat'*

1	K:	*Onaji yooni sokkara-, genba kara tachisari, nige-kaette,*	Just like that... he wanted to leave the scene, run back,
2	R:	*nn.*	Hmm.
3	K:	*Jiitto shite itai to.*	and stay put.
4	W:	*Nigeru [dake desu yo, are wa.*	He just [runs away, that's it.
5	K:	*[are wa akumu datta to.*	[Like it was a nightmare,
6		*de.. futon kabutte netori-tai.*	and... he wanted to cover himself up with a futon and go to sleep.
7		*Nee, gaki ga daijiken o okoshite shimatte,*	You know, like a brat who caused a big trouble,
8		*nee, futon o kabutte netoritai to.*	you know, he just wanted to sleep with a futon over his head.
9		*Sono shinkyoo wa wkaru yo.*	I understand how he feels, (but . . . .)
10	W:	*Demo paatonaa kunda aite ga ,*	But his partner is
11		*hh [zairu ni tsunagarete,*	hh [still tied to a rope, and ...
12	K:	*[Dakedo soredemo,*	[But still,
13	W:	*ima-=*	now-=
14	K:	*=demo otona dattara,*	=but if he is a decent adult,
15		*sono sinkyoo o kakanakya naran.*	he has to write down his feelings about it (in the report).

EXCERPT 8.2 Yoochi *'childish'*

1	K:	*Dakara are wa nee,*	So that was, you know,
2		*yoosuruni,*	in short,
3		*hontoni,*	really,
4		*futon kabutte naitotta kuseni sa:.*	like he was crying with a futon over himself.
5	W:	*soo na no?*	Is that so?
6	K:	*Iya kekkyoku,*	Well, I mean,
7		*soo- sore to onaji da gaya.*	that- it is basically the same.
8	W:	*Aa::.*	Oh ...
9	K:	*Iyaa, (soo)nanda kedo,*	Well, that's the case, I mean,
10		*warui koto shite kite ne,*	when a small kid did something bad,
11		*soshite futon kabutte naitotta ne, osanai ko ga ne,*	and was crying under a futon, you know,
12		*nde, futon age tara ato wa nani mo nakatta yoo ni,*	but once he puts away the futon, he is pretending
13		*tsukuro-ttoru dake nan-da.*	as if nothing happened.
14		*(2.0) Hontoni yoochi da yo.*	(2.0) It's really childish.
15		*Mukatsuku na.*	It's disgusting.
16		*Dakara sooyuu mono ga=*	Given all this, he's=
17	W:	*=sekininkan ga nasa-sugiru.*	=totally irresponsible.

In line 4, K says that "(he [J] was crying) with a futon over himself" (with the hyperbolic description of J's crying), which was actually questioned by W (line 5). Admitting that it is just a metaphor (line 7), K compares this to typical behavior by a small kid (line 11), and declares J to be "childish" again (line 14). W's utterance in line 17 refers exactly to J's lack of responsibility, which implicitly refers back to his failure to submit a detailed report.

Behaviors that are incomprehensible to a mature adult are often regarded to be characteristic of infancy as well as of poor mental function. In other words, a state of "infantilization" is another aspect of "pathologization." As Sontag (1978) has previously argued, using the metaphorical imagery of cancer and tuberculosis, disease tends to be seen as a manifestation of personality. When framed in the context of moral decadence, disease has been the basis for the social condemnation of infected individuals as morally deficient. As we will see, the participants build on this common perception that J's behaviors deviate from the norms shared among mature adults.

8.4.1.2 Pathologization

The abovementioned process developed as the gossip proceeded based on various levels of epistemic and deontic interpretation. As well as infantilization, another strategy that has been repeatedly used is to compare the gossip target to a person with pathological or mental problems. The following statement was made by another participant, M, who was the manager of the lodge where the gossip session took place. He was in a position to glean more details about the accident because he was close to both friends of the victim and members of the alpine club to which she belonged (Excerpt 8.3). In response to his comments, K describes J's behaviors after the accident as being *okashii*, which can mean "strange," "wrong," or even "crazy" depending on context (lines 13 and 15).[2]

In Excerpt 8.3, K calls it *okashii* that J continues to guide other clients even after his climbing partner's death. Even though J had also been involved in the accident, he was behaving as if he felt no remorse or grief. In the segment that follows (Excerpt 8.4), this "strangeness" comes to mean moral and ethical aberration, and to imply a huge lack of empathy. When the insinuated abnormality is unanimously confirmed by participants (lines 6–9), M describes J's behaviors with the metaphor "punch-drunker," which now apparently implies poor mental capacity (line 10). It should be remembered that apart from the original meaning, the loanword *panchi-dorankaa* in Japanese often refers to a boxer with (permanent) cerebral damage. This sort of pathological image is a source of metaphor for mental deficiency and abnormality (cf. a conceptual metaphor: "Inappropriate conditions are illness" (Kövecses 2002: 134; see also Sontag 1978).[3]

As shown in Excerpts 8.3 and 8.4 above, J continues to guide people in the mountains (smiling as he does so) despite being strongly dissuaded by the local community. This fact is regarded as the basis for attributing a mental disorder to J, as well as regarding him as someone who lacks remorse and moral judgment. The above metaphor-based slander about a lack of social responsibility seems to go hand in hand with the common sense and decency required of climbers as ordinary citizens.

EXCERPT 8.3 Okashii 'strange/wrong/crazy'

1	M:	*Futsuu nara ne, aayuu baai wa ne,*	Normally, in a case like that,
2		*J- J ga totta taido-tte yuu no wa ne,*	J-, the attitude that J took is (unacceptable).
3		*jibun no koto ni taisuru sono: shokuzai ishiki ga ne,*	If he feels the ah: remorse for his actions,
4		*nakanaka koren yo.*	he won't be able to come here.
5	W:	↑*Hontto soo omou-n ya te.*	I really feel the same way.
6	M:	*Aitsu maishuu kite,*	That guy comes back here every week,
7	W:	*Sugu kiteta yo!*	He came here right away! (after the accident)
8	M:	*Mada maishuu hito tsurete aruitoru yaro.*	and still take people around every week.
9	K:	↑*Oo: tsure-toru.*	Yeah, he does!
10		*Konshuu mo tsure-totta.*	He was with someone this week too.
11	M:	*mm.*	Hmm.
12	W:	*Gaido yatte-nda yo.*	He's guiding people.
13	K:	<u>*Okashii*</u>.	He's <u>wrong</u>.
14	W:	*Ikeshaashaa to.*	Shamelessly.
15	K:	<u>*Okashii*</u>.	Just <u>wrong</u>.
16	W:	*Shiranai hito ga kawaisoo yo.*	I feel sorry for people who don't know about it.

EXCERPT 8.4 Panchi dorankaa 'punch-drunkard'

1	N:	*Minna ga toobun kunna-tte ittan dakedo ne:.*	Everybody told him not to come here for a while.
2	M:	*mm.*	Yeah.
3	W:	*Hee(k)kina kao shite hito to kuru.*	He blatantly comes here with people.
4		*Ni(k)ko-niko niko-niko shite heeki de kuru mon ne:.*	He impudently comes with people with a big big smile on his face.
5		*(1.2) Sugu chokugo kara.*	(1.2) Right after (the accident).
6	T:	*Dakara yappari chotto <u>okashii</u>-n'ya.*	So there's something totally <u>wrong</u> with him.
7	M:	<u>*Okashii*</u>.	He's <u>wrong</u>.
8	W:	<u>*Okashii*</u>.	He's <u>wrong</u>.
9	M:	<u>*Okashii*</u>.	He's <u>wrong</u>.
10		*Yappa ne, arya chotto <u>panchi-dorankaa</u> ya.*	I knew that. He is something like a <u>punch-drunker</u>.
11	W:	*Aa::, S-chan, fuun yattan ya wa.*	Oh: S-chan, you had such a bad luck.
12		*Hontoni aite ga warukatta.*	You really had a bad (climbing) partner.
13	M:	<u>*Panchi-dorankaa ya*</u>.	(He's a) <u>punch-drunker</u>!

8.4.2 Hidden Text of Mountaineering Ethics

The location and attribution of responsibility is judged in light of the socialized and shared norms of a particular group (here, the climbing community). Developmental and psychological deviances are often institutionalized pathologically in modern society, but in mountaineering activities—where participants' lives are at stake—a somewhat different sense of decency seems to be expected and reinforced. In this respect, I argue that behind the following slander of J lies an implicitly constructed and shared "cultural model" (D'Andrade and Strauss 1992) in interpreting the significance and consequences of the accident.

The beginning of the insult to J can be traced to K's initial statement (Excerpt 8.5), which started with his nonfluent, fragmented utterances (lines 1 3), a rather ambiguous summary (lines 4–6), and a long pause before he topicalizes J (line 8). They all suggest that he was hesitant at first but finally determined to bring up the topic in this conversation.

The techniques of denunciation that were observed in the previous section were used when the criticism of J reached its peak. However, in order for these techniques to be communally effective, there should be some sort of a shared standard of value judgments. Such a shared standard is an unwritten rule and common sense among mountaineers who are committed to and engaged in climbing not simply for amusement, but for self-realization and social achievement. Summarizing the preceding discussion, K continues in Excerpt 8.6 that "If you can't do it, don't climb mountains" (line 1). Here "it" means that, in the event of an accident in the mountains,

EXCERPT 8.5 *The beginning of gossip*

1	K:	*Tokoroga,*	But . . .
2		*nn . . . nn . . .*	uhm. . . ahh . . .
3		*sono . . . nnn . . . nn.*	I mean. . .uhm hmm,
4		*un no warui-tte yuu ka,*	should we say it was a bad luck, or
5		*jibun no seeshin jootai o waruku suru-tte koto ga,*	things do happen that make our mental states worse
6		*yo no naka de okoru wake desho.*	in the world, you know.
7	R:	*Mm.*	Uh hum.
8	K:	(2.0) *J-chan no hanashi ja nai kedo,*	(2.0) I don't wanna bring up J-chan here, but
9		*hakkiri yuu kedo . . nazashi de sa:.*	I have to say it clearly, naming the name.
10		*Dakedo mo:,*	Bu::t,
11		*soo yuu koto ga okoru to ne:,*	something like that does happen,
12		*monosugoi fuyukai ni narun dawa.*	and it makes me really disgusted, you know.

EXCERPT 8.6 Hooritsu "Law"

1	K:	Sore ga dekinai mono wa:	If you can't do it (conform to implicit rules),
2		tozan nanka yaccha ikan.	you shouldn't climb mountains.
3	R:	Mm.	Hmm.
4	W:	Hx	Hx.
5	K:	Yaccha ikan noda yo=	You just shouldn't=
6		=date sono ruuru wa nai-n'da mon.	=because there are no (written) rules.
7		<u>Hooritsu</u> wa nai-n'da mon.	There are no <u>laws</u>, you know.
8	R:	Mm.	Hmm.
9	K:	Sora fubui-toru toki wa,	Like, when a blizzard is blowing,
10		soko arui-tara ikemasen nante yuu <u>kanban</u> datte yo:,	there's no <u>sign</u> that says "Don't walk there," and
11	W:	hx@	hx@
12	K:	okashita mono wa [bakkin torare tari nanka shite nai yo,	the offender isn't [fined or anything, you know,
13	W:	[hx hx@@	[hx hx@@
14	K:	kootsuu jiko mitai ni.	like a traffic accident.
15	R:	Hm hm.	Hmm hmm.
16	K:	↑Nai-n'da mon.	There's nothing like that.
17		Naku[te,	There's [nothing, and
18	T:	[soo ya na.	[You're right.
19	K:	jibun no ude ya ne, gijutsu ya,	it's all about your skills, your expertise,
20	W:	shinyoo[shite yatteru-n'da mon ne, otagai.	We can do it cuz we [trust each other, don't we?
21	K:	[migaite iku wake dakara ne.	[that you have to polish.

one should do all they can on the spot and give a sincere report on what was done (or not).

I assume that this autonomy and responsibility is still largely expected of climbers, especially in organized expeditions and high-altitude climbing (but possibly less so in commercialized expeditions). It is their responsibility to assure safety in climbing by training constantly and taking active steps to improve their skills. K's statement, which warns against abusing liberally due to the absence of particular "laws" for climbers, is endorsed instantly with overlapping utterances by several participants, especially by T (M's wife) (line 18) and W (K's ex-wife), who follows it up with confirmation (line 20).

However, even in this discussion, the participants are keenly aware that a code of mountaineering ethics should not deviate from general societal norms (Excerpt 8.7). As shown above, touching on J's inadequacy of not submitting a full report (lines 1–8), the climbers' awareness of societal norms comes to be validated. Evidently, this exchange, which confirms that a code of mountaineering ethics should not be fundamentally different from societal norms (lines 10–13), serves as a process to collaboratively sanction both climbing ethics and the idea that mountaineers are mature members of society. This process emerges schematically as a dichotomous

EXCERPT 8.7 Ippan no hito 'the general public'

1	W:	Chotto yappari ne kichinto kejime tsukena akan te.	Well, you know, he's got to fix things up, saying
2		<Q Mooshiwake arimasen deshita! Q>-tte ne,	<Q "I'm very sorry!," Q> and
3		mitomete ne:,	admit it,
4		hansee shite,	repent it,
5		de,	and,
6	K:	See ippai ya[ru.	Does his [best.
7	W:	[kore kara onaji koto o kurikaesanai yooni ne:.	[never let it happen again.
8		Yappari: hookokusho o dasana akan te.	Either way, he has to hand in a report.
9	K:	Dakara--	So--
10	W:	Ima soo shina=	If he doesn't do that now,
11	T:	=yamaya-san* te kon'na mon ka-tte *ippan no hito* ni omowareru wa na.	the general public will think that mountaineers are people like that.
12	W:	Soo yate.	That's right.
13	K:	Omowareru te.	They will think that.

* Yamaya-san: a jargon for "mountaineers"

evaluation between opposites, qualitatively reflecting "those who adhere to mountaineering ethics" and "those who lack them," "those enlightened" and "those not enlightened," that is, "us" and "J" (Excerpt 8.8).

Mountaineers, especially those who practice alpine climbing in extreme conditions, are expected to behave in accordance with principles of conduct that are shared by the community. Although these principles have changed over time, the traditional spirit of service and sacrifice to the party was largely maintained in the alpine climber community at the time of this data collection (mid-1990s). This can be seen in W's statement at the beginning of Excerpt 8.8 that the "martyr-like devotion of the guide" is an expected virtue (lines 3–4).[4] However, K, who has also experienced a Himalayan expedition, is well aware of the demands of high-altitude mountaineering, which cannot be addressed by virtue alone. Thus, he does not immediately agree with the statement (line 5), and keeps silent until line 22.

Imitating the voice of "Kazu-san (pseudonym)" (lines 8–16), M employs an extensive "free direct speech" (FDS: shown in "<Q ... Q>" without a quotation marker) to condemn J's irresponsible behavior in leaving his troubled partner without checking on her location and condition. This perception is echoed by N's statement that it goes against the common sense of *yatteru yamaya* ("experienced climbers"; line 21), a sentiment confirmed repeatedly by other participants (lines 19–28).

Furthermore, the possibility of a more serious defect is projected by introducing a "hypothetical narrative" (one type of "small story": Bamberg 2007) about J, who keeps ignoring the importance of accountability (Excerpt 8.9).

EXCERPT 8.8 Yatteru yamaya 'Committed climbers'

1	W:	Hh datte Kazu-san ga Everest de jiko yatta ano,	hh .. but when Kazu-san had an accident on Everest,
2		riidaa datte,	as the leader,
3		ano yowatta hito ni hitoban tsukiatte jibun mo inochi o otoshita jan ne.	a guide spent the night with that exhausted man and lost his life, didn't he?,
4		Sekininkan de ne:, gaido ga.	out of his responsibility, you know, the guide.
5	K:	(0.5) Hmmm.	(0.5) Weeell
6	W:	Erai chigai [da yo.	There's a huge[difference.
7	M:	[Iya Kazu-san ni iware totta.	[You know, Kazu-san told him.
8		<Q Watashi wa nee, Q>	<Q Even if I am-, Q>.
9		<Q Jibun wa nee, Q>	<Q Even if I am-, Q>
10		<Q ikura batebate ni natto-ttemo nee, Q>	<Q no matter how exhausted I am, Q>
11	K:	Mm	hmm
12	M:	<Q shinu kamo wakaran to omo-tte mo zettai, Q>	<Q and even if I know I may die, I'll definitely— Q>.
13		Ano:::	Um . . .
14		Zairu . . .(1.5) chanto kotee-shite arun dakara ne,	since the rope (1.5) is properly fixed, you know,
15	W:	Soo::	Right.
16	M:	<Q watashi wa moo sore tsutawatte oriru yo. Q>	<Q I will definitely climb down with it. Q>
17	W:	hh[n	hh[n.
18	K:	[mmm	[hmm
19	W:	(1.2) Kakunin suru yo ne=	(1.2) (We) will check her condition, won't (we)?=
20	M:	=un!	=Yeah!
21	N:	Maa <u>yatteru yamaya</u>-san nara zettai soo suru [yone.	Yeah any <u>experienced climbers</u> will do that, [won't they?
22	K:	[Zettai da.	[Definitely.
23	W:	Futsuu da yo ne.	That's normal.
24	K:	Dakara basho mo jooken mo ne.	I mean, given the location and condition.
25	M:	Mm	Hmm.
26	K:	Ano: zettai da.	Uhm, absolutely.
27		Zettai oriru beki [toko- tokoro da.	Absolutely he [should have done that.
28	M:	[hm hm	[Uhun. Uhun.

Excerpt 8.9 introduces an extremely contestable issue (lines 1–7). M offers a critical conjecture that casts doubt on the integrity of J, who omits important details of the accident (lines 1-7). From around here, M becomes highly talkative, and extensively acts as a ventriloquist of *Kenji-san*' voice using FDS (lines 18–23). M's FDSs appear consecutively, embodying *Kenji-san*'s parlance that criticizes J's silence about the accident.

EXCERPT 8.9 Utaga-cchau 'cannot help but doubt'

1	M:	Ano:::	You knooow, like,
2		jibun ga ochite,	he himself fell, and
3		S-chan o: hikizuri konde,	dragged S-chan in, and
4	W:	Watashi soo omotta!	I thought so!
5	M:	kowaku natte,	got scared, and
6	T:	Sore mo kangae rareru wa na.	That's another possibility.
7	M:	tooboo shita to.	ran away, you know.
8	W:	Aredake dama-tteru [to sooyuu koto mo kangae rare chau no.	As long as he keeps silent, [we can't help thinking that.
9	T:	[Waruku ieba--	[To put it badly--
10	W:	Soo ja naka-ttara jibun de hakkiri yuu yo,	If it wasn't so, he should have said so himself,
11		<Q soo ja nai! Q>-ttutte.	like <Q: That's not true! Q>
12	M:	Hm	Hmm
13	W:	Sore o nani yuwaretemo damattoru-tte koto [wa sa,	The fact that he remains silent about it, no matter what people say [to him,
14	M:	[Soo.	[Yes.
15	W:	Nanka utaga-cchau yo ne.	makes us suspicious, doesn't it?
16	M:	Hakkiri to Kenji-san ga saa,	Very clearly, Kenji-san (said), you know,
17	W:	Hmm	Hmm
18	M:	<Q Anta sore ja tekizen tooboo da yo Q>-tte.	<Q you're just running away, Q>
19		<Q Anta- Anta ni totte nee, Q>	<Q and for your own sake, Q>
20		ano:: <Q yuurina: ano: koto wa hitotsu mo okinai yo Q>-tte.	uh::n <Q there is no good thing occurring to you, never. Q>
21	W:	Soo.	Right.
22		[Sono,	[You know,
23	M:	[<Q Zutto furi nanda yo Q>-tte.	[<Q Being silent is never an advantage for you. Q>
24	W:	Sono toori da yo.	That's totally true.

So far, I have examined the escalating process via which J is ostracized from the community and regarded as an ethical exile if not a quasi-criminal. Below, by considering the discussion from a semiotic and meta-pragmatic perspective, I attempt to reconstruct the community-held "cultural model" that would have motivated the process of exclusion. First, it is assumed that contemporary Japan seemingly embraces diverse social values and incorporates "deviances" from community-held "common sense" (Figure 8.2, dashed line). As shown in Excerpt 8.7, it was confirmed by the participants that although mountaineer community ethics are different from the law, they should never be separated from it (i.e., laws ≒ mountaineering ethics) (Figure 8.2, upper part). Accordingly, autonomous and sound-minded mountaineers follow the law and community ethics, and they would not breach them nor spare efforts to rescue climbing partners (dotted line on the left side of Figure 8.2). In a reasonable

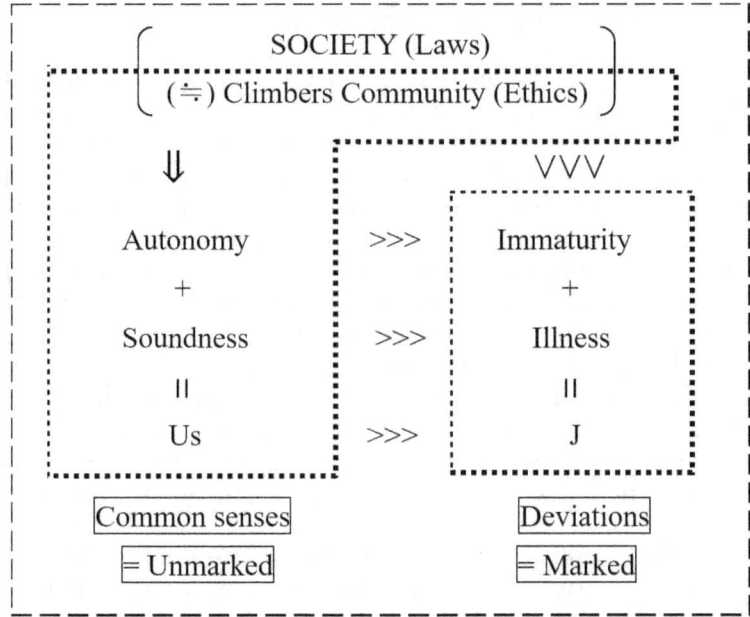

FIGURE 8.2 *A cultural model shared by participants.*

extension, it is "we," not J, who adhere to and embody such climbing/mountaineering norms and ethics.

These relationships are established discursively, such that J was gradually severed as a case of deviation and ostracized from his community through various strategies (dotted line on the right side of Figure 8.2). His personality shows "immature" sociality and lacks autonomy as a respectable citizen. Immaturity is simultaneously equated with incomprehensible and "pathological" behaviors and reactions, implying a deviation from the "sound" mountaineering ethics, and that it was none other than J who acted in such a way.

This ostracization process is reminiscent of Silverstein's (1985) exposition of ideological conflicts in English gender markings, such that the masculine gender is ideologically opposed to the feminine gender, and as seen in the use of "generic 'he'" to refer to humans in general, it incorporates the feminine gender as a "marked" case. In our case, however, it was not through the explicit grammatical system, but rather the accumulation of discursive practices that the deviation from the community ethics was rendered "marked" in the ongoing discourse. In fact, J had belonged to the local climbing community as an unmarked person (i.e., as a local mountain guide), but as a result of the present gossip, he came to be "constructed" as an outsider via metaphors suggesting he was being childish, potentially unwell, and perhaps challenged by poor mental health. In other words, those taking part in the gossip collaboratively marginalized, excluded, and erased J (cf. Irvine and Gal 2000) by characterizing him as, and relegating him to, their ethical antagonist. It is along this oppositional and dichotomic division that J's ethical ostracism was achieved, and their community norms were confirmed and reinforced.

8.4.3 Stance and Reported Speech

We have seen that communal ethics is largely shared among the participants, but the respective "footing" or "stance" (Goffman 1981; Du Bois 2007; Jaffe 2009) for evaluating a target varies depending on available semiotic resources. It is a mode of (dis)alignment that one takes toward others, both animate and inanimate, through a projected self. Recently, such a notion or stance was defined comprehensively by Du Bois (2007: 163) as "a public act by a social actor, achieved dialogically through overt communicative means (language, gesture, and other symbolic forms), through which social actors simultaneously evaluate objects, position subjects (themselves and others), and align with other subjects, with respect to any salient dimension of the sociocultural field." In the present gossip, the participants sometimes resorted to explicit statements condemning J's behavior, while at other times they relied more on implicit calibrations of the *origo* vis-à-vis the target. For the latter practice, their stances toward the gossip target were realized through the management of reporting styles, the configuration of which entails indexical connotations emanating from the interaction.

The degree of indexicality can be determined by the degree to which it is anchored to the *origo*, and is always accompanied by the sense of responsibility (Hill and Irvine 1993; Hill 1995). In other words, different levels of anchorage to the *origo* are reflections of their epistemic stances toward the target. As widely acknowledged, one such device for positioning the self vis-à-vis a target would be differential modes of reported speech (Du Bois 1986; Short and Leech [1981] 2007), used here for facilitating slander against J. Among the participants, such differences are most vividly articulated by K and M—and thus, W, T, and N are excluded from the following discussion due to their relative paucity of reported utterances and actions. Here I assume that by examining the different modes of reporting, we can gain useful insights into their stances as to how J's wrongdoings should be evaluated and censured socially.

In what follows, two sets of three segments will be compared according to where and how M's and K's reporting was heavily exploited. Of practical significance is the difference of their reporting styles, especially in terms of the use of hypothetical narration and FDS. Excerpts (10) and (11) show the segments of such instances, including some portions already presented above. There, the Japanese quotation markers are placed in squares and followed up on the type of reporting (see Figure 8.1 for the abbreviations in parentheses). Also, FDS (free direct speech) and DS (direct speech) are specifically indicated by the notation "<Q ... Q>," identified by recognizable suprasegmental features (such as change of tone of voice, volume, and intonation).

First, Excerpt 8.10 includes segments of K's utterances as to how he described J's behavior. What is characteristic of K's utterances is the heavy use of indirect or hypothetical reports of J's own words and actions.

As is evident from the excerpts, K's reported speech relies heavily on such markers as *-to*, *-(t)te*, and *toka*, which are also frequently used in literary text. Repeated and sequential use of *-to* and *-(t)te* serves to create the image of J's persistence in the described actions (Excerpt 8.10 (1)) and K's claim that J could have behaved differently (Excerpt 8.10 (2, 3)). These markers are used with indirect or hypothetical

EXCERPT 8.10 *K's reporting style*

(1) [Indirect quote]

Sono tento ni nige-kaetta toki wa, dooshitemo . . . abunai to *(IS), kiken da* to *(IS), omotta* to *yuu ne, dakara . . soko ni wa irare nakatta to yuu (IS) keredo mo.*

(I heard that,) when he ran back to that tent, he couldn't help but think that it was definitely dangerous **(IS)**, and (it was) risky **(IS)**, so he couldn't stay there **(IS)**.

(2) [Hypothetical actions]

S-chan toko made ori te *(NRA), ne, kiru-mon o zenbu . . . matotte-, oi* te *(NRA), tabemono o oi* te *(NRA), yoosu o mi* te *(NRA), jibun ga ne, ue no tento ni iku (NRA) nara betsu dakedo, dakedo sonna koto wa-, sono dekin yoona mono wa ne, kakera mo dekin yoona—, sugoi kutabireta* toka *(IS)*, asu no asa no kaisha ga doono-koono* toka *(IS), tondemonai hanashi da.*

Well, if he had gone down to S-chan's location **(NRA)**, put all the clothes on her **(NRA)**, left his food **(NRA)**, made sure of her condition **(NRA)**, and gone back to the tent up above **(NRA)**, then his behaviors were understandable. But if one can't do them at all, saying like he was totally exhausted **(IS)**, and he had to go to work next morning **(IS)** or something, then his behaviors are totally unacceptable.

(3) [Hypothetical Conversation and actions]

Zettai sore o kangaete, J-chan no honto no shisee to- shisee o kichitto soo(yuu)fuuni, kare ga honttoni, hyoogen-shite, <Q tanomu, ore wa zenzen ugoken noda Q> to *(DS), ano dotchi ni— <Q futari ni tayoritai'n dakedomo Q>-*tte *(DS) yutte, dogeza shi-*te *(NRA) sokode tanon-*de *(NRSA), ugoite kurenan- kurenaka-ttemo ne, atarimae no koto nanda yo. Atarimae no koto nanda yo. Dakedo, soo shitara, <Q wakari mashita! Q>-*to *(DS) itte, J ga orite-*tte *(NRA), hitoride tsukisou (NRA) ka dooka nanda.*

If he thought hard enough and expressed his intentions properly, he could have said, "please, I can't move at all **(DS)**," which one— "I need support from both of you **(DS)**," and got down on his knees for help **(NRA)**. Even if he asked for help **(NRSA)** and they didn't comp- comply to do that, it's a matter of course. He/You cannot complain about it. But what matters in this case is whether or not he says "I understand," **(DS)** and go back down **(NRA)** and accompany her **(NRA)** by himself.

* In this analysis, we consider it as "indirect speech" because *kutabireta* 'tired' is a regional dialect of K and it is unclear whether J actually said it that way.

---

speech, either of which gives an impression of a detached and objective stance and perspective toward the target object (J),

Specifically, K criticizes J's lack of climbing/mountaineering ethics by impersonating J's hypothetical utterances and giving voice to what J should have said and done with "constructed dialogue" (Tannen 1989). In this way, K demonstrates a high degree of narrator intervention by assigning (in vain) an ideal persona to J, but not conveying J's voice. K's hypothetical speech (a type of "small story" (Bamberg 2007)) represents an ideal, ethical climber (J's alter ego) who would have acted differently to J.

Next, let us look into M's utterances referring to J. His quotation styles are characterized by unusually high ratios of FDS and DS, here introduced linguistically by zero and -*tte* markers.

EXCERPT 8.11 *M's reporting style*

(1) [**Direct speech**]

hakkirito:, Kenji-san ga saa, <Q anta soreja tekizen tooboo da yo Q>-tte (DS). <Q anta- anta ni totte nee, ano: yurina ano: koto wa hitotsu mo okinai yo Q>-tte (DS). Sono, <Q zutto furi nanda yo Q>-tte (DS).

Very clearly, Kenji-san (said), "You're just running away (**DS**)," and "for your own sake, there's no good thing occurring to you, never! (**DS**)" "Being silent is never an advantage for you (**DS**)."

(2) [**Free direct speech**]

iya, Kazu-san ni iwareto-tta. <Q Watashi wa nee, jibun wa nee, ikura batebateni natto-ttemo nee, shinukamo wakaran to omottemo Zettai, Q> (FDS), <<ano::: zairu ...(1.5) chanto kotee-shite arun'dakara ne,>> <Q watashi wa moo sore tsutawatte oriru yo Q> (FDS).

You know, he was told by Kazu-san. "Even if I am-, even if I am-, no matter how exhausted I am, and even if I know I may die, I'll definitely—," (**FDS**) *<<uh:::m, since the rope (1.5) is properly fixed, you know,>> "I will definitely climb down using it." (**FDS**)

(3) [**Reported report**]

Hmm, J wa moo ikutaku nakatta rashii'n ya (NRSA). <Q koko de moo bibaaku shiyoo Q>-ttu-tte (DS). Mm. Yuutotta. <Q Koko wa dame dakara Q> (FDS). S-chan, mm. <<Yamanaka-kun kara kitan yakedo na.>> S-chan wa, <Q moo iko iko, hayo iko Q>-ttchi-tte (DS). Mm, S-chan nanka genki yatta rashii wa (NRA?). Nanka, koohii nihai- nihai nonde (NRA), de, <Q aa: oishi-katta:: Q> (DS), <Q moo hayo iko iko: Q>-ttchi-tte (DS), De, J- J-kun wa maa moo, tairyoku-tekini bate-bate yatta rashii (NRA?) wa.

Hmm. ... I heard that J didn't want to go any further (**NRSA**). He said, "Let's bivouac here (**DS**)." "No, this place is no good (**FDS**)" (said S-chan). *<<I heard this from Yamanaka-kun, okay.>> And S-chan said, "Hey let's go, let's go, let's go now" (**DS**). I heard S-chan was peppy (**NRA?**), so she drank two cups of coffee (**NRA**), saying "Oh this is so good!" (**DS**), "Hey, let's go, let's go now" (**DS**). And J was like, you know, totally exhausted and could hardly move (**NRA?**).

* "<< >>" denotes an utterance in the "paranarrative" level (McNeill 1992).

What is striking about M's quotation style is the heavy use of *-(t)te* and FDS. In particular, the ratio of FDS is remarkably high compared to other participants' utterances. M relies on a faithful reproduction of the utterances of secondary characters (friends and acquaintances of J), employing a reporting style with a low degree of speaker intervention (Excerpt 8.11 (1, 2)). In particular, M seems to faithfully perform the voices of secondary characters by mimicking their intonation and prosody, but never those of J (Excerpt 8.11 (1, 2, 3)). In this respect, M seems to emphasize the deviant nature of J's conduct by directly quoting other parties' criticisms (in (F)DS) as the real voice of the majority. M also uses an epistemic evidential marker, *rashii* ("seem"), several times to report on J's actions, most likely based on his knowledge gained from the guests at the mountain lodge. This style was available to him specifically mainly because he had chances to discuss the issue with secondary characters at several occasions.

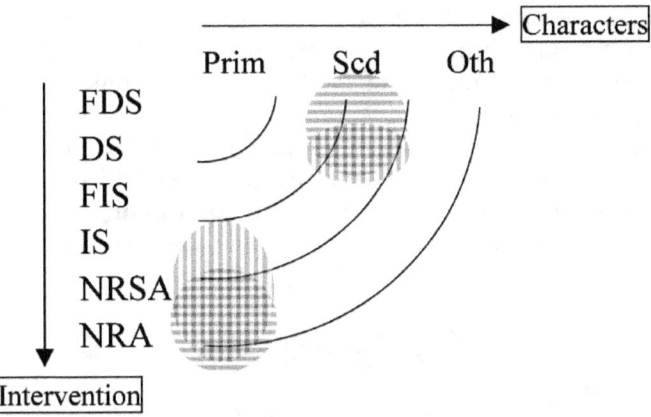

FIGURE 8.3 *Repertoires of K and M's reported speech.*

Notes: ||||| : K   : M
Prim : Primary character (J) Scd : Secondary characters Oth : General public

In fact, "experience" is one of the salient factors that determine the level of evidentiality expressed in conversation (Mushin 2001; Koven 2001). Thus, differential experiences motivate distinctive evidential forms—for example, *-yooda* ("[subjectively] seem"), *-rashii* ("[objectively] appear"), *-sooda* ("hear [that]") in Japanese). In our case, M, as the owner/manager of the mountain lodge, was in a position to gather information widely and directly from the members of the alpine club to which S belonged. K, on the other hand, was a famous climber but belonged to another alpine club, and thus was unable to gather as much detail as M. Therefore, the different reporting styles are likely outcomes of this experiential difference in the availability of indirect/direct knowledge, which was hypothesized or obtained from other parties, but not from J himself. Moreover, the "author" can fundamentally manipulate styles for expressing voices of the characters in literature, but in gossip-driven situations, where what one says about others without conviction can damage their reputation, he/she will have to stick to experiential and evidential bases.

Building on these observations, Figure 8.3 presents a configuration of the types of reported speech (vertical axis) and the types of characters realized in the present gossip (horizontal axis). In Figure 8.3, K's impersonated discourse of J's "alter ego" (10-3) is considered as DS by a "secondary" character.

The notable point here is not whether it was K or M that made a harsher or stronger claim, but the stances adopted by each in a situation where individual "construction" was possible. As seen above, their gossip about J increased in severity from suspicion to slander, and finally to accusation. Despite seeming differences in the proportion of reporting styles used (Excerpts 10, 11), there is a conspicuous similarity in the distribution of those strategies (Figure 8.3). Superficially, given J's taciturnity about the accident, K and M seem to resort to different reporting styles to denounce J's unethical conduct, such as by quoting his hypothetical utterances in the relevant scene (by K) or precisely reporting secondary characters' criticisms (by M). This way, however, both K and M are reporting indirectly on J's behaviors by not recounting what J actually said or did, or ascribing him any agency and autonomy

(Figure 8.3). This method of highlighting the legitimacy of their stances and the heresy of the antagonist through the voices of "others" and *seken* ("the general public") is one of the consequences of the Japanese communicative style of valuing the group-oriented social order (e.g., Watanabe 1991). This practice also shows how the interlocutors displayed their own ethical and moral orientations while gossiping. The management of reporting styles seems to reflect the distinct "voices" of different sources of information and levels of interference, contributing collaboratively to the formation of J's unfavorable social persona through gossip.

8.5 Conclusion

As has been claimed, gossip becomes a locus of recursively projecting one's own values by reasoning and evaluating the actions of a third party who is regarded as deviating from societal norms and expectations. It contributes to the manifestation and reinforcement of group ethics depending on the degree to which the evaluation is sanctioned by the other participants. In this analysis, I tried to uncover the "common sense" and implicit ethics of a climbing community by examining gossip about a fatal accident told by fellow climbers. It was an attempt to identify the unmarked norms indexed through the process of assigning responsibility in a marked event. As a basis for this study, I postulated the existence of an implicit cultural model, and identified some common strategies (i.e., use of metaphors) and individual strategies (i.e., quotation styles) used by the participants.

Although the proportion and availability of these strategies used are different, the participants (especially K and M) are generally and collaboratively oriented to promoting and conforming to the communal norms and ethics. We have also observed that any deviations from healthy, mature, and community-held ethics can evolve into a gossiping scenario. Specifically, due to the fluid and multipurpose nature of gossip, it can also develop into a manifestation of various intentions, contributing to the strengthening of sociality and human relationships among participants. It is this plasticity and chimerical nature of talk that continues to fascinate us.

9

Conclusion

While there are many ways to engage with mountain/rock climbing as an object of research, this book examines how humans participate in it through language and the body. In this chapter, I would like to conclude by reviewing the arguments made in the book and situating them in the context of human interactive activities. As mentioned in Chapter 1, rock climbing developed as a means to reach the summit of a mountain. It has since come to be recognized as a form of alpinism that finds the meaning of life in the act of climbing itself, rather than in climbing done for reasons of religion, hunting, and war. Currently, as many would agree, the cutting-edge forms of alpinism are represented by the alpine-style climbing in the Himalayas, free soloing on big walls, and sport climbing on boulders and extremely challenging routes. In fact, an abundance of media, both public and private, have documented and elaborated on these activities, including travelogues, non-fiction, mountaineering reports, documentaries, and movies, among others. However, few academic endeavors have been undertaken (with the probable exception of some ethnographies of the sherpas) that straightforwardly address language use during climbing activities. In that sense, I hope that this book opens a narrow mountain trail leading to linguistics, discourse studies, and linguistic anthropology in general.

Common images of alpine/rock climbing do not align correctly with reality. As the name implies, the focus has dominantly been placed on the activity of "climbing," and therefore, other activities that accompany it, such as "belaying" and "descending," are often disregarded—perhaps except for falling, which occasionally leads to critical consequences. Also, apart from the incipient era of the Himalayan climbs that relied on polar-style expeditions, climbing activities have been recognized and evaluated in terms of individual achievements. In this vein, alpine-style solo ascents of high-altitude mountains and free-solo climbing of huge walls are admired as the ultimate forms of such achievements. Yet ordinary climbing is a highly collaborative, safety-conscious activity—it is conducted with a partner to safeguard against the tragedy that might come from, for example, slipping or falling. Inevitably, shared protocols are expected for conducting the activity of and standard discourse around climbing, as well as for developing the necessary expertise and knowledge.

Based on these assumptions, Chapter 3 clarified that rock climbing is inherently a linguistic and physical institution formed through the speech–action complex. At the same time, the activity of leading a route can be seen as a narrative consisting of a beginning, middle, and end, which is largely equivalent to "telling a story with the body." In lead climbing, for example, while the beginning and the end consist of distinct linguistic protocols for ensuring safety, the middle performance consists fundamentally of reciprocal actions made possible by tacit, accumulated knowledge. This central activity includes not only climbing actions, but also taking protections (and the partner's belaying actions) to ensure safety—which is nothing other than the collaborative "accomplishment" by the climber and the belayer. Taking a "pro" comprises an action sequence oriented not only to the prior and subsequent actions needed to appropriately accomplish the task at hand, but also to the management of "re-starting," "repairing," and/or "abandoning" of actions on both sides of the rope. Since these actions must be taken instantly and with care on the spot depending on the surrounding environment, they are always subject to the question of "attribution" (Levinson 2013)—who is responsible for those ongoing actions?

As was shown in Chapter 3, the whole sequence of actions, from beginning to end, must be accomplished as a multi-stranded task that is consistent with the purpose of the main activity but which accords with the constraints imposed by sub-tasks. In this respect, the sequence is reminiscent of the gate-keeping process in institutional discourses (Heritage 2005) because it requires fixed steps to be taken, and in order to ensure efficacy and/or safety, it is unacceptable to skip a step along the way. It is also important to know how quickly each step should be completed. As we have observed, there is high degree of similarity between the belayer's reaction time and the general pause length between turns in conversation (Stivers et al. 2009). Although further research is required, it would be intriguing and informative to compare climbing with other activities for determining the optimal reaction time allowed by humans.

The next point of argument in this book is how climbers perceive the activity of climbing and what kind of instruction and learning occurs to enhance their skills. Focusing on the ongoing interaction, Chapter 4 discussed the process by which novices come to recognize certain holds as available and applicable—i.e., as "affordances" (Gibson [1979] 2015) in the "fields of promoted actions" (Reed 1996). In line with this argument, I examined the process of how experts' instructions in bouldering activities are accepted, incorporated, and reflected upon novices' actions in relation to such instruction. First, how do climbers perceive the holds that are available for climbing? Does an expert climber perceive the environment (a climbing wall) and its affordances in the same way as a novice climber? It seems that perception differs, depending on participants' expertise and dexterity. In this sense, the vertical surface, which is a "niche" for climbers to climb, affords different availability of holds to each climber; at the same time, each climber perceives "affordances" (i.e., holds) from the environment differently depending on his or her dexterity (Bernstein 1996).

In general, in discussions of affordance, it has been common to presuppose the same affordances for each animal or species of organism (e.g., a 60cm cube affords "sitting (on it)" to a human adult, but not to a cat due to the body size). However, the fact that a 60cm cube would not afford "sitting" to a two-year-old child—probably only "climbing" instead, presents a possibility of developmental variability of affordance. In other words, the aspect of changes in affordance with growth, development, and learning is a major theme that is also related closely to changes in the perception of affordances. Following this assumption, I presented a case study of how a seemingly un-afforded hold can be made available by providing multisensorial cues, such as visual and tactile. Through the observation of a climbing session among boulderers, it was argued that the fluidity of actors' perception in the "lived space" is key to understanding bodily management on the vertical plane. At the same time, it was confirmed that the instruction provided by an expert to a novice can be "effectivized" when it is provided in the field of promoted actions (FPA; Reed 1996), or within the range of novices' possible and anticipated abilities, as was exemplified in solving bouldering problems. In this sense, finding a "range/leeway" of actions and corresponding instructions that can facilitate a novice's skills are important not only for participants in climbing, but also for learners and instructors in general.

The vertical space offers variable and richer affordances along the development of a climber's skills. In addition, activities in the vertical plane and certain linguistic expressions that accompany them seem to allow for perceptions adapted to that "lived space." Depending on the extent to which these perceptual extensions are represented in language, we know how differently the same stimulus is perceived and internalized during the process of speech. In Chapter 5, I examined such perceptual changes projected onto the utterance and considered a possible range of "collateral effects" (Sidnell and Enfield 2012) by examining Japanese spatial terms *ue/shita* ("up/ down") judged in a shifted (and rotated) "frame of reference" (FOR). Because of the indeterminate dependence on gravity of those terms, the perception of the vertical axis is represented fluidly in linguistic expressions through lived cognition in the field of activity. Although the fluidity and plasticity of such spatial perceptions have already been highlighted in phenomenological investigations in terms of inter-subjectivity/-corporeality (Merleau-Ponty 1962; Ingold 2000), those perceptions have been regarded as readily available as universal human faculty. Rather than assuming them as directly accessible, Chapter 5 focused on the process of reaching the status through an analysis of actual *ba* ("place/space/context"; Hanks et al. 2019).

What I considered in Chapter 5 was the vertical axis of the spatial FOR. Although there have been a number of studies examining the "up/down" relationship in reciprocal actions (Ochs et al. 1996; Roth and Lawless 2002), they have focused on the spatial axis of manipulable objects projected on a screen and/or a drawing board. Very few studies have examined the vertical relationship of the human body in interaction. In addition, the *ue/shita* terms in Japanese are defined as "nouns," but due to their conceptual fluidity, the interpretation of their meanings is largely contingent on the linguistic structure and the context of speech in which they are used. Thus, the "*ue/shita* (+ PosP)" construction can be interpreted as nouns ("upper/ lower surface or part"), adverbs ("up/down"), or adopositions ("above/below" or "over/under") depending on the linguistic context.

To confirm this phenomenon, I first examined variable uses of *ue/shita* along the body axis in a lifesaving session attended by rock climbers to see how the canonical and projected vertical axes are manipulated implicitly to achieve mutual understanding in interactions. I then examined embodied instructions that were mediated by materials, and issued by an expert climber on the vertical plane and given to a novice on the horizontal plane in a climbing situation. It was observed that through the collaborative shifting of the body axes and gaze directions, both participants gradually acclimated into the non-canonical use of vertical expressions by going in and out of the projected space, or through a *mi-wake* ("corporal division"; Ichikawa 1998). Although the analysis of Japanese data alone is not sufficient to confirm the collateral effects, the novelty of this analysis rests in the gradual but ongoing extension of the spatial concept by shifting the focus from the "conceptual" space to the "lived" space on the vertical plane.

Apparently, previous discussions of the concept of space are largely the outcome of pure reasoning, which holds the highest value in human intellectual attainment, and is based on the theorem that human spatial cognition can be instantly and equally achieved. In recent years, however, it has been extensively argued in various fields that the body is both a medium and a source of recognizing reality. Despite such awareness, there has been little analysis of FORs mediated by language and the human body in an ongoing interaction, with the exception of intellectual contemplations and experimental investigations. The above analysis shows the significance of discursively examining the fluidity and relativity of spatial cognition that emerges in interaction.

Chapter 6 addressed the continuing themes in human interaction in/of space in terms of intersubjectivity and intercorporeality. Based on the audio and video data collected at a mountain camp, a multimodal analysis was conducted to investigate the kinds of linguistic and bodily information that contributed to a mutual understanding of space through collaborative wayfinding. In particular, I analyzed a discussion held by members of an alpine club in which they attempted to identify the location of a member's accidental fall during climbing. Since these members climbed different routes as four parties, each party (and member) had different spatial experiences and perceptions about the unidentified location. In other words, it was a joint task for the accumulation and integration of fragmentary spatial information. Such collaborative wayfinding exhibits a process of gradual negotiation. In the data, the participants' perspectives were variable—an expert who closely knew the routes under discussion took a "survey" (similar to a bird's-eye-view) perspective from memory, while some others took a more experience-based, "route" perspective (Linde and Labov 1975; Taylor and Tversky 1996; cf. Danziger 2010).

One of the factors that made the integration possible was the systematic use of the Japanese deictic verbs "go/come." Although the participants had distinct experiences and therefore different degrees of authority to use these verbs, they spontaneously sensed the climbing-route nodes on which they "hitched" their cognitive anchors with these verbs, and proceeded together in an imagined space. Interestingly, the pattern of the appearance of "going" and "coming," which is akin to "leaving" and "arriving" in English, represented a wave-like "poetic" structure consisting of repetition of the "|→ →|" schema that the participants collaboratively imagined. Moreover, when a stable image of the scene came to be shared and agreed by the participants, finger-pointing based on intersubjectified corporeality also came to appear, serving as an index of collaborative construction of the mental map. Notably, this process of mutual understanding and poetic formation in wayfinding developed hand-in-hand based on the "denotational" text and the "interactional" text (Silverstein 1993, 2004) emerging *in situ*.

These space-originated, experience-laden meanings in motion were also discussed in terms of "chronotopes" (Bakhtin 1981). Chapter 7 was one such attempt to view climbing talk from an evaluative point of view of narration. In the act of narrating an experience, the change of space is often assumed to represent a different phase of the narrative plot, and thus index different actions, events, and evaluations. The notion of a "chronotope" is a conceptual epitome of such perceptions. With the passage of time, each place accumulates experiences, emotions, and history attached to it. In the narrative of climbing, especially of falling experiences, the circumstances leading up to the climax and the consequences that ensue are always value-laden. In addition, the narrator's evaluations of the fall scenes may change within the narrative.

Building on this assumption, Chapter 7 centered on how falling experiences are constructed with distinct expressions and bodily depictions. I specifically looked into two narratives: one about falling into a crevasse while climbing in the Himalayas, and the other about a long fall while rock climbing in the Japanese Alps. These events were examined multimodally by identifying specific "(local) chronotopes" in each narrative, and I argued that the phenomenon called "co-eval-ness" (Silverstein 2005), which is characterized by the merger of perspectives, can be viewed as equivalent to the "intersubjective" perspective (Chapter 2) realized through gesturing. Simultaneously, since these narratives are aligned with specific perspectives as the narrated space shifts, I attempted to reveal their systematicity by applying Hymes' (1981, 1996) Verse/Stanza analysis, which is utilized widely in ethnopoetic investigations. As mentioned in Chapter 2, while the mainstream narrative analysis concerns language (i.e., the narrated semantic content), this chapter also focused on gestures, which are considered to be another outlet of the "growth point" (McNeill 2005). I attempted to delineate local chronotopes precisely by combining these ideas with a continuum between O-VPT (observer viewpoint) and C-VPT (character viewpoint)—a classification of perspectivized gestures (McNeill 1992). In so doing, I confirmed that even in a narrative that reiterates a single event, the narrator's different stances can produce distinct local chronotopes with a "co-eval" mode of depictions typically clustering around the climax. In sum, it was pointed out that more diverse and precise (local) chronotopes can be recognized through multi-layered relationships such as narrative components and accompanying bodily perspectives in narration.

The main portion of the book came to a close at Chapter 8, which delineates how climbers' identity is constructed, expressed, and reinforced. The object of analysis is gossip surrounding a partner in a fatal climbing accident in Japan's Northern Alps. This gossip was conveyed by the hosts and guests at a mountain lodge who knew the deceased well. Out of the gossip emerged a certain mountaineering ideology shared among the participants, as well as a mental model about how one should behave in such a serious situation. A mental model is a notional complex that is indexed explicitly or implicitly and formed through daily interactions (D'Andrade 1995), and for the members of the climbing community under discussion, it seemed to serve as a set of desirable and idealized norms that were envisioned and internalized in the process of socialization into the community.

In particular, critical assessments of the gossip target (a surviving partner) paradoxically index a desirable climber persona. In the present data, deviations from such an image were problematized by using metaphors of "infantilization" and "pathologization," as well as emphasized by quoting others' condemning "voices" (Hill 1995). These factors eventually facilitated the target being ostracized from the community as a heretic. Specifically, analysis of the participants' utterances showed that the types of "quotations" (Leech and Short 2007) used were not the utterances of the gossip target, but rather the words and deeds of the people enraged by his conduct (particularly failures therein) and what they thought he might have said, both of which seemed to deprive the target's legitimate agency. These methods combined to buttress the image of authentic climbers, while the target was marginalized with regard to ethics by resorting to the voices of "others" and *seken* ("the public") through the group-oriented social order in Japan.

From the above analyses, I confirmed that a variety of elements is relevant in climbing talk, ranging from exceptional lexical use based on individual climbers' perceptions to indigenous ideology common to the climbing (and possibly Japanese) community. If there are any merits of this study, they would be to show various levels of particularity and universality of climbing through detailed analyses of the actual data. Evidently, climbing is an activity that intertwines aspects of human perception, cognition, language, environment, and culture/history, which are spanned by the themes covered in this book—institutions, affordances, spatial frames of reference, collateral effects, poetics, chronotopes, and identity/ideology.

Because of the scope of such themes and concepts, some could be discussed only briefly. However, considering that the purpose of this book was to show the diversity of climbing activities, this was probably unavoidable. As with many activities, climbing has a specific locale of action and a clear ultimate purpose, which is not often attained easily. That inherent purposefulness would require a sense of agency that is maximized by cultivating space and the body, and a climbing discourse epitomizes such referential and non-referential relationships between them. The discussion of the body in space is obviously longstanding, and it has accumulated a huge body of discussion since the late twentieth century in particular. It is regrettable that this book can only partially address such historical and social backgrounds, but if it offers some paths of analysis to further cultivate the climbing activity as a research subject, I would be delighted.

Language shifts, the body extends, and space flows. They are all mobile and fluid within the leaky boundaries set up by the environment. While a house cannot stand without pillars and frames, it can be stronger if it allows for "play area" at the joints and junctures. It is the degree of leeway that residents can allow that is crucial, and that may or may not be specific to each household.

NOTES

1 Language and Body in Place and Space

1 A long and arduous path to modern alpinism continues in the twentieth century, but it is not an essential background for the present study. There is a vast literature on the historical development of mountaineering and climbing. Among recent works, Mcfarlane (2003) and Hansen (2013) are introductory, but also among the most comprehensive. Hoibian (2017) also provides a concise summary of cultural aspects of mountaineering and climbing.

2 There are other views on the birth of Japanese alpinism. According to Kinji Imanishi (a mountaineer and ecologist), for example, the dawn of modern mountaineering in Japan can be dated to 1918, the end of the First World War.

3 It is expected that at the next Olympic Games (Paris in 2024) lead climbing and bouldering will be placed in one category and speed climbing into the other, constituting two different styles of climbing.

4 There are various types of protection (often referred to as "pro"). Typical pros are pitons and bolts nailed into rock, but they are not always available on free climbing routes. A "nut" is a tapered metal wedge attached to a wire cable to be slipped into a crack as passive pro. Cams are a mainstay of active pro, and typically feature three or four curved pieces of cam lobes. The unit of cams, when the trigger is pulled, slid into a crack, and released, stay in the crack and offer excellent hold as pro. See glossary for other climbing terminology.

5 This style is also called "onsight flash."

6 See also "https://www.rockandice.com/videos/climbing/bolt-wars-conflict-death-and-community-in-the-garden-of-the-gods/" for a specific case.

7 In the current trend of sport climbing, clean climbing is often regarded as out of fashion and indifferent to climbers' safety issues, which serves as a major cause for retro-bolting. For traditional climbers, "(r)etro-bolted routes, as the new convention, require less skill and therefore threatens the standing of bolder climbers. Adding bolts to risky routes increases access to less-skilled leaders, thereby hurting the "reputation" of the route and the first ascensionist (Chouinard 1961; Hamilton 1970: 290; cited in Bogardus 2012: 17)."

8 Studying the socio-psychological aspects of rock climbing is another area in academia. Examples include a wide variety of research from sports sociology, psychology, and tourism studies in terms of climbing as a leisure activity and a lifestyle (Rickly-Boyd 2012), the relation between climbing styles and "whiteness" (Erickson 2005), and a sociological interest in the so-called "bolt wars" that arose between traditional and free climbers (Bogardus 2011). Bunn (2017) advocates Bourdieu's notion of "regulated improvization" by which climbers routinely strive to control inherent risks in the length, remoteness, and severity of a climbing route. Research in climbing can be approached

from physiological and medical perspectives. Seifert et al. (2017) is an advanced and cutting-edge collection of papers in various fields such as physiology, medicine, biomechanics, psychology, and engineering aspects of mountain equipment.

2 Theories and Approaches

1. An example of multiactivity taken by Haddington et al. (2014) is a "car journey," which may at first glance seem like a simple task of driving, but can incorporate different kinds of activities that occur simultaneously, such as talking, texting, using a cellphone, and handling on-vehicle equipment (e.g., air-conditioning or audio). Haddington et al. (2014) listed two major reasons for advocating multiactivity rather than multitasking. First, the term "multitasking" has traditionally been used in the fields of psychology and cognitive science. These disciplines are primarily concerned with mental issues such as cognitive load or deviation from the main activity. Another reason is that when the study of multitasking is conducted in social sciences, it presupposes the "involvement of participants" when engaging in various tasks and has been studied from the perspective that it is a characteristic inherent in the highly technologized activities so prevalent in contemporary society. Given this definition, climbing should be considered as multitasking rather than multiactivity.

2. On the other hand, in conversation analysis it is posited to be an impetus to push forward and continuously renew "alignment" in interaction through such conversational moves as "continuer," "newsmark," "assessment," "formulation," "collaborative completion," and "repair" (Stokes and Hewitt, 1976; Nofsinger, 1991; Schegloff, 1992).

3. The differential focus on the actor and the place is also a fundamental issue in linguistics. Many findings have emerged from the study of *jitai-haaku* ("construal"; how speakers perceive the world), in which a culturally preferred style of viewing a situation is conventionalized. As can be seen in Ikegami's (1981) contrast between "do-languages" (e.g., English) and "become-languages" (e.g., Japanese), languages differ in the degree of tendency to place the "actor" in the central role of the sentence structure or to place the emerging "situation" as the causal element (see also Nisbett 2003 for cross-cultural psychology). This distinction aligns with that drawn between the "person focus" and the "situational focus" described by Hinds and Nishimitsu (1986) and is also seen in various pragmatic situations (e.g., Ide 2006; Nakamura and Uehara 2016).

4. The viewpoint has been an important issue in Japanese linguistics as well, because lexical categories and predicates that specify "uchi/soto" are used widely in Japanese, and honorific expressions that indicate social "hierarchical" relations are abundant (Suzuki 1973; Tsubomoto, Wada, and Hayase 2009). In particular, grammatical subjects such as the transitive verb "to go/to come," the conferring verb "(to) do/(to) give," and the passive sentence have been the main subjects of discussion. So far, there have been numerous analyses of grammatical phenomena related to viewpoint (Sawada 1993), including the concept of "home base" (Ohye 1975) and the "viewpoint hierarchy" (Kuno 1973), as well as many contrastive analyses with other languages (Okutsu 1984; Ogoshi, Kimura, Washio 2008). In particular, Matsumoto (2017) has recently proposed a typology of obligatory perspective-marking by deictic verbs "go/come" based on experimental methods.

   Perspective is also an important theme in the study of Japanese deixis, and it is based on the semantic analysis of "ko/so/a" (proximal/medial/distal) demonstratives. Also, there are a number of studies that treat perspective as an interpersonal operation such as empathy or psychological proximity/remoteness (Sakuma 1951; Kinsui and Takubo 1992: cf. Clark 1974; Nabeshima 2016). However, prior to the rise of Levinson et al.'s spatial frames of reference research, cases dealing with "configurational" (especially discursive) spatial representations are very rare, with the exception of Noda (1987).

5 In spatial memory research, "distortions" or transformations of spatial arrangements that occur in a systematic manner (Tversky 1992) have been cited, and one of most conspicuous causes for the perspectival shift is considered to be the amount of "cognitive load" (Tversky, Lee, and Mainwaring 1999). Also, factors that increase the complexity of operations in wayfinding are assumed to include the route distance, angle of turns, experience in the search space, and the difference between the spatial imagery based on maps and the actual geographical relationship, among others. In addition, the presence of others in interactions (Schober 1993; Filipi and Wales 2004) and the presence of "action" descriptions (Tversky and Hard 2009) have been pointed out as factors that promote the transfer of perspective to others.

6 In fact, this sort of tripartite classification seems to be supported by distinct neural activations in the brain (Committeri et al. 2004).

7 Note that, in Levinson 1996a and 2003, the intrinsic and relative FORs are differentiated in terms of binary and ternary relations. This differentiation motivates the distinction between the often-encountered confusion between relative and deictic reference, the latter being fundamentally binary and speaker-centered and often relying on non-angular specifications such as "here/there" and "this/that." As shown below ((i) and (ii), Levinson 2003: 36–8), the intrinsic FOR is the prototypical case of the relative FOR where there is no floatation of the speaker's viewpoint from the origin—i.e., Origin and Relatum simply overlap.

(i) *The ball is in front of me.*		(ii) *The ball is in front of the tree.*	
Coordinates:	Intrinsic (and deictic)	Coordinates:	Relative
Origin:	Speaker	Origin:	Speaker
Relatum:	Speaker	Relatum:	tree
Relation:	binary	Relation:	ternary

Building on those definitions, Levinson maintained that "deictic and intrinsic are not opposed" (2003: 38), and that "many relative systems can be thought of as *derived intrinsic* ones—systems that utilize relative conceptual relations to extend and supplement intrinsic ones" (2003: 46).

8 Kataoka (2018) differentiated "frame of reference" and "descriptive mode," and proposed a grid of spatial description/depiction in terms of three types of static FORs (intrinsic/relative/absolute) and four styles of dynamic descriptive modes (tour/gaze/survey/integration).

9 Danziger's (2010) direct frame of reference is an integration of what Levinson calls Intrinsic FOR and Relative FOR in a way that the viewer's perspective is laminated onto the intrinsic orientation of the relatum (whether it is an actor or an object). It is equivalent to a viewpoint called "route" or "tour" perspective (Linde and Labov 1975: see Table 2.2). Kataoka (2018) proposed instead that the route/direct perspective should be regarded as a descriptive mode (DM) and differentiated from FOR.

10 In addition, the correlation between the size/height of the pointing gesture and interactional intention about the distance has been pointed out (Enfield, Kita, and de Ruiter 2007). Also, "mismatches" between the content of speech and gestures are often observed in the language development process of children (Church and Goldin-Meadow

1986; Cassell et al. 1999). Similar discrepancies are occasionally observed in adult speech, and in some cases the two are merged under the influence of the listener's presence (Parrill 2009; Furuyama, Matsuzaki, and Sekine 2011). In addition, it is necessary to consider not only the differences in form and frequency of occurrence (McNeill 2005), but also the diversity of preferred/dispreferred bodily representations (e.g., avoidance of gestures made with the left hand because of cultural taboos: Kita and Essegbey 2001).

11 For example, if the speaker makes a gesture of holding a handlebar, saying "when she was riding her bike . . .," that gesture is based on C-VPT in the narrated scene; a hand-sliding gesture that represents the bike's trajectory would be the one based on O-VPT.

12 Although there is no reference to this level in Labov's model, an interviewer's question that triggers the narrative itself (e.g., "Have you ever almost died?") would correspond to the one at this level.

13 Typically in the European literary tradition, most conventional poetic forms cover a variety of stylistic/rhetorical techniques and prosodical/phonological forms, and explore the principles of coordinated sounds (e.g., rhyme) and stress patterns (e.g., meter) (Short 1996; Fabb 2002). In Japanese poetics, in addition to rhythmic formulaicity based on moras, imagistic associations, and melodic/lexico-semantic creativity is highly valued (see Yoshimoto 1990; Yoshimasu 2021).

14 When prosodic contours are available, all three types of Intonation Units (IUs: Chafe 1994) are considered for analysis. *Substantive* and *Regulatory* IUs basically constitute single lines. *Fragmentary* IUs are appended to the beginning of the next new line or to the end of the same line depending on language-specific regulatory patterns. In other words, a fragmentary unit is generally taken to be an abandoned rendition, or a yet-to-be Substantive IU not completed for some reason.

15 As Iwasaki (1993) mentioned, IUs may exhibit language-specific skewing in length of, and proportion of (should "of" be "to"?), preferred units (e.g., lexical, phrasal, or clausal) for achieving IU. He found that Japanese conversation mainly consists of phrasal IUs, whereas American English conversation, of clausal IUs.

16 I say "often" because what is called *up-talk* or *han-gimonkei* 'semi-question style'—which may indicate termination of an IU—is currently a widespread practice among young generations around the world.

17 Bakhtin developed the idea of a chronotope around the 1920s, but was deprived of a chance to publish it because he was a political exile in the next decade. A chronotope thus seems to be a recurring concern for him throughout his career, and it is known that it was published forty years later, just before his death in 1975.

18 In addition, see also Morson and Emerson (1990: 367), who mentioned that ". . . the relation of 'chronotope' to Einsteinian 'time-space' is something weaker than identity, but stronger than mere metaphor or analogy."

19 The following quote precisely represents the difference of Bakthin's notion from Kant's: "The Kantian categories of time and space are so transcendental that their application—even in the most abstruse logical or mathematical formulae—already compromises their status as pure categories. Nevertheless, if time and space have their "natural" home in logic and science, chronotopes have their natural—their only—home in language" (Holquist 2010: 31).

20 "Local" chronotopes are different from "micro" chronotopes, which are units of speech smaller than the sentence, and consists of words and phrases over larger syntactic structures (Ladin 1999: 216). In this sense, micro chronotopes concern more of "form,"

while local chronotopes concern "content," and as any content/meaning leads to consciousness of time and space, together they constitute a "major" chronotope.

3 Rock Climbing as a Site of Embodied Institution

1. Also, more recent belay devices automatically impose friction on rope even if a belayer lets go of it, which makes serious accidents even rarer.
2. A redpoint climb is defined as successfully free-climbing a route after having practiced the route, whether it by hangdogging or top-roping.
3. Interestingly, he is depicted as a quiet young man of Asian heritage, probably because of the widespread myth of Asian "telepathic" communication styles in "high-context" culture.
4. According to the entry for "reaction time (RT)" on Encyclopedia.com, "(w)hen a human subject follows instructions to make a specific response as soon as he can after the presentation of a specific signal, the latency of the response is called reaction time (*RT*). Average values of between 150 and 250 milliseconds (msec.) are typically found." In particular, a case similar to the belaying action (such as stamping on the brakes) is found to take 200 ms.
5. Sometimes it becomes harder to perceive visually or aurally: a climber may be out of sight while on an overhang, for example, and extreme weather conditions (a thunderstorm or torrential rain) can also have an impact. In such cases, the belayer would need to rely on tactile cues gleaned from the movement and speed of the rope in order to gauge the climber's intentions and status.

4 Affordances in Rock Climbing

1. Affordance also depends on species' specific body scale in the sense that a 20 x 20 inch box will afford to sit to a human, but not to a cat.
2. Ingold (2018) pointed out two distinct orientations manifested in Gibson's ([1979] 2015) original writing, calling them "realist" and "relational" as to whether affordances are intrinsic properties of objects (realist) or made available by the activity of a creature (relational). However, Chemero (2003) applies the term "relational" to represent a mediated view toward a relationship between the animal and the environment.
3. Bernstein (1996) defined dexterity in terms of four levels of integration: Level A ("tone": spinal column and support), Level B ("muscular-articular links": formation of motor skills and the automation of movements), Level C ("space": perception of, and ability to use, external space), and Level D ("actions": chain structure and adaptive variability).
4. Knowing the type of route beforehand (face climbing or crack climbing, overhang or slab, etc.), however, is not regarded as "prior knowledge" (also called "beta").
5. The "three-point-contact" rule is one of many safety rules in which three out of the four limbs are in contact at all times with the surface or the hold, and is widely adopted in other activities.
6. Although these cases may seem like a typical case of "mansplaining," that issue is beyond the scope of this analysis and will not be addressed here.

5 *Ue* and *Shita* in Horizontal and Vertical Space

1 Kant claimed that space is endowed with its own reality. He observed that the intrinsic relations that apply to the right hand are similar to those that apply to the left hand, and yet the right hand cannot substitute for the left hand. If this difference cannot be explained as a mere appearance of different relations to each other (and it cannot, he claims, because we cannot put a glove meant for the right hand on the left hand), we must postulate different dispositions with respect to absolute space (see Van Cleve and Frederick 1991 for recent discussions).

2 Kant's theory of space evolved chronologically from "space as absolute" to "space as intuitive" to "space as mind-dependent" (Van Cleve and Frederick 1991: viii). Our discussion focuses on Kant's first treatment of the subject.

3 For vertical spatial expressions, there seems to be a continuum on this point. The relative acceptability of such expressions as "under [here in the sense of "behind"] the screen" and "climbing over the roof [which sticks out horizontally]" shows that "under/over" can be contextually compatible with rotated vertical planes, in contrast to more strictly gravity-defined prepositions such as "up/down" and "above/below," both pairs of which defy applicability to rotated verticality: "*up/*above the screen" in describing the situation represented by "under (or behind) the screen."

4 Although spatial perspective-taking has been shown to be flexible (e.g., Levelt 1984; Logan 1995; and Taylor and Tversky 1992a, 1992b, 1996), there is general agreement that environment-based representation based on gravity is the determining factor in assigning vertical relation terms such as "above" and "below" (Garnham 1989; Friederici and Levelt 1990; Carlson-Radvansky and Irwin 1993).

5 Haugen's (1957) seminal work on Icelandic distinguished two types of orientation, complementarily distributed: "proximate" (corresponding to the absolute or compass directions) and "ultimate" (directions along a line of travel, based on the four quarters of Icelandic geography). Similar absolute systems and/or "dead reckoning" systems are said to exist, for example, in Guugu Yimithirr (Haviland 1993, 1996), in Saulteaux (Hallowell 1955), in Truk (Goodenough 1966), in Puluwat (Gladwin 1970), among Australian Aboriginal peoples (Lewis 1976, Hoffmann 2019)), in Haiḻḻom (Widlok 1996), in Kilivila (Senft 2000), and in Belhare (Bickel 1997). Others have also formulated culture-specific configurations of social space: the "sociocentric" (rather than "ego-centric") frames of reference in the Yucatec Maya (Hanks 1990, 1992), the "action-oriented" embodiment of space in Plains Sign Talk (Farnell 1995), and the relations between gesture and mapping in American Sign Language (e.g., Emmorey and Reilly 1995). However, numerous anthropological studies point to a possibility that the boundary of physical and social spaces are often blurred, or rather "socio-centric" (e.g. Hanks 1990; Duranti 1992; Keating 1998; and Enfield 2003).

6 However, Carlson-Radvansky and Irwin (1994) also confirmed the possibility that other FORs are computed in addition to the environmental (not necessarily "absolute") FOR. Indeed, they have been shown to compete with the environmental FOR for lexical mapping, but not to be prototypically selected, as evidenced by reaction times to spatial cues.

7 Sidnell and Enfield (2012: 313) gave a comparative study of "K-plus (= knowing better than the other) second assessment," for which speakers of different languages (Caribbean English creole, Finnish, and Lao) may employ different linguistic structures, and such structures would lead to changes in how those actions effect changes in language-specific consequences.

8 Japanese also has a transitive version of this pair (*sageru*), but it occurred in my data only in the vertical sense, *sageru₁* ("to lower"). This kind of vertical relationship between interlocutors on horizontal ground is most typical of Japanese honorific verbs such as *sash[age]ru*/*[kuda]saru* ("to give/receive"). both expressions of which include the same Chinese characters as *ue*/*shita*. Other verbs of spatial motion are *(ni)* [aga]*ru* ("(to go [up] to) visit") and *san[joo] suru* ("to go [up] and visit/make oneself appear"), where "up" encodes a metaphorical value of importance and significance.

9 Ikegami (1981) comments specifically on Japanese verbs by using such examples as *moyashita kedo moe nakatta* ("I burned it, but it didn't burn") and *oyu o wakashita kedo wakanakatta* ("I boiled water, but it didn't boil"). These sentences may sound strange in English but are totally acceptable in Japanese. According to Ikegami, this difference inheres in the feature that many Japanese verbs, even those categorized as "achievement/accomplishment verbs" in English (Vendler 1967), do not necessarily have to imply the completion of action, while English ones canonically do (one exception is "invite").

10 That said, Merleau-Ponty seems to assume that special training or mastery is not required to achieve a mind–body union that transcends mind–body dualism. In Nishida's (1989 [1941]) view, however, the state of the "historical body" (i.e., mind–body unity) refers to the ideal state of the mind-body functioning as one, which is achieved through *shugyo* 'training' (as in Zen practice), and to reach this state, one must go through a process of incomplete, ever-changing development (hence the term "historical"). Nevertheless, actions through such creative intuition envisioned by Nishida are in some ways in common with those achieved through the body's sensory-motor circuit posited by Merleau-Ponty (Yuasa 1987).

6 The Body and Deictic Verbs of Motion in Imaginary Space

1 Here, I use the uppercase COME and GO as representing semantically primitive, language-independent notions, which can be a matrix for English *come* and *go*, Japanese *kuru* and *iku*, Indonesian *datang* and *pergi*, German *kommen* and *gehen*, and so forth. See Goddard (1997) for an elaboration of this idea.

2 However, there seems to be dialectal variation for the "speaker orientation" encoded by *kuru*. It is widely known that Kyushu dialects in Japan exhibit the same type of "speaker/hearer orientation" as seen in the English *come*.

3 A canonical use of *kuru* dictates that that it can be used only when the speaker reaches the goal, emphasizing the "subjective" nature of Japanese speakers' perspective-taking (Ohye 1975: 18–19). Also, as Fillmore ([1971] 1997) pointed out, the conditions for *come* and *go* sentences in an "accompaniment" sense are not freely transported across languages (see, for example, Gathercole 1978 and Nakazawa 2002 for cross-linguistic accounts).

4 However, it is observed that in "absolute" FOR languages, pointing to one's chest often means the "back," not "the self" (Levinson 2003).

5 The M Route was first ascended in the 1930s, and it is considered to be a genuinely historic route in the Japanese climbing community.

6 Figure 6.2 was reconstructed from the drawing by C2, who had this accident, and later verified by the other participants.

7 The nodes and landmarks mentioned in the paper are tentative and not necessarily shared in the rock-climbing community. Some guidebooks published in Japan apply different names to some nodes discussed here or simply do not specify them. Still, in a landmark-scarce environment like a rock wall, an overhang, a rock band, a terrace, and an anchor point serve as important landmarks.

8 There is in fact a lasting argument that the *–(r)u/-ta* forms are not exact theoretical equivalents to the present/past tenses, but the degrees of match between *–(r)u/-ta* and PRS/PST are irrelevant in the following analysis because the importance lies in the shift of indexical values induced by the proximal and distal forms in relation to the deictic center (the speaker). Thus, I will refer to these sets of concepts interchangeably.

9 The visual data analyzed here was initially unavailable because it was mostly filmed in low light, and thus it was not used in Kataoka (2004). The current analysis was made possible because of the technical development of the editing software, although some of the plates shown remain of marginal quality for visual analysis.

10 The length of a pitch is basically equivalent to the rope length used in a climb. Forty-meter ropes were dominant in previous times (as in this case), but currently 50- or 60-meter pitches are not rare, especially in big-wall climbing.

11 Some gestures observed here are not easily categorized into a single type. For example, McNeill (2005: 268) mentions that the iconic and deictic gestures are often inseparable because any hand gesture may include a deictic feature such that it usually consists of a movement brought to, and pointed at, a certain gesture space (see also Krauss et al. 2000).

12 For example, Morita (1977: 71–2) pointed out that *iku/kuru* verbs in the *V-te iku/kuru* construction encode four types of spatial motion with respect to the preceding verb *V-te*: (1) coordination of actions: *gohan o tabe-te iku* ("eat a meal and go"); (2) parallel actions: *magat-te iku* ("curve and go"); (3) state/manner of actions: *hasit-te iku* ("go running"); and (4) merged actions: *kare ni tui-te iku* ("going after/following him." Generally speaking, the compound form could be more "experience-near" than the basic form in that it particularly depicts the contingent actions to the agent (see also Matsumoto 2017 for cross-linguistic comparison of COME/GO).

13 The meaning of *iki kakeru* may be ambiguous. This phrase may just mean "be about to go," indicating that the motion has not yet started. However, in my dialect as well as the speaker's, this phrase can also mean that the action has already been partially assumed.

7 Poetic Construction of Vertical Space and Chronotopic Analysis of "Fall" Experiences

1 Leech and Short (1981/2007: 260–1) give some examples of free indirect speech. It is typically characterized by the omission of the reporting clause and preservation of tense and pronoun of indirect speech. Thus, the following sentences are free indirect versions of "He said, 'I'll come back here to see you again tomorrow.'":

—He would return there to see her again the following day.
—He would return there to see her again tomorrow.
—He would come back there to see her again tomorrow.

2 In the English translation, I tried to reflect the use of final particles, connectives, and hesitation markers, but I must admit that some expressions sound awkward. My intention was simply to show how they play major roles in demarcating the lines and verses.

3 The status of *wake* and *'nda* (*no da*) as final particles is still dubious, but current vernacular usage does show similar characteristics to final particles. In that sense, they are most likely undergoing grammaticalization (see a special issue of grammaticalization in Japanese (*Nihongo no Kenkyu*, 1 (3)) for other examples).
4 Cho Oyu is considered to be the easiest 8,000-meter peak to climb (from a normal route). Following the climb, the narrator made a historical (and arguably the first) winter ascent of the southeast face of Mt. Everest on December 20, 1993, as a member of the Japanese expedition team. According to Nepalese regulations, December is considered "winter," and this climb qualified for a winter ascent. However, the international mountaineering standards dictate that "winter climbing (in the Himalayas) should start no earlier than December 21st and should end before March 21st." Unfortunately, according to the international standard, his ascent is not regarded officially as the first winter ascent.
5 Also, in Hymes (1981, 1996), the same kind of components are defined in terms of Exposition, Complication, Climax, and Denouement.
6 For this section, I completely re-analyzed the transcription and included the audio-visual data here. The result is a significant revision of the previous analysis shown in Kataoka (1998a).
7 As to the moraic organization of Japanese traditional poems, some scholars (e.g., Bekku 1977) have arguably claimed that the inclusion of a one-beat rest after odd-number moras points to the ubiquity of even-numbered units.
8 Linguistic mimetics is usually used in a limited sense, as ideophones. Broadly speaking, however, the act of mimesis involves numerous sorts of imitation including ideophones, onomatopoeia, reported speech/quotation, pastiche, and simulacre, among others (Lempert 2014). That said, there cannot be identical "repetitions" in interaction because even the complete repetition of speech or action across speakers involves the transfer of the *origo*, and the deictic manipulation of some sort is inevitable.
9 It is widely acknowledged that there are two essential elements in the description of spatial movement: the path and the manner, which can be typified in terms of how they are lexicalized (Talmy 1983). Japanese is what is called a "verb-framed" language, in which the "path" information tends to be included in the predicate elements (mainly verbs), while the "manner" information is incorporated into the supplementary elements called "satellites" (e.g., postpositional phrases and adverbial elements). English, on the other hand, is a "satellite-framed" language, in which semantic information about path is encoded in satellites (e.g., prepositions and prepositional phrases), while that of manner tends to be encoded in a predicate. In short, the lexicalization patterns of incorporating path and manner information are typologically different. How these types of lexicalization relates to cross-linguistic embodiment of gestures has been the subject of much debate (Kita and Özyürek 2003; Allen et al. 2007; Brown and Chen 2013).
10 On the other hand, Kita and Özyürek (2003) did not find a significant difference between Japanese and English speakers' use of C-VPT or what they call "event-internal perspective" gestures.

8 Views from Mountaineer Ethics and Deviations

1 In the present analysis, I will address the reporting of both speech and thought under the cover term of "reported speech."
2 *Okashii* also means "funny" and "amusing" if used in an appropriate context.

3 The extreme manifestation of this is the physical exclusion of heretics and dissenters, as exemplified by the unjust segregation policy against leprosy patients, as was institutionally practiced until the 1980s in Japan.

4 Before the 1980s, the "polar method" of large-group mountaineering expeditions was in full swing. The members were expected to be cogs in the machine, and the priority was placed on the hierarchical system via which the elite climbers can eventually reach the summit.

REFERENCES

Agha, A. (2007a), *Language and Social Relations*, Cambridge: Cambridge University Press.
Agha, A. (2007b), "Recombinant Selves in Mass Mediated Spacetime," *Language & Communication*, 27: 320–35
Agha, A. (2015), "Chronotopic Formulations and Kinship Behaviors in Social History," *Anthropological Quarterly*, 88(2): 549–64.
Alim, H. S. (2006), *Roc the Mic Right: The Language of Hip Hop Culture*, London: Routledge.
Allen, S., A. Özyürek, S. Kita, A. Brown, R. Furman, T. Ishizuka, and M. Fujii (2007), "Language-specific and Universal Influences in Children's Syntactic Packaging of Manner and Path: A Comparison of English, Japanese, and Turkish," *Cognition*, 102: 16–48.
Bakhtin, M. M. (1981), "Forms of Time and of the Chronotope in the Novel," in M. Holquist (ed.), *The Dialogic Imagination: Four Essays By M. M. Bakhtin*, Austin: University of Texas Press.
Bakhtin, M. M. (1990a), *Art and Answerability: Early Philosophical Works by M.M. Bakhtin*, ed. M. Holquist and V. Liapunov, trans. V. Liapunov, Austin, TX: University of Texas Press.
Bamberg, M. (2007), "Stories: Big or Small: Why Do We Care?," in M. Bamberg (ed.), *Narrative: State of the Art*, 165–74, Amsterdam: John Benjamins.
Banfield, A. (1993), "Where Epistemology, Style, and Grammar Meet Literary History: The Development of Represented Speech and Thought," in J. A. Lucy (ed.), *Reflexive Language: Reported Speech and Metapragmatics*, 339–64, Cambridge: Cambridge University Press.
Basso, K. H. (1990), *Western Apache Language and Culture: Essays in Linguistic Anthropology*, Tucson, AZ: University of Arizona Press.
Bauman, R. (1986), *Story, Performance, and Event: Contextual Studies of Oral Narrative*. New York: Cambridge University Press.
Bauman, R., and C. L. Briggs (1990), "Poetics and Performance as Critical Perspectives on Language and Social Life," *Annual Review of Anthropology*, 19: 59–88.
Bauman, R., ed. (1992), *Folklore, Cultural Performances, and Popular Entertainments*, Oxford: Oxford University Press.
Bekku, S. (1977), *Nihongo no Rizumu: Yonbyoushi Bunkaron / The Rhythm of Japanese: A Cultural Theory of Four Beat*, Tokyo: Kodansha.
Bemong, N., and P. Borghart (2010), "Bakhtin's Theory of the Literary Chronotope: Reflections, Applications, Perspectives," in N. Bemong, P. Borghart, M. De Dobbeleer, K. Demoen, K. De Temmerman, and B. Keunen (eds), *Bakhtin's Theory of the Literary Chronotope: Reflections, Applications, Perspectives*, 1–16, Ghent: Academia Press.
Bennardo, G. (2009), *Language, Space, and Social Relationships: A Foundational Cultural Model in Polynesia*, Cambridge: Cambridge University Press.
Bergmann, J. (1993), *Discreet Indiscretions: The Social Organization of Gossip*, trans. J. Bednarz, Jr., New York: Aldine.
Berlin, B., and P. Kay (1969), *Basic Color Terms: Their Universality and Evolution*, Berkeley and Los Angeles, CA: University of California Press.

Bernstein, N. A., (1996), "On Dexterity and Its Development," in M. L. Latash and M. T. Turvey (eds), Dexterity and Its Development, 1–244, trans. M. L. Latash, Mahwah, NJ: Lawrence Erlbaum Associates.
Besnier, N. (1989), "Information Withholding as a Manipulative and Collusive Strategy in Nukulaelae Gossip," *Language in Society*, 18(3): 315–41.
Besnier, N. (2009), *Gossip and Everyday Production of Politics,* Honolulu, HI: University of Hawai'i Press.
Besnier, N., S. Brownell, and T. F. Carter (2018), *The Anthropology of Sport: Bodies, Borders, Biopolitics,* Oakland, CA: University of California Press.
Bickel, B. (1997), "Spatial Operations in Deixis, Cognition, and Culture: Where to Orient Oneself in Belhare," in E. Pederson and J. Nuyts (eds), *Language and Conceptualization,* 46–83, Cambridge: Cambridge University Press.
Blommaert, J. (2006), "Applied Ethnopoetics," *Narrative Inquiry,* 16(1): 181–90.
Blommaert, J. (2007), "Sociolinguistic Scales," *Intercultural Pragmatics,* 4(1): 1–19.
Blommaert, J. (2009), "Ethnography and Democracy: Hymes's Political Theory of Language," *Text & Talk,* 29(3): 257–76.
Blommaert, J. (2015), "Chronotopes, Scales, and Complexity in the Study of Language in Society," *Annual Review of Anthropology,* 44:105–16.
Blommaert, J. (2018), *Dialogues with Ethnography: Notes on Classics, and How I Read Them,* Bristol: Multilingual Matters.
Blommaert, J., and A. De Fina (2017), "Chronotopic Identities: On the Spacetime Organization of Who We Are," in A. De Fina, D. Ikizoglu, and J. Wegner (eds), *Diversity and Super-Diversity: Sociocultural Linguistic Perspectives,* 1–15, Washington D.C.: Georgetown University Press.
Boas, F. (1911), "Introduction," in *Handbook of American Indian Languages,* Vol. 1: 1–83, Bureau of American Ethnology, Bulletin 40, Washington D. C.: Government Print Office.
Bogardus, L. M. (2012), "The Bolt Wars: A Social Worlds Perspective on Rock Climbing and Intragroup Conflict," *Journal of Contemporary Ethnography,* 41(3): 283–308.
Bourdieu, P. (1977), *Outline of a Theory of Practice,* trans. R. Nice, Cambridge: Cambridge University Press.
Bourdieu, P. (1990), *The Logic of Practice,* trans. R. Nice, Palo Alto, CA: Stanford University Press.
Bredel, U. (2002), "'You Can Say *You* to Yourself': Establishing Perspectives with Personal Pronouns," in C. F. Graumann and W. Kallmeyer (eds), *Perspective and Perspectivation in Discourse,* 167–80, Amsterdam: John Benjamins.
Brenneis, D. (1992), "Gossip," in R. Bauman (ed.), *Folklore, Cultural Performance, and Poplar Entertainment,* 150–53, Oxford: Oxford University Press.
Brenneis, D. ([1987] 1996), "Grog and Gossip in Bhatgaon: Style and Substance in Fiji Indian Conversation," in D. Brenneis and R. K. S. Macaulay (eds), *The Matrix of Language,* 209–23, Boulder, CO: Westview Press.
Briggs, C. L. (2021), *Unlearning: Rethinking Poetics, Pandemics, and the Politics of Knowledge,* Logan, UT: Utah State University Press.
Bright, W. (1984), *American Indian Linguistics and Literature,* Berlin: De Gruyter Mouton.
Brown, A., and J. Chen (2013), "Construal of Manner in Speech and Gesture in Mandarin, English, and Japanese," *Cognitive Linguistics,* 23(4): 605–31.
Brown, G. (1995), *Speakers, Listeners, and Communication: Explorations in Discourse Analysis,* Cambridge: Cambridge University Press.
Brown, P. (1999), "Repetition," *Journal of Linguistic Anthropology,* 9(2): 223–26.
Brown, P., and S. C. Levinson (1993), "Uphill" and "Downhill" in Tzeltal," *Journal of Linguistic Anthropology,* 3(1): 46–74.

Brugman, C. M. (1988), *The Story of Over: Polysemy, Semantics, and the Structure of the Lexicon*, New York: Garland Publishing Inc.
Bruner, J. S. (1975), "The Ontogenesis of Speech Acts," *Journal of Child Language*, 2(1): 1–19.
Bruner, J. S. (1983), *Child's Talk: Learning to Use Language*. Oxford: Oxford University Press.
Bryant, D. J., B. Tversky, and N. Franklin, (1992), "Internal and External Spatial Frameworks for Representing Described Scenes," *Journal of Memory and Language*, 31: 74–98.
Bucholtz, M. (2000), "The Politics of Transcription," *Journal of Pragmatics*, 32: 1439–65.
Bühler, K. ([1934] 1982), "The Deictic Field of Language and Deictic Words," in R. Jarvella and W. Klein (eds), *Speech, Place, and Action: Studies in Deixis and Related Topics*, 9–30, Chichester and New York: John Wiley.
Bunn, M. (2015), "'I'm gonna do this over and over and over forever!': Overlapping Fields and Climbing Practice," *International Review for the Sociology of Sport*, 52 (5): 1–14.
Bunn, M. (2017), "A Disposition of Risk: Climbing Practice, Reflexive Modernity and the Habitus," *Journal of Sociology* 53 (1): 3–17.
Campbell, J. (1993), "The Role of Physical Objects in Spatial Thinking," in N. Eilan, R. McCarthy, and B. Brewer (eds), *Spatial Representation*, Oxford: Blackwell.
Carlson-Radvansky, L. A., and D. E. Irwin (1993), "Frames of Reference in Vision and Language: Where Is Above?," *Cognition*, 46: 223–44.
Carlson-Radvansky, L. A., and D. E. Irwin (1994), "Reference Frame Activation During Spatial Term Assignment," *Journal of Memory and Language*, 33: 646–71.
Carr, E. S. (2010), "Enactments of Expertise," *Annual Review of Anthropology*, 39: 17–32.
Carr, S., and M. Lempert, eds (2016), *Scale: Discourse and Dimensions of Social Life*, Oakland, CA: University of California Press.
Cassell, J., and D. McNeill (1991), "Gesture and the Poetics of Prose," *Poetics Today*, 12(3): 375–404.
Cassell, J., D. McNeill, and K. McCullough (1999), "Speech-gesture Mismatches: Evidence for One Underlying Representation of Linguistic and Nonlinguistic Information," *Pragmatics & Cognition*, 7(1): 1–34.
Cekaite, A., and L. Mondada, eds (2020), *Touch in Social Interaction: Touch, Language and Body*, London: Taylor & Francis.
Chafe W. L. (1980), "The Deployment of Consciousness in the Construction of Narrative," in W. Chafe (ed.), *The Pear Stories: Cognitive, Cultural, and Linguistic Aspects of Narrative Production*, 9–50, Norwood: Ablex.
Chafe, W. (1994), *Discourse Consciousness, and Time: The Flow and Displacement of Conscious Experience in Speaking and Writing*, Chicago: The University of Chicago Press.
Chafe, W. L. (1987), "Cognitive Constraints on Information Flow," in R. S. Tomlin (ed.), *Coherence and Grounding in Discourse*, 21–51, Amsterdam: John Benjamins.
Chemero, A. (2003), "An Outline of a Theory of Affordances," *Ecological Psychology*, 15(2): 181–95.
Chemero, A. (2009), *Radical Embodied Cognitive Science*, Cambridge, MA: MIT Press.
Chemero, A., and S. Käufer (2016), "Pragmatism, Phenomenology, and Extended Cognition," in M. S. Jung and R. Madzia (eds), *Pragmatism and Embodied Cognitive Science: From Bodily Intersubjectivity to Symbolic Articulation*, 57–72, De Gruyter.
Chilton, P. (2004), *Analyzing Political Discourse: Theory and Practice*, London and New York: Routledge.
Chouinard, Y. (1961), "Are Bolts Placed by Too Many Climbers?" *Summit Magazine*, March.
Church, R. B., and S. Goldin-Meadow (1986), "The Mismatch Between Gesture and Speech as an Index of Transitional Knowledge," *Cognition*, 23(1), 43–71.

Cicourel, A. V. (1973), *Cognitive Sociology: Language and Meaning in Social Interaction*, London: Penguin.
Cienki, A. (2016), "Cognitive Linguistics, Gesture Studies, and Multimodal Communication," *Cognitive Linguistics*, 27 (4): 603–18.
Clark, A. (2006), "Language, embodiment, and the cognitive niche," *Trends in Cognitive Sciences*, 10(8): 370–4.
Clark, E. V. (1974), "Normal States and Evaluative Viewpoints," *Language*, 50(2): 316–32.
Cohn, C. (1987), "Sex and Death in the Rational World of Defense Intellectuals," *Sign*, 12(4): 687–718.
Committeri, G., G. Galati, A.-L. Paradis, L. Pizzamiglio, A. Berthoz, and D. LeBihan (2004), "Reference Frames for Spatial Cognition: Different Brain Areas Are Involved in Viewer-, Object-, and Landmark-centered Judgments About Object Location," *Journal of Cognitive Neuroscience*, 16(9): 1517–35.
Coopmans, C., J. Vertesi, M. Lynch, and S. Woolgar (2014), *Representation in Scientific Practice Revisited*, Cambridge, MA: MIT Press.
Coupland, J., ed (2003), "Special Issue: Small Talk: Social Functions," *Research on Language and Social Interaction* 36 (1).
Csordas, T. J. (2008), "Intersubjectivity and Intercorporeality," *Subjectivity*, 22: 110–21.
Dancigier, B. (2011), *The Language of Stories: A Cognitive Approach*, Cambridge: Cambridge University Press.
D'Andrade, R. (1992), "Schemas and Motivation," in R. D'Andrade and C. Strauss (eds), *Human Motives and Cultural Models*, 23–44, Cambridge: Cambridge University Press.
D'Andrade, R. (1995), *The Development of Cognitive Anthropology*, Cambridge: Cambridge University Press.
D'Andrade, R., and C. Strauss, eds (1992), *Human Motives and Cultural Models*, Cambridge: Cambridge University Press.
Danziger, E. (2010), "Deixis, Gesture, and Cognition in Spatial Frame of Reference typology," *Studies in Language*, 34: 167–85.
Davidse, K., L. Vandelanotte and H. Cuyckens, eds (2010), *Subjectification, Intersubjectification and Grammaticalization*, Berlin: De Gruyter Mouton.
De Fina, A. (2017), "Narrative analysis," in R. Wodak and B. Forchtner (eds), *The Routledge Handbook of Language and Politics*, 233–46, London: Routledge.
De Fina, A., and S. Perrino (2020), "Introduction: Chronotopes and Chronotopic Relations," *Language & Communication*, 70(3): 67–70.
De Ruiter, J. P. (2007), "Postcards from the Mind: The Relationship Between Speech, Imagistic Gesture and Thought," *Gesture*, 7(1): 21–38.
Desjarlais, R., and J. Throop (2011), "Phenomenological Approaches in Anthropology," *Annual Review of Anthropology*, 40: 87–102.
Diessel, H. (2014), "Demonstratives, Frames of Reference, and Semantic Universals of Space," *Language and Linguistics Compass*, 1–17.
Dilley, R. E., and S. J. Scraton (2010), "Women, Climbing and Serious Leisure," *Leisure Studies*, 29(2): 125–41.
Dingemanse, M. (2013), "Ideophones and Gesture in Everyday Speech," *Gesture*, 13(2): 143–65.
Drew, P., and Heritage, J. (1992), "Analyzing Talk at Work: an introduction," in P. Drew and J. Heritage (eds), *Talk At Work: Interaction in Institutional Setting*, 3–65, Cambridge: Cambridge University Press.
Du Bois, J. (1986), "Self-evidence and Ritual Speech," in W. L. Chafe and J. Nichols (eds), *Evidentiality: The Linguistic Coding of Epistemology*, 313–36, Norwood, NJ: Ablex.
Du Bois, J. (2007), "The Stance Triangle," in R. Englebretson (ed.), *Stancetaking in Discourse: Subjectivity, Evaluation, Interaction*, 139–82, Amsterdam: John Benjamins.

REFERENCES

Du Bois, J. (2014), "Towards a Dialogic Syntax," *Cognitive Linguistics*, 25(3): 359–410.
Du Bois, J., S. Schuetze-Coburn, S. Cumming, and D. Paolino. (1993), "Outline of Discourse Transcription," in J. Edwards and M. Lampert (eds), *Talking Data: Transcription and Coding Methods for Language Research*, 45–89, Hillsdale, NJ: Lawrence Erlbaum Associates.
Dunbar, R. (1996), *Grooming, Gossip and the Evolution of Language,* London: Faber.
Dunbar, R. (2004), "Gossip in Evolutionary Perspective," *Review of General Psychology,* 8(2): 100–10.
Duranti, A. (1992), "Language and Bodies in Social Space: Samoan Ceremonial Greetings," *American Anthropologist*, 94(3): 657–91.
Duranti, A. (2009), "The Relevance of Husserl's Theory to Language Socialization," *Journal of Linguistic Anthropology*, 19(2): 205–26.
Duranti, A. (2010), "Husserl, Intersubjectivity and Anthropology," *Anthropological Theory* 10(1): 1–20.
Duranti, A., and D. Brenneis (1986), "The Audience as Co-author (Special Issue)," *Text*, 6(3).
Duranti, A., and M. McCoy (2020), "Language and Creativity: Improvisation," in James Stanlaw (ed.), *The International Encyclopedia of Linguistic Anthropology,* Chichester: Wiley.
Ehrich, V., and C. Koster (1983), "Discourse Organization and Sentence Form: The Structure of Room Descriptions in Dutch," *Discourse Processes*, 6: 169–95.
Eliot, J. (1987), *Models of Psychological Space: Psychometric, Developmental, and Experimental Approaches*, New York: Springer-Verlag.
Emmorey. K., and J. Reilly (1995), *Language, Gesture, and Space*, Hillsdale, NJ: Lawrence Erlbaum Associates.
Enfield, N. J. (2003), "Producing and Editing Diagrams Using Co-speech Sesture: Spatializing Nonspatial Relations in Explanations of Kinship in Laos," *Journal of Linguistic Anthropology,* 13(1): 7–50.
Enfield, N. J. (2014), *Natural Causes of Language: Frames, Biases, and Cultural Transmission,* Berlin: Language Science Press.
Enfield, N. J. (2015), "Linguistic Relativity from Reference to Agency," *Annual Review of Anthropology*, 44: 207–24.
Enfield, N., and S. C. Levinson, eds (2006), *Roots of Human Sociality: Culture, Cognition and Interaction*, Cambridge: Cambridge University Press.
Enfield, N., and T. Stivers (2007), *Person Reference in Interaction: Linguistic, Cultural, and Social Perspectives*, Cambridge: Cambridge University Press.
Enfield, N., S. Kita and J. P. de Ruiter (2007), "Primary and Secondary Pragmatic Functions of Pointing Gestures," *Journal of Pragmatics*, 39: 1722–41.
Erickson, B. (2005), "Style Matters: Explorations of Bodies, Whiteness, and Identity in Rock Climbing," *Sociology of Sport Journal*, 22(3): 373–96.
Evaldsson, A. C. (2002), "Boys' Gossip Telling: Staging Identities and Indexing (Unacceptable) Masculine Behavior," *Text*, 22(2): 199–225.
Fabb, N. (2002), *Language and Literary Structure: The Linguistic Analysis of Form in Verse and Narrative*, Cambridge: Cambridge University Press.
Farnell, B. (1995), *Do You See What I Mean: Plains Indian Sign Talk and the Embodiment of Action*, Austin, TX: University of Texas Press.
Fauconnier, G. (1994), *Mental Spaces*, 2nd edn, Cambridge: Cambridge University Press.
Fauconnier, G., and E. Sweetser, eds (1996), *Spaces, Worlds, and Grammar,* Chicago: University of Chicago Press.
Feld, Steven, and Basso, Keith H. (1996), *Senses of Place,* School of American Research Press, Santa Fe, NM.

Fillipi, A., and R. Wales (2004), "Perspective-taking and Perspective-shifting As Socially Situated and Collaborative Actions," *Journal of Pragmatics,* 36(10): 1851–84.
Fillmore, C. J. (1982a), "Frame Semantics," in Linguistic Society of Korea (ed.), *Linguistics in the Morning Calm,* Seoul: Hanshin, 111–38.
Fillmore, C. J. (1982b), "Descriptive Framework for Spatial Deixis," in R. J. Jarvella and W. Klein (eds), *Speech, Place, and Action,* 31–59, Chichester: John Wiley.
Fillmore, C. J. (1997), *Lectures on Deixis,* Stanford, CA: CSLI Publications.
Fine, G. A. (1986), "The Social Organization of Adolescent Gossip: The Rhetoric of Moral Evaluation," in J. Cook-Gumperz, W. A. Corsaro, and J. Streeck (eds), *Children's Worlds and Children's Language,* 405–23, New York: De Gruyter Mouton.
Fleischman, S. (1990), *Tense and Narrativity.* Austin, TX: University of Texas Press.
Frank, B., and C. Trevarthen (2012), "Intuitive Meaning: Supporting Impulses for Interpersonal Life in the Sociosphere of Human Knowledge, Practice and Language," in A. Foolen, U. Lüdtke, T. Racine and J. Zlatev (eds), *Moving Ourselves, Moving Others: Motion and Emotion in Intersubjectivity, consciousness and Language,* 261–303, Amsterdam, John Benjamins.
Friederici, A. D., and W. J. M. Levelt (1990), "Spatial Reference in Weightlessness: Perceptual Factors and Mental Representations," *Perception & Psychophysics,* 47(3): 253–66.
Friedrich, P. (2001), "Lyric Epiphany," *Language in Society,* 30(2): 217–47.
Friedrich, P. (2006), "Maximizing Ethnopoetics: Fine-Tuning Anthropological Experience," in C. Jordan and K. Tuite (eds), *Language, Culture, and Society,* 217–47, Cambridge: Cambridge University Press.
Fuchs, T. (2013), "The Phenomenology and Development of Social Perspectives," *Phenomenology and the Cognitive Sciences,* 12: 655–83.
Furukawa, F. (2020), *Sherupa to Michi no Jinruigaku / Anthropology of Sherpas and Trails,* Tokyo: Aki Shobo.
Furuyama, N., Matsusaki, H. Sekine, K. (2011), "Miburi ni okeru maiukro surippu to shiten no jizokusei "Microslips and the continuity of viewpoints in spontaneous gestures'," *Japanese Journal of Language in Society,* 14(1): 5–19.
Garfinkel, H. (1967), *Studies in Ethnomethodology.* Englewood Cliffs, NJ: Prentice-Hall.
Garnham, A. (1989), "A Unified Theory of the Meaning of Some Spatial Relational Terms," *Cognition,* 31(1): 45–60.
Gathercole, V. C. (1978), "Toward a Universal for Deictic Verbs of Motion," *Kansas Working Papers in Linguistics,* 3: 72–88.
Gavins, J., and G. Steen (2003), *Cognitive Poetics in Practice,* London: Taylor & Francis.
Gee, J. P. (1986), "Units in the Production of Narrative Discourse," *Discourse Processes,* 9: 391–422.
Gee, J. P. (1989), "Two Styles of Narrative Construction and Their Linguistic and Educational Implications," *Discourse Processes,* 12: 287–307.
Gee, J. P. (2014), *An Introduction to Discourse Analysis: Theory and Method.* 4th edn, London: Routledge.
Georgakopoulou, A. (2008), "'On MSN with buff boys': Self- and Other-identity Claims in the Context of Small Stories," *Journal of Sociolinguistics* 12: 597–626.
Gibson, J. J. ([1979] 2015), *The Ecological Approach to Visual Perception,* New York: Psychology Press.
Gillespie, A., and F. Cornish (2009), "Intersubjectivity: Towards a Dialogic Analysis," *Journal for the Theory of Social Behaviour,* 40(1): 19–45.
Gladwin, T. (1970), *East is a Big Bird: Navigation and Logic on Puluwat Atoll,* Cambridge, MA: Harvard University Press.
Goddard, C. (1997), "The Semantics of Coming and Going," *Pragmatics,* 7(2): 147–62.
Goffman, E. (1959), *The Presentation of Self in Everyday Life,* New York: Doubleday.

Goffman, E. (1974), *Frame Analysis*, Oxford: Blackwell.
Goffman, E. (1981), *Forms of Talk*, Philadelphia: University Pennsylvania Press.
Goodenough, W. H. (1966), "Notes on Truk's Place Names," *Micronesica*, 2: 95–129.
Goodrich, A. (2004), "Scaling Culture: Rock Climbing and the Embodied Nature of Spatial Knowledge," *Anthropology Southern Africa*, 27(2): 27–34.
Goodwin, C. (1981), *Conversational Organization: Interaction between Speakers and Hearers*, New York: Academic Press.
Goodwin, C. (1994), "Professional Vision," *American Anthropologist*, 96(3): 606–33.
Goodwin, C. (1995), "Seeing in Depth," *Social Studies of Science*, 25: 237–74.
Goodwin, C. (2000), "Action and Embodiment Within Situated Human Interaction," *Journal of Pragmatics*, 32(10): 1489–1522.
Goodwin, C. (2003), "The Body in Action," in J. Coupland and R. Gwyn (eds), *Discourse, the Body and Identity*, 19–42, New York: Palgrave/Macmillan.
Goodwin, C. (2006), "Retrospective and Prospective Orientation in the Construction of Argumentative Moves," *Text & Talk*, 26(4/5): 443–61.
Goodwin, C. (2007a), "Environmentally Coupled Gestures," in S. Duncan, J. Cassell, and E. Levy (eds), *Gesture and the Dynamic Dimensions of Language*, 195–212, Amsterdam/Philadelphia: John Benjamins.
Goodwin, C. (2007b), "Interactive Footing," in E. Holt and R. Clift (eds), *Reporting talk: Reported Speech in Interaction*, 16–46, Cambridge: Cambridge University Press.
Goodwin, C. (2017), *Co-Operative Action*, Cambridge: Cambridge University Press.
Goodwin, C., and M. H. Goodwin. (1996), "Seeing as a Situated Activity: Formulating Planes," in Y. Engeström and D. Middleton (eds), *Cognition and Communication at Work*, 61–95, Cambridge: Cambridge University Press.
Goodwin, C., and M. H. Goodwin (1992), "Assessments and the Construction of Context," in A. Duranti and C. Goodwin (eds), *Rethinking Context: Language as an Interactive Phenomenon*, 147–89, Cambridge: Cambridge University Press.
Goodwin, M. H. (1990), *He-Said-She-Said: Talk as Social Organization among Black Children*, Bloomington, IN: Indiana University Press.
Goodwin, M. H. (1997), "By-play: Negotiating Evaluation in Story-telling," in G. R. Guy, C. Feagin, D. Schriffin, and J. Bough (eds), *Towards a Social Science of Language: Papers in Honor of William Labov 2*, 77–102, Amsterdam and Philadelphia: John Benjamins.
Goodwin, M. H., and A. Kyratzis (2007), "Children Socializing Children: Practices for Negotiating the Social Order Among Peers," *Research on Language and Social Interaction*, 40(4): 279–89.
Grice, P. (1989), *Studies in the Way of Words*, Cambridge, MA: Harvard University Press.
Grimes, J. E. (1972), "Outlines and Overlays," *Language*, 48 (3): 513–24.
Gumperz, J. (1982), *Discourse Strategies*, Cambridge University Press, Cambridge.
Gumperz, J. J., and S. C. Levinson, eds (1996), *Rethinking Linguistic Relativity*, Cambridge: Cambridge University Press.
Haddington, P., T. Keisanen, L. Mondada, and M. Nevile, eds (2014), *Multiactivity in Social Interaction: Beyond Multitasking*, Amsterdam: John Benjamins.
Halliday, M. A. K., and R. Hasan (1976), *Cohesion in English*, London: Longman.
Hallowell, A. I. (1955), "Chapter 9: Cultural Factors in Spatial Orientation," in *Culture and Experience*, 184–202, Philadelphia: University of Pennsylvania Press.
Haneda, O. (2010), *Yama no Sounan: Anata no Yama-nobori ha Daijoubu ka / Mountaineering Accidents: Is Your Mountaineering All Right?*, Tokyo: Heibonsha.
Hanks, W. (1987), "Discourse Genres in a Theory of Practice," *American Ethnologist*, 14(4): 668–92.
Hanks, W. (1989), "Text and Textuality," *Annual Review of Anthropology*, 18: 95–127.

Hanks, W. F. (1990), *Referential Practice: Language and Lived Space among the Maya*, Chicago, IL: University of Chicago Press.

Hanks, W. F. (1992), "The Indexical Ground of Deictic Reference," in A. Duranti and C. Goodwin (eds), *Rethinking Context: Language as an Interactive Phenomenon*, 43–76, Cambridge: Cambridge University Press.

Hanks, W., S. Ide, Y. Katagiri, S. Saft, Y. Fujii, and K. Ueno (2019), "Communicative Interaction in Terms of *Ba* Theory: Towards an Innovative Approach to Language Practice," *Journal of Pragmatics*, 145: 63–71.

Hansen, P. H. (2013), *The Summits of Modern Man. Mountaineering after the Enlightenment*, Cambridge, MA: Harvard University Press.

Hansen, P. H. (2013), *The Summits of Modern Man*, Cambridge, MA: Harvard University Press.

Harkness, N. (2015), "The Pragmatics of Qualia in Practice," *Annual Review of Anthropology*, 44: 573–89.

Haugen, E. (1957), "The Semantics of Icelandic Orientation," *Word*, 13: 447–59.

Haun, D. B. M., C. J. Rapold, J. Call, G. Janzen and S. C. Levinson (2006), "Cognitive Cladistics and Cultural Override in Hominid Spatial Cognition," *PNAS*, 103(46): 17568–73.

Haviland, J. B. (1977), "Gossip as Competition in Zinacantan," *Journal of Communication*, 27(1): 186–91.

Haviland, J. B. (1993), "Anchoring, Iconicity and Orientation in Guugu Yimidhirr Pointing Gestures," *Journal of Linguistic Anthropology*, 3(1), 3–45.

Haviland, J. B. (1996), "Projections, Transpositions, and Relativity," in J. J. Gumperz and S. C. Levinson (eds), *Rethinking Linguistic Relativity*, 271–323, Cambridge, Cambridge University Press.

Haviland, J. B. (2000), "Pointing, Gesture Spaces, and Mental Maps," in D. McNeill (ed.), *Language and Gesture*, 13–46, Cambridge: Cambridge University Press.

Heath, C., and P. Luff. (2000), *Technology in Action*, Cambridge: Cambridge University Press.

Heft, H. (2001), *Ecological Psychology in Context: James Gibson, Roger Barker, and the Legacy of William James's Radical Empiricism*, Mahwah, NJ: Lawrence Erlbaum Associates.

Heine, B. (1997), *Cognitive Foundations of Grammar*, New York: Oxford University Press.

Heritage, J. (1984), "A Change-of-state Token and Aspects of Its Sequential Placement," in J. M. Atkinson and J. Heritage (eds), *Structures of Social Action*, 245–99, Cambridge: Cambridge University Press.

Heritage, J. (2004), "Conversation Analysis and Institutional Talk," in K. L. Fitch and R. E. Sanders (eds), *Handbook of Language and Social Interaction*, 103–47, Mahwah, NJ: Lawrence Erlbaum Associates.

Heritage, J., and D. Greatbatch (1989), "On the Institutional Character of Institutional Talk: The Case of News Interviews," *Selected papers from a seminar arranged by the Department of Communication Studies: On Communication*, 5: 47–98, University of Linköping.

Hill, C. (1982), "Up/down, front/back, left/right: A Contrastive Study of Hausa and English," in J. Weissenborn and W. Klein (eds), *Here and There: Cross-linguistic Studies on Deixis and Demonstration*, 13–42, Amsterdam: John Benjamins.

Hill, J. H. (1985), "The Grammar of Consciousness and the Consciousness of Grammar," *American Ethnologist* 12(4): 725–37.

Hill, J. H. (1995), "The Voices of Don Gabriel: Responsibility and Self in a Modern Mexicano Narrative," in D. Tedlock and B. Mannheim (eds), *The Dialogic Emergence of Culture*, 97–147, Urbana, IL: University of Illinois Press.

Hill, J. H. (2005), "Finding Culture in Narrative," in N. Quinn (ed.), *Finding Culture in Talk: Culture, Mind and Society*, 157–202, New York: Palgrave Macmillan.
Hill, J. H., and B. Mannheim (1992), "Language and World View," *Annual Review of Anthropology*, 21: 381–406.
Hill, J. H., and J. Irvine, eds (1993), *Responsibility and Evidence in Oral Discourse*, Cambridge: Cambridge University Press.
Hinds, J., and Y. Nishimitsu (1986), *Situation vs. Person Focus*, Kurosio Publishers.
Hoffmann, D. (2019), "Restrictions on the Usage of Spatial Frames of Reference in Location and Orientation Descriptions: Evidence from Three Australian Languages," *Australian Journal of Linguistics*, 39(1): 1–31.
Hoibian, O. (2017), "A Cultural History of Mountaineering and Climbing," in L. Seifert, P. Wolf, and A. Schweizer (eds), *The Science of Climbing and Mountaineering*, 1–16, London: Routledge.
Holland, D., and N. Quinn, eds (1987), *Cultural Models in Language and Thought*, New York: Cambridge University Press.
Holquist, M. (2010), "The Figure of Chronotope," in N. Bemong, P. Borghart, M. De Dobbeleer, K. Demoen, K. De Temmerman, and B. Keunen (eds), *Bakhtin's Theory of the Literary Chronotope: Reflections, Applications, Perspectives*, 19–33, Ghent, Academia Press.
Howard, K. M. (2009), "Breaking in and Spinning out: Repetition and Decalibration in Thai Children's Play Genres," *Language in Society*, 38(3): 339–63.
Human, L., D. Kriek, and S. Potgieter (2007), "Laughter in the Crags: Exploring Discourse During Rock Climbing," *African Journal for Physical, Health Education, Recreation and Dance*, 13(4): 368–79.
Hutchins, E. (1995), *Cognition in the Wild*, Cambridge, MA: MIT Press.
Hymes, D. (1966), "Two Types of Linguistic Relativity," in W. Bright (ed.), *Sociolinguistics*, 114–58, The Hague: De Gruyter Mouton.
Hymes, D. (1981), *In Vain I Tried to Tell You: Essays in Native American Ethnopoetics*, Philadelphia: University of Pennsylvania Press.
Hymes, D. (1994), "Ethnopoetics, Oral-formulaic Theory, and Editing Texts," *Oral Traditions*, 9(2): 330–70.
Hymes, D. (1996), *Ethnography, Linguistics, Narrative Inequality*, Bristol, PA: Taylor & Francis Inc.
Hymes, D. (2003), *Now I Know Only So Far: Essays in Ethnopoetics*, Omaha, NE: University of Nebraska Press.
Iacoboni, M. (2009), "Imitation, Empathy, and Nirror Beurons," *Annual Review of Psychology*, 60: 653–70.
Ichikawa, H. (2001), *Shintairon Shuusei / Thoughts on the Body*, ed. Y. Nakamura, Tokyo: Iwanami.
Ide, S. (2006), *Wakimae no Goyouron / Pragmatics of Discernment*, Tokyo: Taishukan.
Ikegami, Y. (1981), *"Suru' to "Naru' no Gengogaku / Linguistics of DO and BECOME*, Tokyo: Taishukan.
Ingold, T. (2000), *The Perception of the Environment: Essays on Livelihood, Dwelling and Skill*, London: Routledge.
Ingold, T. (2014), "That's Enough About Ethnography!,", *Hau: Journal of Ethnographic Theory*, 4(1): 383–95.
Ingold, T. (2018), "Back to the Future with the Theory of Affordances," *HAU: Journal of Ethnographic Theory*, 8 (1/2): 39–44.
Irvine, J., and S. Gal (2000), "Language Ideology and Linguistic Differentiation," in P. V. Kroskrity (ed.), *Regimes of Language: Ideologies, Polities, and Identities*, 35–84, Santa Fe: School of American Research Press.

Iwasaki, S. (1993), "The Structure of the Intonation Unit in Japanese," *J/K Linguistics* 3: 39–53.
Iwasaki, S., M. Bartlett, H. Manns, and L. Willoughby (2019), "The Challenges of Multimodality and Multi-sensoriality: Methodological Issues in Analyzing Tactile Signed Interaction," *Journal of Pragmatics*, 143: 215–27.
Jackendoff, R. (1983), *Semantics and Cognition*, Cambridge, MA: MIT Press.
Jaffe, A. (2009), "The Sociolinguistics of Stance," in A. Jaffe (ed.), *Stance: Sociolinguistic Perspectives*, 3–28, Oxford: Oxford University Press.
Jakobson, R. (1960), "Linguistics and Poetics," in T. Sebeok (ed.), *Style in Language*, 350–77, Cambridge, MA: MIT Press.
Jakobson, R. (1966), "Grammatical Parallelism and its Russian Facet," *Language*, 42: 399–429.
Jakobson, R. (1985), "Poetry of Grammar and Grammar of Poetry," in K. Pomorska and S. Rudy (eds), *Verbal Art, Verbal Sign, Verbal Time*, 37–46, Minneapolis, MN: University of Minnesota Press.
Jefferson, G. (1978), "Sequential Aspects of Storytelling in Conversation," in J. Schenkein (ed.), *Studies in the Organization of Conversational Interaction*, 219–48, New York: Academic Press.
Jefferson, G. (1996), "On the Poetics of Ordinary Talk," *Text and Performance Quarterly*, 16(1): 1–61.
Jefferson, G. (2004), "Glossary of Transcript Symbols with an Introduction," in G. H. Lerner (ed.), *Conversation Analysis: Studies from the First Generation*, 13–31, Amsterdam: John Benjamins.
Johnson, M. (1990), *The Body in the Mind: The Bodily Basis of Meaning, Imagination, and Reason*, Chicago: The University of Chicago Press.
Johnstone, B., ed. (1994), *Repetition in Discourse: Interdisciplinary Perspectives*, Norwood, NJ: Ablex.
Kamada, O. (2000), *Nihongo no In'you / Quotation in Japanese*, Tokyo: Hituzi Shobo.
Kant, I. ([1768] 1991), "On the First Ground of the Distinction of Regions in Space," in J. Van Cleve and R. E. Frederick (eds), *The Philosophy of Right and Left: Incongruent Counterparts and the Nature of Space*, 27–33, Dordrecht: Kluwer Academic Publishing.
Kärkkäinen, E. (2006), "Stance Taking in Conversation: From Subjectivity to Intersubjectivity," *Text & Talk*, 26(6): 699–731.
Kataoka, K. (1998a), "The Vertical Experience in English and Japanese Discourse," Ph.D. Diss., The University of Arizona.
Kataoka, K. (1998b), "Gravity or Levity: Vertical Space in Japanese Rock Climbing Instructions," *Journal of Linguistic Anthropology*, 8(2): 222–48.
Kataoka, K. (2004), "Co-construction of a Mental Map in Spatial Discourse: A Case Study of Japanese Rock Climbers' Use of Deictic Verbs of Motion," *Pragmatics*, 14(4): 409–38.
Kataoka, K. (2005), "Variability of Spatial Frames of Reference in the Wayfinding Discourse on Commercial Signboards," *Language in Society*, 34(4), 593–632.
Kataoka, K. (2009), "A Multi-modal Ethnopoetic Analysis (Part 1): Text, Gesture, and Environment in Japanese Spatial Narrative," *Language & Communication*, 29(4): 287–311.
Kataoka, K. (2010), "A Multi-modal Ethnopoetic Analysis (Part 2): Catchment, Prosody, and Frames of Reference in Japanese Spatial Narrative," *Language & Communication*, 30(2): 69–89.
Kataoka, K. (2012a), "Toward Multimodal Ethnopoetics," *Applied Linguistics Review*, 3(1): 101–30.
Kataoka, K. (2012b), "The "Body Poetics': Repeated Rhythm as a Cultural Asset for Japanese Life-saving Instruction," *Journal of Pragmatics*, 44: 680–704.

Kataoka, K. (2014), "On Intersubjective Co-construction of Virtual Space Through Multimodal Means: A Case of Japanese Route-finding Discourse," in M. Yamaguchi, D. Tay, and B Blount (eds), *Approaches to Language, Culture, and Cognition: The Intersection of Cognitive Linguistics and Linguistic Anthropology*, 181–216, Basingstoke: Palgrave Macmillan.

Kataoka, K. (2017), "Maruchi-moodaru no shakaigengogaku (Multimodal sociolinguistics)," in I. Inoue (ed.), *Taishou Shakaigengogaku / Contrastive Sociolinguistics*, 82–106, Tokyo: Asakura Shoten.

Kataoka, K. (2018), "Kuukanteki shitendori ruikei to taishou kenkyuu he no ouyou ni tsuite (Applying a Perspective-Taking Typology to Contrastive Studies)" *Japanese Journal of Language in Society*, 21(1): 19–34.

Kataoka, K. (2020), "Scale of "Relevance' and Complementarity: Focusing on Schematic and Poetic Formations of Interaction," *Journal of Asian Linguistic Anthropology*, 2(3): 77–109.

Kataoka, K., and Y. Asahi (2015), "Synchronic and Diachronic Variation in the Use of Spatial Frames of Reference: An Analysis of Japanese Route Instruction," *Journal of Sociolinguistics*, 19(2): 133–60.

Kataoka, K., M. Takekuro, and T Enomoto, eds (2022), *Poethikusu no Shin-Tenkai / The State-of-the-Art in Poetics*, Tokyo: Hituzi Shobo.

Käufer, S., and A. Chemero (2015), *Phenomenology: An Introduction*, Malden, MA: Polity Press.

Keane, W. (2011), "Indexing Voice: A Morality Tale," *Journal of Linguistic Anthropology*, 21(2): 166–78.

Keating, E. (1998), *Power Sharing: Language, Rank, Gender and Social Space in Pohnpei, Micronesia*, Oxford: Oxford University Press.

Keating, E. (2015), "Discourse, Space, and Place," in D. Tannen, H. E. Hamilton, and D. Schiffrin (eds), *The Handbook of Discourse Analysis*, 2nd edn, 244–61, New York: Wiley.

Keating, E., and C. Sunakawa. (2010), "Participation Cues: Coordinating Activity and Collaboration in Complex Online Gaming Worlds," *Language in Society*, 39: 331–56.

Keating, E., and G. Mirus (2003), "American Sign Language in Virtual Space: Interactions Between Deaf Users of Computer-mediated Video Communication and the Impact of Technology on Language Practices," *Language in Society*, 32(5): 693–714.

Keenan, E. L., and B. Comrie (1977), "Noun Phrase Accessibility and Universal Grammar," *Linguistic Inquiry* 8: 63–99.

Kemp Smith, N. ([1918] 1991), "The Paradox of Incongruous Counterparts," in J. Van Cleve and R. E. Frederick (eds), *The Philosophy of Right and Left: Incongruent Counterparts and the Nature of Space*, 43–7, Dordrecht: Kluwer Academic Publishing.

Kendon, A. (1990), *Conducting Interaction: Patterns of Behavior in Focused Encounters*, Cambridge: Cambridge University Press

Kendon, A. (2004), *Gesture: Visible Action as Utterance*, Cambridge: Cambridge University Press.

Kidwell, M. (2000), "Common Ground in Cross-cultural Communication: Sequential and Institutional Contexts in Front Desk Service Encounters," *Issues in Applied Linguistics*, 11(1): 17–37.

Kikuchi, T. (2003), *Kita Arupusu: Kono Hyakunen / The North Alps: The last 100 Years*, Tokyo: Bungei Shunju.

Kinsui, S., and Y. Takubo (1992), "Daiwa kanri riron kara mita Nihongo no shijishi," in S. Kinsui and Y. Takubo (eds), *Shijishi*, 123–49, Tokyo: Hituzi Shobo.

Kita, S. (1997), "Two-dimensional Semantic Analysis of Japanese Mimetics," *Linguistics*, 35(2): 379–415.

Kita, S. (2002), *Jesuchaa: Kangaeru Karada* ("Gesture: Thinking Body"), Tokyo: Kaneko Shobo.

Kita, S., ed. (2003a), *Pointing: Where Language, Culture and Cognition Meet*, Mahwah, NJ: LEA.

Kita, S. (2003b), "Interplay of Gaze, Hand, Torso Orientation, and Language in Pointing," in S. Kita (ed.), *Pointing: Where Language, Culture and Cognition Meet*, 307–28, Mahwah, NJ: LEA.

Kita, S., and J. Essegbey (2001), "Pointing Left in Ghana. How a Taboo on the Use of the Left Hand Influences Gestural Practice," *Gesture*, 1: 73–95.

Kita, S., and A. Özyürek (2003), "What Does Cross-linguistic Variation in Semantic Coordination of Speech and Gesture Reveal?: Evidence for an Interface Representation of Spatial Thinking and Speaking," *Journal of Memory and language*, 48(1): 16–32.

Klein, W. (1982), "Local Deixis in Route Directions," in R. J. Jarvella and W. Klein (eds), *Speech, Place, and Action: Studies in Deixis and Related Topics*, 161–82, Chichester: John Wiley.

Klein, W. (1983), "Deixis and Spatial Orientation in Route Directions," in H. L. Pick Jr. (ed.), *Spatial Orientation: Theory, Research, and Application*, 283–311, New York: Plenum Press.

Klima, E. S., and U. Bellugi (1983), "Poetry Without Sound," in J. Rothenberg and D. Rothenberg (eds), *Symposium of the Whole*, 291–302, Berkeley, CA: University of California Press.

Koizumi, T. (1990), *Gengai no Gengogaku: Nihongo Goyooron / Implicational Linguistics: Japanese Pragmatics*, Tokyo: Sanseidoo.

Kövecses, Z. (2002), *Metaphor: A Practical Introduction*, New York: Oxford University Press.

Koven, M. (2001), "Comparing Bilinguals' Quoted Performances of Self and Others in Tellings of the Same Experience in Two Languages," *Language in Society*, 30: 513–558.

Koven, M. (2002), "An Analysis of Speaker Role Inhabitance in Narratives of Personal Experience," *Journal of Pragmatics*, 34(2): 167–217.

Koven, M. (2012), "Speaker Roles in Personal Narratives," in J. A. Holstein, and J. F. Gubrium (eds), *Varieties of Narrative Analysis*, 151–80, London: SAGE Publishing.

Koven, M. (2015), "Speaker Roles in Personal Narratives," in J. A. Holstein and J. F. Gubrium (eds), *Varieties of Narrative Analysis*, 151–80, Los Angeles: SAGE Publishing.

Koven, M. (2016), "Essentialization strategies in the storytellings of Young Luso-descendant Women in France: Narrative Calibration, Voicing, and Scale," *Language & Communication*, 46: 19–29.

Krauss, R., Y. Chen, and R. F. Gottesman (2000), "Lexical Gestures and Lexical Access: A Process Model," in D. McNeill (ed.), *Language and Gesture*, 261–83, Cambridge Cambridge University Press.

Kristiansen, G., and R. Dirven, eds (2008), *Cognitive Sociolinguistics: Language Variation, Cultural Models, Social Systems,* Berlin and New York: De Gruyter Mouton.

Kroskrity, P. V., and A. K. Webster (2015), *The Legacy of Dell Hymes: Ethnopoetics, Narrative Inequality, and Voice*, Bloomington, IN: Indiana University Press.

Kuno, S. (1973), *The Structure of the Japanese Language*, Cambridge, MA: MIT Press.

Kuno, S., and E. Kaburaki (1977), "Empathy and Syntax," *Linguistic Inquiry*, 8(4): 627–72.

Labov, W. (1972), *Language in the Inner City*, Philadelphia: University of Pennsylvania Press.

Labov, W. (2013), *The Language of Life and Death: The Transformation of Experience in Oral Narrative*, Cambridge: Cambridge University Press.

Labov, W., and J. Waletzky (1967), "Narrative Analysis," in J. Helm (ed.), *Essays on the Verbal and Visual Arts*, 12–44, Seattle, WA: University of Washington Press.

Ladin, J. (1999), "Fleshing Out the Chronotope," in C. Emerson (ed.), *Critical Essays on Mikhail Bakhtin*, 212–36, New York: Hall.
Ladin, J. (2010), "'It was not death': The Poetic Career of the Chronotope," in N. Bemong, P. Borghart, M. De Dobbeleer, K. Demoen, K. De Temmerman, and B. Keunen (eds), *Bakhtin's Theory of the Literary Chronotope: Reflections, Applications, Perspectives*, 131–55, Ghent: Academia Press.
Lakoff, G. (1987), *Women, Fire, and Dangerous Things*, Chicago, IL: University of Chicago Press.
Lakoff, G., and M. Johnson (1980), *Metaphors We Live By*, Chicago: University of Chicago Press.
Langacker, R. W. (1987), *Foundations of Cognitive Grammar, 2 vols*, Stanford, CA: Stanford University Press.
Langacker, R. W. (1990), *Concept, Image, and Symbol: The Cognitive Basis of Grammar*, Berlin: De Gruyter Mouton.
Langacker, R. W. (1999), *Grammar and Conceptualization*, Berlin: De Gruyter Mouton.
Langseth, T., and Ø. Salvesen (2018), "Rock Climbing, Risk, and Recognition. *Frontiers in Psychology*, 24, https://doi.org/10.3389/fpsyg.2018.01793.
Latour, B. (2005), *Reassembling the Social: An Introduction to Actor-Network Theory*, Oxford: Oxford University Press.
Latour, B., and S. Woolgar (1987), *Laboratory Life: The Construction of Scientific Facts*, 2nd edn, Princeton, NJ: Princeton University Press.
Leech, G., and M. Short ([1981] 2007), *Style in Fiction: A Linguistic Introduction to English Fictional Prose*, 2nd edn, Harlow: Pearson.
Lempert, M. (2008), "The Poetics of Stance: Text-metricality, Epistemicity, Interaction," *Language in Society*, 37: 569–92.
Lempert, M. (2014), "Imitation," *Annual Review of Anthropology*, 43(1): 379–95.
Lempert, M. (2018), "On the Pragmatic Poetry of Pose: Gesture, Parallelism, Politics," *Signs and Society*, 6(1): 120–46.
Lempert, M., and M. Silverstein (2012), *Creatures of Politics: Media, Message, and the American Presidency*, Bloomington, IN: Indiana University Press.
Levelt, W. J. M. (1989), *Speaking: From Intention to Articulation*, Cambridge, MA: MIT Press.
Levelt, W. J. M. (1996), "Perspective Taking and Ellipsis in Spatial Descriptions," in P. Bloom, M. A. Peterson, L. Nadel and M. F. Garrett (eds), *Language and Space*, 77–107, Cambridge, MA: MIT Press.
Levinson, S. C. (1983), *Pragmatics*, Cambridge: Cambridge University Press.
Levinson, S. C. (1992), "Activity Types and Language," in P. Drew and J. Heritage (eds), *Talk at Work: Interaction in Institutional Settings*, 66–100, Cambridge: Cambridge University Press.
Levinson, S. C. (1996a), "Frames of Reference and Molyneux's Question: Crosslinguistic Evidence," in P. Bloom, M. A. Peterson, L. Nadel, and M. F. Garrett (eds), *Language and Space*, 109–69, Cambridge, MA: MIT Press.
Levinson, S. C. (1996b), "Language and Space," in W. H. Durham, E. V. Daniel, and B. B. Schieffelin (eds), *Annual Review of Anthropology*, 25: 353–82.
Levinson, S. C. (2003), *Space in Language and Cognition: Explorations in Cognitive Diversity*, Cambridge: Cambridge University Press.
Levinson, S. C. (2006), "On the Human 'Interaction Engine'," in N. Enfield and S. C. Levinson (eds), *Roots of Human Sociality: Culture, Cognition and Interaction*, 39–69, Cambridge: Cambridge University Press.
Levinson, S. C. (2013), "Action formation and ascription," in J. Sidnell and T. Stivers (eds), *The Handbook of Conversation Analysis*, 103–130. Chichester: Wiley-Blackwell.

Levinson, S. C. (2019), "Interactional Foundations of Language: The Interaction Engine Hypothesis," in P. Hagoort (ed.), *Human Language: From Genes and Brain to Behavior*, 189–200. Cambridge: MIT Press.
Levinson, S. C., and P. Brown (1994), "Immanuel Kant among the Tenejapans," *Ethos*, 22(1): 3–41.
Levinson, S. C., and D. P. Wilkins, eds (2006), *Grammars of Space: Explorations in Cognitive Diversity*, Cambridge: Cambridge University Press
Lewis, D. (1976), "Observations on Route to Finding and Spatial Orientation Among the Aboriginal Peoples of the Western Desert Region of Central Australia," *Oceania* XLVI (4): 249–82.
Linde, C., and W. Labov (1975), "Spatial Networks as a Site for the Study of Language and Thought," *Language,* 51: 924–39.
Lindstrom, J., R. Laury, A. Perakyla, and M.-L. Sorjonen, eds (2021), *Intersubjectivity in Action*, Amsterdam: John Benjamins.
Llewellyn, D. J., and X. Sanchez (2008), "Individual Differences and Risk Taking in Rock Climbing," *Psychology of Sport and Exercise*, 9(4): 413–26.
Logan, G. D. (1995), "Linguistic and Conceptual Control of Visual Spatial Attention," *Cognitive Psychology*, 28: 103–74.
Long, J. (2010), *How to Rock Climb!*, 5th edn, Gullford, CT: Globe Pequot Press.
Longacre, R. E. (1996), *The Grammar of Discourse*, 2nd edn, New York: Plenum Press.
Lucy, J. A. (1992), *Language Diversity and Thought: A Reformulation of the Linguistic Relativity Hypothesis*, Cambridge: Cambridge University Press.
Lusthaus, D. (2003), *Buddhist Phenomenology: A Philosophical Investigation of Yogacara Buddhism and the Ch'eng Wei-shih Lun,* London: Routledge.
Macfarlane, R. (2003), *Mountains of the Mind*, London: Granta.
Malinowski, B. (1926), *Myth in Primitive Psychology*, New York: W.W. Norton.
Malloch, S., and C. Trevarthen (2009), *Communicative Musicality: Exploring the Basis of Human Companionship*, Oxford: Oxford University Press.
Mandler, G. (1984), *Mind and Body: Psychology of Emotion and Stress*, New York: Norton.
Masuda, H. (1999), "Verse Analysis and the Nature of Creole Discourse: Universals and Substrata," *Journal of Pidgin and Creole Languages*, 14(2): 285–337.
Matoesian, G. M. (2001), *Law and the Language of Identity: Discourse in the William Kennedy Smith Rape Trial*, New York: Oxford University Press.
Matoesian, G. M. (2010), "Multimodal Aspects of Victim Narration in Direct Examination," in M. Coulthard and A. Johnson (eds), *Routledge Handbook of Forensic Linguistics*, 541–57, New York: Routledge.
Matoesian, G., and K. E. Gilbert (2018), *Multimodal Conduct in the Law: Language, Gesture and Materiality in Legal Interaction*, Cambridge: Cambridge University Press.
Matsumoto, Y. (1996), "Subjective Motion and English and Japanese Verbs," *Cognitive Linguistics*, 7 (2): 183–226.
Matsumoto, Y., ed. (2017), *Idou Hyougen no Ruikeiron* "Typology of Motion Expressions," Tokyo: Kurosio Publishers.
Mauss, M. (1973), "Techniques of the Body," *Economy and Society*, 2(1): 70–88.
McNeill, D. (1992), *Hand and Mind: What Gestures Reveal about Thought*, Chicago: University of Chicago Press.
McNeill, D. (2003), "Pointing and Morality in Chicago," in S. Kita (ed.), *Pointing: Where Language, Culture, and Cognition Meet*, 293–306, Hillsdale: NJ: Lawrence Erlbaum Associates.
McNeill, D. (2005), *Gesture & Thought*, Chicago: University of Chicago Press.
McNeill, D., and S. Duncan (2000), "Growth Points in Thinking-for-Speaking," in D. McNeill (ed.), *Language and Gesture*, 141–61, Cambridge: Cambridge University Press.

McNeill, D., E. T. Levy, and S. D. Duncan (2015), "Gesture in discourse," in D. Tannen, H. E. Hamilton, and D. Schiffrin (eds), *The Handbook of Discourse Analysis*, 2nd edn, 262–89, Chichester: Wiley.

Mehan, H. (1979), *Learning Lessons: Social Organization in the Classroom*, Cambridge, MA: Harvard University Press.

Merleau-Ponty, M. (1962), *Phenomenology of Perception*, trans. C. Smith, London: Routledge.

Merleau-Ponty, M. (1964), *Signs*, trans. R. C. McCleary, Evanston, IL: Northwestern University Press.

Meyer, C., J. Streeck, and J. Scott Jordan (2017), "Introduction," in C. Meyer, J. Streeck and J. Scott Jordan (eds), *Intercorporeality: Emerging Socialities in Interaction*, xiv–xlix, Oxford: Oxford University Press.

Miller, M. (2017), "An Exploration of Sherpas' Narratives of Living and Dying in Mountaineering," Ph.D. Diss., The University of Waterloo.

Minami, M., and A. McCabe (1991), "Haiku as a Discourse Regulation Device: A Stanza Analysis of Japanese Children's Personal Narratives," *Language in Society*, 20: 577–99.

Minamoto, R., ed. (1992), *Kata to Nihon / Kata and Japan*, Tokyo: Sobunsha.

Mohammad, A., and C. Vásquez (2015), "'Rachel's not here': Constructed Dialogue in Gossip," *Journal of Sociolinguistics*, 19(3): 351–71.

Mondada, L. (2003), "Working with Video: How Surgeons Produce Video Records of Their Actions," *Visual Studies*, 18(1): 58–73.

Mondada, L. (2012), "Talking and Driving: Multiactivity in the Car," *Semiotica*, 191(1/4): 223–56.

Mondada, L. (2016), "Challenges of multimodality: Language and the body in social interaction," *Journal of Sociolinguistics*, 20(3): 336–66.

Moore, C., and P. Dunham (1995), *Joint Attention: Its Origins and Role in Development*, Mahwah, NJ: Lawrence Erlbaum Associates.

Moore, E., and R. Podesva (2009), "Style, Indexicality, and the Social Meaning of Tag Questions," *Language in Society*, 38: 447–85.

Morita, Y. (1977), *Kiso Nihongo—Imi to Tsukaikata / Fundamentals of Japanese: Meaning and Use*, Tokyo: Kadokawa Shoten.

Morson, G. S., and C. Emerson (1990), *Mikhail Bakhtin: Creation of a Prosaics*, Stanford, CA: Stanford University Press.

Mukařovský, J. (1964), "Standard Language and Poetic Language," in P. Garvin (ed.), *A Prague School Reader on Esthetics, Literary Structure, and Style*, 17–30, Washington D.C.: Georgetown University Press.

Murata, K., and R. Ide, eds (2016), *Zatsudan no Bigaku / The Kaleidoscope of Small Talk: A Linguistic Approach*, Tokyo: Hituzi Shobo.

Murphy, K. M. (2005), "Collaborative Imagining: The Interactive Use of Gestures, Talk, and Graphic Representation in Architectural Practice," *Semiotica*, 156 (1/4): 113–45.

Murphy, K. M. (2012), "Transmodality and Temporality in Design Interactions," *Journal of Pragmatics*, 44(14): 1966–81.

Mushin, I. (2001), *Evidentiality and Epistemological Stance: Narrative Retelling*, Amsterdam: John Benjamins.

Nabeshima, K. (2016), *Metafaa to Shintaisei / Metaphor and Corporeality*, Tokyo: Hituzi Shobo.

Nagy, E. (2008), "Innate Intersubjectivity: Newborns' Sensitivity to Communication Disturbance," *Developmental Psychology*, 44(6): 1779–84.

Nakassis, C. (2019), "Poetics of Praise and Image-Texts of Cinematic Encompassment," *Journal of Linguistic Anthropology*, 29(1): 69–94.

Nakazawa, T. (2002), "'Kuru' to 'iku' no toochaku suru tokoro" / "Where *come* and *go* reach," in N. Ogoshi (ed.), *Taishoo Ggenngogaku "Contrastive Linguistics,"* 281–304, Tokyo: Tokyo University Press.

Nisbett, R. E. (2003), *The Geography of Thought: How Asians and Westerners Think Differently . . . and Why*, New York: Free Press.
Nishida, K. ([1941] 1989), "Rekishi-teki keisei sayou to shiteno geijutsu-teki sousaku" / "Artistic Creation as Historical Production," in *Nishida Kitaro Tetsugaku Ronshu III* [Selected Writings of Kitaro Nishida, Vol. 3], ed. S. Ueda, 85–176, Tokyo: Iwanami.
Noda, H. (1987), "Dotchi ga migi de dotchi ga hidari?: Sootaitekina kankei o arawasu kotoba o tsukau toki no shiten," *Gengogaku no Shiten: Koizumi Tamotsu Kyooju Kanreki Kinen Ronbunshuu*, 223–242, Tokyo: Daigaku-shorin.
Nofsinger, R. E. (1991), *Everyday Conversation*, Thousand Oaks, CA: SAGE Publishing.
Norrick, N. (2000), *Conversational Narrative: Storytelling in Everyday Talk*, Amsterdam: John Benjamins.
Ochs, E., P. Gonzales, and S. Jacoby (1996), "'When I come down I'm in a domain state': Grammar and Graphic Representation in the Interpretive Activity of Physicists," in E. Ochs, E. A. Schegloff, and S. A. Thompson (eds), *Interaction and Grammar*, 328–69. Cambridge: Cambridge University Press.
Ogoshi, N., H. Kimura, and R. Washio, eds (2008), *Voisu noTaishou Kenkyuu: Higashi Ajia Shogo kara no Shiten / Contrastive Studies of Voice: Perspectives from East Asian Languages*, Tokyo: Kurosio Publishers.
Oh, Y. H. (2016), *Sherpa Intercultural Experiences in Himalayan Mountaineering: A Pragmatic Phenomenological Perspective*. Unpublished Dissertaion, University of California, Riverside.
Ohye, S. (1975), *Nichi-Eigo no Hikaku Kenkyuu: Shukansei o Megutte / A Comparative Study of Japanese and English: On Subjectivity*, Tokyo: Nan'undoo.
Ortner, S. B. (1999), *Life and Death on Mt. Everest: Sherpas and Himalayan Mountaineering*, Princeton, NJ: Princeton University Press.
Ozawa-De Silva, C. (2002), "Beyond the Body/Mind? Japanese Contemporary Thinkers on Alternative Sociologies of the Body," *Body & Society*, 8(2): 21–38.
Parrill, F. (2009), "Dual Viewpoint Gestures," *Gesture*, 9(3): 271–89.
Payne, T. E. (1984), "Locational Relations in Yagua Narrative," in D. C. Derbyshire (ed.), *Work Papers of the Summer Institute of Linguistics: University of North Dakota Session*, 28: 157–92, Huntington Beach, CA: SIL Inc.
Pederson, E. (1993), "Geographic and Manipulable Space in Two Tamil Linguistic Systems," in A. U. Frank and I. Campari (eds), *Spatial Information Theory*, 294–311, Berlin: Springer Verlag.
Pederson, E. (1995), "Language as Context, Language as Means: Spatial Cognition and Habitual Language Use," *Cognitive Linguistics*, 6(1): 33–62.
Pederson, E., E. Danziger, D. Wilkins, S. C. Levinson, S. Kita, and G. Senft (1998), "Semantic Typology and Spatial Conceptualization," *Language*, 74: 557–89.
Peirce, C. S. (1955), "Logic as Semiotic: The Theory of Signs," in J. Buchler (ed.), *Philosophical Writings by Peirce*, 98–119, New York: Dover.
Perrino, S. (2005), "Participant Transposition in Senegalese Oral Narrative," *Narrative Inquiry* 15(2): 345–75.
Perrino, S. (2007), "Cross-chronotope Alignment in Senegalese Oral Narrative," *Language & Communication*, 27(3): 227–44.
Perrino, S. (2011), "Chronotopes of Sory and Storytelling Event in Interviews," *Language in Society*, 40: 91–103.
Perrino, S. (2015), "Chronotopes: Time and Space in Oral Narrative," in A. De Fina and A. Georgakopoulou (eds), *The Handbook of Narrative Analysis*, 140–59, Chichester: Wiley Blackwell.
Pinxten, R. (1976), "Epistemic Universals: A Contribution to Cognitive Anthropology," in R. Pinxten (ed.), *Universalism versus Relativism in Language and Thought:*

Proceedings of a Colloquium on the Sapir-Whorf Hypothesis, 117–75, The Hague: De Gruyter Mouton.

Pozzer-Ardenghi, L., and W.-M. Roth (2008), "Catchments, Growth Points, and the Iterability of Signs in Classroom Communication," *Semiotica*, 172(1/4): 389–409.

Radden, G. (1996), "Motion Metaphorized: The Case of *Coming* and *Going*," in E. H. Casad (ed.), *Cognitive Linguistics in the Redwoods: The Expansion of a New Paradigm in Linguistics*, 423–58, Berlin: De Gruyter Mouton.

Rak, J. (2007), "Social Climbing on Annapurna: Gender in High-altitude Mountaineering Narratives," *English Studies in Canada*, 33(1–2): 109–46.

Reed, E. S. (1991), "Cognition as the Cooperative Appropriation of Affordances," *Ecological Psychology*, 3(2): 135–58.

Reed, E. S., and B. Bril (1996), "The Primacy of Action in Development," in M. L. Latash and M. T. Turvey (eds), *Dexterity and Its Development*, 431–51, Mahwah, NJ: Lawrence Erlbaum Associates.

Reed, E. S. (1996), *Encountering the World: Toward an Ecological Psychology*, Oxford: Oxford University Press.

Rickly-Boyd, J. (2012), "Lifestyle Climbing: Toward Existential Authenticity," *Journal of Sport & Tourism*, 17(2): 85–104.

Rieger, C. L. (2003), "Repetitions as Self-repair Strategies in English and German Conversations," *Journal of Pragmatics*, 35(1): 47–69.

Rietveld, E., and J. Kiverstein (2014), "A Rich Landscape of Affordances," *Ecological Psychology*, 26: 325–52.

Rogoff, B. (1990), *Apprenticeship in Thinking: Cognitive Development in Social Context*, Oxford: Oxford University Press.

Rogoff, B. (2003), *The Cultural Nature of Human Development*, New York: Oxford University Press.

Rosborough, A. (2016), "Understanding Relations Between Gesture and Chronotope: Embodiment and Meaning-Making in a Second-Language Classroom," *Mind, Culture, and Activity*, 23(2): 1–17.

Rossano, F. (2013), "Gaze in Conversation," in J. Sidnell and T. Stivers (eds), *The Handbook of Conversation Analysis*, 308–29. Oxford: Blackwell.

Rossiter, P. (2007), "Rock Climbing: On Humans, Nature, and Other Nonhumans," *Space and Culture*, 10(2): 292–305.

Roth, W. M., and D. V. Lawless (2002), "When Up Is Down and Down Is Up: Body Orientation, Proximity, and Gestures as Resources," *Language in Society* 31(1): 1–28.

Rothenberg, J. ([1967] 2017), *Technicians of the Sacred*, 3rd edn, Oakland, CA: University of California Press.

Rothenberg, J., and D. Rothenberg (eds) (1983), *Symposium of the Whole: A Range of Discourse Toward An Ethnopoetics*, Berkeley, CA: University of California Press.

Rumsey, A. L. (2007), "Musical, Poetic, and Linguistic Form in 'Tom Yaya' Sung Narratives from Papua New Guinea," *Anthropological Linguistics*, 49(3/4): 235–82.

Rumsey, A., and J. F. Weiner (2000), *Emplaced Myth: Space, Narrative, and Knowledge in Aboriginal Australia and Papua New Guinea*, Honolulu: University of Hawai'i Press.

Rumsey, A. L. (1990), "Wording, Meaning and Linguistic Ideology," *American Anthropologist*, 92: 346–61.

Sacks, H., E. A. Schegloff, and G. Jefferson. (1974), "A Simplest Systematics for the Organization of Turn-taking for Conversation," *Language*, 50(4): 696–735.

Sakita, T. (2002), *Reporting Discourse, Tense and Cognition*, Amsterdam: Elsevier.

Sakuma, K. (1952), *Gendai Nihongohoo no Kenkyuu / A Study of Modern Japanese*, Tokyo: Kouseikaku.

Sapir, E. (1921), *Language: An Introduction to the Study of Speech*, New York: Harcourt, Brace and Co.

Sawada, J. (2016), "Nihongo no chokuji idou doushi 'iku/kuru' no rekishi: Rekishi goyouron-teki/ruikeiron-teki apuroochi / "A History of the Japanese Deictic Motion Verbs 'Go/Come': A Historical Pragmatic and Typological Approach," in M. Yamanashi (ed.), *Ninchi Gengogaku Ronkou / Studies in Cognitive Linguistics,* 13: 185–259, Tokyo: Hituzi Shobo.

Sawada. H. (1993), *Shiten to Shukansei: Nichi-Ei-go Jodoushi no Bunseki / Perspectives and Subjectivity: Analysis of Japanese and English Auxiliaries,* Tokyo: Hituzi Shobo.

Sawyer, K. (2002), *Creating Conversations: Improvisation in Everyday Discourse,* New York: Hampton Press.

Schank, R., and R. Abelson (1977), *Scripts, Plans, Goals and Understanding,* Hillsdale, NJ: Lawrence Erlbaum Associates.

Schegloff, E. A. (1968), "Sequencing in Conversational Openings," *American Anthropologist,* 70(6): 1075–95.

Schegloff, E. A. (1972), "Notes on a Conversational Practice: Formulating Place," in D. Sudnow (ed.), *Studies in Social Interaction,* 75–119, New York: Free Press.

Schegloff, E. A. (1984), "On Some Gestures' Relation to Talk," in J. M. Atkinson and J. Heritage (eds), *Structures of Social Action: Studies in Conversation Analysis,* 266–96, Cambridge: Cambridge University Press.

Schegloff, E. A. (1992), "Repair after Next Turn: The Last Structurally Provided Defense of Intersubjectivity in Conversation," *American Journal of Sociology,* 97: 1295–1345.

Schegloff, E. A. (1997), "Narrative Analysis: Thirty Years Later," *Journal of Narrative and Life History,* 7: 97–106.

Schegloff, E. A. (1997), "Practices and Actions: Boundary Cases of Other-initiated Repair," *Discourse Processes* 23(3): 499–547.

Schegloff, E. A. (1998), "Body Torque," *Social Research,* 65(3): 535–96.

Schegloff, E. A. (2007), *Sequence Organization in Interaction: A Primer in Conversation Analysis: Vol. 1,* Cambridge: Cambridge University Press.

Schiffrin, D. (1981), "Tense Variation in Narrative," *Language,* 57(1): 45–62.

Schober, M. (1993), "Spatial Perspective-taking in Conversation," *Cognition,* 47: 1–24.

Scollon, R., and S. W. Scollon (2004), *Nexus Analysis: Discourse and the Emerging Internet,* London and New York: Routledge.

Seifert, L., P. Wolf, and A. Schweizer, eds (2017), *The Science of Climbing and Mountaineering,* London: Routledge.

Senft, G. (1997), *Referring to Space: Studies in Austronasian and Papuan Languages,* Oxford: Clarendon Press.

Senft, G. (2000), ""COME and GO in Kilivila", in Bill Palmer and Paul Geraghty (eds), *SICOL. Proceedings of the Second International Conference on Oceanic Linguistics: vol. 2, Historical and descriptive studies,*" Pacific Linguistics Series, 105–36: Canberra: Australian National University.

Seuren, L. M. (2018), "Assessing Answers: Action Ascription in Third Position," *Research on Language and Social Interaction,* 51(1): 33–51.

Shepard, R. N., and S. Hurwitz (1984), "Upward Direction, Mental Rotation, and Discrimination of Left and Right Turns in Maps," *Cognition,* 18: 161–93.

Shimizu, H. (2003), *Ba no Shiso / Philosophy of Ba,* Tokyo: University of Tokyo Press.

Short, M. (1996), *Exploring the Language of Poems, Plays, and Prose,* London: Taylor & Francis.

Sicoli, M. (2016), "Formulating Place, Common Ground, and a Moral Order in Lachixio Zapotec," *Open Linguistics,* 2: 180–210.

Sicoli, M. (2020), *Saying and Doing in Zapotec: Multimodality, Resonance, and the Language of Joint Actions*, London: Bloomsbury.

Sidnell, J., and N. J. Enfield (2012), "Language Diversity and Social Action: A Third Locus of Linguistic Relativity," *Current Anthropology*, 53(3): 302–21.

Sidnell, J., and T. Stivers, eds (2012), *The Handbook of Conversation Analysis*, Chichester: Wiley-Blackwell.

Silverstein, M. (1976), "Shifters, Linguistic Categories, and Cultural Description," in: K. H. Basso and H. A. Selby (eds), *Meaning in Anthropology*, 11–55, Albuquerque, NM: University of New Mexico Press.

Silverstein, M. (1985), "Language and the Culture of Gender: At the Intersection of Structure, Usage, and Ideology," in E. Mertz and R. J. Parmentier (eds), *Semiotic Mediation: Sociocultural and Psychological Perspectives*, 219–59, Ghent: Academic Press.

Silverstein, M. (1985), "On the Pragmatic 'Poetry' of Prose: Parallelism, Repetition, and Cohesive Structure in the Time Course of Dyadic Conversation," in D. Schiffrin (ed.), *Meaning, Form, and Use in Context: Linguistic Applications*, 181–99, Washington, D.C.: Georgetown University Press.

Silverstein, M. (1993), "Metapragmatic Discourse and Metapragmatic Function," in J. Lucy (ed.), *Reflexive Language: Speech and Metapragmatics*, 33–58, Cambridge: Cambridge University Press.

Silverstein, M. (2003), "Indexical Order and the Dialectics of Sociolinguistic Life," *Language & Communication*, 23: 193–229.

Silverstein, M. (2004), "'Cultural' Concepts and the Language-culture Nexus," *Current Anthropology*, 45(5): 621–52.

Silverstein, M. (2005). "Axes of Evals: Token Versus Type Interdiscursivity," *Journal of Linguistic Anthropology*, 15(1): 6–22.

Silverstein, M., and G. Urban, eds (1996), *Natural Histories of Discourse*, Chicago: University of Chicago Press

Sontag, S. (1977), *Illness as Metaphor*, New York: Farrar, Straus & Giroux.

Stivers, T., N. J. Enfield, P. Brown, C. Englert, M. Hayashi, T. Heinemann, G. Hoymann, F. Rossano, J. P. de Ruiter, K.-E. Yoon, and S. C. Levinson (2009), "Universals and Cultural Variation in Turn-taking in Conversation," *PNAS*, 106(26): 10587–92.

Stokes, R., and J. P. Hewitt (1976), "Aligning Actions," *American Sociological Review*, 41(5): 838–49.

Streeck, J., C. Goodwin, and C. LeBaron, eds (2011), *Embodied Interaction: Language and Body in the Material World*, Cambridge: Cambridge University Press.

Suzuki, M. (2015), *Sangaku Shinkou: Nihon Bunka no Kontei wo Saguru / Mountain Religions: Inquiry into the Source of Japanese Culture*, Tokyo: Chuo Koronsha.

Suzuki, T. (1973), *Kotoba to Bunka / Language and Culture*, Tokyo: Iwanami.

Swann, J., and J. Maybin (2007), "Introduction: Language Creativity in Everyday Contexts," *Applied Linguistics*, 28(4): 491–6.

Talmy, L. (1983), "How Language Structures Space," in H. L. Pick Jr., and L. P. Acredolo (eds), *Spatial Orientation: Theory, Research, and Application*, 225–82, New York: Plenum Press.

Tanaka, S., ed. (1987), *Kihondoushi no Imiron: Koa to Purototaipu / Semantics of Basic Verbs: The Core and Prototypes*, Tokyo: Sanyusha Pub. Co.

Tannen, D. (1989), *Talking Voices*, Cambridge: Cambridge University Press.

Taylor, H. A., and B. Tversky (1992a), "Descriptions and Depictions of Environments," *Memory and Cognition*, 20: 483–96.

Taylor, H. A., and B. Tversky (1992b), "Spatial Mental Models Derived from Survey and Route Descriptions," *Journal of Memory and Language*, 31: 261–92.

Taylor, H. A., and B. Tversky (1996), "Perspective in Spatial Descriptions," *Journal of Memory and Language*, 35: 371–91.
Tedlock, D. (1983), *The Spoken Word and the Work of Interpretation*, Philadelphia: University of Pennsylvania Press,.
Tedlock, D. (1999), *Finding the Center: The Art of the Zuni Storyteller*, 2nd edn, Lincoln, NE: University of Nebraska Press.
The Ice Maiden. National Geographic. 2006. ISBN 9780792259121.
Tierney, J. (2009), "Can You Believe How Mean Office Gossip Can Be?", *The New York Times*, November 2, 2009.
Tokieda, M. ([1941] 2007), *Kokugogaku Genron/ Principles of Japanese Linguistics*, Tokyo: Iwanami.
Tomasello, M. (1999), *The Cultural Origins of Human Cognition*. Cambridge, MA: Harvard University Press.
Tomasello, M. (2008), *Origins of Human Communication*. Cambridge, MA: The MIT Press.
Tomasello, M., and M. Carpenter (2007), "Shared Intentionality," *Developmental Science*, 10(1): 121–5.
Trafton, J. G., S. B. Trickett, C. A. Stitzlein, L. Saner, C. D. Schunn, and S. S. Kirschenbaum (2006), "The Relationship Between Spatial Transformations and Iconic Gestures," *Spatial Cognition and Computation*, 6(1): 1–29.
Traugott, E. C. (1995), "Subjectification in Grammaticalization," in D. Stein and S. Wright (eds), *Subjectivity and Subjectivisation*, 37–54, Cambridge: Cambridge University Press.
Trevarthen, C. (1999), "Intersubjectivity," in R. Wilson and F. Keil (eds), *The MIT Encyclopedia of the Cognitive Sciences*, 413–16, Cambridge, MA: MIT Press.
Tsubomoto, A., N. Wada, and N. Hayase (2009), *Uchi to Soto no Gengogaku / Linguistics of Inside and Outside*, Tokyo: Kaitakusha.
Turner, V. (1978), "A Review of Ethnopoetics," *Boundary 2*, 6(2): 583–90.
Turvey, M. (1992), "Affordances and Prospective Control: An Outline of the Ontology," *Ecological Psychology*, 4: 173–87.
Tversky, B. (1992), "Distortions in Cognitive Maps," *Geoforum*, 23(2): 131–8.
Tversky, B. (1996), "Spatial Perspective in Descriptions," in P. Bloom, M. A. Peterson, L. Nadel, and M. F. Garrett (eds), *Language and Space*, 463–91, Cambridge, MA: MIT Press.
Tversky, B. (2009), "Spatial Cognition: Embodied and Situated," in M. Aydede and P. Robbins (eds), *The Cambridge Handbook of Situated Cognition*, 201–16, Cambridge: Cambridge University Press.
Tversky, B., P. Lee, and S. Mainwaring (1999), "Why Do Speakers Mix Perspectives?" *Spatial Cognition and Computation*, 1(4): 399–412.
Tversky, B., and B. M. Hard (2009), "Embodied and Disembodied Cognition: Spatial Perspective-taking," *Cognition*, 110: 124–9.
Ullmer-Ehrich, V. (1982), "The Structure of Living Space Descriptions," in R. J. Jarvella and W. Klein (eds), *Speech, Place, and Action*, 219–49, Chichester: Wiley.
Urban, G. (1991), *A Discourse-Centered Approach to Culture: Native South American Myths and Rituals*, Austin, TX: University of Texas Press.
Valli, C. (1993), "Poetics of American Sign Language Poetry," Ph.D. Diss., Union Institute Graduate School.
Van Cleve, J., and R. E. Frederick, eds (1991), *The Philosophy of Right and Left: Incongruent Counterparts and the Nature of Space*, Dordrecht: Kluwer Academic Publishers.
Van Wolputte, S. (2004), "Hang on to Your Self: Of Bodies, Embodiment, and Selves," *Annual Review of Anthropology*, 33: 251–69.

Varela, F. J., E. Thompson, and E. Rosch (1991), *The Embodied Mind: Cognitive Science and Human Experience*, Cambridge, MA: MIT Press.

Vendler, Z. (1967), *Linguistics in Philosophy*, Ithaca, NY: Cornell University Press.

Vygotsky, L. S. (1978), *Mind in Society: The Development of Higher Psychological Processes*. Cambridge, MA: Harvard University Press.

Vygotsky, L. S. (1986), "Thought and Word (Chapter 7)," in A. Kozulin (ed.), *Thought and Language*, 210–56, Cambridge, MA: MIT Press.

Watanabe, S. (1993), "Cultural Differences in Framing: American and Japanese Group Discussions," in D. Tannen (ed.), *Framing in Discourse*, 176–209, New York: Oxford University Press.

Watts, P. B., L. M. Joubert, A. K. Lish, J. D. Mast, and B. Wilkins (2003), "Anthropometry of Young Competitive Sport Rock Climbers," *British Journal of Sports Medicine*, 37: 420–4.

Watts, P., V. Newbury, and J. Sulentic (1996), "Acute Changes in Handgrip Strength, Endurance, and Blood Lactate with Sustained Sport Rock Climbing," *Journal of Sports Medicine and Physical Fitness*, 36: 255–60.

Whorf, B. L. (1956), *Language, Thought, and Reality: Selected Writings of Benjamin Lee Whorf*, ed. J. B. Carroll, Cambridge, MA: MIT Press.

Widlok, T. (1997), "Orientation in the Wild: The Shared Cognition of Hai om Bushpeople," *The Journal of the Royal Anthropological Institute*, 3(2): 317–32.

Wigglesworth, J. C. (2021), "Feminist Ethnography of Indoor and Outdoor Sport Climbing and Bouldering," Ph.D. Diss. Queen's University.

Wolfson, N. (1978), "A Feature of Performed Narrative: The Conversational Historical Present," *Language in Society*, 7: 215–37.

Woodbury, A. C. (1985), "The Functions of Rhetorical Structure: A Study of Central Alaskan Yupik Eskimo Discourse," *Language in Society*, 14: 153–90.

Yamaguchi, H. (2009), *Meisekina In'you, Shinayakana In'you: Wahou no Nichi-Ei Taishou Kenkyuu / Lucid Quotation and Flexible Quotation: A Contrastive Study of Japanese-English Quotations*, Tokyo: Kurosio Publishers.

Yamaguchi, M. (2012), "Finding Culture in 'Poetic' Structures: The Case of a 'Racially-Mixed' Japanese/New Zealander," *Journal of Multicultural Discourses*, 7(1): 1–19.

Yoshida, E. (2011), *Referring Expressions in English and Japanese: Patterns of Use in Dialogue Processing*, Amsterdam: John Benjamins.

Yoshimoto, T. (1990), *Teihon: Gengo ni totte Bi to ha Nani ka / What is Beauty for Language? I, II: Standard Edition*, Tokyo: Kadokawa.

Yuasa, Y. *The Body: Toward an Eastern Mind-Body Theory*. Albany, NY: State University of New York Press.

Zimmerman, D. H. (1984), "Talk and Its Occasion: The Case of Calling the Police," in D. Schiffrin (ed.), *Meaning, Form and Use in Context: Linguistic Applications*, 210–28, Washington, DC: Georgetown University Press.

Zimmerman, D. H. (1992), "The Interactional Organization of Calls for Emergency Assistance," in P. Drew and J. Heritage (eds), *Talk at Work. Interaction in Institutional Settings*, 418–69, Cambridge: Cambridge University Press.

Zlatev, J. (2008), "The Co-evolution of *Intersubjectivity* and Bodily Mimesis," in J. Zlatev, T. Racine, C. Sinha, and E. Itkonen (eds), *The Shared Mind: Perspectives on Intersubjectivity*, 215–44. Amsterdam: John Benjamins.

Zlatev, J., T. Racine, C. Sinha, and E. Itkonen (2008), "Intersubjectivity: What Makes Us Human?," in J. Zlatev, T. Racine, C. Sinha, and E. Itkonen (eds), *The Shared Mind: Perspectives on Intersubjectivity*, 1–14, Amsterdam: John Benjamins.

INDEX

Note: References in *italic* and **bold** refer to figures and tables. References followed by "n" refer to endnotes.

absolute FOR 21–2, 22, 24, 31; *see also* spatial frames of reference (FOR)
  pointing 110
action ascription 16, 45
aesthetic/expressive art, gossip/gossiping as 173
affordance-reading ability (ARA) 63–5, 76
affordances 9, 12, 61–77
  bouldering (*see* bouldering)
  Chemero's concept 62
  climbing styles 63–5
  dispositional view 62
  features 61
  Gibson's concept 61
  intersubjectivity 18, 19
  as percepts 19
  relational view 62
  selectionist view 62
Agha, A. 37, 38, 41
alpine climbing 3, 4, 42, 193
  chronotopic values 138
alpinism 2–4, 193; *see also* rock climbing
  gender 9
  genres/types 4
  Japanese 3–4
  literature 8
  outdoor activities 4
American-style free climbing 3–4, 6
ascription 16, 45
Atkinson, Robert William 3
audiovisual data 11

back clipping 12, 94–104, *94*
Bakhtin, M. M. 39–41, 42, 137, 202n17
ba(sho) in/of discourse 19–20
Basso, K. H. 137, 172
Bauman, R. 32

belayer/belaying 1, 12, 43–60
  audiovisual data 46
  climbing situation *vs.* canonical setting 4–5
  commands 48
  communication protocols 48
  decision-making 45
  discursive perspective 44–6
  dynamic belaying 55–7, *56*
  lead climbing (*see* lead climbing)
  middle phase actions 50–3
  non-dynamic belaying 53–5
  role and skills 44
  starting/ending protocols 48–50
  top-rope climbing (*see* top-rope climbing)
Bernstein, N. A. 62, 203n3
Blommaert, J. 42
bodily coordinates 92, 124
bolted protection 6
bolt wars 7
bouldering 5–6, 66–77
  drop knee 72–6
  lunge move 67–8, 72, 76
  moves/techniques 67–75
  problems 6–7
  sidepull 70, 71, 72, 75–6
  undercling move 68–72, 75–6
Brenneis, D. 172, 173
Briggs, C. L. 32, 36
Bril, B. 77
Brown, P. 81
Buhler, K. 92, 124

Campbell, J. 81
canonical setting *vs.* climbing situation 4–5
carabiner 12, 45, 48, 93–4, 99, 100–1
Carlson-Radvansky, L. A. 82, 204n6
Cassell, J. 28, 30, 32

catchment 32, 37, 141, 152
Chafe, W. L. 34
chain complex 45–6, 105
Character-external perspective 26; see also intersubjectivity, perspectivization
Character Viewpoint (C-VPT) 30–1, 30
  internal, spatial description/depiction 117–18
Chemero, A. 19, 41, 62, 106, 203n2
chronotopes 39–42, 137–9, 196–7; see also narratives
  crevasse-falling narrative 149–54
  invocation 41–2
  invokable histories 42
  major 40
  massive fall narrative 163–7
Clark, A. 41
climbing gym 66
climbing party 1, 45
climbing situation vs. canonical setting 4–5
co-eval (cross-chronotopic) alignments 41, 138, 139, 168
cognitive/mental map 7
collaborative imagining 108
collaborative wayfinding, see wayfinding
collateral effects 9, 80, 83–4
  as side effect 84
communication 8, 9, 17–18, 20, 38, 44; see also belayer/belaying
  cross-cultural 83
  gossip 172
  long-distance 59
  tacit 8
  telecommunication 17, 44, 59
conditional relevance 45
constructed dialogue 173, 177
contextualization cues 45
corporal division 19, 108
co-speech gestures 10, 113
creativity 33
crevasse-falling narrative 142–54
  chronotopes 149–54
  denotational text analysis 142–8
cross-chronotope alignment 41
cultural models 173, 182–7

data collection 10–11, 12
decentration of perspective-taking 81
deiconic gestures 115
deictic gestures 29, 30, 31, 107
deictic management 177

deictic verbs of motion (DVM) 109
  clauses 112
  denotational and interactional texts 125–34
  indexical ground 110
  Japanese vs. English 109–10
deixis 20–1, 108, 109–10
  linguistic theories 109
  pointing 110
  spatio-temporal 108, 110, 128
denotational indexical 177
denotational text 108, 110
  crevasse falling 142–8
  deictic verbs of motion (DVM) 125–34
  massive fall narrative 154–63
  poetic construction 124–34
depicting gestures 29; see also iconic gestures
descriptive modes 22–3, 24; see also spatial frames of reference (FOR)
dexterity 62–3, 64, 203n3
diachronic repetition 32
direct speech (DS) 175, *175*, **176**, 177, 188, 189–90; see also free direct speech (FDS)
dispositional view of affordance 62
Drew, P. 17, 45
drop knee 72–6; see also bouldering
Du Bois, J. 11, 32, 33, 142, 175, 188
Duranti, A. 17–18
dynamic belaying 55–7, 56

egocentrism/egocentricity 80–3
Ehrich, V. 23
Einstein, A. 39
emblems 28; see also gestures
environmental affordances, see affordances
epistolae familiares (Petrarch) 2
ethics, clean climbing 7
ethnography 8–9
ethnopoetics 12, 31; see also Verse/Stanza Analysis
  as a movement 34
  multimodal 34–7
  nonverbal aspects 36–7
ethno-semantics 36
European-style free climbing 4, 6

falling experiences 142–67, 197; see also near-death narratives

crevasse 142–54
  massive 154–67
fatal accident, gossip analysis of 177–92
  conceptual metaphors 178–82
  cultural model 182–7
  infantilization 178–80
  pathologization 180–2
  stance and reported speech 188–92
FDS, *see* free direct speech
field of promoted actions (FPA) 63, 77
field of view 5
Fiji Indians 173
Fillmore, C. J. 81, 109, 205n3
first-person perspective 18
FIS, *see* free indirect speech
flash 6, 63, 64; *see also* lead climbing
FOR, *see* spatial frames of reference
free actions 77
free direct speech (FDS) 175, *175*, **176**,
    177, 184, 185, 188, 189–90
free indirect speech (FIS) 138, 152, 168,
    175, *175*, **176**
free solo 6, 43
Friederici, A. D. 82
Friedrich, P. 32, 36
Fuchs, T. 18
futon (thick bedquilt) 178

gaki (hungry devil) 178, 179
Gathercole, V. C. 109
Gee, J. P. 34
gender 9, 187
gestures 28–31, 107
  catchment 32, 37, 141, 152
  classification 28–9, *29*
  co-speech 10
  crevasse-falling narrative 149–54
  emblems 28
  FOR grid 31
  massive fall narrative 163–7
  narratives/narration 30–1, *30*
  perspectivization 27–8, *28*
  poetic features 36–7
  pointing 110
  representational 25, 29
  spatial descriptions and depictions
    113–24
  spontaneous 28
  transcription system 29
  unit 29, *29*
Gibson, J. J. 19, 61, 62, 63, 203n2

Goodrich, A. 8
Goodwin, C. 16, 37
Goodwin, M. 33, 37
gossip/gossiping 10, 12, 171–92, 197–8
  as an aesthetic/expressive art 173
  concept 171
  cultural model 182–7
  fatal accident 177–92
  infantilization 178–80
  Japanese words 171
  malicious intentions 172
  as moral awareness 172–3
  pathologization 180–2
  as a social activity 172
  social interaction 173
  stance and reported speech 188–92
  as a three-pronged tongue 172
  types and features 171–4
Gowland, W. 3
gravity 80–1, 88, 89, 103, 105; *see also*
    vertical space
  climbing situation *vs.* canonical
    setting 5
  up and down expression 95–9, 104
Growth Point Hypothesis 25
gyaku kurippu, see back clipping

hangdogging 6, 44
Hanks, W. 32
Haun, D. B. M. 81
Heft, H. 19
Heritage, J. 17, 45
Hill, J. H. 172–3
historical body 20
Holland, D. 173
Holquist, M. 40, 41
Honnold, A. 6
horizontal space 2, 5; *see also* vertical space
Human, L. 8
Husserl, E. 17, 20
Hymes, D. 34–5, 139, 141, 148, 160, 163,
    168, 197, 207n5

Ichikawa, H. 19
iconic gestures 29, 30, 107; *see also*
    depicting gestures
Ikegami, Y. 102, 200n3, 205n9
incongruent counterparts 79, 80, 81
indexicality 45
indirect free style of narration, *see* free
    indirect speech (FIS)

indirect speech (IS) 175, *175*, 176, **176**, 206n1; *see also* free indirect speech (FIS)
infantilization 178–80; *see also* gossip/gossiping
Ingold, T. 8, 18, 41, 106, 203n2
institutional constraints 17
institutional discourse 45
institutional interaction 17
interaction(s) 8, 9, 10, 15–19
　institutional 17
　second-person 18
　vertical space 102–4
interactional text 107–8, 110
　deictic verbs of motion (DVM) 125–34
　poetic construction 124–34
intercorporeality 1, 9, 15–16, 19, 20, 41
　as carnal intersubjectivity 79
　cooperative actions 19
　social interaction 108
Interface Hypothesis 27
intersubjectified corporeality 99–104
　interactional attunement 102–4
　linguistic choice 101–2
　perceptual environment 99–101
intersubjectivity 1, 9, 15–16, 24, 26, 41, 107, 108
　affordances 18, 19
　cognitive sciences 18
　defined 17–18
　embodiment 108
　Husserlian 17, 20
　perspectivization 18–19, 26–8, 119–24
　as a precondition to communication 18
　spatial construction 119–24
　vertical perception 80
intrinsic FOR 21, *22*, 24, 31; *see also* spatial frames of reference (FOR)
Irwin, D. E. 82, 204n6

Jakobson, R. 31, 110
James, W. 19
Japan Alpine Club 3
Jefferson, G. 11
joint attention 18, 19

Kant, I. 39–40, 79, 80–1, 104, 202n19, 204n1–2
Kataoka, K. 8, 82, 83, 201n8–9, 206n9, 207n6

Käufer, S. 62
Kendon, A. 11, 28, 29, 113
kevlar rope 54–5
Kita, S. 28
Koster, C. 23
Kriek, D. 8
Kroskrity, P. V. 32

Labov, W. 21, 23
Ladin, J. 138
language; *see also* linguistic relativity
　rock climbing 1, 2
　spatial relations (*see* spatial descriptions and depictions)
　verticality 83–106 (*see also* spatial lexicon)
language socialization 173; *see also* gossip/gossiping
laughter as a discursive tool 8
Lawless, D. V. 82
lead climbing 5–6, 7, 193–4
　avoiding back clipping 92–104
　belaying 46, 47, 49–50, 55–7
　dynamic belaying 55–7, *56*
　starting/ending protocols 49–50
leading a route 6
Levelt, W. J. M. 82
Levinson, S. C. 16, 17, 21–4, 26, 31, 81, 83, 105, 110, 201n7, 201n9
lifesaving training session 84–92
Linde, C. 21, 23
linguistic choice 101–2
linguistic markers 176–7
linguistic relativity 83–4
Logan, G. D. 82
Lowth, Robert 33
lunge move 67–8, 72, 76; *see also* bouldering
Lusthaus, D. 20, 108

malicious intentions 172; *see also* gossip/gossiping
map drawings 11
Map Task study 82
massive fall narrative 154–67
　chronotopes 163–7
　denotational text 154–63
Matsumoto, Y. 109, 200n4
Mauss, M. 43
Max Planck Institute for Psycholinguistics 46

McNeill, D. 28, 30–2, 36–7, 139, 140, 206n11
mental model 169, 197
mental problems, see pathologization
Merleau-Ponty, M. 20, 62, 63, 79, 105–6, 205n10
Messner, R. 3
meta-narrative level 30, 140
metaphoric gestures 29, 30; see also depicting gestures
metapragmatic poetics 37–9
Meyer, C. 19, 79, 106, 108
mindful reflection 106
mi-wake, see corporal division
Mohammad, A. 173
Mont Ventoux 2
moral awareness, gossip/gossiping as 172–3
Morita, Y. 109, 206n12
mountaineering, see alpinism
Mukarovsky, J. 33
multimodal analysis methods 10
multimodal ethnopoetics 34–7; see also Verse/Stanza Analysis
multi-stranded task 194
Muromachi period (1336–1573) 3
Murphy, K. M. 82

narrated event *vs.* narrating event 41, 138
narrative report of action (NRA) 175, *175*, **176**, 189, 190; see also reported speech
narrative report of speech acts (NRSA) 175, *175*, **176**, 189, 190; see also reported speech
narratives
  chronotopes (see chronotopes)
  crevasse falling 142–54
  gestures and 30–1, *30*, 139, 140–1
  levels of 30, 140–1
  massive fall 154–67
  near-death and fall incidents 9–10, 12, 141–69
navigation 8; see also wayfinding
near-death narratives 9, 12, 141–69
  crevasse falling 142–54
  massive fall 154–67
Newtonian "absolute" space 80
non-dynamic belaying 53–5, *54*
NRSA, see narrative report of speech acts

Observer-external perspective 113–15
Observer-internal perspective 115–17
Observer Viewpoint (O-VPT) 30–1, *30*
Ochs, E. 82
onomatopoeia 141, 147, 148, 151, 161
onsight a route 6, 64–5; see also lead climbing
orientation, climbing situation *vs.* canonical setting 4
origo (origin of cognition) 20–1, 41, 107, 188
  deictic expressions 109
  notion 109
  shift 109
Ortner, S. B. 8–9
other-consciousness 18
Otzi 2
Otztal Alps 2

parallelism 32, 33–4; see also repetition
para-narrative level 30, 140–1
participant observation method 11
participation frameworks 44
party-style climbing 7
pathologization 180–2; see also gossip/gossiping
perception; see also affordances
  as an omni-corporeal phenomenon 63
  cognition 75
  ecological principles 62
  external world 63
  space (see spatial perception)
Perrino, S. 139
perspectivization 20–8
  combination/integration 24–8
  concept 24
  decentration 81
  gaze 23, 24
  intersubjective 18–19, 26–8, 119–24
  multiplicity 20–31
  route/tour 23–4
  speech/gesture (verbal/gestural) 27–8
  survey 23, 24
  wayfinding (see wayfinding)
phatic communion 172
Pinxten, R. 105
poetics 31–9
  concept 31
  equivalence 31
  metapragmatic poetics 37–9
  multimodal ethnopoetics 34–7

Prague School's approach 33
repetition and parallelism 32–4
Russian formalism 33
pointing gestures 110
polygon 67–72; *see also* bouldering
Polynesia, Nukulaelae people of 173
postposition (PosP) 92
Potgieter, S. 8
pro-clipping carabiner 48, 93, *94*
professional vision 16, 45

Quinn, N. 173
quotation 175, **176**; *see also* reported speech
denotational content 177

redpoint 6, 53, 64; *see also* lead climbing
Reed, E. S. 62, 77
relational view of affordance 62
relative FOR 21, *22*, 24, 31; *see also* spatial frames of reference (FOR)
pointing 110
repetition 32–3; *see also* parallelism
creativity 33
defined 32
diachronic 32
forms of participation 33
interactional functions 33
synchronic 32
reported speech 175–7, *175*
cline of speech presentation 175
deictic management 177
denotational indexical 177
linguistic markers 176–7
models 175
stance and 188–92
representational gestures 25, 29
rope 43–4, 93
rope-clipping carabiner 48, 93, 94, *94*
Roth, W. M. 82
Rothenberg, J. 34
Russian formalism of poetics 33

Saeki Ariyori 3
safety 43, 48–9
Satow, Ernest Mason 3
Sawada, J. 109
second-person perspective 18
selectionist view of affordance 62
self-consciousness 18
sherpas 8–9
shifting of perspectives 21

sidepull 70, 71, 72, 75–6; *see also* bouldering
Silverstein, M. 37, 41, 139, 168, 187
Snyder, G. 34
social activity, gossip/gossiping as a 172
social grooming, gossiping as 172
socially distributed cognition 19
space
body or bodily depiction (*see* spatial descriptions and depictions)
concept 7–8, 80
Newtonian "absolute" 80
perception (*see* spatial perception)
vertical representations (*see* vertical space)
spatial descriptions and depictions 107–34; *see also* deictic verbs of motion (DVM)
Character-internal VPT 117–18
intersubjective perspective 119–24
Observer-external perspective 113–15
Observer-internal perspective 115–17
poetic construction 124–34
verbal and gestural 113–24
spatial frames of reference (FOR) 8, 20, 21–2
absolute 21–2, *22*, 24, 31
descriptive modes *vs.* 22–3, 24
gesture types 31
intrinsic 21, *22*, 24, 31
pointing gestures 110
relative 21, *22*, 24, 31
tripartite typology 21–2, *22*
spatial lexicon 8, 9, 22, 77, 84–106
horizontal space 105
lifesaving training session 84–92
ue (and *saki*) expression 85–92
ue/shita (up/down) 12, 65, 66, 77, 79–80, 90–2, 95–104
spatial perception 79–80; *see also* vertical space
egocentricity and verticality 80–3
gravity 80–1
spatio-temporally displaced communication 44
spontaneous gestures 28; *see also* gestures
stair-climbing 62, 76
stance and reported speech 188–92
structural coupling 106
style of climbing 5–7; *see also* affordances; *specific style*
synchronic repetition 32

Taicho 3
Tannen, D. 32
Taylor, H. A. 23
Tedlock, D. 34, 139
telecommunication 17, 44, 59
Tenejapan Mayans 81
tenses 131
Theory of Ba 20
third-person perspective 18
three-point contact method 67
time-space, Einstein's theory of 39
top-rope climbing 6, 44
  belaying 46–9, 53–5
  non-dynamic belaying 53–5, *54*
  starting/ending protocols 48–9
trading places 18, 83, 107, 108, 113, 122, 134
traditional protection 6
Trafton, J. G. 107
transcription 11
transgredience 40
Tversky, B. 23, 82

ue (and *saki*) expression 85–92
ue/shita (up/down) 12, 65, 66, 77, 79–80, 90–2, 95–104
undercling move/techniques 68–72, 75–6; see also bouldering
up and down expression, *see ue/shita* (up/down)

Varela, F. J. 106
Vasquez, C. 173
Verse/Stanza Analysis 34–5, 36, 139–40, 197
  crevasse-falling narrative 142–54
  massive fall narrative 154–67
  schematic formation 35, *36*
  units 34–5
vertical dimensions 81
vertical space 2
  body movement 5
  gravity (*see* gravity)
  interactional attunement 102–4
  intersubjectified corporeality 99–104
  lifesaving training session 84–92
  linguistic choice 101–2
  over-determination 79, 80–3
  perceptual environment 99–101
  spatial frames of reference 8
  up and down expression 95–9
vision, *see* professional vision
Vygotsky, L. S. 77, 105

wayfinding 8, 12, 107; *see also* navigation; spatial descriptions and depictions
  data and informants 111–12
  individual and collaborative perspectives 113–19
  intersubjectified corporeality 119–24
Webster, A. K. 32
Western scientific tradition 108
Weston, Walter 3
Whorf, B. L. 83, 104
Woodbury, A. C. 32
"The World's Best Belayer" video 59

zero anaphora 173
Zimmerman, D. H. 58
Zlatev, J. 18
zone of proximal development (ZPD) 63, 77

www.ingramcontent.com/pod-product-compliance
Lightning Source LLC
Chambersburg PA
CBHW071825300426
44116CB00009B/1435